Collectives and the Design
of Complex Systems

Springer

New York
Berlin
Heidelberg
Barcelona
Hong Kong
London
Milan
Paris
Singapore
Tokyo

Kagan Tumer
David Wolpert
Editors

Collectives and the Design of Complex Systems

 Springer

Kagan Tumer
David Wolpert
Computational Sciences Division
NASA Ames Research Center
Moffett Field, CA 94035
USA

Library of Congress Cataloging-in-Publication Data
Tumer, Kagan.
  Collectives and the design of complex systems / Kagan Tumer, David Wolpert.
    p. cm.
  Includes bibliographical references and index.
  ISBN 0-387-40165-2 (hc. : alk. paper)
    1. Electronic data processing—Distributed processing. 2. Intelligent agents (Computer
  software) 3. System design. I. Wolpert, David H. II. Title.

  QA76.9.D5T84 2003
  006.3–dc22   2003061105

ISBN 0-387-40165-2   Printed on acid-free paper.

Printed in the United States of America.   (TXQ/EB)

9 8 7 6 5 4 3 2 1   SPIN 10932650

Springer-Verlag is a part of *Springer Science+Business Media*

springeronline.com

Contents

Preface vii

1. A Survey of Collectives
Kagan Tumer and David Wolpert 1

2. Theory of Collective Intelligence
David Wolpert 43

3. On Learnable Mechanism Design
David C. Parkes 107

4. Asynchronous Learning in Decentralized Environments:
A Game-Theoretic Approach
Eric J. Friedman 133

5. Competition between Adaptive Agents: Learning and
Collective Efficiency
Damien Challet 145

6. Managing Catastrophic Changes in a Collective
David Lamper, Paul Jefferies, Michael Hart, and Neil F. Johnson 161

7. Effects of Interagent Communications on the Collective
Zoltán Toroczkai, Marian Anghel, György Korniss, and Kevin E. Bassler 185

8. Man and Superman: Human Limitations, Innovation, and
Emergence in Resource Competition
Robert Savit, Katia Koelle, Wendy Treynor, and Richard Gonzalez 199

9. Design Principles for the Distributed Control of Modular
Self-Reconfigurable Robots
Arancha Casal and Tad Hogg 213

10. Two Paradigms for the Design of Artificial Collectives
Kristina Lerman and Aram Galstyan 231

11. Efficiency and Equity in Collective Systems of Interacting Heterogeneous Agents
Akira Namatame and Saori Iwanaga 257

12. Selection in Coevolutionary Algorithms and the Inverse Problem
Sevan Ficici, Ofer Melnik, and Jordan Pollack 277

13. Dynamics of Large Autonomous Computational Systems
Tad Hogg and Bernardo A. Huberman 295

Index 317

About the Editors 323

Preface

Many complex systems found in nature can be viewed as function optimizers. In particular, they can be viewed as such optimizers of functions in extremely high-dimensional spaces. Given the difficulty of performing such high-dimensional optimization with modern computers, there has been a lot of exploration of computational algorithms that try to emulate those naturally-occurring function optimizers. Examples include simulated annealing (SA [15, 18]), genetic algorithms (GAs) and evolutionary computation [2, 3, 9, 11, 20–22, 24, 28]. The ultimate goal of this work is an algorithm that can, for any provided high-dimensional function, come close to extremizing that function. Particularly desirable would be such an algorithm that works in an adaptive and robust manner, without any explicit knowledge of the form of the function being optimized. In particular, such an algorithm could be used for distributed adaptive control—one of the most important tasks engineers will face in the future, when the systems they design will be massively distributed and horribly messy congeries of computational systems.

Unfortunately, no optimization algorithm outperforms random search over the space of all optimization functions [26, 27]. If the algorithm is not well matched to the function being optimized, it may do even *worse* than random search. Indeed, it has not even been established that the optimization algorithms in nature outperform random search. As an example, the algorithm of natural selection is non-teleological; it has no optimization goal whatsoever, and any ability in achieving such a goal is a side effect. Moreover, to the degree that it does achieve a particular goal, at least a large part of its success is due to its brute force massive parallelism. The number of genomes mutating and recombining simultaneously in the terrestrial biosphere may exceed Avogadro's number.

To understand what kinds of optimization functions are well matched to these naturally occurring complex systems, we need a unifying way of viewing those systems. One feature shared by many of these naturally occurring complex systems is that they can be viewed as though the underlying variables were self-interested adaptive agents. In some of these systems this is overt, the underlying variables being controlled by agents engaged in a noncooperative game, their equilibrium joint state (hopefully) maximizing the provided "world utility" function G [1,4,5,13,14,16,23].

Examples of such systems are auctions and clearing of markets. Typically in the computational algorithms inspired by such systems, each agent is a separate machine learning algorithm [7, 8, 10, 17], e.g., a reinforcement learning (RL) algorithm [25, 29].

Other complex systems found in nature that have inspired function-maximization algorithms are not usually considered in terms of noncooperative game theory. However even these systems are very often viewed as though their underlying variables were controlled by self-interested agents. Examples include spin glasses (agents are particles trying to extremize their free energies) genomes undergoing neo-Darwinian natural selection (each genome is an agent trying to maximize its reproductive fitness), and eusocial insect colonies. These have been translated into SA, GAs and evolutionary computation, and swarm intelligence [6, 12, 19], respectively.

One crucial issue concerning the systems that are explicitly noncooperative games is whether the payoff function g_η of each player η is sufficiently sensitive to the coordinate η controls in comparison with the other coordinates, so that it is feasible for η to discern how to set its coordinates to achieve high payoff. A second crucial issue is the need for all of the g_η to be aligned with G, so that as the players individually learn how to increase their payoffs, G also increases. A particularly important issue with collectives that are not explicitly noncooperative game is the exploration/exploitation tradeoff.

Clearly then, both to be able to better understand the behavior of these natural systems, as well as perform high-dimensional optimization, we need a thorough overarching understanding of collectives, that is in understanding systems in which there is a provided world utility, and in which at least some of the system's variables can be viewed as self-interested adaptive agents. This book, compiling recent research from the fields of physics, economics, computer science and biology, is a first foray into such an understanding.

In assembling this book, we resisted the temptation to group chapters into sections connected to well-established fields (e.g., economics-based approaches, physics-based approaches). Though such sections may provide some order, they also would obscure the underlying theme of the book: the emerging field of collectives is connected to many current disciplines, but cannot be wholly captured by one or even a simple combination of those existing fields. Furthermore, such sections would suggest that a closer similarity, or a certain homogeneity among chapters within a section exists, which is not generally true. Chapter 13, for example, could be at a broad brush grouped with other chapters on computational economies, though doing so would hide the groundbreaking work of the authors in bringing statistical mechanics concepts and computational market approaches into the engineering and computer science communities. Finally such sections would make it difficult to classify work that uses ideas from more than one field. Chapter 10 could fit within a physics section due to its analysis techniques, a biology section due to its first approach, and finally an economics section due to its second approach. Any of these choices though would not only hide the nature of the work, but also de-emphasize the practical and engineering contributions of the work.

Instead, we let the chapters stand on their own as examples of work in collectives. The first chapter in this volume provides a broad survey of the emerging field of collectives. By formally defining what constitutes a collective, and discussing their various properties, it aims to provide a common language with which to approach this field. This introduction is followed by a brief overview of the various fields (multi-agent systems, mechanism design, game theory, statistical physics etc.) that are related to collectives. The second chapter provides a theory of the "collective intelligence" framework, which focuses on the inverse problem of initializing and updating the collective's structure (including the agents' utility functions) so as to induce high values of the world utility. Through formal mathematics this chapter provides both an analysis of existing techniques and suggests new agent utility functions in collectives.

Chapter 3 discusses how mechanism design can be used in the control of a collective. This chapter addresses the challenges traditional mechanism design faces in large distributed systems, and provides a *learnable mechanism design* framework drawing parallels with the collective intelligence framework. It is an extremely fresh look at traditional concepts. Chapter 4 focuses on cases where the collective's overall goal (i.e., the world utility) is based on the agents' utilities, and the designers have fewer options in inducing behavior that would benefit the collective. This interesting situation is detailed with an application example from the Internet.

Chapter 5 analyzes how the efficiency (the world utility is indirectly set as the variance of the agents' private utilities, hence the name "efficiency") of a system depends on the learning properties of the agents in a collective using statistical physics. The minority game (also called the "El Farol Bar problem") is used as the testbed. Chapter 6 focuses on the difficult task of predicting and controlling catastrophic changes in a collective. It shows how large macroscopic (e.g., system level) changes are encoded in the microscopic (e.g., agent level) dynamics. This leads to either design stage modifications to a collective to avoid catastrophic changes or run-time monitoring to alleviate the effect of such changes. Chapter 7 focuses on the effect of communication on the evolution of a collective. Using the minority game as a testbed, it shows that local social networks can override global information and thus totally change the evolution of a collective.

Chapter 8 provides the only work in this book which focuses solely on human agents. In this chapter, minority game experiments conducted on students suggest that many of the results obtained on computer agents (e.g., often simpler strategies yield better results for the agents) also hold for human agents.

Chapter 9 presents techniques designing self-reconfigurable robots. This fascinating problem, where many simple modules can form complex shapes presents a unique distributed control problem. This chapter addresses those challenges by using *local* rules only, providing a decentralized solution to this problem. Chapter 10 presents two approaches to the distributed control of collectives. Both a biology-inspired solution based on local interactions leading to global behavior and a market-based mechanism are presented in the context foraging in a group of robots and resource allocation. Chapter 11 provides an analysis of how the information presented to the agents and the heterogeneity of the agents influences the world utility, showing that local interactions can lead to higher world utility than global interactions.

Chapter 12 provides a look at the inverse problem of designing collectives from a evolutionary algorithm viewpoint. It shows how certain selection and fitness-sharing methods used in coevolution can be used in the design of a collective. Finally Chapter 13 provides a market-based "computational ecosystem" approach to collectives. It presents theory describing the dynamics of the agents, and experimentally shows that very sophisticated agents can lead to undesirable behavior. Then it shows that such undesirable global behavior can be prevented by applying local control.

With the variety in both the approaches used by the authors and the types of problems selected, this book presents a broad view of the current state of the art in the field of collectives. We hope that this book along with the interaction it might engender among scientists from different disciplines will lead to the emergence of a new and exciting field of collectives and the design of complex systems.

Moffett Field, CA   *Kagan Tumer*
July 2003   *David Wolpert*

References

1. R.J. Aumann and S. Hart. *Handbook of Game Theory with Economic Applications, Volumes I and II*. North-Holland Press, 1992.
2. R. Axelrod. *The Evolution of Cooperation*. Basic Books, NY, 1984.
3. T. Back, D. B. Fogel, and Z. Michalewicz, editors. *Handbook of Evolutionary Computation*. Oxford University Press, 1997.
4. T. Basar and G.J. Olsder. *Dynamic Noncooperative Game Theory*. Academic Press, 1982.
5. K. Binmore. *Fun and Games: A Text on Game Theory*. D. C. Heath and Company, Lexington, MA, 1992.
6. E. Bonabeau, M. Dorigo, and G. Theraulaz. Inspiration for optimization from social insect behaviour. *Nature*, 406(6791):39–42, 2000.
7. G. Caldarelli, M. Marsili, and Y. C. Zhang. A prototype model of stock exchange. *Europhysics Letters*, 40:479–484, 1997.
8. D. Challet and N. F. Johnson. Optimal combinations of imperfect objects. *Physical Review Letters*, 89:028701, 2002.
9. K. Chellapilla and D.B. Fogel. Evolution, neural networks, games, and intelligence. *Proceedings of the IEEE*, pages 1471–1496, September 1999.
10. R. H. Crites and A. G. Barto. Improving elevator performance using reinforcement learning. In D. S. Touretzky, M. C. Mozer, and M. E. Hasselmo, editors, *Advances in Neural Information Processing Systems - 8*, pages 1017–1023. MIT Press, 1996.
11. J. de Boer, B. Derrida, H. Flyvberg, A. D. Jackson, and T. Wettig. Simple model of self-organized biological evolution. *Physical Review Letters*, 73(6):906–909, 1994.
12. M. Dorigo and L. M. Gambardella. Ant colony systems: A cooperative learning approach to the travelling salesman problem. *IEEE Transactions on Evolutionary Computation*, 1(1):53–66, 1997.

13. D. Fudenberg and D. K. Levine. *The Theory of Learning in Games*. MIT Press, Cambridge, MA, 1998.

14. D. Fudenberg and J. Tirole. *Game Theory*. MIT Press, Cambridge, MA, 1991.

15. S. Geman and D. Geman. Stochastic relaxation, Gibbs distribution and the Bayesian restoration of images. *IEEE Transactions on Pattern Analysis and Machine Intelligence*, 6:721–741, 1984.

16. A. Greif. Economic history and game theory: A survey. In R. J. Aumann and S. Hart, editors, *Handbook of Game Theory with Economic Applications*, volume 3. North Holland, Amsterdam, 1999.

17. B. A. Huberman and T. Hogg. The behavior of computational ecologies. In *The Ecology of Computation*, pages 77–115. North-Holland, 1988.

18. S. Kirkpatrick, C. D. Jr Gelatt, and M. P. Vecchi. Optimization by simulated annealing. *Science*, 220:671–680, May 1983.

19. M.J.B. Krieger, J.-B. Billeter, and L. Keller. Ant-like task allocation and recruitment in cooperative robots. *Nature*, 406:992–995, 2000.

20. T. M. Lenton. Gaia and natural selection. *Nature*, 394:439–447, 1998.

21. M. Mesterton-Gibbons and E. S. Adams. Animal contests as evolutionary games. *American Scientist*, 86:334–341, 1998.

22. J. H. Miller. The coevolution of automata in the repeated prisoner's dilemma. *Journal of Economic Behavior and Organization*, 29(1):87–112, 1996.

23. M. Osborne and A. Rubenstein. *A Course in Game Theory*. MIT Press, Cambridge, MA, 1994.

24. T. S. Ray. Evolution, complexity, entropy and artificial life. *Physica D*, 1995.

25. R. S. Sutton and A. G. Barto. *Reinforcement Learning: An Introduction*. MIT Press, Cambridge, MA, 1998.

26. D. H. Wolpert. The existence of a priori distinctions between learning algorithms. *Neural Computation*, 8:1391–1420, 1996.

27. D. H. Wolpert. The lack of a priori distinctions between learning algorithms. *Neural Computation*, 8:1341–1390, 1996.

28. D. H. Wolpert and W. G. Macready. No free lunch theorems for optimization. *IEEE Transactions on Evolutionary Computation*, 1(1):67–82, 1997. Best Paper Award.

29. D. H. Wolpert, K. Wheeler, and K. Tumer. Collective intelligence for control of distributed dynamical systems. *Europhysics Letters*, 49(6), March 2000.

1

A Survey of Collectives

Kagan Tumer[1] and David Wolpert[2]

Summary. Due to the increasing sophistication and miniaturization of computational components, complex, distributed systems of interacting agents are becoming ubiquitous. Such systems, where each agent aims to optimize its own performance, but there is a well-defined set of system-level performance criteria, are called **collectives**. The fundamental problem in analyzing and designing such systems is in determining how the combined actions of a large number of agents lead to "coordinated" behavior on the global scale. Examples of artificial systems that exhibit such behavior include packet routing across a data network, control of an array of communication satellites, coordination of multiple rovers, and dynamic job scheduling across a distributed computer grid. Examples of natural systems include ecosystems, economies, and the organelles within a living cell.

No current scientific discipline provides a thorough understanding of the relation between the structure of collectives and how well they meet their overall performance criteria. Although still very young, research on collectives has resulted in successes in both understanding and designing such systems. It is expected that as it matures and draws on other disciplines related to collectives, this field will greatly expand the range of computationally addressable tasks. Moreover, in addition to drawing on them, such a fully developed field of collective intelligence may provide insight into already established scientific fields, such as mechanism design, economics, game theory, and population biology. This chapter provides a survey of the emerging science of collectives.

1 Just What Is a "Collective"?

As computing power increases, becomes cheaper, and is packed into smaller units, a new computational paradigm based on adaptive distributed computing is emerging. Whether used for control or optimization of complex engineered systems or the analysis of natural systems, this new paradigm offers new and exciting solutions to the problems of the twenty-first century. However, before the full strength of this

[1] NASA Ames Research Center, Mailstop 269-4, Moffett Field, CA, 94035
   ktumer@mail.arc.nasa.gov
[2] NASA Ames Research Center, Mailstop 269-4, Moffett Field, CA, 94035
   dhw@ptolemy.arc.nasa.gov

powerful computational paradigm can be harnessed, some fundamental issues need to be addressed.

In this chapter we provide a survey of approaches to large distributed systems called **collectives**. A collective is a large system of agents,[3] where each agent has a **private utility** function it is trying to maximize using adaptive utility-maximizing algorithms, called **agents**, along a **world utility** function that measures the full system's performance.[4]

Many fields provide partial solutions to the design and study of collectives. In particular, game theory [11, 19, 30, 87], mechanism design [82, 87], and multiagent reinforcement learning [53, 56, 112, 192] are fields that grapple with some of the issues encountered in the field of collectives. However, although these fields provide some of the ingredients required for a Full-fledged field of collectives, they fall short of providing a suitable starting point for the development of such a field. Furthermore, merging concepts from one of these fields with another is generally cumbersome due to the various assumptions—rarely explicit—deeply rooted in each field. What is needed for the field of collectives to develop and mature is a common language describing the various properties of collectives, a set of desirable properties, a theoretical framework, and a set of problems that will provide good testing grounds for new ideas in this field.

1.1 Distinguishing Characteristics of Collectives

Collectives can be characterized through many different distinguishing characteristics. Because the chapters in this volume focus on various design and analysis aspects of collectives, we briefly synopsize some distinguishing characteristics of collectives. These include the presence or absence of a well-defined world utility function; the forward or inverse approach; the presence or absence of centralized control or communications; the presence or absence of a model; and scalability, robustness, and adaptivity.

World Utility Function

Having a well-defined world utility function that concerns the behavior of the entire distributed system is crucial in the study of collectives. Such a world utility function provides an objective quantification of how well the system is performing. In that light, in a collective, we are not concerned with an unquantifiable "emergent" behavior of the system. Rather we are interested in how the system maximizes the specified world utility function (of course, nothing precludes the world utility from depending on the emergent behavior of the system, assuming such behavior can be quantified).

---

[3] We use the term **agent** to refer to the components of the system, although the various fields surveyed use different terminology (i.e., player in game theory).

[4] The world utility can be provided as part of the specifications of the system or "constructed" by the designer, as discussed later.

The most natural type of world utility is a *provided* utility, one that comes as part of the problem definition and specifies the overall performance criteria that the collective needs to meet. Examples of such world utilities include total throughput in a data network, total scientific information gathered by a team of deployables, total information downloaded by a constellation of satellites, the valuation of a company, or the percentage of available free energy exploited by an ecosystem.

However, the lack of a provided world utility does not preclude a collective-based approach to a problem. In such a case, assuming the agents have some utility functions associated with them, a world utility can be constructed (e.g., construct a social welfare function in economics). Examples of such world utilities include sum of agent utilities, sum of agent utilities and variances, and the utility of the worst-off agent. Note that maximizing each of these *constructed* world utilities would result in different system behavior. What is particularly interesting in such problems is the relationship between the agents' initial utility functions and the utility functions that they ought to pursue in order to maximize the constructed world utility function.

Forward (Analysis) vs. Inverse (Design) Problem

Whether it has a provided or constructed world utility, a collective can be approached from two very different perspectives: analysis or the forward problem and design or the inverse problem.

The **forward problem** focuses on how the localized attributes of a collective induce global behavior and thereby determine system performance. Generally, this problem arises in the study of already existing complex systems and is most naturally applicable to biological systems or systems that can be viewed as such. Examples of such systems include ecosystems or a living cell, where in each case, the local interactions (species and organelles, respectively) lead to complex emergent behavior on a large scale.

Engineered systems such as processes (e.g., the space shuttle maintenance and refurbishment process) or (economic) organizations, can also be viewed as forward problems in collectives. In those cases, the analysis approach can lead to predictive models and detect interactions among components of the system that may lead to breakdowns (e.g., determining whether a component considered "safe" can cause a critical malfunction when it interacts with another "safe" component).

The **inverse problem**, on the other hand, arises when we wish to design a system to induce behavior that maximizes the world utility. Here, the designer either has the freedom to assign the private utility functions of the agents (e.g., determine what each satellite or router should be doing) or needs to design incentives that will be added to the preexisting private utilities of the agents (e.g., economics, where agents are humans). In either case, though, the focus is on guiding toward states where the world utility is high.

Centralized Communication or Control

Though not in the formal definition of a collective, many collectives are decentralized systems. With few exceptions, it is difficult, if not impossible, to have centralized control in a collective, not only because reaching each agent may be problematic, but more fundamentally, because in many cases a centralized algorithm may not be able to determine what each agent should do.

Similarly, though some amount of global communication (e.g., broadcasting) may be possible, in general there will be little to no centralized communication, where a small subset of agents not only communicates with all the other agents but communicates differently with each of those other agents. Establishing the amount of allowed (or possible) centralized communication and control will be one of the fundamental issues in a collective.

Model-Based vs. Model-Free Approaches

Another important characteristic of a collective is the presence or absence of a model describing the dynamics of the system. A **model-based** approach consists of:

1. constructing a detailed model of the dynamics governing the collective;
2. learning the function that maps the parameters of the model to the resulting dynamics of the system (in practice, this step can involve significant hand-tuning); and
3. (a) drawing conclusions about this system based on the model (forward problem) and (b) determining parameters of the model that will yield the desired behavior (inverse problem).

A fundamentally different approach, however, is to dispense with building a model altogether, on the grounds that large complex systems are generally noisy, faulty, and often operate in nonstationary environments. In such cases, coming up with a detailed model that captures the dynamics in an accurate manner is often extraordinarily difficult.

A **model-free** approach relies on agents "reacting" to the environment (e.g., through a reinforcement learning mechanism). As such they avoid explicitly modeling the system in which they operate, and they avoid the potentially infinite regress when one agent tries to model another's behavior and the other agent is itself modeling the first agent's behavior.

The model-based-vs.-model-free choice has significant consequences on how the system can adapt and scale up and on how lessons learned from one domain can map to another. A model-based approach may be the choice for domains where the designer can develop detailed models and have a moderate degree of control over the environment. However, in domains where detailed models are not available or where there is reason to believe changes in the environment can lead to significant deviations from any model, a model-free approach is preferable.

Scalability

One of the implicit defining properties of a collective is that it is a *large* system of distributed agents. As such, scalability is a fundamental property of any approach that aims to study or design a collective. Although this does not preclude extending extant analysis and design tools appropriate for single (or small) systems to large systems, it does suggest that in most instances, new ways of approaching the problem are likely to be more appropriate (e.g., a game-theoretic equilibrium analysis for a million nanodevices is unlikely to provide useful insight into the behavior of the collective).

Adaptivity

Although scalability does not require that the system be adaptive, it provides a strong impetus to move in that direction. Any approach that allows adaptivity or learning will have a significant advantage over one that does not, simply because the larger a system, the more difficult it will be to know a priori all the "right moves" for each agent.

Furthermore, the need for adaptivity extends beyond each agent in the collective. Indeed, the structure of the collective itself (e.g., the communication channels among the agents and the agents' utility function) in many cases is adaptive. In natural collectives this system-level adaptivity is generally implicit (e.g., the interaction among species in an ecosystem or the relationship among employees in a company), whereas in artificial systems it must be built in.

Robustness

Another desirable property of a collective is that it be robust, i.e., that in order to reach good values of the world utility, the collective not require that many parameters be set "just right," that each agent operate failure-free, and that their interaction be carefully constructed. Clearly, as the number of agents in a system increases and their interaction with one another and the environment becomes more complex, it will be increasingly difficult to predict conditions that will lead the system to maximize the world utility. It is therefore imperative that the collective be insensitive to the specific values of some parameters or the specific operation of a small subset of its agents (e.g., in general, the poor performance of one employee does not bring a company down, or the demise of a single individual does not result in the extinction of a species).

1.2 Canonical Experimental Domains

The previous section provided a list of distinguising characteristics of collectives. The usefulness of defining these characteristics is in their providing a common language for a field of collectives. For example, a particular instance of data routing in a telecommunications network can be characterized as "a model-free inverse problem involving a provided world utility function where there is limited broadcast information but no form of global control."

We now provide examples of both engineered and natural systems that are ideally suited to be studied as collectives. For each, we provide one or more world utility functions, discuss how it can be approached (e.g., forward or inverse problem), and list the assumptions (e.g., is it model-based?) and restrictions (e.g., is global communication possible?) present.

- *Control system for constellations of communication satellites:* A candidate world utility for this problem is a measure of (potentially importance-weighted) information transferred. It is an example of an inverse problem, where centralized communication or control is likely to be difficult or impossible due to physical constraints (e.g., time lag) and where a model of the data flow is likely to be inadequate.
- *Control system for constellations of planetary exploration vehicles:* A potential world utility for such a problem is a measure of the quality of scientific data collected. Although this can be viewed as an example of an inverse design problem (as with constellations of satellites), it can also be approached as a forward problem, particularly if the vehicles have characteristics that cannot be altered (e.g., vehicles are built and we are confronted with the problem of predicting the behavior of the collective).
- *Control system for routing over a communication network:* An obvious world utility for this problem is the total throughput of the communication network. Centralized communication or control in such a network is all but impossible, but some amount of broadcast information can filter its way to all the agents at regular time intervals. As an inverse problem, one would be required to design the private utility functions of the agents. As a forward problem on an already functioning network, one could determine the stress points of the system or the states that would cause the most congestion in the network.
- *Air space management:* Given a problem specification where there is some leeway in modifying the course and speed of airplanes, a potential world utility is the total delay at airports. The system designers are faced with the inverse problem of determining the incentives for the agents (whether they be pilots or air traffic controllers) so that their behavior (e.g., arrival times in the airport's airspace) optimizes the world utility. This is a case where global communication is possible, but global control is not.
- *Managing a power grid:* A world utility based on the efficiency of the grid would be a good starting point for an inverse problem, involving some degree of centralized communication or control. An alternative world utility may be robustness. In such a case a forward problem would involve finding how quickly the system responds to certain disturbances and how the system interactions can be modified to limit the propagation of those disturbances.
- *Job scheduling across a computational grid:* A candidate world utility is the efficiency in processing the jobs entering the system. This problem is very similar to managing a power grid but provides a glimpse of the inverse problem: How should one set the rewards of the computational nodes so that they process the highest number of jobs collectively? A model-free solution involving learners at the computational nodes would be based on limited global communication.

- *Control of the elements of a nanocomputer:* A potential world utility for this problem is how well certain computations are carried out by the nanocomputer.[5] In an inverse problem, one would focus on determining the structure of the adaptive system, which would lead the agents to perform the desired computations. A particular instance of an inverse problem of this nature is the selection of subsets of faulty devices, where the world utility is the total aggregate error of the selected devices.

- *Study of a protocell:* A potential world utility for this problem is the length of time the protocell[6] maintains its functionality. As a forward problem, this problem consists of modeling the behavior of the system based on the organelles and their functions and interactions. With more leeway in the definition of the functions the organelles perform, one can view this as an interesting inverse problem: What should the organelles try to achieve to maintain the structure and functionality of the protocell?

- *Study and design of an ecosystem:* One world utility for the study of an ecosystem is the total biomass of the ecosystem. In a model-based forward problem, one can study the effect of various interactions on the world utility. Alternatively, as an inverse problem, one can investigate how to design an ecosystem that will provide the best sustainable biodiversity for a given mass (e.g., for a long-term space mission).

- *Design of incentives in a company:* A "simple" world utility for a company is the valuation of the company (share price times the number of outstanding shares). The inverse problem consists of determining how to design incentives that will induce the company's valuation to go up (e.g., what set of salaries, benefits, and stock options will induce the employees to take actions that will benefit the corporation).

All of these problems share the property that they are inherently distributed systems where the interactions among the agents lead to complex behavior. Although each can be approached by conventional methods, how those methods need to be modified to suit the particular application will be different in each case. The aim of this chapter is to both accentuate the similarities among these problems and to highlight the need for a general approach, which would address all these problems within the same framework.

2 Review of the Literature Related to Collectives

There are many approaches to analyzing and designing collectives that do not exactly meet the needs of a "field of collectives" yet provide some part of the equation. The rest of this section consists of brief presentations of some of these approaches and characterizes them in terms of the properties of collectives discussed earlier.

---

[5] A **nanocomputer** is a computer with nano-scale components.

[6] A **protocell** is a vessicle lacking conventional genetic material and organelles, especially an artificially constructed one used to investigate cellular homeostasis.

2.1 Artificial Intelligence and Machine Learning

There is an extensive body of work in artificial intelligence (AI) and machine learning related to the design of collectives. Indeed, one of the most famous speculative works in the field can be viewed as an argument that AI should be approached as a design of collectives problem [163]. We will discuss some topics relevant to collectives from this domain.

Distributed Artificial Intelligence

The field of distributed artificial intelligence (DAI) has arisen as more traditional AI tasks have migrated toward parallel implementation. The most direct approach to such implementations is to directly parallelize AI production systems or the underlying programming languages [79,189]. An alternative and more challenging approach is to use distributed computing, where not only the individual reasoning, planning, and scheduling AI tasks are parallelized, but there are *different modules* with different such tasks, concurrently working toward a common goal [118,119,143].

In a DAI, one needs to ensure that the task has been modularized in a way that improves efficiency. Unfortunately, this usually requires a central controller whose purpose is to allocate tasks and process the associated results. Moreover, designing that controller in a traditional AI fashion often results in brittle solutions. Accordingly, there has recently been a move toward both more autonomous modules and fewer restrictions on the interactions among the modules [194].

Despite this evolution, DAI maintains the traditional AI concern with a prefixed set of *particular* aspects of intelligent behavior (e.g., reasoning, understanding, and learning) rather than on their *cumulative* character. As the idea that intelligence may have more to do with the interaction among components started to take shape [41,42], focus shifted to concepts (e.g., multiagent systems) that better incorporated that idea [121].

Multiagent Systems

The field of multiagent systems (MAS) is concerned with the interactions among the members of such a set of agents [40,92,121,204,222], as well as the inner workings of each agent in such a set (e.g., their learning algorithms) [36–38]. As in computational ecologies and computational markets (discussed later), a well-designed MAS is one that achieves a global task through the actions of its components. The associated design steps involve [121]:

1. decomposing a global task into distributable subcomponents, yielding tractable tasks for each agent;
2. establishing communication channels that provide sufficient information to each of the agents for it to achieve its task, but that are not too unwieldly for the overall system to sustain; and

3. coordinating the agents in a way that ensures that they cooperate on the global task, or at the very least does not allow them to pursue conflicting strategies in trying to achieve their tasks.

Step 3 is rarely trivial; one of the main difficulties encountered in MAS design is that agents act selfishly and artificial cooperation structures have to be imposed on their behavior to enforce cooperation [13]. An active area of research, which holds promise for addressing the design of collectives problem, is to determine how selfish agents' "incentives" have to be engineered to avoid problems such as the tragedy of the commons (TOC) [209]. (This work draws on the economics literature, which we review separately later.) When simply providing the right incentives is not sufficient, one can resort to strategies that actively induce agents to cooperate rather than act selfishly. In such cases, coordination [205], negotiations [135], coalition formation [193, 195, 249], or contracting [3] among agents may be needed to ensure that they do not work at cross purposes.

Unfortunately, all of these approaches share with DAI and its offshoots the problem of relying on hand-tailoring and therefore are difficult to scale and often nonrobust. In addition, except as noted in the next subsection, they involve little to no adaptivity, and therefore the constituent computational elements are usually not as robust as they need to be to provide the foundation for the field of collectives.

Reinforcement Learning

The maturing field of reinforcement learning (RL) provides a much needed tool for the types of problems addressed by collectives. The goal of an RL algorithm is to determine how, using those reward signals, the agent should update its action policy to maximize its utility [123, 220, 221, 232]. Because RL generally provides model-free[7] and "online" learning features, it is ideally suited for the distributed environment where a "teacher" is not available and the agents need to learn successful strategies based on "rewards" and "penalties" they receive from the overall system at various intervals. It is even possible for the learners to use those rewards to modify *how* they learn [199, 200].

Although work on RL dates back to Samuel's checker player [191], relatively recent theoretical [232] and empirical results [56, 224] have made RL one of the most active areas in machine learning. Many problems, ranging from controlling a robot's gait to controlling a chemical plant to allocating constrained resources, have been addressed with considerable success using RL [97, 114, 166, 186, 247]. In particular, the RL algorithms $TD(\lambda)$ (which rates potential states based on a *value function*) [220] and Q–learning (which rates action-state pairs) [232] have been investigated extensively. A detailed investigation of RL is available in [123, 221, 232].

Intuitively, one might hope that RL would help us solve the distributed control problem, because RL is adaptive and, in general, mode-free. However, by itself, conventional single-agent RL does not provide a means for controlling large distributed systems. The problem is that the space of possible action policies for such systems

---

[7] There are some model-based variants of traditional RL. See, for example, [8].

is too big to be searched. So although powerful and widely applicable, solitary RL algorithms will not generally perform well on large distributed heterogeneous problems. It is, however, natural to consider deploying many RL algorithms rather than a single one for these large distributed problems.

Reinforcement Learning–Based Multiagent Systems

Because it requires neither explicit modeling of the environment nor a "teacher" that provides the "correct" actions, the approach of having the individual agents in a MAS use RL is well-suited for MASs deployed in domains where one has little knowledge about the environment or other agents. There are two main approaches to designing such MASs:

1. One has "team game agents" that don't know about each other and whose RL rewards are given by the performance of the entire system (so the joint actions of all other agents form an "inanimate background" contributing to the reward signal each agent receives).
2. One has "social agents" that explicitly model each other and take each others' actions into account.

Both 1 and 2 can be viewed as ways to (try to) coordinate the agents in a MAS in a robust fashion.

Team game agents: MASs with team game agents have been successfully applied to a multitude of problems [56, 96, 107, 192, 198]. However, scaling to large systems is a major issue with team game agents. The problem is that each agent must be able to discern the effect of its actions on the overall performance of the system, because that performance constitutes its reward signal. However, as the number of agents increases, the effects of any one agent's actions (signal) will be swamped by the effects of other agents (noise), making the agent unable to learn well, if at all. In addition, of course, team game agents cannot be used in situations lacking centralized calculation and broadcast of the single global reward signal.

Social agents: MASs whose agents take the actions of other agents into account synthesize RL with game-theoretic concepts (e.g., Nash equilibrium). They do this to try to ensure that the overall system both moves toward achieving the overall global goal and avoids often deleterious oscillatory behavior [53, 85, 111–113]. To that end, the agents incorporate internal mechanisms that actively model the behavior of other agents. In general, this approach involves hand-tailoring for the problem, and there are some well-studied domains (the El Farol Bar problem) in which such modeling is self-defeating [5, 238].

2.2 Game Theory

Game theory is the branch of mathematics concerned with formalized versions of "games," in the sense of chess, poker, nuclear arms races, and the like [11, 19, 30, 66,

73, 87, 148, 207]. It is perhaps easiest to describe it by loosely defining some of its terminology, which we do here and in the next section.

The simplest form of a game is that of the "noncooperative single-stage extensive-form" game, which involves the following situation: There are two or more agents (called **players**), each of which has a pre-specified set of possible actions that it can follow. (A "finite" game has finite sets of possible actions for all the players.) In addition, each agent i has a utility function (also called a **payoff matrix** for finite games). This maps any "profile" of the action choices of all agents to an associated utility value for agent i. (In a "zero-sum" game, for every profile, the sum of the payoffs to all the agents is zero.)

The agents choose their actions in a sequence, one after the other. The structure determining what each agent knows concerning the action choices of the preceding agents is known as the "information set."[8] Games in which each agent knows exactly what the preceding (leader) agent did are called **Stackelberg games**.

In a multistage game, after all the agents choose their first action, each agent is provided some information concerning what the other agents did. The agent uses this information to choose its next action. In the usual formulation, each agent gets its payoff at the end of all of the game's stages.

An agent's strategy is the rule it elects to follow mapping the information it has at each stage of a game to its associated action. It is a pure strategy if it is a deterministic rule. If the agent's action is chosen by randomly sampling from a distribution, that distribution is known a mixed strategy. Note that an agent's strategy concerns *all* possible sequences of provided information, even those that cannot arise due to the strategies of the other agents.

Any multistage extensive-form game can be converted into a normal-form game, which is a single-stage game in which each agent is ignorant of the actions of the other agents, so that all agents choose their actions simultaneously. This conversion is achieved by having the "actions" of each agent in the normal-form game correspond to an entire strategy in the associated multistage extensive-form game. The payoffs to all the agents in the normal-form game for a particular strategy profile is then given by the associated payoff matrices of the multistage extensive-form games.

Nash Equilibrium

A solution to a game, or an **equilibrium**, is a profile in which every agent behaves "rationally." This means that every agent's choice of strategy maximizes its utility subject to a prespecified set of conditions. In conventional game theory those conditions involve, at a minimum, perfect knowledge of the payoff matrices of all other players and, often, specification of what strategies the other agents adopted. In particular, a **Nash equilibrium** is a a profile where each agent has chosen the best strategy

---

[8] Although stochastic choices of actions are central to game theory, most of the work in the field assumes the information in information sets is in the form of definite facts, rather than a probability distribution. Accordingly, there has been relatively little work incorporating Shannon information theory into the analysis of information sets.

it can, *given the choices of the other agents*. A game may have no Nash equilibrium, one equilibrium, or many equilibria in the space of pure strategies. A beautiful and seminal theorem due to Nash proves that every game has at least one Nash equilibrium in the space of mixed strategies [171].

There are several reasons one might expect a game to result in a Nash equilibrium. One is that it is the point that perfectly rational Bayesian agents would adopt, assuming the probability distributions they used to calculate expected payoffs were consistent with one another [10, 124]. A related reason, arising even in a non-Bayesian setting, is that a Nash equilibrium provides "consistent" predictions, in that if all parties predict that the game will converge to a Nash equilibrium, no one will benefit by changing strategies. Having a consistent prediction does not ensure that all agents' payoffs are maximized, however. The study of small perturbations around Nash equilibria from a stochastic dynamics perspective is just one example of a "refinement" of a Nash equilibrium, which provides a criterion for selecting a single equilibrium state when more than one is present [154].

Cooperative Game Theory

In cooperative game theory the agents are able to enter binding contracts with one another and thereby coordinate their strategies. This allows the agents to avoid being "stuck" in Nash equilibria that are Pareto-inefficient, that is being stuck at equilibrium profiles in which all agents would benefit if only they could agree to all adopt different strategies, with no possibility of betrayal. The *characteristic function* of a game involves subsets ('coalitions') of agents playing the game. For each such subset, it gives the sum of the payoffs of the agents in that subset that those agents can guarantee if they coordinate their strategies. An *imputation* is a division of such a guaranteed sum among the members of the coalition. It is often the case that for a subset of the agents in a coalition, one imputation *dominates* another, meaning that under threat of leaving the coalition that subset of agents can demand the first imputation rather than the second. So the problem each agent i is confronted with in a cooperative game is which set of other agents to form a coalition with, given the characteristic function of the game and the associated imputations i can demand of its partners. There are several kinds of solution for cooperative games that have received detailed study, varying in how the agents address this problem of who to form a coalition with. Some of the more popular are the "core," the "Shapley value," the "stable set solution," and the "nucleolus."

In the real world, the actual underlying game the agents are playing does not only involve the actions considered in cooperative game theory's analysis of coalitions and imputations. The strategies of that underlying game also involve bargaining behavior, considerations of trying to cheat on a given contract, bluffing and threats, and the like. In many respects, by concentrating on solutions for coalition formation and their relation with the characteristic function, cooperative game theory abstracts away these details of the true underlying game. Conversely though, progress has recently been made in understanding how cooperative games can arise from noncooperative games, as they must in the real world [11].

Evolution and Learning in Games

Not surprisingly, game theory has come to play a large role in the field of multiagent systems. In addition, due to Darwinian natural selection, one might expect game theory to be important in population biology, in which the "utility functions" of the individual agents can be taken to be their reproductive fitness. There is an entire subfield of game theory concerned with this connection with population biology, called "evolutionary game theory" [155, 157].

To introduce evolutionary game theory, consider a game in which all players share the same space of possible strategies and there is an additional space of possible "attribute vectors" that characterize an agent, along with a probability distribution g across that new space. (Examples of attributes in the physical world could be things like size and speed.) We select a set of agents to play a game by randomly sampling g. Those agents' attribute vectors jointly determine the payoff matrices of each agent. (Intuitively, the benefit that accrues to an agent for taking a particular action depends on its attributes and those of the other agents.) However, each agent i has limited information concerning both its attribute vector and that of the other players in the game, information encapsulated in an "information structure." The information structure specifies how much each agent knows about the game it is playing.

In this context, we enlarge the meaning of the term "strategy" to not just a mapping from information sets and the like to actions, but from entire information structures to actions. In addition to the distribution g over attribute vectors, we have a distribution over strategies, h. A strategy s is a "population strategy" if h is a delta function about s. Intuitively, we have a population strategy when each animal in a population "follows the same behavioral rules," rules that take as input what the animal is able to discern about its strengths and weaknesses relative to other members of the population and produce as output how the animal will act in the presence of such animals.

Given g, a population strategy centered about s, and its own attribute vector, any player i in the support of g has an expected payoff for any strategy it might adopt. When i's payoff could not improve if it were to adopt any strategy other than s, we say that s is "evolutionary-stable." Intuitively, an evolutionary-stable strategy is one that is stable with respect to the introduction of mutants into the population.

Now consider a sequence of such evolutionary games. Interpret the payoff that any agent receives after being involved in such a game as the "reproductive fitness" of that agent, in the biological sense. So the higher the payoff the agent receives, in comparison to the fitnesses of the other agents, the more "offspring" it has that get propagated to the next game. In the continuum time limit, where games are indexed by the real number t, this can be formalized by a differential equation that specifies the derivative of g_t evaluated for each agent i's attribute vector, as a monotonically increasing function of the relative difference between the payoff of i and the average payoff of all the agents. (We also have such an equation for h.) The resulting dynamics is known as "replicator dynamics," with an evolutionary-stable population strategy, if it exists, being one particular fixed point of the dynamics.

Now consider removing the reproductive aspect of evolutionary game theory and instead have each agent propagate to the next game, with "memory" of the events of the preceding game. Furthermore, allow each agent to modify its strategy from one game to the next by "learning" from its memory of past games in a bounded rational manner. The field of learning in games is concerned with exactly such situations [12,17,26,70,86,126,173,178]. Most of the formal work in this field involves simple models for the learning process of the agents. For example, in "fictitious play" [86], in each successive game, each agent i adopts what would be its best strategy if its opponents chose their strategies according to the empirical frequency distribution of such strategies that i has encountered in the past. More sophisticated versions of this work use simple Bayesian learning algorithms, or reinventions of some of the techniques of the RL community [190]. Typically in learning in games one defines a payoff to the agent for a sequence of games, for example, as a discounted sum of the payoffs in each of the constituent games. Within this framework one can study the long-term effects of strategies such as cooperation and see if they arise naturally, and if so, under what circumstances.

Many aspects of real-world games that do not occur very naturally otherwise arise spontaneously in these kinds of games. For example, when the number of games to be played is not prefixed, it may behoove a particular agent i to treat its opponent better than it would otherwise, because i may have to rely on that other agent's treating it well in the future, if they end up playing each other again. This framework also allows us to investigate the dependence of evolving strategies on the amount of information available to the agents [159]; the effect of communication on the evolution of cooperation [160,162]; and the parallels between auctions and economic theory [108,161].

In many respects, learning in games is even more relevant to the study of collectives than is traditional game theory. However, in general, it lacks a well-defined world utility and is almost exclusively focused on the forward problem, making it a difficult starting point for a field of collectives.

2.3 Other Social Science–Inspired Systems

Some human economies provides examples of naturally occurring systems that can be viewed as a (more or less) well-performing collective. However, the field of economics provides much more. Both empirical economics (e.g., economic history, experimental economics) and theoretical economics (e.g., general equilibrium theory [4], theory of optimal taxation [164]) provide a rich literature on strategic situations where many parties interact. In fact, much of economics can be viewed as concerning how to maximize certain constrained kinds of world utilities, when there are certain (very strong) restrictions on the individual agents and their interactions, in particular when we have limited freedom in setting the utility functions of those agents.

Mechanism Design

One way to try to induce a large collective to reach an equilibrium point without centralized control is via an auction.[9] (This is the approach usually used in computational markets, as discussed later.) Along with optimal taxation and public good theory [137], the design of auctions is the subject of the field of mechanism design. Broadly defined, mechanism design is concerned with the incentives that must be applied to any set of agents that interact and exchange goods [87, 164, 229] in order to get those agents to exhibit desired behavior. Usually the desired behavior concerns prespecified "inherent" utility functions of some sort for each agent. In particular, mechanism design is often concerned with the incentives that must be superimposed on such inherent utility functions to guide the agents to a "(Pareto)-efficient" (or "Pareto-optimal") point, that is, to a point in which no agent's inherent utility can be improved without hurting another agent's inherent utility [86, 87].

One particularly important type of such an incentive scheme is an auction. When many agents interact in a common environment there often needs to be a structure that supports the exchange of goods or information among those agents. Auctions provide one such (centralized) structure for managing exchanges of goods. For example, in the English auction all the agents come together and "bid" for a good, and the price of the good is increased until only one bidder remains, who gets the good in exchange for the resource bid. As another example, in the Dutch auction the price of a good is decreased until one buyer is willing to pay the current price.

All auctions perform the same task: They match supply and demand. As such, auctions are one of the ways in which price equilibration among a set of interacting agents can be achieved. However, very few world utilities have their maximum occur at a point that is Pareto-optimal for the preset inherent utility functions. Accordingly, unless we are very fortunate in the relation between those inherent utility functions and the (in general, separately specified) world utility, knowing how to induce such a Pareto-optimal point is of little value. For example, in a transaction in an English auction both the seller and the buyer benefit. They may even have arrived at an allocation that is efficient. However, because the winner may have been willing to pay more for the good, such an outcome may confound the goal of the market designer, if that designer's goal is to maximize revenue. This point is returned to later, in the context of computational economics.

Another, perhaps more intuitive, perspective is to view the restrictions of mechanism design as concerning the private utility functions of the individual agents. Typically in mechanism design the private utility function for each agent η, which maps states of the entire world (including the internal state of the agent itself) to $\mathcal{R}$, is of the form $\gamma_\eta(x_{\eta,1}, x_{\eta,2}, ..., x_{\eta,n}, T_\eta(y_{\eta,1}, y_{\eta,2}, ..., y_{\eta,m}))$, where $\gamma_\eta(\cdot)$ is agent η's prefixed inherent utility function; the $x_{\eta,1}, x_{\eta,2}, ..., x_{\eta,n}$ constitute the first n of

---

[9] We do not discuss general equilibrium theory in detail here, because although it deals with the interaction among multiple markets to set the market "clearing" price for goods, it is not appropriate for the study of collectives: It requires centralized control (Walrasian auctioneer), does not allow for dynamic interactions, and in general, there is no reason to believe that having the markets clear maximizes a world utility.

the $n + k$ variables that that function depends on; and $T_\eta(\cdot)$ is the $\mathcal{R}^k$-valued "mechanism" function the designer can set, the $y_{\eta,1}, y_{\eta,2}, ..., y_{\eta,m}$ being the variables making up its arguments. Unlike the private utility, world utility can depend on all of the $x_{\eta,1}, ..., x_{\eta,n}, y_{\eta,1}, y_{\eta,2}, ..., y_{\eta,m}$ directly (as well as on other entirely different variables). As an example, the $y_{\eta,1}, y_{\eta,2}, ..., y_{\eta,m}$ could be a set of all agents' bids at an auction; $T_\eta(\cdot)$ could be $\mathcal{R}^2$-valued, giving the amount of change in η's owned quantities of both money and the item up for bid; and the $x_{\eta,1}, ..., x_{\eta,n}$ could parameterize η's happiness trade-off relating owned quantities of the good and of money.

Typically $\gamma_\eta(\cdot)$ and the choice of what variables make up the arguments $y_{\eta,1}, y_{\eta,2}, ..., y_{\eta,m}$ to T_η are fixed a priori, with only the function $T_\eta(\cdot)$ allowed to vary in the design. In addition, often there are a priori restrictions on the functional form of the T_η. For example, often the T_η are not allowed to vary with η. More precisely, usually they must be invariant under the transformation $\eta \to \eta'$ in both the index to the function and the indices to its arguments. This means, in particular, that the designer can't "cheat" and have the functional forms of the T_η vary from one η to another in a way that reflects the variations across the (often predetermined) associated vectors $(x_{\eta,1}, ..., x_{\eta,n})$. For example, typically an auction mechanism determines who gets what goods for what price in a manner that is independent of the identities of the bidding agents and does not directly reflect any internal happiness trade-off parameters of the agents that aren't reflected in their bids.

From the perspective of a collective, these kinds of restrictions on private utilities only hold in a small subset of the potential computational problems and constitute a severe handicap in other scenarios. Another limitation of most of the work on mechanism design is that either it assumes a particular computational model for the agent or (more commonly) it focuses on (game-theoretic) equilibria. This limited nature of the treatment of off-equilibrium scenarios is intimately related to the restrictions on the form of the private utility. If there are no restrictions on the private utilities, then there is a trivial solution for how to set such utilities to maximize the world utility at equilibrium: Have each such utility simply equal the world utility, in a so-called "team game." To have the analysis be nontrivial, restrictions like those on the private utilities are needed.

In practice though, no real system is at a game-theoretic equilibrium, due to bounded rationality. In particular, it means that if one considers mechanism design in the limiting case of no restrictions on $\gamma(\cdot)$, the associated "mechanism design solution" of a team game often will result in poor performance [238]. Team theory [105, 153] is one approach that has been tried to circumvent this problem. The idea there is to remove all notions of a private or inherent utility and solve directly for the strategy profile that will maximize the world utility. Needless to say, though, such an approach becomes extraordinarily difficult for all but the simplest problems and requires centralized, completely personalized control and communication and exact modeling of the system's dynamics.

Computational Economics

"Computational economies" are schemes inspired by economics, and more specifically, by general equilibrium theory and mechanism design theory, for managing the components of a distributed computational system. They work by having a "computational market," akin to an auction, guide the interactions among those components. Such a market is defined as any structure that allows the components of the system to exchange information on relative valuation of resources (as in an auction), establish equilibrium states (e.g., determine market clearing prices), and exchange resources (i.e., engage in trades).

Such computational economies can be used to investigate real economies and biological systems [31, 34, 35, 128]. They can also be used to design distributed computational systems. For example, such computational economies are well-suited to some distributed resource allocation problems, where each component of the system can either directly produce the "goods" it needs or acquire them through trades with other components. Computational markets often allow for far more heterogeneity in the components than do conventional resource allocation schemes. Furthermore, there is both theoretical and empirical evidence suggesting that such markets are often able to settle to equilibrium states. For example, auctions find prices that satisfy both the seller and the buyer, which results in an increase in the utility of both (else one or the other would not have agreed to the sale). Assuming that all parties are free to pursue trading opportunities, such mechanisms move the system to a point where all possible bilateral trades that could improve the utility of both parties are exhausted.

Now restrict attention to the case, implicit in much of computational market work, with the following characteristics: First, world utility can be expressed as a monotonically increasing function F, where each argument i of F can in turn be interpreted as the value of a prespecified utility function f_i for agent i. Second, each of those f_is is a function of an i-indexed "goods vector" x_i of the nonperishable goods "owned" by agent i. The components of that vector are $x_{i,j}$, and the overall system dynamics is restricted to conserve the vector $\sum_i x_{i,j}$. (There are also some other, more technical conditions.) As an example, the resource allocation problem can be viewed as concerning such vectors of "owned" goods.

Due to the second of our two conditions, one can integrate a market-clearing mechanism into any system of this sort. Due to the first condition, because in a market equilibrium with nonperishable goods no (rational) agent ends up with a value of its utility function lower than the one it started with, the value of the world utility function must be higher at equilibrium than it was initially. In fact, so long as the individual agents are smart enough to avoid all trades in which they do not benefit, any computational market can only improve this kind of world utility, even if it does not achieve the market equilibrium.

This line of reasoning provides one of the main reasons to use computational markets in those situations in which they can be applied. Conversely, it underscores one of the major limitations of such markets: Starting with an arbitrary world utility function with arbitrary dynamical restrictions, it may be quite difficult to cast that function as a monotonically increasing F taking as arguments a set of agents' goods-vector-based utilities f_i, if we require that those f_i be well-enough behaved that we can reasonably expect the agents to optimize them in a market setting.

One example of a computational economy being used for resource allocation is Huberman and Clearwater's use of a double-blind auction to solve the complex task of controlling the temperature of a building. In this case, each agent (individual temperature controller) bids to buy or sell cool or warm air. This market mechanism leads to an equitable temperature distribution in the system [116]. Other domains where market mechanisms were successfully applied include purchasing memory in an operating system [50], allocating virtual circuits [75], "stealing" unused CPU cycles in a network of computers [69, 230], predicting option futures in financial markets [185], and numerous scheduling and distributed resource allocation problems [138, 142, 210, 218, 234, 235].

Computational economics can also be used for tasks not tightly coupled to resource allocation. For example, following the work of Maes [151] and Ferber [74], Baum shows how by using computational markets many agents can interact and cooperate to solve a variant of the blocks world problem [22, 23]. However, market-based computational economics relies on both centralized communication and centralized control to some degree, raising scalability issues. Furthermore, in practice, the applicability of computational economies depends greatly on the domain [225], making it a difficult starting point for a field of collectives.

2.4 Biologically Inspired Systems

Properly speaking, biological systems do not involve utility functions and search across them with learning algorithms. However, it has long been appreciated that there are many ways in which viewing biological systems as involving searches over such functions can lead to a deeper understanding of them [203, 244]. Conversely, some have argued that the mechanism underlying biological systems can be used to help design search algorithms [109].[10]

These kinds of reasoning, which relate utility functions and biological systems have traditionally focused on the case of a single biological system operating in some external environment. If we extend this kind of reasoning to a set of biological systems that are coevolving with one another, then we have essentially arrived at biologically based collectives. This section discusses how some previous work in the literature bears on this relationship between collectives and biology.

Population Biology and Ecological Modeling

The fields of population biology and ecological modeling are concerned with the large-scale "emergent" processes that govern the systems that consist of many (relatively) simple entities interacting with one another [24, 99]. As usually cast, the

----

[10] See [150, 236] for some counterarguments to the particular claims most commonly made in this regard.

"simple entities" are members of one or more species, and the interactions are a mathematical abstraction of the process of natural selection as it occurs in biological systems (involving processes like genetic reproduction of various sorts, genotype-phenotype mappings, inter- and intra-species competitions for resources, etc.). Population biology and ecological modeling in this context address questions concerning the dynamics of the resultant ecosystem, in particular how its long-term behavior depends on the details of the interactions between the constituent entities. Broadly construed, the paradigm of ecological modeling can even be broadened to study how natural selection and self-regulating feedback create a stable planetwide ecological environment known as Gaia [144].

The underlying mathematical models of other fields can often be usefully modified to apply to the kinds of systems in which population biology is interested [14]. (See also the discussion in the earlier section on game theory.) Conversely, the underlying mathematical models of population biology and ecological modeling can be applied to other nonbiological systems. In particular, those models shed light on social issues such as the emergence of language or culture, warfare, and economic competition [71, 72, 88]. They also can be used to investigate more abstract issues concerning the behavior of large complex systems with many interacting components [89, 98, 156, 176, 184].

Going a bit further afield, an approach that is related in spirit to ecological modeling is "computational ecologies." These are large distributed systems where each component of the system acts (seemingly) independently, resulting in complex global behavior. Those components are viewed as constituting an "ecology" in an abstract sense (although much of the mathematics is not derived from the traditional field of ecological modeling). In particular, one can investigate how the dynamics of the ecology is influenced by the information available to each component and how cooperation and communication among the components affect that dynamics [115, 117].

Although in some ways the most closely related to collectives of the current ecology-inspired research, the fields of population biology and computational ecologies do not provide a full science of collectives. These fields are primarily concerned with the "forward problem" of determining the dynamics that arises from certain choices of the underlying system. Unless one's desired dynamics is sufficiently close to some dynamics that was previously catalogued (during one's investigation of the forward problem), one has very little information on how to set up the components and their interactions to achieve that desired dynamics.

Swarm Intelligence

The field of "swarm intelligence" is concerned with systems that are modeled after social insect colonies, so that the different components of the system are queen, worker, soldier, etc. It can be viewed as ecological modeling in which the individual entities have extremely limited computing capacity or action sets and in which there are very few types of entities. The premise of the field is that the rich behavior of social insect colonies arises not from the sophistication of any individual entity in the colony, but from the interaction among those entities. The objective of current research is to uncover kinds of interactions among the entity types that lead to prespecified behavior of some sort.

More speculatively, the study of social insect colonies may also provide insight into how to achieve learning in large distributed systems. This is because at the level of the individual insect in a colony, very little (or no) learning takes place. However, across evolutionary time scales, the social insect species as a whole functions as if the various individual types in a colony had "learned" their specific functions. The "learning" is the direct result of natural selection. (See the discussion on this topic in the section on ecological modeling.)

Swarm intelligences have been used to adaptively allocate tasks [33, 136], solve the traveling salesman problem [62, 63] and route data efficiently in dynamic networks [32, 201, 219]. However, there is no general framework for adapting swarm intelligences to maximize particular world utility functions. Accordingly, such intelligences generally need to be hand-tailored for each application.

2.5 Physics-Based Systems

Statistical Physics

Equilibrium statistical physics is concerned with the stable-state character of large numbers of very simple physical objects, interacting according to well-specified local deterministic laws, with probabilistic noise processes superimposed [6, 188]. Typically, there is no sense in which such systems can be said to have centralized control, because all particles contribute comparably to the overall dynamics.

Aside from mesoscopic statistical physics, the numbers of particles considered are usually huge (e.g., 10^{23}), and the particles themselves are extraordinarily simple, typically having only a few degrees of freedom. Moreover, the noise processes usually considered are highly restricted, formed by "baths" of heat, particles, and the like. Similarly, almost all of the field restricts itself to deterministic laws that are readily encapsulated in Hamilton's equations (Schrodinger's equation and its field-theoretic variants for quantum statistical physics). In fact, much of equilibrium statistical physics isn't even concerned with the dynamic laws by themselves (as, for example, stochastic Markov processes are). Rather, it is concerned with invariants of those laws (e.g., energy), invariants that relate the states of all of the particles. Deterministic laws without such readily discoverable invariants are outside the purview of much of statistical physics.

One potential use of statistical physics for collectives involves taking the systems that statistical physics analyzes, especially those analyzed in its condensed matter variant (e.g., spin glasses [213, 214]), as simplified models of a class of collectives. This approach is used in some of the analyses of the El Farol Bar problem, also called the minority game (discussed later) [5, 48]. It is used more overtly in (for example) the work of Galam [90], in which the equilibrium coalitions of a set of "countries" are modeled in terms of spin glasses. This approach cannot provide a general collectives framework, however. This is due to its not providing a general solution to arbitrary collectives inversion problems, being only concerned with the kinds of systems discussed earlier, and to its not using RL algorithms.[11]

Another contribution that statistical physics can make is with the mathematical techniques it has developed for its own purposes, such as mean field theory, self-averaging approximations, phase transitions, Monte Carlo techniques, the replica trick, and tools to analyze the thermodynamic limit in which the number of particles goes to infinity. Although such techniques have not yet been applied to collectives,[12] and they have been successfully applied to related fields. This is exemplified by the use of the replica trick to analyze two-player zero-sum games with random payoff matrices in the thermodynamic limit of the number of strategies in [27]. Other examples are the numeric investigation of the iterated prisoner's dilemma played on a lattice [223], the analysis of stochastic games by expressing deviation from rationality in the form of a "heat bath" [154], and the use of topological entropy to quantify the complexity of a voting system studied in [158].

Other recent work in the statistical physics literature is formally identical to that in other fields but has a novel perspective. A good example of this is [211], which is concerned with the problem of controlling a spatially extended system with a single controller using an algorithm identical to a simple-minded proportional RL algorithm (in essence, a rediscovery of RL).

Action Extremization

Much of the theory of physics can be cast as solving for the extremization of an actional, which is a functional of the worldline of an entire (potentially many-component) system across all time. The solution to that extremization problem constitutes the actual worldline followed by the system. In this way the calculus of variations can be used to solve for the worldline of a dynamic system. As an example, simple Newtonian dynamics can be cast as solving for the worldline of the system that extremizes a quantity called the "Lagrangian," which is a function of that worldline and certain parameters (e.g., the "potential energy") governing the system at hand. In this instance, the calculus of variations simply results in Newton's laws.

If we take the dynamic system to be a collective, we are assured that its worldline automatically maximizes a "world utility" consisting of the value of the associated actional. If we change physical aspects of the system that determine the functional form of the actional (e.g., change the system's potential energy function), then we change the world utility, and we are assured that our collective maximizes that new world utility. Counterintuitive physical systems, like the strings-and-springs systems

---

[11] In regard to the latter point, however, it's interesting to speculate about recasting statistical physics as a collective, by viewing each of the particles in the physical system as running an "RL algorithm" that perfectly maximizes the "utility function" of its Lagrangian, given the "actions" of the other particles. In this perspective, many-particle physical systems are multistage games that are at Nash equilibrium in each stage. So, for example, a frustrated spin glass is such a system at a Nash equilibrium that is not Pareto-optimal.

[12] Preliminary results in combining Monte Carlo techniques with collectives has yielded improvements of several orders of magnitude over traditional Monte Carlo techniques [240].

that exhibit Braess' paradox [20], are simply systems for which the world utility implicit in our human intuition is extremized at a point different from the one that extremizes the system's actional.

The challenge in exploiting this to solve the design of collectives problem is in translating an arbitrary provided global goal for the collective into a parameterized actional. Note that that actional must govern the dynamics of the collective, and the parameters of the actional must be physical variables in the collective, variables whose values we can modify.

Active Walker Models

The field of active walker models [21, 100, 101] is concerned with modeling "walkers" (be they human walkers or simple physical objects) crossing fields along trajectories, where those trajectories are a function of several factors, including the trails already worn into the field. Often the kind of trajectories considered are those that can be cast as solutions to actional extremization problems so that the walkers can be explicitly viewed as agents maximizing a private utility.

One of the primary concerns with the field of active walker models is how the trails worn in the field change with time to reach a final equilibrium state. The problem of how to design the cement pathways in the field (and other physical features of the field) so that the final paths actually followed by the walkers will have certain desirable characteristics is then one of solving for parameters of the actional that will result in the desired worldline. This is a special instance of the inverse problem of how to design a collective.

Using active walker models this way to design collectives, like action extremization in general, probably has limited applicability. It is also not clear how robust such a design approach might be or whether it would be scalable and exempt from the need for hand-tailoring.

2.6 Other Related Subjects

This section presents a "catch-all" of other fields that have little in common with one another and, while either still nascent or not extremely closely related to collectives, bear some relation to collectives.

Stochastic Fields

An extremely well-researched body of work concerns the mathematical and numeric behavior of systems for which the probability distribution over possible future states conditioned on preceding states is explicitly provided. This work involves many aspects of Monte Carlo numerical algorithms [172], all aspects of Markov chains [80, 177, 215] and especially of Markov fields, a topic that encompasses the Chapman-Kolmogorov equations [91] and their variants: Liouville's equation, the Fokker-Plank equation, and the detailed-balance equation. Nonlinear dynamics is also related to this body of work (see the synopsis of iterated function systems and the synopsis of cellular automata later), as is Markov competitive decision processes (see the earlier synopsis of game theory).

Formally, one can cast the problem of designing a collective as fixing each of the conditional transition probability distributions of the individual elements of a stochastic field so that the aggregate behavior of the overall system is a desired form.[13]

Amorphous Computing and Control of Smart Matter

Amorphous computing grew out of the idea of replacing traditional computer design, with its requirements for high reliability of the components of the computer, with a novel approach in which widespread unreliability of those components would not interfere with the computation [1, 2]. Some of its more speculative aspects are concerned with "how to program" a massively distributed, noisy system of components that may consist in part of biochemical or biomechanical components [131, 233]. Work here has tended to focus on schemes for how to robustly induce desired geometric dynamics across the physical body of the amorphous computer—an issue closely related to morphogenesis—and thereby lend credence to the idea that biochemical components are a promising approach.

Especially in its limit of computers with very small constituent components, amorphous computing is closely related to the fields of nanotechnology [64]. As the prospect of nanotechnology-driven mechanical systems gets more concrete, the daunting problem of how to robustly control, power, and sustain protean systems made up of extremely large sets of nano-scale devices looms more important [95, 96, 107]. If this problem were to be solved, one would in essence have "smart matter." For example, one would be able to "paint" an airplane wing with such matter and have it improve drag and lift properties significantly.

Self-Organizing Systems

The concepts of self-organization and self-organized criticality [15] were originally developed to help understand why many distributed physical systems are attracted to critical states that possess long-range dynamic correlations in the large-scale characteristics of the system. It provides a powerful framework for analyzing both biological and economic systems. For example, natural selection (particularly punctuated equilibrium [68, 93]) can be likened to self-organizing dynamical system, and

---

[13] In contrast, in the field of Markov decision processes discussed in [45], the full system may be a Markov field, but the system designer only sets the conditional transition probability distribution of at most a few of the field elements, to the appropriate "decision rules." Unfortunately, it is hard to imagine how to use the results of this field to design collectives because of major scaling problems. Any decision process must accurately model likely future modifications to its own behavior—often an extremely daunting task [150]. What's worse, if multiple such decision processes are running concurrently in the system, each such process must also model the others, potentially in their full complexity.

some have argued that it shares many properties (e.g., scale invariance) of such systems [57]. Similarly, one can view the economic order that results from the actions of human agents as a case of self-organization [59]. The relationship between complexity and self-organization is a particularly important one, in that it provides the potential laws that allow order to arise from chaos [125].

Adaptive Control Theory

Adaptive control [7,196], and in particular adaptive control involving locally weighted RL algorithms [9, 165], constitute a broadly applicable framework for controlling small, potentially inexactly modeled systems. Augmented by techniques in the control of chaotic systems [52, 60, 61], they constitute a very successful way of solving the "inverse problem" for such systems. Unfortunately, it is not clear how one could even attempt to scale such techniques up to the massively distributed systems of interest in collectives.

3 COIN Framework

The previous section provided a summary of different fields that address various issues pertinent to the field of collectives. In this section, we summarize the COIN (collective intelligence) framework, which is one of the first frameworks that aims to bridge the gap between the needs of the field of collectives and the extant analysis and design methods.[14]

3.1 Central Equation

Let Z be an arbitrary vector space whose elements z give the joint move of all agents in the system (i.e., z specifies the full "worldline" consisting of the actions and states of all the agents). The **world utility** $G(z)$, is a function of the full worldline, and we are concerned with the problem of finding the z that maximizes $G(z)$.

In addition to G, for each agent η, there is a **private utility function** $\{g_\eta\}$. The agents act to improve their individual private utility functions, even though we, as system designers, are only concerned with the value of the world utility G. To specify all agents other than η, we will use the notation $\hat{\eta}$.

Our uncertainty concerning the behavior of the system is reflected in a probability distribution over Z. Our ability to control the system consists of setting the value of some characteristic of the agents, e.g., setting the private functions of the agents. Indicating that value by s, our analysis revolves around the following central equation for $P(G \mid s)$, which follows from Bayes' theorem:

$$P(G \mid s) = \int d\epsilon_G P(G \mid \epsilon_G, s) \int d\epsilon_g P(\epsilon_G \mid \epsilon_g, s) P(\epsilon_g \mid s) \,, \tag{1}$$

---

[14] The full COIN theory is presented in Chapter 2.

where ϵ_g is the vector of the "intelligences" of the agents with respect to their associated private functions and ϵ_G is the vector of the intelligences of the agents with respect to G. Intuitively, these vectors indicate what percentage of η's actions would have resulted in lower utility.[15] In this chapter, we use intelligence vectors as decomposition variables for Equation 1.

Note that $\epsilon_{g_\eta}(z) = 1$ means that player η is fully rational at z, in that its move maximizes the value of its utility given the moves of the players. In other words, a point z where $\epsilon_{g_\eta}(z) = 1$ for all players η is one that meets the definition of a game-theory Nash equilibrium. On the other hand, a z at which all components of $\epsilon_G = 1$ is a local maximum of G (or, more precisely, a critical point of the $G(z)$ surface). If we can get these two vectors to be identical, then if the agents do well enough at maximizing their private utilities we are assured to be near a local maximum of G.

To formalize this, consider our decomposition of $P(G \mid s)$. If we can choose s so that the third conditional probability in the integrand, $P(\epsilon_g \mid s)$, is peaked around vectors ϵ_g, all of whose components are close to 1 (that is, agents are able to "learn" their tasks), then we have likely induced large private utility intelligences (this issue is traditially addressed in the field of machine learning). If we can also have the second term, $P(\epsilon_G \mid \epsilon_g, s)$, be peaked about ϵ_G equal to ϵ_g (that is, the private and world utilities are aligned), then ϵ_G will also be large (this issue is traditionally addressed in mechanism design). Finally, if the first term in the integrand, $P(G \mid \epsilon_G, s)$, is peaked about high G when ϵ_G is large, then our choice of s will likely result in high G, as desired (this issue arises in fields such as operations research and evolutionary programming).

3.2 Factoredness and Learnability

For high values of G to be achieved in a collective, the private utility functions of the agents need to satisfy two properties (i.e., have good form for the second and third term of Equation 1).[16] First, the private utility functions need to be "aligned with G," a need expressed in the second term of Equation 1. In particular, regardless of the details of the stochastic environment in which the agents operate, or of the details of the learning algorithms of the agents, if ϵ_g equals ϵ_G exactly *for all* z, the desired form for the second term in Equation 1 is assured. For such systems, we have:

$$g_\eta(z) \geq g_\eta(z') \Leftrightarrow G(z) \geq G(z') \qquad \forall\, z, z'\ s.t.\ z_{\hat\eta} = z'_{\hat\eta}.$$

Intuitively, for all pairs of states z and z' that differ only for agent η, a change in η's state that increases its private utility cannot decrease the world utility. We call such a

---

[15] Intelligence is formally defined in Chapter 2.

[16] Nongame theory–based function maximization techniques like simulated annealing instead address how to have term 1 have the desired form. They do this by trying to ensure that the local maxima that the underlying system ultimately settles near have high G, by "trading off exploration and exploitation." One can combine such term-1-based techniques with the techniques presented here. The resultant hybrid algorithm, addressing all three terms, outperforms simulated annealing by more than two orders of magnitude [240].

system **factored**. In game theory language, the private utility function Nash equilibria of a factored system are local maxima of G. In addition to this desirable equilibrium behavior, factored systems automatically provide appropriate off-equilibrium incentives to the agents (an issue generally not considered in the game theory and mechanism design literature).

Second, we want the agents' private utility functions to have high **learnability**, intuitively meaning that an agent's utility should be sensitive to its own actions and insensitive to the actions of others. This requirement that private utility functions have high "signal-to-noise" ratios arises in the third term. As an example, consider a "team game" where the private utility functions are set to G [56]. Such a system is tautologically factored. However, team games often have low learnability, because in a large system an agent will have a difficult time discerning the effects of its actions on G. As a consequence, each η may have difficulty achieving high g_η in such a system. Loosely speaking, agent η's learnability is the ratio of the sensitivity of g_η to η's actions to the sensitivity g_η to the actions of all other agents. So at a given state z, the higher the learnability, the more $g_\eta(z)$ depends on the move of agent η, i.e., the better the associated signal-to-noise ratio for η. Intuitively then, higher learnability means it is easier for η to achieve a large value of its utility.

3.3 Difference Utilities

It is possible to solve for the set of all private utilities that are factored with respect to a particular world utility. Unfortunately, in general it is not possible for a collective both to be factored and to have perfect learnability for all of its players (i.e., no dependence of any g_η on any agent other than η) for all of its agents [238]. However, consider **difference** utilities, which are of the form:

$$DU(z) = G(z) - \Gamma(f(z)), \tag{2}$$

where $\Gamma(f)$ is independent of z_η. Such difference utilities are factored [238]. In addition, under usually benign approximations, learnability is maximized over the set of difference utilities by choosing

$$\Gamma(f(z)) = E(G \mid z_{\hat{\eta}}, s) \tag{3}$$

up to an overall additive constant. We call the resultant difference utility the **Aristocrat** utility (AU). If each player η uses an appropriately rescaled version of the associated AU as its private utility function, then we have ensured good form for both the second and third terms in Equation 1.

Using AU in practice is sometimes difficult, due to the need to evaluate the expectation value. Fortunately, there are other utility functions that, while easier to evaluate than AU, still are both factored and possess superior learnability to the team game utility, $g_\eta = G$. One such private utility function is the **Wonderful Life** utility (WLU). The WLU for player η is parameterized by a prefixed **clamping parameter** CL_η chosen from among η's possible moves:

$$
\begin{array}{c}
z \\
\begin{array}{l}
\eta_1 \\
\eta_2 \\
\eta_3 \\
\eta_4
\end{array}
\begin{bmatrix}
1 & 0 & 0 \\
0 & 0 & 1 \\
1 & 0 & 0 \\
0 & 1 & 0
\end{bmatrix}
\end{array}
\quad
\begin{array}{c}
\Longrightarrow \\
\text{Clamp} \\
\eta_2 \text{ to} \\
\text{``null''}
\end{array}
\quad
\begin{array}{c}
(z_{\hat{\eta}_2}, \mathbf{0}) \\
\begin{bmatrix}
1 & 0 & 0 \\
0 & 0 & 0 \\
1 & 0 & 0 \\
0 & 1 & 0
\end{bmatrix}
\end{array}
$$

$$
\begin{array}{c}
\Longrightarrow \\
\text{Clamp} \\
\eta_2 \text{ to} \\
\text{``average''}
\end{array}
\quad
\begin{array}{c}
(z_{\hat{\eta}_2}, \mathbf{a}) \\
\begin{bmatrix}
1 & 0 & 0 \\
.33 & .33 & .33 \\
1 & 0 & 0 \\
0 & 1 & 0
\end{bmatrix}
\end{array}
$$

Figure 1. This example shows the impact of the clamping operation on the joint state of a four-agent system where each agent has three possible actions and each such action is represented by a three-dimensional unary vector. The first matrix represents the joint state of the system z where agent 1 has selected action 1, agent 2 has selected action 3, agent 3 has selected action 1, and agent 4 has selected action 2. The second matrix displays the effect of clamping agent 2's action to the "null" vector (i.e., replacing z_{η_2} with $\mathbf{0}$). The third matrix shows the effect of instead clamping agent 2's move to the "average" action vector $\mathbf{a} = \{.33, .33, .33\}$, which amounts to replacing that agent's move with the "illegal" move of fractionally taking each possible move ($z_{\eta_2} = \mathbf{a}$).

$$
WLU_\eta \equiv G(z) - G(z_{\hat{\eta}}, CL_\eta) . \tag{4}
$$

WLU is factored no matter what the choice of clamping parameter. Furthermore, while not matching the high learnability of AU, WLU usually has much better learnability than does a team game, because most of the "noise" due to other agents is removed from η's utility. Therefore, WLU generally results in better performance than does team game utilities [228, 238].

Figure 1 provides an example of clamping. As in that example, in many circumstances there is a particular choice of clamping parameter for agent η that is a "null" move for that agent, equivalent to removing that agent from the system. For such a clamping parameter WLU is closely related to the economics technique of "endogenizing a player's (agent's) externalities," for example, with the Groves mechanism [87, 174, 175].

However, it is usually the case that using WLU with a clamping parameter that is as close as possible to the expected move defining AU results in much higher learnability than does clamping to the null move. Such a WLU is roughly akin to a mean-field approximation to AU.[17] For example, in Figure 1, if the probabilities of player 2 making each of its possible moves was $1/3$, then one would expect that

---

[17] Formally, our approximation is exact only if the expected value of G equals G evaluated at the expected joint move (both expectations being conditioned on given moves by all players other than η). In general, however, for relatively smooth G, we would expect such a mean-field approximation to AU, to give good results, even if the approximation does not hold exactly.

a clamping parameter of **a** would be close to optimal. Accordingly, in practice, use of such an alternative WLU derived as a "mean-field approximation" to AU almost always results in better values of G than does the "endogenizing" WLU.

Intuitively, collectives having factored and highly learnable private utilities like AU and WLU can be viewed as akin to well-run human companies. G is the "bottom line" of the company, the players η are identified with the employees of that company, and the associated g_η given by the employees' performance-based compensation packages. For example, for a "factored company," each employee's compensation package contains incentives designed such that the better the bottom line of the corporation, the greater the employee's compensation. As an example, the CEO of a company wishing to have the private utilities of the employees be factored with G may give stock options to the employees. The net effect of this action is to ensure that what is good for the employee is also good for the company. In addition, if the compensation packages are "highly learnable," the employees will have a relatively easy time discerning the relationship between their behavior and their compensation. In such a case, the employees will both have the incentive to help the company and be able to determine how best to do so. Note that in practice, providing stock options is usually more effective in small companies than in large ones. This makes perfect sense in terms of the formalism summarized earlier because such options generally have higher learnability in small companies than in large companies, in which each employee has a hard time seeing how his or her moves affect the company's stock price.

3.4 Summary of COIN Results to Date

In earlier work, we tested the WLU for distributed control of network packet routing [241], achieving substantially better throughput than by using the best possible shortest-path-based system [241], even though that SPA-based system has information denied the agents in the WLU-based collective. In related work we have shown that use of the WLU automatically avoids the infamous Braess' paradox, in which adding new links can actually decrease throughput, a situation that readily ensnares SPAs [228, 239].

We have also applied the WLU to the problem of controlling communication across a constellation of satellites to minimize the importance-weighted loss of scientific data flowing across that constellation [237]. We have also shown that agents using utility functions derived from the COIN framework significantly improve performance in the problem of job scheduling across a heterogeneous computing grid [227].

In addition, we have explored COIN-based techniques on variants of congestion games [238, 242, 243], in particular of a more challenging variant of Arthur's El Farol Bar attendance problem [5] (also known as the "minority game" [48]). In this work we showed that use of the WLU can result in performance *orders of magnitude* superior to that of team game utilities. We have also successfully applied COIN techniques to the problem of coordinating a set of autonomous rovers to maximize the importance-weighted value of a set of locations they visit [226].

Finally, we have also explored applying COIN techniques to problems that are explicitly cast as search. These include setting the states of the spins in a spin glass to minimize energy; the conventional bin-packing problem of computer science, and a model of human agents connected in a small-world network who have to synchronize their purchase decisions [240].

4 Applications and Problems Driving Collectives

The previous sections focused on fields that provide solutions to problems arising in the field of collectives. To complement them, in this section we present three problems that are particularly suited to being approached from the field of collectives and that provide fertile ground for testing novel theories of collectives.

4.1 El Farol Bar Problem (Minority Game)

The "El Farol" Bar problem (also known as the minority game) and its variants provide a clean and simple testbed for investigating certain kinds of interactions among agents [5, 44, 47, 206]. In the original version of the problem, which arose in economics, at each time step (each "night"), each agent needs to decide whether to attend a particular bar. The goal of the agent in making this decision depends on the total attendance at the bar on that night. If the total attendance is below a preset capacity then the agent should have attended. Conversely, if the bar is overcrowded on the given night, then the agent should not attend. (Because of this structure, the bar problem with capacity set to 50% of the total number of agents is also known as the "minority game"; each agent selects one of two groups at each time step, and those that are in the minority have made the right choice). The agents make their choices by predicting ahead of time whether the attendance on the current night will exceed the capacity and then taking the appropriate course of action.

What makes this problem particularly interesting is that it is impossible for each agent to be perfectly "rational," in the sense of correctly predicting the attendance on any given night. This is because if most agents predict that the attendance will be low (and therefore decide to attend), the attendance will actually be high, and if they predict the attendance will be high (and therefore decide not to attend) the attendance will be low. (In the language of game theory, this essentially amounts to the property that there are no pure-strategy Nash equilibria [49, 246].) Alternatively, viewing the overall system as a collective, it has a prisoner's dilemma–like nature, in that "rational" behavior by all the individual agents thwarts the global goal of maximizing total enjoyment (defined as the sum of all agents' enjoyment and maximized when the bar is exactly at capacity).

This frustration effect is a crisp example of the difficulty that can arise when agents try to model agents that are in their turn modeling the first agents. It is similar to what occurs in spin glasses in physics, and it makes the bar problem closely related to the physics of emergent behavior in distributed systems [46–48, 248]. Researchers

have also studied the dynamics of the bar problem to investigate economic properties like competition, cooperation, and collective behavior and their relationship to
market efficiency [58, 122, 197].

4.2 Data Routing in a Network

Packet routing in a data network [28, 94, 110, 127, 212, 231] presents a particularly
interesting domain for the investigation of collectives. In particular, with such routing:

1. the problem is inherently distributed;
2. for all but the most trivial networks it is impossible to employ global control;
3. the routers only have access to local information (routing tables);
4. it constitutes a relatively clean and easily modified experimental testbed; and
5. there are potentially major bottlenecks induced by "greedy" behavior on the part
   of the individual routers, where the behavior constitutes a readily investigated
   instance of the tragedy of the commons (TOC).

Many of the approaches to packet routing incorporate a variant on RL [39, 43,
51, 147, 152]. Q-routing is perhaps the best known such approach and is based on
routers using reinforcement learning to select the best path [39]. Although generally
successful, Q-routing is not a general scheme for inverting a global task. This is
true even if one restricts attention to the problem of routing in data networks; there
exists a global task in such problems, but that task is directly used to construct the
algorithm.

A particular version of the general packet-routing problem that is acquiring increased attention is the quality of service (QoS) problem, where different communication packets (voice, video, data) share the same bandwidth resource but
have widely varying importances to both the user and (via revenue) the bandwidth
provider. Determining which packet has precedence over other packets in such cases
is not only based on priority in arrival time but more generally on the potential effects
on the income of the bandwidth provider. In this context, RL algorithms have been
used to determine routing policy, control call admission, and maximize revenue by
allocating the available bandwidth efficiently [43, 152].

Many researchers have exploited the noncooperative game-theoretic understanding of the TOC to explain the bottleneck character of empirical data networks' behavior and suggest potential alternatives to current routing schemes [25, 67, 132,
133, 139, 141, 179, 180, 208]. Closely related is work on various "pricing"-based
resource-allocation strategies in congestable data networks [149]. This work is at
least partially based on current understanding of pricing in toll lanes and traffic flow
in general. All of these approaches are of particular interest when combined with
the RL-based schemes mentioned earlier. Due to these factors, much of the current
research on a general framework for collectives is directed toward the packet-routing
domain (see the next section).

4.3 Traffic Theory

Traffic congestion typifies the tragedy of the commons public good problem: Everyone wants to use the same resource, and all parties greedily try to maximize their use of that resource worsens global behavior and *their own* private utility (e.g., if everyone disobeys traffic lights, everyone gets stuck in traffic jams). Indeed, in the well-known Braess' paradox [20, 54, 55, 134], keeping everything else constant—including the number and destinations of drivers—but opening a new traffic path can *increase* everyone's time to get to their destination. (Viewing the overall system as an instance of the prisoner's dilemma, this paradox in essence arises through the creation of a novel "defect-defect" option for the overall system.) Greedy behavior on the part of individuals also results in very rich global dynamic patterns, such as stop-and-go waves and clusters [102, 103].

Much of traffic theory employs and investigates tools that have previously been applied in statistical physics [102, 129, 130, 183, 187] (see the preceeding section). In particular, the spontaneous formation of traffic jams provides a rich testbed for studying the emergence of complex activity from seemingly chaotic states [102,104]. Furthermore, the dynamics of traffic flow is particularly amenable to the application and testing of many novel numerical methods in a controlled environment [16, 29, 202]. Many experimental studies have confirmed the usefulness of applying insights gleaned from such work to real-world traffic scenarios [102, 169, 170].

5 Challenge Ahead

A collective is any multiagent system in which each agent adaptively tries to maximize its own private utility function, while at the same time there is an overall world utility that rates the behavior of the entire system. Collectives are quite common in the natural world, canonical examples being human organizations (e.g., a company), an ecosystem, or organelles in a living cell. In addition, as computing becomes ubiquitous, artificial systems that constitute collectives are rapidly increasing. Such systems include data networks, arrays of communication satellites, teams of rovers, amorphous computers, and national airspace.

The fundamental problem in analyzing and designing such systems is in determining how the combined actions of many agents lead to "coordinated" behavior on the global scale. Unfortunately, though they provide valuable insight on *some* aspects of collectives, none of the fields discussed in this survey can be modified to meet all the requirements of a "field" of collectives. This is not too surprising because none of those fields were explicitly formed to design or analyze collectives, but rather they touched on certain aspects of collectives. What is needed is a fundamentally new approach, one that may borrow from the various fields but will not simply extend an existing field.

To that end, this survey provides a common language for studying collectives and highlights the benefits and shortcomings of the many fields related to collectives. Furthermore, it outlines some of the work ahead if a *science of collectives* is to emerge. The types of answers that future work on collectives can and will uncover are difficult to predict. It is a vast and rich area of research, a new field at the intersection of new needs and new capabilities. And although this survey does not provide those answers, it is our hope that it provides some of the essential questions that need to be addressed if the fledging field of collectives is to mature into a new science.

Acknowledgments. We would like to thank Adrian Agogino, David Parkes, and Neil Johnson for valuable discussions.

References

1. H. Abelson, D. Allen, D. Coore, C. Hanson, G. Homsy, T. F. Knight, Jr., R. Nagpal, E. Rauch, G. J. Sussman, and R. Weiss. Amorphous computing. *Communications of the ACM*, 43(5), May 2000.
2. H. Abelson and N. Forbes. Morphous-computing techniques may lead to intelligent materials. *Computers in Physics*, 12(6):520–2, 1998.
3. M. R. Anderson and T. W. Sandholm. Leveled commitment contracts with myopic and strategic agents. In *Proceedings of the Fifteenth National Conference on Artificial Intelligence*, pages 36–45, 1998.
4. K. Arrow and G. Debreu. The existence of an equilibrium for a competitive equilibrium. *Econometrica*, 22:265–90, 1954.
5. W. B. Arthur. Complexity in economic theory: Inductive reasoning and bounded rationality. *The American Economic Review*, 84(2):406–11, May 1994.
6. W. Ashcroft and N. D. Mermin. *Solid State Physics*. W. B. Saunders, Philadelphia, 1976.
7. J.J. Astrom and B. Wittenmark. *Adaptive Control*. Addison–Wesley, 1994.
8. C. G. Atkeson. Nonparametric model-based reinforcement learning. In *Advances in Neural Information Processing Systems—10*, pages 1008–14. MIT Press, 1998.
9. C. G. Atkeson, S. A. Schaal, and A. W. Moore. Locally weighted learning. *Artificial Intelligence Review*, 11:11–73, 1997.
10. R. J. Aumann. Correlated equilibrium as an expression of Bayesian rationality. *Econometrica*, 55(1):1–18, 1987.
11. R.J. Aumann and S. Hart. *Handbook of Game Theory with Economic Applications, Volumes I and II*. North-Holland Press, 1992.
12. R. Axelrod. *The Evolution of Cooperation*. Basic Books, New York, 1984.
13. R. Axelrod. *The Complexity of Cooperation: Agent-Based Models of Competition and Collaboration*. Princeton University Press, New Jersey, 1997.
14. P. Bak and K. Sneppen. Punctuated equilibrium and criticality in a simple model of evolution. *Physical Review Letters*, 71(24):4083–6, 1993.
15. P. Bak, C. Tang, and K. Wiesenfeld. Self-organized criticality. *Physical Review A*, 38: 364, 1988.
16. M. Bando, K. Hasebe, A. Nakayama, A. Shibata, and Y. Sugiyama. Dynamical model of traffic congestion and numerical simulation. *Physical Review E*, 51(2):1035–42, 1995.
17. S. Bankes. Exploring the foundations of artificial societies: Experiments in evolving solutions to the iterated N–player prisoner's dilemma. In R. Brooks and P. Maes, editors, *Artificial Life IV*, pages 337–42. MIT Press, 1994.
18. Y. Bar-Yam, editor. *The Dynamics of Complex Systems*. Westview Press, 1997.

19. T. Başar and G. J. Olsder. *Dynamic Noncooperative Game Theory*, second edition. Siam, Philadelphia, 1999.

20. T. Bass. Road to ruin. *Discover*, 13(5):56–61, May 1992.

21. M. Batty. Predicting where we walk. *Nature*, 388:19–20, July 1997.

22. E. Baum. Toward a model of mind as a laissez-faire economy of idiots. In L. Saitta, editor, *Proceedings of the 13th International Conference on Machine Learning*, pages 28–36. Morgan Kaufman, 1996.

23. E. Baum. Toward a model of mind as an economy of agents. *Machine Learning*, 1999 (in press).

24. M. Begon, D. J. Thompshon, and M. Mortimer, editors. *Population Ecology: A Unified Study of Animals and Plants*. Blackwell Science Inc., 1996.

25. A. M. Bell and W. A. Sethares. The El Farol problem and the internet: Congestion and coordination failure. In *Fifth International Conference of the Society for Computational Economics*, Boston, 1999.

26. J. Bendor and P. Swistak. The evolutionary advantage of conditional cooperation. *Complexity*, 4(2):15–18, 1996.

27. J. Berg and A. Engel. Matrix games, mixed strategies, and statistical mechanics. *Physics Review Letters*, 81:4999–5002, 1998. preprint cond-mat/9809265.

28. D. Bertsekas and R. Gallager. *Data Networks*. Prentice Hall, Englewood Cliffs, NJ, 1992.

29. O. Biham and A. A. Middleton. Self-organization and a dynamical transition in traffic-flow models. *Physical Review A*, 46(10):R6124–7, 1992.

30. K. Binmore. *Fun and Games: A Text on Game Theory*. D. C. Heath and Company, Lexington, MA, 1992.

31. L. E. Blume and D. Easley. Optimality and natural selection in markets. Preprint: econ-wpa 9712003.pdf, 1997.

32. E. Bonabeau, F. Henaux, S. Guerin, D. Snyders, P. Kuntz, and G. Theraulaz. Routing in telecommunications networks with "smart" and-like agents (Preprint), 1999.

33. E. Bonabeau, A. Sobkowski, G. Theraulaz, and J.-L. Deneubourg. Adaptive task allocation inspired by a model of division of labor of social insects (Preprint), 1999.

34. V. S. Borkar, S. Jain, and G. Rangarajan. Collective behaviour and diversity in economic communities: Some insights from an evolutionary game. In *Proceedings of the Workshop on Econophysics*, Budapest, Hungary, 1997.

35. V. S. Borkar, S. Jain, and G. Rangarajan. Dynamics of individual specialization and global diversification in communities. *Complexity*, 3(3):50–6, 1998.

36. C. Boutilier. Planning, learning and coordination in multiagent decision processes. In *Proceedings of the Sixth Conference on Theoretical Aspects of Rationality and Knowledge*, Holland, 1996.

37. C. Boutilier. Learning conventions in multiagent stochastic domains using likelihood estimates (Preprint), 1999.

38. C. Boutilier, Y. Shoham, and M. P. Wellman. Editorial: Economic principles of multi-agent systems. *Artificial Intelligence Journal*, 94:1–6, 1997.

39. J. A. Boyan and M. Littman. Packet routing in dynamically changing networks: A reinforcement learning approach. In *Advances in Neural Information Processing Systems—6*, pages 671–8. Morgan Kaufman, 1994.

40. J. M. Bradshaw, editor. *Software Agents*. MIT Press, 1997.

41. R. A. Brooks. Intelligence without reason. In *Proceedings of the Twelfth International Joint Conference on Artificial Intelligence*, pages 569–95, 1991.

42. R. A. Brooks. Intelligence without representation. *Artificial Intelligence*, 47:139–59, 1991.

43. T. X. Brown, H. Tong, and S. Singh. Optimizing admission control while ensuring quality of service in multimedia networks via reinforcement learning. In *Advances in Neural Information Processing Systems—11*. MIT Press, 1999.

44. G. Caldarelli, M. Marsili, and Y. C. Zhang. A prototype model of stock exchange. *Europhysics Letters*, 40:479–84, 1997.

45. A. R. Cassandra, L. P. Kaelbling, and M. L. Littman. Acting optimally in partially observable stochastic domains. In *Proceedings of the 12th National Conference on Artificial Intelligence*, 1994.

46. A. Cavagna. Irrelevance of memory in the minority game. Preprint cond-mat/9812215, December 1998.

47. D. Challet and Y. C. Zhang. Emergence of cooperation and organization in an evolutionary game. *Physica A*, 246(3-4):407, 1997.

48. D. Challet and Y. C. Zhang. On the minority game: Analytical and numerical studies. *Physica A*, 256:514, 1998.

49. J. Cheng. The mixed strategy equilibria and adaptive dynamics in the bar problem. Technical report, Santa Fe Institute Computational Economics Workshop, 1997.

50. D. R. Cheriton and K. Harty. A market approach to operating system memory allocation. In S. E. Clearwater, editor, *Market-Based Control: A Paradigm for Distributed Resource Allocation*. World Scientific, 1995.

51. S. P. M. Choi and D. Y. Yeung. Predictive Q-routing: A memory based reinforcement learning approach to adaptive traffic control. In D. S. Touretzky, M. C. Mozer, and M. E. Hasselmo, editors, *Advances in Neural Information Processing Systems—8*, pages 945–51. MIT Press, 1996.

52. D. J. Christini and J. J. Collins. Using noise and chaos control to control nonchaotic systems. *Physical Review E*, 52(6):5806–9, 1995.

53. C. Claus and C. Boutilier. The dynamics of reinforcement learning cooperative multiagent systems. In *Proceedings of the Fifteenth National Conference on Artificial Intelligence*, pages 746–52, Madison, WI, June 1998.

54. J. E. Cohen and C. Jeffries. Congestion resulting from increased capacity in single-server queueing networks. *IEEE/ACM Transactions on Networking*, 5(2):305–10, 1997.

55. J. E. Cohen and F. P. Kelly. A paradox of congestion in a queueing network. *Journal of Applied Probability*, 27:730–4, 1990.

56. R. H. Crites and A. G. Barto. Improving elevator performance using reinforcement learning. In D. S. Touretzky, M. C. Mozer, and M. E. Hasselmo, editors, *Advances in Neural Information Processing Systems—8*, pages 1017–23. MIT Press, 1996.

57. J. de Boer, B. Derrida, H. Flyvberg, A. D. Jackson, and T. Wettig. Simple model of self-organized biological evolution. *Physical Review Letters*, 73(6):906–9, 1994.

58. M. A. R. de Cara, O. Pla, and F. Guinea. Competition, efficiency and collective behavior in the "El Farol" Bar model. *European Physical Journal B*, 10:187, 1999.

59. A. de Vany. The emergence and evolution of self-organized coalitions. In M. Gilli, editor, *Computational Methods in Economics*. Kluwer Scientific Publishers, 1999 (to appear).

60. W. L. Ditto, S. N. Rauseo, and M. L. Spano. Experimental control of chaos. *Physics Review Letters*, 65:3211, 1990.

61. W. L. Ditto and K. Showalter. Introduction: Control and synchronization of chaos. *Chaos*, 7(4):509–11, 1997.

62. M. Dorigo and L. M. Gambardella. Ant colonies for the travelling salesman problem. *Biosystems*, 39, 1997.

63. M. Dorigo and L. M. Gambardella. Ant colony systems: A cooperative learning approach to the travelling salesman problem. *IEEE Transactions on Evolutionary Computation*, 1(1):53–66, 1997.

64. K. E. Drexler. *Nanosystems: Molecular Machinery, Manufacturing, and Computation.* John Wiley and Sons, 1992.

65. B. Drossel. A simple model for the formation of a complex organism. Preprint adap-org/9811002, November 1998.

66. J. Eatwell, M. Milgate, and P. Newman. *The New Palgrave Game Theory.* Macmillan Press, 1989.

67. A. A. Economides and J. A. Silvester. Multi-objective routing in integrated services networks: A game theory approach. In *IEEE Infocom '91: Proceedings of the Conference on Computer Communication*, volume 3, 1991.

68. N. Eldredge and S. J. Gould. Punctuated equilibria: An alternative to phyletic gradualism. In J. M. Schopf, editor, *Models in Paleobiology*, pages 82–115. Greeman, Cooper, 1972.

69. C. M. Ellison. The Utah TENEX scheduler. *Proceedings of the IEEE*, 63:940–5, 1975.

70. J. M. Epstein. Zones of cooperation in demographic prisoner's dilemma. *Complexity*, 4(2):36–48, 1996.

71. J. M. Epstein. *Nonlinear Dynamics, Mathematical Biology, and Social Science.* Addison Wesley, Reading, MA, 1997.

72. J. M. Epstein and R. Axtell. *Growing Artificial Societies: Social Sciences from the Bottom Up.* MIT Press, 1996.

73. N. Feltovich. Equilibrium and reinforcement learning with private information: An experimental study. Preprint, Dept. of Economics, U. of Houston, July 1997.

74. J. Ferber. Reactive distributed artificial intelligence: Principles and applications. In G. O'Hare and N. Jennings, editors, *Foundations of Distributed Artificial Intelligence*, pages 287–314. John Wiley and Sons, 1996.

75. D. F. Ferguson, C. Nikolaou, and Y. Yemini. An economy for flow control in computer networks. In *IEEE Infocom '89*, pages 110–8, 1989.

76. S. G. Ficici and J. B. Pollack. Challenges in coevolutionary learning: Arms-race dynamics, open-endedness, and mediocre stable states. In C. Adami et al., editor, *Artificial Life VI*, pages 238–47. MIT Press, 1998.

77. J. Filar and K. Vrieze. *Competitive Markov Decision Processes.* Springer-Verlag, 1997.

78. D. B. Fogel. An overview of evolutionary programming. In L. D. Davis, K. De Jong, M. D. Vose, and L. D. Whitley, editors, *Evolutionary Algorithms*, pages 89–109. Springer, 1997.

79. C. L. Forgy. RETE: A fast algorithm for the many pattern/many object patent match problem. *Artificial Intelligence*, 19(1):17–37, 1982.

80. D. Freedman. *Markov Chains.* Springer-Verlag, 1983.

81. E. Friedman. Strategic properties of heterogeneous serial cost sharing. In *Mathematical Social Sciences*. 2000.

82. E. Friedman and D. C. Parkes. Pricing WiFi at Starbucks – Issues in online mechanism design. In *Fourth ACM Conf. on Electronic Commerce*, 2003.

83. E. Friedman and S. Shenker. Learning and implementation in the Internet. Available from www.orie.cornell.edu/~friedman, 2002.

84. J. W. Friedman. *Game Theory with Applications to Economics.* Oxford University Press, New York, 1986.

85. D. Fudenberg and D. K. Levine. Steady state learning and Nash equilibrium. *Econometrica*, 61(3):547–73, 1993.

86. D. Fudenberg and D. K. Levine. *The Theory of Learning in Games*. MIT Press, 1998.

87. D. Fudenberg and J. Tirole. *Game Theory*. MIT Press, 1991.

88. Gabora. Autocatalytic closure in a cognitive system: A tentative scenario for the origin of culture. *Psycoloquy*, 9(67), December 1998.

89. V. V Gafiychuk. Distributed self-regulation induced by negative feedbacks in ecological and economic systems. Preprint, adap-org/98110011, November 1998.

90. S. Galam. Spontaneous coalition forming: A model from spin glass. Preprint cond-mat/9901022, January 1999.

91. C. W. Gardiner. *Handbook of Stochastic Methods*. Springer-Verlag, New York, 1985.

92. C. V. Goldman and J. S. Rosenschein. Emergent coordination through the use of cooperative state-changing rules (Preprint), 1999.

93. S. J. Gould and N. Eldredge. Punctuated equilibria: The tempo and mode of evolution reconsidered. *Paleobiology*, 3:115–51, 1977.

94. W. Grover. Self organizing broad band transport networks. *Proceedings of the IEEE*, 85(10):1582–1611, 1997.

95. O. Guenther, T. Hogg, and B. A. Huberman. Learning in multiagent control of smart matter. In *AAAI-97 Workshop on Multiagent Learning*, 1997.

96. O. Guenther, T. Hogg, and B. A. Huberman. Market organizations for controlling smart matter. In *Proceedings of the International Conference on Computer Simulation and Social Sciences*, 1997.

97. E. A. Hansen, A. G. Barto, and S. Zilberstein. Reinforcement learning for mixed open-loop and closed loop control. In *Advances in Neural Information Processing Systems—9*, pages 1026–32. MIT Press, 1998.

98. I Hanski. Be diverse, be predictable. *Nature*, 390:440–1, 1997.

99. A. Hastings. *Population Biology : Concepts and Models*. Springer-Verlag, 1997.

100. D. Helbing, J. Keltsch, and P. Molnar. Modeling the evolution of the human trail systems. *Nature*, 388:47–9, July 1997.

101. D. Helbing, F. Schweitzer, J. Keltsch, and P. Molnar. Active walker model for the formation of human and animal trail systems. *Physical Review E*, 56(3):2527–39, 1997.

102. D. Helbing and M. Treiber. Jams, waves, and clusters. *Science*, 282:200–1, December 1998.

103. D. Helbing and M. Treiber. Phase diagram of traffic states in the presence of inhomogeneities. *Physics Review Letters*, 81:3042, 1998.

104. M. Herrmann and B. S. Kerner. Local cluster effect in different traffic flow models. *Physica A*, 225:163–8, 1998.

105. Yu-Chi Ho. Team decision theory and information structures. *Proceedings of the IEEE*, 68(644-54), 1980.

106. T. Hogg and B. A. Huberman. Achieving global stability through local controls. In *Proceedings of the Sixth IEEE Symposium on Intelligent Control*, pages 67–72, 1991.

107. T. Hogg and B. A. Huberman. Controlling smart matter. *Smart Materials and Structures*, 7:R1–R14, 1998.

108. J. Holland and J. H. Miller. Artificial adaptive agents in economic theory. *American Economic Review*, 81:365–70, May 1991.

109. J. H. Holland, editor. *Adaptation in Natural and Artificial Systems*. MIT Press, 1993.

110. M.-T. T. Hsiao and A. A. Lazar. Optimal flow control of multi-class queueing networks with decentralized information. In *IEEE Infocom '89*, pages 652–61, 1987.

111. J. Hu and M. P. Wellman. Self-fulfilling bias in multiagent learning. In *Proceedings of the Second International Conference on Multiagent Systems*, pages 118–25, 1996.

112. J. Hu and M. P. Wellman. Multiagent reinforcement learning: Theoretical framework and an algorithm. In *Proceedings of the Fifteenth International Conference on Machine Learning*, pages 242–50, June 1998.

113. J. Hu and M. P. Wellman. Online learning about other agents in a dynamic multiagent system. In *Proceedings of the Second International Conference on Autonomous Agents*, pages 239–46, May 1998.

114. M. Huber and R. A. Grupen. Learning to coordinate controllers—Reinforcement learning on a control basis. In *Proceedings of the 15th International Conference of Artificial Intelligence*, volume 2, pages 1366–71, 1997.

115. B. A. Huberman, editor. *The Ecology of Computation*. North-Holland, Amsterdam, 1988.

116. B. A. Huberman and S. H. Clearwater. A multi-agent system for controlling building environments. In *Proceedings of the International Conference on Multiagent Systems*, pages 171–6, 1995.

117. B. A. Huberman and T. Hogg. The behavior of computational ecologies. In *The Ecology of Computation*, pages 77–115. North-Holland, 1988.

118. M. E. Huhns, editor. *Distributed Artificial Intelligence*. Pittman, London, 1987.

119. R. V. Iyer and S. Ghosh. DARYN, a distributed decision-making algorithm for railway networks: Modeling and simulation. *IEEE Transaction of Vehicular Technology*, 44(1):180–91, 1995.

120. P. Jefferies, M. L. Hart, and N. F. Johnson. Deterministic dynamics in the minority game. *Physical Review E*, 65 (016105), 2002.

121. N. R. Jennings, K. Sycara, and M. Wooldridge. A roadmap of agent research and development. *Autonomous Agents and Multi-agent Systems*, 1:7–38, 1998.

122. N. F. Johnson, S. Jarvis, R. Jonson, P. Cheung, Y. R. Kwong, and P. M. Hui. Volatility and agent adaptability in a self-organizing market. Preprint cond-mat/9802177, February 1998.

123. L. P. Kaelbling, M. L. Littman, and A. W. Moore. Reinforcement learning: A survey. *Journal of Artificial Intelligence Research*, 4:237–85, 1996.

124. E. Kalai and E. Lehrer. Rational learning leads to Nash equilibrium. *Econometrica*, 61(5):1019–45, 1993.

125. S. A. Kauffman. *At Home in the Universe: The Search for the Laws of Self-Organization and Complexity*. Oxford University Press, 1995.

126. L. Keller and H. K. Reeve. Familiarity breeds cooperation. *Nature*, 394:121–2, 1998.

127. F. P. Kelly. Modeling communication networks, present and future. *Philosophical Trends Royal Society of London A*, 354:437–63, 1996.

128. J. O. Kephart, J. E. Hanson, and J. Sairamesh. Price and niche wars in a free-market economy of software agents. *Artificial Life*, 4:1–13, 1998.

129. B. S. Kerner, P. Konhauser, and M. Schilke. Deterministic spontaneous appearance of traffic jams in slightly inhomogeneous traffic flow. *Physical Review E*, 51(6):6243–6, 1995.

130. B. S. Kerner and H. Rehborn. Experimental properties of complexity in traffic flow. *Physical Review E*, 53(5):R4275–8, 1996.

131. T. F. Knight and G. J. Sussman. Cellular gate technology. In *Proceedings of the First International Conference on Unconventional Models of Computation*, Auckland, January 1998.

132. Y. A. Korilis, A. A. Lazar, and A. Orda. Achieving network optima using Stackelberg routing strategies. *IEEE/ACM Transactions on Networking*, 5(1):161–73, 1997.

133. Y. A. Korilis, A. A. Lazar, and A. Orda. Capacity allocation under noncooperative routing. *IEEE Transactions on Automatic Control*, 42(3):309–25, 1997.

134. Y. A. Korilis, A. A. Lazar, and A. Orda. Avoiding the Braess paradox in noncooperative networks. *Journal of Applied Probability*, 36:211–22, 1999.

135. S. Kraus. Negotiation and cooperation in multi-agent environments. *Artificial Intelligence*, pages 79–97, 1997.

136. M. J. B. Krieger, J.-B. Billeter, and L. Keller. Ant-like task allocation and recruitment in cooperative robots. *Nature*, 406:992–5, 2000.

137. V. Krishna and P. Motty. Efficient mechanism design. (Preprint), 1997.

138. J. F. Kurose and R. Simha. A microeconomic approach to optimal resource allocation in distributed computer systems. *IEEE Transactions on Computers*, 35(5):705–17, 1989.

139. R. J. La and V. Anantharam. Optimal routing control: Game theoretic approach (Submitted to *IEEE transactions on Automatic Control*), 1999.

140. M. Lauer and M. Riedmiller. An algorithm for distributed reinforcement learning in cooperative multi-agent systems. In *Proceedings of the Seventeenth International Machine Learning Conference*, pages 535–42. Morgan Kauffman, 2000.

141. A. A. Lazar, A. Orda, and D. E. Pendarakis. Capacity allocation under noncooperative routing. *IEEE Transactions on Networking*, 5(6):861–71, 1997.

142. A. A. Lazar and N. Semret. Design, analysis and simulation of the progressive second price auction for network bandwidth sharing. Technical Report 487-98-21 (Rev 2.10), Columbia University, April 1998.

143. T. S. Lee, S. Ghosh, J. Liu, X. Ge, and A. Nerode. A mathematical framework for asynchronous, distributed, decision-making systems with semi-autonomous entities: Algorithm synthesis, simulation, and evaluation. In *Fourth International Symposium on Autonomous Decentralized Systems*, Tokyo, 1999.

144. T. M. Lenton. Gaia and natural selection. *Nature*, 394:439–447, 1998.

145. K. Lerman and A. Galstyan. Mathematical model of foraging in a group of robots: Effect of interference. *Autonomous Robots*, 13(2), 2002.

146. M. L. Littman. Markov games as a framework for multi-agent reinforcement learning. In *Proceedings of the 11th International Conference on Machine Learning*, pages 157–63, 1994.

147. M. L. Littman and J. Boyan. A distributed reinforcement learning scheme for network routing. In *Proceedings of the 1993 International Workshop on Applications of Neural Networks to Telecommunications*, pages 45–51, 1993.

148. R. D. Luce and H. Raiffa. *Games and Decisions*. Dover Press, 1985.

149. J. K. MacKie-Mason and R. V. Hal. Pricing congestible network resources. *IEEE Journal on Selected Areas of Communications*, 13(7):1141–49, 1995.

150. W. G. Macready and D. H. Wolpert. Bandit problems and the exploration/exploitation tradeoff. *IEEE Transactions on Evolutionary Computation*, 2:2–22, 1998.

151. P. Maes. *Designing Autonomous Agents*. MIT Press, 1990.

152. P. Marbach, O. Mihatsch, M. Schulte, and J. Tsisiklis. Reinforcement learning for call admission control and routing in integrated service networks. In *Advances in Neural Information Processing Systems—10*, pages 922–8. MIT Press, 1998.

153. J. Marschak and R. Radner. *Economic Theory of Teams*. Yale University Press, New Haven, CT, 1972.

154. M. Marsili and Y.-C. Zhang. Stochastic dynamics in game theory. Preprint cond-mat/9801309, January 1998.

155. J. Maynard Smith. *Evolution and the Theory of Games*. Cambridge University Press, 1982.

156. D. McFarland. Toward robot cooperation. In *From Animals to Animats 3: Proceedings of the Third International Conference on Simulation of Adaptive Behavior*, pages 440–3. MIT Press, 1994.

157. M. Mesterton-Gibbons, J. H. Marden, and L. A. Dugatkin. On wars of attrition without assessment. *Journal of Theoretical Biology*, 181:65–83, 1992.

158. D. A. Meyer and T. A. Brown. Statistical mechanics of voting. *Physics Review Letters*, 81(8):1718–21, 1998.

159. J. H. Miller. The coevolution of automata in the repeated prisoner's dilemma. *Journal of Economic Behavior and Organization*, 29(1):87–112, 1996.

160. J. H. Miller. Evolving information processing organizations (Preprint), 1996.

161. J. H. Miller and J. Andreoni. Auctions with adaptive artificial agents. *Journal of Games and Economic Behavior*, 10:39–64, 1995.

162. J. H. Miller, C. Butts, and D. Rode. Communication and cooperation (Preprint), 1998.

163. M. Minsky. *The Society of Mind*. Simon and Schuster, 1988.

164. J. Mirrlees. An exploration in the theory of optimal income taxation. *Review of Economic Studies*, 38:175–208, 1974.

165. A. W. Moore, C. G. Atkeson, and S. Schaal. Locally weighted learning for control. *Artificial Intelligence Review*, 11:75–113, 1997.

166. R. Munos and P. Bourgine. Reinforcement learning for continuous stochastic control problems. In *Advances in Neural Information Processing Systems—10*, pages 1029–35. MIT Press, 1998.

167. R. Nagpal. Programmable pattern-formation and scale-independence. In *Proceedings of the 4th International Conference on Complex Systems*, New Hampshire, June 2002.

168. R. Nagpal. Programmable self-assembly using biologically-inspired multi-agent control. In *Proceedings of the 1st International Joint Conference on Autonomous Agents and Multi-agent Systems*, July 2002.

169. K. Naigel. Experiences with iterated traffic microsimulations in Dallas. Preprint adap-org/9712001, December 1997.

170. K. Naigel, P. Stretz, M. Pieck, S. Leckey, R. Donnelly, and C. Barrett. TRANSIMS traffic flow characteristics. Preprint adap-org/9710003, October 1997.

171. J. F. Nash. Equilibrium points in N-person games. *Proceedings of the National Academy of Sciences of the United States of America*, 36(48–49), 1950.

172. R. M. Neal. *Bayesian Learning for Neural Networks, Lecture Notes in Statistics, No. 118*. Springer-Verlag, New York, 1996.

173. A. Neyman. Bounded complexity justifies cooperation in the finitely repeated prisoner's dilemma. *Economics Letters*, 19:227–30, 1985.

174. W. Nicholson. *Microeconomic Theory*, seventh edition. The Dryden Press, 1998.

175. N. Nisan and A. Ronen. Algorithmic mechanism design. *Games and Economic Behavior*, 35:166–96, 2001.

176. S. I. Nishimura and T. Ikegami. Emergence of collective strategies in a prey-predator game model. *Artificial Life*, 3:243–360, 1997.

177. J. Norris. *Markov Chains*. Cambridge University Press, 1998.

178. M. A. Nowak and K. Sigmund. Evolution of indirect reciprocity by image scoring. *Nature*, 393:573–7, 1998.

179. S. Olafsson. Games on networks. *Proceedings of the IEEE*, 85(10):1556–62, 1997.

180. A. Orda, R. Rom, and M. Sidi. Minimum delay routing in stochastic networks. *IEEE/ACM Transactions on Networking*, 1(2):187–98, 1993.

181. D. C. Parkes. *Iterative Combinatorial Auctions: Theory and Practice*. Ph.D. thesis, University of Pennsylvania, 2001.

182. D. C. Parkes. Price-based information certificates for minimal-revelation combinatorial auctions. In *Agent Mediated Electronic Commerce IV: Designing Mechanisms and Systems*, volume 2531 of *Lecture Notes in Artificial Intelligence*. 2002.

183. L. A. Pipes. An operational analysis of traffic dynamics. *Journal of Applied Physics*, 24(3):274–81, 1953.

184. G. A. Polls. Stability is woven by complex webs. *Nature*, 395:744–5, 1998.

185. M. Potters, R. Cont, and J.-P. Bouchaud. Financial markets as adaptive ecosystems. Preprint cond-mat/9609172 v2, June 1997.

186. D. Prokhorov and D. Wunsch. Adaptive critic design. *IEEE Transactions on Neural Networks*, 8(5):997–1007, 1997.

187. Z. Qu, F. Xie, and G. Hu. Spatiotemporal on-off intermittency by random driving. *Physical Review E*, 53(2):R1301–4, 1996.

188. F. Reif. *Fundamentals of Statistical and Thermal Physics*. McGraw–Hill, 1965.

189. E. Rich and K. Knight. *Artificial Intelligence*, second edition. McGraw-Hill, Inc., 1991.

190. A. E. Roth and I. Erev. Learning in extensive-form games: Experimental data and simple dynamic models in the intermediate term. *Games and Economic Behavior*, 8:164–212, 1995.

191. A. Samuel. Some studies in machine learning using the game of checkers. *IBM Journal of Reseach and Development*, 3:210–29, 1959.

192. T. Sandholm and R. Crites. Multiagent reinforcement learning in the iterated prisoner's dilemma. *Biosystems*, 37:147–66, 1995.

193. T. Sandholm, K. Larson, M. Anderson, O. Shehory, and F. Tohme. Anytime coalition structure generation with worst case guarantees. In *Proceedings of the Fifteenth National Conference on Artificial Intelligence*, pages 46–53, 1998.

194. T. Sandholm and V. R. Lesser. Issues in automated negotiations and electronic commerce: Extending the contract net protocol. In *Proceedings of the Second International Conference on Multi-agent Systems*, pages 328–35. AAAI Press, 1995.

195. T. Sandholm and V. R. Lesser. Coalitions among computationally bounded agents. *Artificial Intelligence*, 94:99–137, 1997.

196. S. Sastry and M. Bodson. *Adaptive Control, Stability, Convergence, and Robustness*. Prentice Hall, 1989.

197. R. Savit, R. Manuca, and R. Riolo. Adaptive competition, market efficiency, phase transitions and spin-glasses. Preprint cond-mat/9712006, December 1997.

198. A. Schaerf, Y. Shoham, and M. Tennenholtz. Adaptive load balancing: A study in multi-agent learning. *Journal of Artificial Intelligence Research*, 162:475–500, 1995.

199. J. Schmidhuber, J. Zhao, and N. N. Schraudoiph. Reinforcement learning with self-modifying policies. In S. Thrun and L. Pratt, editors, *Learning to Learn*, pages 293–309. Kluwer, 1997.

200. J. Schmidhuber, J. Zhao, and M. Wiering. Shifting inductive bias with success-story algorithm, adaptive Levin search, and incremental self-improvement. *Machine Learning*, 28:105–30, 1997.

201. R. Schoonderwoerd, O. Holland, and J. Bruten. Ant-like agents for load balancing in telecommunication networks. In *Autonomous Agents 97*, pages 209–16. MIT Press, 1997.

202. M. Schreckenberg, A. Schadschneider, K. Nagel, and N. Ito. Discrete stochastic models for traffic flow. *Physical Review E*, 51(4):2939–49, 1995.

203. J. Schull. Are species intelligent? *Behavioral and Brain Sciences*, 13:63–108, 1990.

204. S. Sen. *Multi-agent Learning: Papers from the 1997 AAAI Workshop (Technical Report WS-97-03*. AAAI Press, Menlo Park, CA, 1997.

205. S. Sen, M. Sekaran, and J. Hale. Learning to coordinate without sharing information (Preprint), 1999.

206. W. A. Sethares and A. M. Bell. An adaptive solution to the El Farol problem. In *Proceedings. of the Thirty-Sixth Annual Allerton Conference on Communication, Control, and Computing*, Allerton, IL, 1998.

207. R. Sethi. Stability of equilibria in games with procedural rational players. Preprint, Dept of Economics, Columbia University, November 1998.

208. S. J. Shenker. Making greed work in networks: A game-theoretic analysis of switch service disciplines. *IEEE Transactions on Networking*, 3(6):819–31, 1995.

209. Y. Shoham and K. Tanaka. A dynamic theory of incentives in multi-agent systems. In *Proceedings of the International Joint Conference on Artificial Intelligence*, 1997.

210. J. Sidel, P. M. Aoki, S. Barr, A. Sah, C. Staelin, M. Stonebreaker, and Yu A. Data replication in mariposa. In *Proceedings of the 12th International Conference on Data Engineering*, 1996.

211. S. Sinha and N. Gupte. Adaptive control of spatially extended systems: Targeting spatiotemporal patterns and chaos. *Physical Review E*, 58(5):R5221–4, 1998.

212. W. Stallings. *Data and Computer Communications*. MacMillian Publishing Co., New York, 1994.

213. J. Stein. Critical exponents of the $u(n)$ vector spin glasses. *Europhysics Letters*, 34(9):717–21, 1996.

214. J. Stein. Critical properties of a spin glass with anisotropic Dzyaloshinskii-Moriya interaction. *Journal of Physics A*, 29:963–71, 1996.

215. W. J. Stewart. *Introduction to the Numerical Solution of Markov Chains*. Princeton University Press, 1995.

216. P. Stone. TPOT-RL applied to network routing. In *Proceedings of the Seventeenth International Machine Learning Conference*, pages 935–42. Morgan Kauffman, 2000.

217. P. Stone and M. Veloso. Multiagent systems: A survey from a machine learning perspective. *Autonomous Robots*, 8(3), 2000.

218. M. Stonebreaker, P. M. Aoki, R. Devine, W. Litwin, and M. Olson. Mariposa: A new architecture for distributed data. In *Proceedings of the 10th International Conference on Data Engineering*, 1994.

219. D. Subramanian, P. Druschel, and J. Chen. Ants and reinforcement learning: A case study in routing in dynamic networks. In *Proceedings of the Fifteenth International Conference on Artificial Intelligence*, pages 832–8, 1997.

220. R. S. Sutton. Learning to predict by the methods of temporal differences. *Machine Learning*, 3:9–44, 1988.

221. R. S. Sutton and A. G. Barto. *Reinforcement Learning: An Introduction*. MIT Press, 1998.

222. K. Sycara. Multiagent systems. *AI Magazine*, 19(2):79–92, 1998.

223. G. Szabo and C. Toke. Evolutionary prisoner's dilemma game on a square lattice. *Physical Review E*, 58(1):69–73, 1998.

224. G. Tesauro. Practical issues in temporal difference learning. *Machine Learning*, 8:33–53, 1992.

225. P. Tucker and F. Berman. On market mechanisms as a software techniques. Technical Report CS96–513, University of California, San Diego, December 1996.

226. K. Tumer, A. Agogino, and D. Wolpert. Learning sequences of actions in collectives of autonomous agents. In *Proceedings of the First International Joint Conference on Autonomous Agents and Multi-agent Systems*, pages 378–85, Bologna, Italy, July 2002.

227. K. Tumer and J. Lawson. Collectives for multiple resource job scheduling across heterogeneous servers. In *Proceedings of the Second International Joint Conference on Autonomous Agents and Multi-agent Systems*, Melbourne, Australia, July 2003.

228. K. Tumer and D. H. Wolpert. Collective intelligence and Braess' paradox. In *Proceedings of the Seventeenth National Conference on Artificial Intelligence*, pages 104–9, Austin, TX, 2000.

229. W. Vickrey. Counterspeculation, auctions and competitive sealed tenders. *Journal of Finance*, 16:8–37, 1961.

230. C. A. Waldspurger, T. Hogg, B. A. Huberman, J. O. Kephart, and W. S. Stornetta. Spawn: A distributed computational economy. *IEEE Transactions of Software Engineering*, 18(2):103–17, 1992.

231. J. Walrand and P. Varaiya. *High-Performance Communication Networks*. Morgan Kaufmann, San Fransisco, 1996.

232. C. Watkins and P. Dayan. Q-learning. *Machine Learning*, 8(3/4):279–92, 1992.

233. R. Weiss, G. Homsy, and R. Nagpal. Programming biological cells. In *Proceedings of the 8th International Conference on Architectural Support for Programming Languages and Operating Systems*, San Jose, NZ, 1998.

234. M. P. Wellman. A market-oriented programming environment and its application to distributed multicommodity flow problems. In *Journal of Artificial Intelligence Research*, 1993.

235. M. P. Wellman. A computational market model for distributed configuration design. In *Proceedings of the 12th National Conference on Artificial Intelligence*, 1994.

236. D. H. Wolpert and W. G. Macready. No free lunch theorems for optimization. *IEEE Transactions on Evolutionary Computation*, 1(1):67–82, 1997. Best Paper Award.

237. D. H. Wolpert, J. Sill, and K. Tumer. Reinforcement learning in distributed domains: Beyond team games. In *Proceedings of the Seventeenth International Joint Conference on Artificial Intelligence*, pages 819–24, Seattle, 2001.

238. D. H. Wolpert and K. Tumer. Optimal payoff functions for members of collectives. *Advances in Complex Systems*, 4(2/3):265–79, 2001.

239. D. H. Wolpert and K. Tumer. Collective intelligence, data routing and Braess' paradox. *Journal of Artificial Intelligence Research*, 16:359–87, 2002.

240. D. H. Wolpert, K. Tumer, and E. Bandari. Improving search algorithms by using intelligent coordinates. 2003, submitted.

241. D. H. Wolpert, K. Tumer, and J. Frank. Using collective intelligence to route Internet traffic. In *Advances in Neural Information Processing Systems—11*, pages 952–8. MIT Press, 1999.

242. D. H. Wolpert, K. Wheeler, and K. Tumer. General principles of learning-based multi-agent systems. In *Proceedings of the Third International Conference of Autonomous Agents*, pages 77–83, 1999.

243. D. H. Wolpert, K. Wheeler, and K. Tumer. Collective intelligence for control of distributed dynamical systems. *Europhysics Letters*, 49(6), March 2000.

244. S. Wright. The roles of mutation, inbreeding, crossbreeding and selection in evolution. *Proceedings of the XI International Congress of Genetics*, 8:209–22, 1932.

245. H. P. Young. The evolution of conventions. *Econometrica*, 61(1):57–84, 1993.

246. E. Zambrano. Rationalizable bounded rational behavior (Preprint), 1999.

247. W. Zhang and T. G. Dietterich. Solving combinatorial optimization tasks by reinforcement learning: A general methodology applied to resource-constrained scheduling. *Journal of Artificial Intelligence Research*, 2000.

248. Y. C. Zhang. Modeling market mechanism with evolutionary games. *Europhysics Letters*, March/April 1998.

249. G. Zlotkin and J. S. Rosenschein. Coalition, cryptography, and stability: Mechanisms for coalition formation in task oriented domains (Preprint), 1999.

2

Theory of Collective Intelligence

David Wolpert*

Summary. In this chapter an analysis of the behavior of an arbitrary (perhaps massive) collective of computational processes in terms of an associated "world" utility function is presented We concentrate on the situation where each process in the collective can be viewed as though it were striving to maximize its own private utility function. For such situations the central design issue is how to initialize and update the collective's structure, in particular the private utility functions, so as to induce the overall collective to behave in a way that has large values of the world utility. Traditional "team game" approaches to this problem simply set each private utility function equal to the world utility function. The "collective intelligence" (COIN) framework is a semiformal set of heuristics that have recently been used to construct private utility functions that in many experiments have resulted·in world utility values up to orders of magnitude superior to that ensuing from use of the team game utility. In this chapter we introduce a formal mathematics for analyzing and designing collectives. We also use this mathematics to suggest new private utilities that should outperform the COIN heuristics in certain kinds of domains. In accompanying work we use that mathematics to explain previous experimental results concerning the superiority of COIN heuristics. In that accompanying work we also use the mathematics to make numerical predictions, some of which we then test. In this way these two papers establish the study of collectives as a proper science, involving theory, explanation of old experiments, prediction concerning new experiments, and engineering insights.

1 Introduction

This chapter concerns distributed systems, some of whose components can be viewed as though they were agents, adaptively "trying" to induce large values of their associated private utility functions. When combined with a world utility function that rates the possible behaviors of that system, the system is known as a **collective** [17, 20, 23, 26].

Given a collective, there is an associated inverse design problem: how to configure or modify the system so that in their pursuit of their private utilities the agents

* NASA Ames Research Center, Mailstop 269-2, Moffett Field, CA, 94035
  dhw@ptolemy.arc.nasa.gov

also maximizes the world utility. Solving this problem may involve determining or modifying the number of agents and how they interact with each other and what degrees of freedom of the overall system each controls (i.e., the very definition of the agents). When the agents are machine learning algorithms overtly trying to maximize their private utilities, the inverse problem may also involve determining or modifying the algorithms used by those agents, as well as precisely what private utilities each is trying to maximize.

This chapter presents a mathematical framework for the investigation of collectives, in particular the investigation of this design problem. A crucial feature of this framework is that it involves no modeling of the underlying system or of the algorithms controlling the agents. For example, only the behavior of an agent (or, more precisely, certain broad aspects of it) is formally related to what private utility that agent is "trying" to maximize; nothing of what goes on "under the hood" is assumed. This behaviorist approach is crucial because in the real world, collectives are often so complicated that no tractable model can bear more than a cursory similarity with the system it is supposed to represent. More generally, this approach is crucial to have the framework be broad enough to encompass, for example, the collectives of spin glasses and human economies.

In the next section we will introduce generalized coordinates. These allow us to avoid any restrictions on the kinds of variables comprising the system—they can be uncountable, countable, or combinations thereof; with or without an underlying topology or metric; and except where explicitly indicated otherwise, all the results of the framework apply. The underlying variables can include time or not, and if they do, the associated underlying dynamics is arbitrary. The variables can be broken up explicitly into separate agents or not, and if they are, there can be arbitrary restrictions on which of the conceivable joint moves of the agents are physically allowed. In addition, how the variables are broken up into agents and the number of agents are arbitrary and can be modified dynamically (if time is included in the underlying variables). Moreover, if time is included as an underlying variable, then some of the agents can have their decision "simultaneously" fix the state of one or more variables of the system *at distinct moments in time*. (This is reminiscent of what is decided in settling on a contract in cooperative game theory.) Again, all of this can be varied in an arbitrary fashion.

Using these generalized coordinates, a central equation can be derived that determines how well any of these kinds of systems perform. It does so by breaking performance down into three terms. These terms loosely reflect the concerns of the fields of high-dimensional search, economics, and machine learning; the central equation is the bridge that couples those fields.

The following section uses this mathematical framework to introduce a (model-independent) formalization of the assumption that a particular component of the system is a "utility-maximizing ... agent". That formalization is then used to derive the Aristocrat and Wonderful Life private utility functions, two utility functions previously intuited that have been found to result in much better world utility than conventional techniques [17]. This derivation also uncovers (relatively rare) conditions under which those utilities should not perform very well. That section ends by deriving many new results, including the collapsed private utility, and ways to modify other agents to help a particular agent, along with specification of the scenarios in which such techniques should result in good world utility.

An accompanying paper [22] presents this mathematical framework in a more pedagogical manner, including many examples, commentary, and some discussion of related fields (e.g., mechanism design in game theory). That paper also discusses recent experiments involving a set of previous semiformal heuristics (including the Aristocrat and Wonderful Life private utilities) that have been found to be very useful for the design of collectives. It uses the mathematical framework to explain the efficacy of those techniques. It then goes on to make numerical predictions based on that framework, and then presents some experimental tests of those predictions. It ends by making other (testable) predictions and presents a sample of future research topics and open issues.

This chapter exhaustively presents all of the currently elaborated mathematics of the framework, including the details omitted in [22]. In particular, this chapter contains theorems not presented there, extensions of the theorems presented there, proofs of all theorems, detailed application of the framework to multistep games, and the important example of applying the framework to gradient ascent over categorical variables. (For pedagogical reasons, the latter two occur as appendices.) Combined, these two papers present a mathematical theory along with associated predictions, experiments, and engineering recommendations. In this, they lay the foundation for a full-fledged science of collectives.

2 The Central Equation

2.1 Generalized Coordinates and Intelligence

We are interested in addressing optimization problems by decomposing them into many subproblems, each of which is solved separately. We will not try to choose such subproblems so that they are independent of one another or find a way to coordinate their solutions. Rather we will choose the subproblems so that each of them is relatively easy to solve, *given the context of a particular current solution to the other subproblems*, and then solve them in parallel.

To formalize this, let ζ be an arbitrary space with elements z called **worldpoints**. Let $C \subseteq \zeta$ be the set of elements of ζ that are actually allowed, for example, in that they are consistent with the laws of physics.[1] Define a **generalized coordinate variable** as a function from C to associated **coordinate values**. (When the context makes the precise meaning clear, we will sometimes use the term "coordinate" to refer to a generalized coordinate variable and sometimes to a value of that variable.) We will sometimes view a coordinate variable ρ as an exhaustive partition of C

---

[1] Whenever expressing a particular system as a collective, it is a good rule to write out the functional dependencies presumed to specify $C(\cdot)$ as explicitly as one can, to check that what one has identified as the space ζ does indeed contain all the important variables.

into nonempty subsets, with $\rho(z)$ being the element of the partition that contains z. Accordingly, we will sometimes write a coordinate value $r = \rho(z)$ as "$r \in \rho$" and a worldpoint z' sharing that value as "$z' \in r$."[2] Intuitively, each "subproblem" of our overall optimization problem will be formalized in terms of such a partition ρ, as finding the optimal z within the $r \in \rho$ specified by the current solutions to the other subproblems.

Often we implicitly assume that the set of values that any coordinate variable we are discussing can take on forms a measurable set, as does the set of worldpoints having any such value. (All integrals are implicit with respect to such measures.)

As an example, C might consist of the possible joint actions of a set of computational agents engaged in a noncooperative game [2, 3, 5, 7, 10]. $\rho(z \in C)$ could then be the actions of all agents *except* some particular agent identified with ρ. In this case, by fixing all other degrees of freedom, the value of the coordinate ρ implicitly specifies the degrees of freedom that are still "available to be set" by the agent identified with ρ.

A frequently occurring type of coordinate variable is one whose values are contained in the real numbers. A particularly important example is a **world utility** function $G : C \to \mathfrak{R}$ that ranks the possible worldpoints of the system. We are always provided a G; the goal in the problem of designing collectives is to maximize G.

Our mathematics does not concern G alone, but rather its relationship with some **coordinate utilities** $g_\rho : C \to \mathfrak{R}$.[3] Each coordinate utility ranks the possible values of those degrees of freedom still allowed once the worldpoint has been restricted to a set of worldpoints $r \in \rho$. Given a set of coordinate variables, $\{\rho\}$, we are interested in inducing a z that each g_ρ ranks highly (relative to the other worldpoints in the associated set $r = \rho(z)$), and in the relation between those rankings of z and G's ranking of z. To analyze these issues we need to standardize utility functions so that the numeric value they assign to z only reflects their relative ranking of z (potentially just in comparison to the other worldpoints sharing some associated coordinate value).[4]

Generically, we indicate such a standardization by N, and for any utility function U, coordinate ρ, and $z \in C$, we write the associated value of such a standardization of the utility U as $N_{\rho,U}(z)$. Define "sgn[x]" to equal $+1$, 0, or -1 in the usual way. Then we only need to require of a standardization N that $N_{\rho,U}(z)$ be a $[0, 1]$-valued, ρ-parameterized functional of the pair $(U, U(z))$, one that meets the following two conditions as we vary U or z:

(i) $\forall z \in C$, if for a pair of utilities V and W, sgn$[W(z') - W(z)] = $ sgn$[V(z') - V(z)] \; \forall z' \in \rho(z)$, then $N_{\rho,W}(z) = N_{\rho,V}(z)$.

---

[2] In general, we try to use lowercase Greek letters for coordinates and the associated lowercase roman letter for the value of that coordinate.

[3] In previous work, roughly analogous utilities were called "personal utilities" [17].

[4] It turns out that there never arises a reason to consider the relation between such a standardization and the axioms conventionally used to derive utility theory [10], in particular those axioms concerning behavior of expectation values of utility.

(ii) With U and $r \in \rho$ fixed, $\forall \, z, z' \in r$, $\mathrm{sgn}[N_{\rho,U}(z) - N_{\rho,U}(z')] = \mathrm{sgn}[U(z) - U(z')]$.

We call the value of $N_{\rho,U}$ at z the "**intelligence** of z (given ρ) with respect to U for coordinate ρ."[5],[6] If ρ consists of a single set (all of C), we simply write $N_U(z)$. An example of an intelligence operator based on percentiles is provided in Appendix A. Unless explicitly stated otherwise, whenever calculating intelligence values in any examples, we will use this choice of the intelligence operator.

Often there will be uncertainly in the worldpoint z, in particular on the part of the system designer (e.g., when worldpoints are worldlines of a physical system, such uncertainty arises if the designer is not able to calculate exactly how the system evolves). Such uncertainty is captured by a distribution $P(z)$ that equals 0 off of C.[7] Accordingly, coordinates ρ are not only partitions, but also random variables, taken values $r \in \rho$.

All aspects of the designer's ability to manipulate the system are encapsulated in the selection of an element s from some **design coordinate** σ. In particular, because the (sub)problem of finding a $z \in r$ with maximal ρ-intelligence will vary as r varies, it cannot be addressed with conventional algorithms for maximizing a static function. Instead, its solution requires techniques—like those in reinforcement learning—tailored for dynamically varying or uncertain functions. Accordingly, we will often consider the case where (among other things) s specifies which of a set of allowed **private utility** functions to associate with some coordinate ρ, $g_{\rho,s} : z \to \mathfrak{R}$. Such a function is one that we view intuitively as the "payoff function" for a self-

---

[5] Note that for fixed U, the function $N_{\rho,U}(\cdot)$ from $C \to \mathfrak{R}^+$ can be viewed as a utility function and therefore as a coordinate. In particular, $N_{\rho,N_{\rho,U}} = N_{\rho,U}$. This follows from condition (i) in the definition of intelligence with $V = U$, $W = N_{\rho,V}$, and the equality of sgn's following from condition (ii) in the definition of intelligence.

[6] Although this chapter concentrates on $\mathfrak{R}$-valued utility functions, much of its analysis can be extended to functions having different ranges. Examples include vector-valued functions having range $\mathfrak{R}^n$—appropriate for analyzing intelligence with respect to several distinct Us at once—and functions whose range is a set of non-overlapping contiguous subintervals of $\mathfrak{R}$. In particular, given some such range Q and any associated antisymmetric preference function $F : Q \times Q \to \{-1, 0, 1\}$, we can replace the sgn function with F throughout (i) and (ii) when we specify our intelligence operator. Much of the sequel (e.g., Theorem 1) still holds under this modification. If Q is also a field over the reals, we can also form the average value of such an intelligence, and some of the theorems presented herein concerning expected intelligence values will go through.

[7] If there is uncertainty in C itself we express that with a distribution $P(C)$, to go with the distributions $P(z \mid C)$. In particular, if probabilities reflect the system designer's uncertainty about C, then $P(z)$ may be nonzero even for points z off of the actual C. Fixing C exactly is analogous to fixing the energy exactly in statistical physics (the microcanonical ensemble); allowing C to vary is analogous to uncertainty in the energy (the canonical ensemble). Unless explicitly stated otherwise, in this chapter we will consider C to be fixed. In a similar fashion, if probabilities reflect uncertainty in how a coordinate κ partitions C, then it could be that $P(z \mid k)$ is nonzero even for points z where $\kappa(z) \neq k$. (For simplicity, we will usually assume this is not the case.)

interested computational agent, embodied in C, that uses a "learning algorithm" to "control" position within any particular element of ρ.[8] A priori, a coordinate need not have an associated private utility; in particular, nonlearning agents need not. Informally, when we have a "learning agent" associated with coordinate ρ we refer to ρ as either the **agent coordinate** or the agent's **context coordinate**, with the value of that coordinate being the agent's **context**. (These definitions are made more formal later.)

Properly interpreted, the rules of set theory hold when coordinate variables play the role of sets. Under this interpretation any coordinate variable κ arising in a set-theoretic expression should be read as "every (subset of ζ that constitutes an) element of κ." For example, $\kappa \subset \lambda$ means "every element of κ is a proper subset of every element of λ," so that the value k fixes l; see Appendix B.

As a notational matter, we adopt the usual convention that probability of a coordinate value is shorthand that the associated random variable takes on that value, e.g., $P(a)$ means $P(\alpha = a)$. As usual, though, this convention is not propagated to expectation values: $E(U(a, \beta) \mid c) \equiv \int db U(a, b) P(b \mid c)$. Delta functions are either Kronecker or Dirac as appropriate (although always written as arguments rather than as subscripts). Similarly, integrals are assumed to have a point-mass measure (i.e., reduce to a sum) as appropriate. For any function $\phi : C \to \Re$ and coordinate κ, with $y \in [0, 1]$, we write $\mathrm{CDF}_\phi(y \mid k)$ to mean the cumulative distribution function $P(\phi \leq y \mid k) \equiv \int_{-\infty}^{y} dt \int dz\, P(z \mid k) \delta(\phi(z) - t)$, and just write $\mathrm{CDF}(\phi \mid k)$ to refer to the entire function over y. In addition, "supp" is shorthand for the support operator, and "$\mathfrak{B}$" indicates the Booleans. $O(A)$ means the cardinality of the set A. For any two functions f_1 and f_2 with the same domain $x \in X$, "$f_1 < f_2$" means that $\forall x\ \ f_1(x) \leq f_2(x)$, and $\exists x$ such that $f_1(x) < f_2(x)$. All proofs that are not in the text are provided in Appendix C.

2.2 The Central Equation

Our analysis revolves around the following **central equation** for $P(U \mid s)$, which follows from applying Bayes' theorem twice in succession:

$$P(U \mid s) = \int d\mathbf{N}_U\, P(U \mid \mathbf{N}_U, s) \int d\mathbf{N}_g\, P(\mathbf{N}_U \mid \mathbf{N}_g, s) P(\mathbf{N}_g \mid s), \qquad (1)$$

where usually we are interested in having $U = G$. g is the vector of the values of a set of coordinate utilities, and $\mathbf{N}_g$ is an associated vector of intelligences with respect to those utilities. Here we concentrate on the case where each of those intelligences is for the associated coordinate, i.e., for the set of coordinates $\{\rho\}$ it is the ρ-indexed vector with components $\{\mathbf{N}_{\rho, g_\rho}(z)\}$. $\mathbf{N}_U$ is also a coordinate-variable-indexed vector of intelligence values, only for utility U. We will concentrate on the

---

[8] Note that, formally speaking, the learning algorithm itself is embodied in C. Hence the quotation marks around the term "control."

case where $\mathbf{N}_U$ is indexed with the same coordinates as $\mathbf{N}_g$. In this situation $\mathbf{N}_U$ has components $\mathbf{N}_{\rho,U}(z)$ and is identical to $\mathbf{N}_g$ except in its choice of utility functions.[9]

If we can choose s so that term 3 in the integrand in Equation 1 is peaked around vectors $\mathbf{N}_g$, all of whose components are close to 1, then we have likely induced large intelligences. If in addition to such a good term 3 we can have term 2 peaked about $\mathbf{N}_U$ equal to $\mathbf{N}_g$, then $\mathbf{N}_U$ will also be large. If term 1 in the integrand is also peaked about high U when $\mathbf{N}_U$ is large, then our choice of s will likely result in high U, as desired.

In the next section we analyze what coordinate utilities give the desired form of term 2 in the central equation for our choice of $\mathbf{N}_G$ and $\mathbf{N}_g$. We then present examples illustrating such systems and more generally illustrating generalized coordinates. We end this section with a brief discussion of term 1. In the next section we analyze what coordinate utilities give the desired form of term 3 in the central equation. It is only here that the use of agents to control some coordinate values becomes crucial. We end that section by combining these analyses to derive coordinate utilities that have the desired forms for both terms 2 and 3.

This formalism applies to many more scenarios than those involving dynamical systems with values z specifying behavior across time. It also applies even in scenarios that are not conventionally viewed as instances of game theory. Nonetheless, as an example of the formalism, Appendix D is a detailed exposition of multistep games in terms of this formalism.

2.3 Term 2—Factoredness

We say that U_1 and U_2 are (mutually) **factored** at a point z for coordinate ρ if $N_{\rho,U_1}(z') = N_{\rho,U_2}(z') \ \forall \ z' \in \rho(z)$.[10] Note that factoredness is transitive. If we do not specify U_2, it is taken to be G, and we sometimes say that U "is factored" or "is factored with respect to G" when U and G are mutually factored. If $\forall \ \rho$ in a set of coordinates that we are using to analyze a system, the utility g_ρ is factored with respect to G for coordinate ρ at a point z, we simply say that the system is factored at z or that the $\{g_\rho\}$ are factored with respect to G there.

There is a very tight relation between factoredness and game theory. For example, consider the case where we have Pareto superiority of a point z' over some other point z with respect to the coordinate utility intelligences [2, 3, 5, 7, 10]. Say that those associated utilities also form a factored system with respect to the world utility G. These imply the Pareto superiority of z' over z with respect to world utility. The converse also holds. However, these properties relating factoredness, coordinate and

---

[9] Because the distributions in Equation 1 are conditioned on s, when we have a percentile-style intelligence, a natural choice for the associated measure $d\mu(z)$ is given by the values $r = \rho(z)$ and s, as $P(z \mid r)P(r \mid s)$ (see Appendix A). In other words, given that we are within a particular r, the measure extends across that entire context—including points inconsistent with s—according to the distribution $P(z \mid r)$.

[10] In previous work we defined **factoredness** only to mean that $\text{sgn}[U_1(z') - U_1(z)] = \text{sgn}[U_2(z') - U_2(z)] \ \forall \ z' \in \rho(z)$. This is a necessary (but not sufficient) condition that $N_{\rho,U_1}(z') = N_{\rho,U_2}(z') \ \forall \ z' \in \rho(z)$; see Theorem 1 and the definition of intelligence.

world utilities only hold for Pareto superiority for intelligences (rather than for raw coordinate utility values), in general. In addition, by taking $U_2 = G$, the following theorem provides the basis for relating game-theoretic concepts like Nash equilibria and nonrational behavior with world utility in factored systems.

Theorem 1. U_1 and U_2 are mutually factored at $z \in C$ for coordinate ρ iff

$$\text{sgn}[U_1(z') - U_1(z'')] = \text{sgn}[U_2(z') - U_2(z'')] \qquad \forall \, z', z'' \in \rho(z).$$

Note that this holds regardless of the precise choice of N, so long as it meets the formal definition of an intelligence operator.

By Theorem 1, for a system whose coordinate utilities are factored with respect to G, the set of Nash equilibria of those coordinate utilities equals the set of points that are maxima of the world utility along each coordinate individually (which of course does not mean that they are maxima along off-axis directions).[11] In addition to this desirable equilibrium structure, factoredness ensures the appropriate off-equilibrium structure; so long as for each coordinate the associated intelligence is high (with respect to that coordinate's utility), the system will be close to a local maximum of world utility. This is because, for each coordinate ρ, given a (fixed) associated coordinate value r, any change in $z \in r$ that decreases ρ's coordinate utility—which is almost all changes if ρ's intelligence is high—will assuredly decrease world utility. Note, however, that having g_ρ factored with respect to G does not preclude deleterious side effects on the other coordinate utilities of such a g_ρ-improving change within r. All such factoredness tells us is whether world utility gets improved by such changes (see the end of Appendix D).[12]

The following theorem gives the entire equivalence class of utilities that are mutually factored at a point.

---

[11] An immediate game-theoretic corollary is that any game whose utilities can be expressed as coordinate utilities of a system that is factored with respect to a world utility having critical points has at least one pure strategy Nash equilibrium. However, consider an arbitrary vector ε all of whose components lie in $[0, 1]$. Then it is not the case that every factored system has a pure strategy joint profile with each player's intelligence given by the associated component of ε. This is even true if every component of ε is either a 0 or a 1. As a simple example, choose $g_1 = g_2 = G$, and have $\varepsilon = (0, 1)$. Have $G = z_1$ for $z_2 > 1/2$, and equal $1 - z_1$ otherwise, where both z_1 and $z_2 \in [0, 1]$. Then if $z_2 > 1/2$, $z_1 = 1$, because $N_1 = 1$. However, if $z_1 = 1$, then $z_2 \in [0, 1/2]$ because $N_2 = 0$. If $z_2 \le 1/2$, however, $z_1 = 0$, which means that $z_2 \in (1/2, 1]$. **QED**.

[12] Factoredness is simply a bit; a system is factored or it isn't. As such it cannot quantify situations in which term 2 has a good form although it is not exactly a delta function. Nor can it characterize "super-factored" situations in which that conditional distribution is *better* than a delta function, being biased toward N_G values that exceed the N_g values. One way to address this deficiency is to define a "degree of factoredness." One example of such a measure is $1 - \int dz \, P(z \mid s)[N_G - N_g]^2 \in [0, 1]$. Another is $\int dz \, P(z \mid s)[N_G - N_g]$, which extends from "partially factored" systems (negative values), to perfectly factored systems (value 0), to super-factored systems (value greater than 0). Other definitions arise from consideration of Theorem 1. For example, one might quantify factoredness for coordinate ρ as the probability that a random move within a context changes G and g_ρ the same way:

Theorem 2. U_1 *and* U_2 *are mutually factored at* z *for coordinate* ρ *iff* $\forall\ z' \in r \equiv$ $\rho(z)$, *we can write*

$$U_1(z') = \Phi_r(U_2(z'))$$

for some r-*indexed function* Φ_r *that is a strictly increasing function of its argument across the set of all values* $U_2(z' \in r)$. *(The form of* U_1 *for other arguments is arbitrary.)*

Using some notational overloading of the Φ function, by Theorem 2 we can ensure that the system is factored by having each $g_\rho(z) = \Phi_\rho(G(z), \rho(z)) \ \forall\ z \in \zeta$ for some functions Φ_ρ whose first partial derivative is strictly increasing everywhere. Note that this factoredness holds regardless of C or $P(z \mid s)$. The canonical example of such a case is a **team game** (also known as an **exact potential game** [4, 6, 12]), where $g_\rho = G$ for all ρ. Alternatively, by only requiring that $\forall\ z \in C$ does g_ρ take on such a form, we can access a broader class of factored utilities, a class that *does* depend on aspects of C.

As an example, define a **difference** utility for coordinate ρ with respect to utility D_1 as a utility taking the form $D_\rho(z) = \beta(z)[D_1(z) - D_2(z)]$ for some function D_2 and positive function $\beta(\cdot)$, where both $\beta(\cdot)$ and $D_2(\cdot)$ have the same value for any pair of points z and $z' \in C$ for which $\rho(z) = \rho(z')$. (We will sometimes refer to D_1 as the **lead utility** of such a difference utility, with D_2 being the **secondary utility**.) Because both $\beta(z)$ and $D_2(z)$ can be written purely as a function of $\rho(z)$, by Theorem 2, a difference utility is factored with respect to D_1. As explained in the next section, for such a utility with $D_1 = G$, term 3 in the central equation can be vastly superior to that of a team game, especially in large systems. In addition, as a practical matter, often D_ρ can be evaluated much more easily than can D_1.

2.4 Term 1 and Alternate Forms of the Central Equation

Assuming term 3 results in a large value of $\mathbf{N}_g$, having factoredness then ensures that we have a large value of $\mathbf{N}_G$ as well. In this situation term 1 will determine how good G is. Intuitively, term 1 reflects how likely the system is to get caught near local maxima of G. If any maximum of G the system finds is likely to be the global maximum, then term 1 has a good form. (For factored systems, in such scenarios it is likely that a system near a Nash equilibrium it is near the highest possible G.)

So for factored systems, for our choice of $\mathbf{N}_G$ and $\mathbf{N}_g$, term 1 can be viewed as a formal encapsulation of the issue underpinning the much-studied exploration–exploitation trade-off of conventional search algorithms. That trade-off can manifest

$$\int dz\, dz'\, P(z \mid s)P(z' \mid s)\delta(z' \in \rho(z))\Theta([G(z) - G(z')][g_\rho(z) - g_\rho(z')]).$$

Especially when one has a percentile-type intelligence, all these possibilities suggest yet other variants in which the measure $d\mu(z)$ replaces the distribution(s) $P(z \mid s)$. Similarly, one can define "local" (degree of factoredness) about some point z'' by introducing into the integrands of all these variants Heaviside functions restricting the worldpoint to be near z''.

itself both within the learning algorithms of the individual agents and in a centralized process determining whether those agents are allowed to make proposed changes in their state ([25]). In this paper we will not consider such issues but instead will concentrate on terms 2 and 3.

As mentioned, term 2 in the central equation is closely related to issues considered in economics and game theory (cf. Theorem 1 and note the relation between factoredness and the concept of incentive compatibility in mechanism design [2, 7, 8, 10, 13–16, 27]. On the other hand, as expounded later, term 3 is closely related to signal-noise issues often considered in machine learning (but essentially never considered in economics). Finally, as just mentioned, term 1 is related to issues considered by the search community. So the central equation can be viewed as a way of integrating the fields of economics, machine learning, and search.

Finally, an important alternative to the choice of $\mathbf{N}_U$ investigated in this chapter is where it is the scalar $N_{\emptyset,U}$. In this situation, $\mathbf{N}_U$ is a monotonic transformation of U *over all of* C, rather than just within various partition elements of C. For this choice, term 1 in the central equation becomes moot, and that equation effectively reduces to $P(U \mid s) = \int d\mathbf{N}_g P(U \mid \mathbf{N}_g, s) P(\mathbf{N}_g \mid s)$. The analysis presented later of the $P(\mathbf{N}_g \mid s)$ term in the central equation is unchanged by this change. However, the analysis of the $P(\mathbf{N}_U \mid \mathbf{N}_g, s)$ term is now replaced by analysis of $P(U \mid \mathbf{N}_g, s)$. For reasons of space, we do not investigate this alternative choice of $\mathbf{N}_U$ in this chapter.

3 The Three Premises

3.1 Coordinate Complements, Moves, and Worldviews

Because intelligence is bounded above by 1, we can roughly encapsulate the quality of term 3 in the central equation as the associated expected intelligence. Accordingly, our analysis of term 3 will be expressed in terms of expected intelligences.

We will consider only one coordinate at a time together with the associated expected coordinate intelligence. This simplifies the analysis to only concern one of the components of ε_g together with the dependence of that component on associated variations in s, our choice of the element of the design coordinate. For now we further restrict attention to agent coordinate utilities, reserve ρ to refer only to such an agent coordinate with some associated learning algorithm, and take $g_\rho = g_{\rho,s}$.[13] The context will always make clear whether ρ specifies a coordinate (as when it subscripts a private utility), refers to the values the coordinate can assume (as in $r \in \rho$), indicates the associated random variable (as in expressions like $P(U(x, \rho)) = \int dr\, P(r) U(x, r)$), etc.

---

[13] Note that changing ρ's coordinate utility while leaving s unchanged has no effect on the probability of a particular G value; g_ρ is just an expansion variable in the central equation. Conversely, leaving ρ's coordinate utility the same while changing its private utility (and therefore s, and therefore in general the associated distribution over ζ, $P(z \mid s)$) changes the probability distribution across G values. Setting those two utilities equal is what allows the expansion of the central equation to be exploited to help determine s.

As a notational matter, define two partitions of some $T \subseteq \zeta$, π_1 and π_2, to be **complements** over $T \subseteq \zeta$ if $z \in T \rightarrow (\pi_1(z), \pi_2(z))$ is invertible, so that, intuitively speaking, π_1 and π_2 jointly form a "coordinate system" for T.[14,15] When discussing generalized coordinates, this nomenclature is used with T implicitly taken to be C. (π_1 and π_2 are coordinate variables in the formal sense if $T = C$.) We adopt the convention that for any coordinate ρ, $\hat{}\rho$, having labels or values written $\hat{}r$, is shorthand for some coordinate that is complementary to ρ (the precise such coordinate will not matter) and that $\hat{}\hat{}\rho = \rho$. We do not take the "$\hat{}$" operator to refer to values of a coordinate, only to coordinates as a whole. So, for example, there is no a priori relationship implied between a particular element of $\hat{}\rho$ that we write as $\hat{}r$, and some particular element of ρ that we write as r.

We always have $E(N_{\rho,U} \mid s) = \int dr \, dn \, dx \, P(r \mid s) P(n \mid r, s) P(x \mid n) N_{\rho,U}(x, r)$. Accordingly, if we knew $P(r \mid s)$ and one of $P(n \mid r, s)$ and $P(x \mid n)$ but not the other, then we could in principle solve for that other distribution to optimize expected intelligence.[16] Unfortunately, we usually do not know two of those three distributions, and so we must take a more indirect approach.

The analysis presented here for agent coordinates revolves around the issue of how sensitive g_ρ is to changes within an element of ρ as opposed to changes between those elements of ρ. To conduct this analysis we will need to introduce two coordinates in addition to σ and ρ: ξ and υ.[17] Given some $\hat{}\rho$, rather than the precise element $\hat{}r \in \hat{}\rho$, in general the agent associated with ρ can only control in which of several sets of possible elements $\hat{}r$ the system is. This is formalized with the coordinate $\xi \supseteq \hat{}\rho$. We refer to ξ as the **move variable** of the agent, and we refer to an $x \in \xi$ or the set of z that that x specifies, as the **move value** of the agent. For convenience, we assume that for all such contexts r and moves x there exists at least one $z \in C$ such that $\rho(z) = r$ and $\xi(z) = x$. In general, what we identify as the ξ of a particular ρ need not be unique. Intuitively, such a partition ξ delineates a set of $r \rightarrow z$ maps, each such map giving a way that the agent associated with ρ is allowed to vary its behavior to reflect in what context r it is. An agent's move is a selection among such a set of allowed variations. An important example of move variables involving dynamic processes is presented in Appendix D.

---

[14] This characterization as a coordinate system is particularly apt if π_1 and π_2 are **minimal** complements, by which is meant that there is neither a coarser partition $\pi' \supseteq \pi_1$ such that π' and π_2 are complements nor a coarser partition $\pi'' \supseteq \pi_2$ such that π'' and π_1 are complements.

[15] Note that it is not assumed that $T \rightarrow (p_1, p_2)$ taking points z to partition element pairs is surjective.

[16] Formally, to implement this would require making an associated change to s, which in the case of solving for $P(x \mid n)$ would have to be reflected in the value of n.

[17] Properly speaking, ξ and υ should be indexed by ρ, as should the coordinates $\sigma_{\underline{g}}$ and $\sigma_{\hat{}\underline{g}}$ introduced later; for reasons of clarity, here all such indices are implicit.

We assume that $\xi(z)$ and $\rho(z)$ jointly set the value of $G(z)$ and of any $\underline{g}_{\rho,s}$ we will consider.[18] Accordingly, we write $\underline{\gamma}_\rho^{\cdot}$ when we mean the coordinate whose partition elements are identical to σ's but whose values are instead the private utility functions of ρ: $\underline{\gamma}_\rho : s \in \sigma \to \underline{g}_{\rho,s}$. Similarly, we will write N_ρ when we mean the function $(x, r, s) \to N_{\rho, \underline{g}_{\rho,s}(x,r)}$.

We refer to ν as the **worldview variable** of the agent, and we refer to a $n \in \nu$, or the set of possible z that that ν specifies, as the **worldview value** of the agent. Intuitively, n specifies all the information—all training data, all knowledge of how the training data are formed (including, potentially, knowledge of its own private utility), all observations, all external commands, all externally set prior biases—that ρ's agent uses to determine its move, and nothing else. It is the contents of the (perhaps distorting) "window" through which the learning algorithm receives information from the external world.

Formally, there are three properties a coordinate must possess for it to qualify as a worldview of an agent. First, if the agent does indeed use all the information in n, then the agent's preference in moves must change in response to any change in the value of n. This means that $\forall n_1, n_2 \in \nu$, for at least one of the $x \in \xi$, $P(x \mid n_1) \neq P(x \mid n_2)$.[19] Second, if the worldview truly reflects everything the agent uses to make its move, then any change to any variable must be able to affect the distribution over moves only insofar as it affects n. This means that with Ω defined as the set of all non-ξ coordinate we will consider in our analysis (e.g., σ, ρ for some other agent, their intersection, etc.), $P(x \mid n, W) = P(x \mid n) \; \forall x \in \xi$, $n \in \nu$ and $W \in \Omega$ such that $P(x, n, W) \neq 0$.[20,21,22] Finally, of all coordinates obeying these two properties, the worldview must be among those whose information maximizes the expected performance of the associated Bayes-optimal guessing,[23] i.e., $\forall s \in \sigma, \beta \neq \nu$,

$$\int db P(b \mid s) E\left(\underline{\gamma}_\rho \left[\operatorname*{argmax}_{x'}\{E(\underline{\gamma}_\rho(x', \rho) \mid b)\}, \rho\right] \mid b\right)$$

$$\leq \int dn P(b \mid s) E\left(\underline{\gamma}_\rho \left[\operatorname*{argmax}_{x'}\{E(\underline{\gamma}_\rho(x', \rho) \mid n)\}, \rho\right] \mid n\right).$$

---

[18] Phrased differently, given the utility function and the associated ξ and ρ, the minimal choice for ζ is $\xi \times \rho$. If the value s is not fixed by $x \times r$, i.e., if it is not the case that $\sigma \supseteq \xi \cap \rho$, then σ must also be contained in ζ, and similarly for ν.

[19] When worldviews are numeric-valued, we can modify this requirement to be that the distribution $P(x \mid n)$ has to be a function of n sufficiently sensitive over all of ν.

[20] Note that if *all* W are allowed, then in general the only choice for ν obeying this restriction is $\nu = \xi$.

[21] As a result of this requirement, $P(r \mid x, n, W) = P(r \mid n, W)$, $P(x, r \mid n, W) = P(x \mid n) P(r \mid n, W)$, etc.

[22] For any $P(z)$ and coordinates α and β, one can always construct a coordinate $\delta \neq \alpha$ such that $P(a \mid b, d)$ varies with d. So our assumption about ξ, ν, and Ω constitutes a restriction on what coordinates we will consider in our analysis.

[23] If it were not for this requirement, ξ could double as the worldview and often so could σ.

So $P(n \mid s)$ is how the worldview varies with s, and $P(x \mid n)$ is how the agent's learning algorithm uses the resultant information. The $P(x \mid s)$ induced by these two distributions is how the move of the agent varies with s. Alternatively, $P(r \mid s)$ is the distribution over contexts caused by our choice of design coordinate value, and the distribution $P(x \mid r, s) = \int dn P(x \mid n) P(n \mid r, s)$ gives all salient aspects of the agent's learning algorithm and technique for inferring information about r; the integral over r of the product of these two distributions says how the choice of s determines the distribution over moves.

We will find it convenient to decompose $\sigma = \sigma_{\gamma_\rho} \cap \sigma_{\hat{\gamma}_\rho}$, where σ_{γ_ρ} is a coordinate whose value gives $\underline{g}_{\rho,s}$, and there is no coordinate $\omega \supset \sigma_{\gamma_\rho}$ with this property. (Intuitively, σ_{γ_ρ}'s value is a component of s that specifies $\underline{g}_{\rho,s}$ and nothing more.) Also, from now on, we will often drop the ρ index whenever its implicit presence is clear. So, for example, we will often write $s_{\underline{g}}$ instead of s_{γ_ρ}.

3.2 Ambiguity

Because we do not know $P(x \mid n)$ in general, we cannot directly say how n sets the distribution over x. Fortunately we do not need such detailed information. We only need to know the effect that certain changes to n have on particular characteristics of the associated distribution $P(x \mid n)$ (e.g., the effect certain changes to n have on the "characteristic of $P(x \mid n)$" given by an n-conditioned expected intelligence $E(N_U \mid n)$).

If there were a universal rule for how such characteristics affect expected intelligence, then without any assumptions we could use such a rule to deduce that some particular choices of n are superior to others. However, that has been proven to be impossible [18, 21]. Accordingly, we must make some presumption about the nature of the learning algorithm that must be as conservative as possible if it is to apply to all reasonable algorithms.

To see what presumption we can safely make concerning such effects, first note that the worldview n encapsulates all the information the agent might try to exploit concerning the x-dependence of the likely values of the private utility. That encapsulation given by n takes the form of the distribution over the Euclidean vector of private utility values $(y^1, y^2, \cdots)$ given by $\int dr ds \ \delta(\underline{g}_{\rho,s}(x^1, r) - y^1) \delta(\underline{g}_{\rho,s}(x^2, r) - y^2) \cdots P(r, s \mid n)$. The agent works by "trying" to use this encapsulation to appropriately set its move. Our presumption must concern aspects of how it does this. Furthermore, if that presumption is to apply to a wide variety of learning algorithms, it must *only* involve the encapsulated information and not (for example) any characteristics of some class of learning algorithms to which the agent belongs.

For simplicity, consider the case where there are only two possible moves, x^1 and x^2. The encapsulated information provided by n induces a pair of distributions of likely utility values at those two xs, $\int dr ds \ \delta(\underline{g}_{\rho,s}(x^1, r) - y) \ P(r, s \mid n)$ and $\int dr ds \ \delta(\underline{g}_{\rho,s}(x^2, r) - y) \ P(r, s \mid n)$, which we can write in shorthand as $P(y; \underline{\gamma}_\rho; n, x^1)$ and $P(y; \underline{\gamma}_\rho; n, x^2)$, respectively. (Note that unlike n, the x^i value in this semicolon notation is a parameter to the random variable γ_ρ, not a conditioning event for that random variable.) By definition of Von Neumann utility functions, for worldview n, the optimal move is x^1 if the expected value $E(y; \underline{\gamma}_\rho; n, x^1) > E(y; \underline{\gamma}_\rho; n, x^2)$, and x^2 otherwise. In general, though, the learning algorithm of the agent will not (and often cannot) have its distribution over x set to a delta function this way. Aspects of $P(y; \underline{\gamma}_\rho; n, x^1)$ and $P(y; \underline{\gamma}_\rho; n, x^2)$ in addition to the difference in their first moments will affect how $P(x \mid n)$ changes in going from one n to the other. For example, it may be that if $E(y; \underline{\gamma}_\rho; n, x^1) > E(y; \underline{\gamma}_\rho; n, x^2)$, then if n is changed so that both the probability of a relatively large y value at x^2 and the probability of a relatively small y value at x^1 shrinks, while the first moments of those distributions are unchanged, then the algorithm is more likely to choose x^1 with the new n than with the original one.

In light of this, we want to err on the side of caution in presuming how changes to $P(y; \underline{\gamma}_\rho; n, x^1)$ and $P(y; \underline{\gamma}_\rho; n, x^2)$ induced by changing n affect the associated distribution $P(x \mid n)$. The most unrestrictive such presumption we can make is that if the *entire distributions* $P(y; \underline{\gamma}_\rho; n, x^1)$ and $P(y; \underline{\gamma}_\rho; n, x^2)$ are "further separated" from one another after the change in n, then $P(x \mid n)$ gets weighted more to the higher of those two distributions. Such a presumption is the most conservative one we can make that holds for any learning algorithm, i.e., that is cast purely in terms of the set of posterior distributions $\{P(y; \underline{\gamma}_\rho; n, x)\}$ without any reference to attributes of the learning algorithm. This can be viewed as a first-principles justification that applies to any learning algorithm not horribly mis-suited to the learning problem at hand.[24]

To formalize the foregoing, consider the quantity

$$P(\underline{g}^1 = y^1, \underline{g}^2 = y^2; n, x^1, x^2) \equiv P(\underline{g}_\sigma(x^1, \rho) = y^1 \mid n) P(\underline{g}_\sigma(x^2, \rho) = y^2 \mid n),$$

which expands into the distribution

$$\int dr^1 \, dr^2 \, ds^1 \, ds^2 \, \delta(\underline{g}_{s^1}(x^1, r^1) - y^1) \delta(\underline{g}_{s^2}(x^2, r^2) - y^2) P(r^1, s^1 \mid n) P(r^2, s^2 \mid n).$$

This is the distribution generated by sampling $P(r', s' \mid n)$ to get values of $\underline{\gamma}_\rho$ at x^1, and then doing this again (in an IID manner) to get values at x^2. This "semicolon" distribution is the most accurate possible distribution of private utilities values at x^1 and x^2 that the agent could possibly employ to decide which x to adopt to optimize that private utility, based solely on n.

Now fix a utility U that is a single-valued function of x. Our "most accurate distribution" induces the convolution distribution $P(y = y^1 - y^2; n, x^1, x^2)$. The more weighted this convolution is toward values of y that are large and that have the same sign as $U(x^1) - U(x^2)$, the less likely we expect the agent to be "led astray, as

---

[24] If the learning algorithm and underlying distribution over utility values do not adhere to this presumption, then in essence that underlying distribution is "adversarially chosen" for the learning algorithm—that algorithm's implicit assumptions concerning the learning problem are such a poor match to the actual ones—that the algorithm is likely to perform badly for that underlying distribution *no matter what one does* to s, n, or the like.

far as $U(\cdot)$ is concerned" in "deciding between x^1 and x^2," when the worldview is n. On the other hand, if the convolution distribution is heavily weighted around the value 0, then we expect the agent is more likely to be mistaken (again, as far as U is concerned) in its choice of x.

Consider changing n^a to n^b in such a way that the associated convolution distribution, $P([g^1 - g^2] \operatorname{sgn}[U(x^1) - U(x^2)]; n^a, x^1, x^2)$ is more weighted upward than is $P([g^1 - g^2] \operatorname{sgn}[U(x^1) - U(x^2)]; n^b, x^1, x^2)$. Say this is the case for *all* pairs of x values (x^1, x^2), i.e., with worldview n^a, the agent is less likely to be led astray for all decisions between a pair of x values than it is with worldview n^b. Our assumption is that whenever such a situation arises, if we truly have an adaptive agent operating in a learnable environment, then the agent has higher intelligence with respect to U, on average, with worldview n^a.

In general, we can encapsulate how much a stochastic process over C weights some random variable V upward, given some coordinate value $l \in \lambda$, with $\mathrm{CDF}_V(y \mid l)$—the smaller this cumulative distribution function, the larger the l-conditioned values of V tend to be.[25] Accordingly, we can use such a CDF to quantify how much more "weighted upward" our convolution distribution for n^a is in comparison to the one for n^b. (See Appendix A for how this CDF is related to intelligence.)

To formalize this we extend the semicolon notation introduced earlier. Given a coordinate χ whose value c is a single-valued function of (x, r, s) and arbitrary coordinate λ, define the (x^1, x^2, l)-parameterized distribution over values c^1, c^2,

$$
\begin{aligned}
P(&\chi^1, \chi^2; l, x^1, x^2) \\
&\equiv P_\chi(c^1, c^2; l, x^1, x^2) \\
&= \int dr^1 \, dr^2 \, ds^1 \, ds^2 \, P(r^1, s^1 \mid l) P(r^2, s^2 \mid l) \\
&\quad \times \delta(\chi(x^1, r^1, s^1) - c^1) \delta(\chi(x^2, r^2, s^2) - c^2).
\end{aligned}
$$

Thus, in this expression χ is a random variable that is (being treated as) parameterized by x, and we are considering its l-conditioned distributions at x^1 and x^2. This notation is sometimes simplified when the meaning is clear, e.g., $P_\chi(c^1, c^2; l, x^1, x^2)$ is written as $P(c^1, c^2; l, x^1, x^2)$.

Expectations, variances, marginalizations, and CDFs of this distribution and of functionals of it are written with the obvious notation. In particular, $P_\chi(c; l, x) = P(\chi(x, \rho, \sigma) = c \mid l)$, so $P_\chi(c^1, c^2; l, x^1, x^2) = P_\chi(c^1; l, x^1) P_\chi(c^2; l, x^2)$. As another example, say that χ is the real-valued coordinate ψ taking values y^i at (x^i, r^i, s^i). Then for any function $f : \mathfrak{R}^2 \to \mathfrak{R}$, for any l,

---

[25] Let $\bar{u}$ be a real-valued random variable and $F : \mathfrak{R} \to \mathfrak{R}$ a function such that $F(y) > y; \; \forall \, y \in \mathfrak{R}$. Then $P(F(\bar{u}) < y) \leq P(\bar{u} < y) \; \forall \, y$, i.e., the monotonically increasing function F applied to the underlying random variable pushes the CDF down. Conversely, if $\mathrm{CDF}_1 < \mathrm{CDF}_2$, then the function $F(u) = \mathrm{CDF}_1^{-1}(\mathrm{CDF}_2(u))$ is a monotonically increasing function that transforms CDF_1 into CDF_2.

$$\text{CDF}_{f(y^1,y^2)}(y; l, x^1, x^2)$$

$$\equiv \int_{-\infty}^{\infty} dy^1 \, dy^2 \, P(y^1, y^2; l, x^1, x^2) \Theta[y - f(y^1, y^2)]$$

$$= \int dr^1 \, dr^2 \, ds^1 \, ds^2 \, P(r^1, s^1 \mid l) P(r^2, s^2 \mid l)$$

$$\times \Theta[y - f(\psi(x^1, r^1, s^1), \psi(x^2, r^2, s^2))].$$

Using this notation, for any single-valued function $U : x \rightarrow \Re$, we define the **(ordered) ambiguity** of U and ψ, for l, x^1, x^2, as the CDF of the associated convolution distribution:

$$A(y; U, \psi; l, x^1, x^2) \equiv \text{CDF}_{(y^1-y^2)\,\text{sgn}[U(x^1)-U(x^2)]}(y; l, x^1, x^2) \,.$$

Note that the argument of the sgn is just a constant as far as the integrations giving the CDF are concerned. That sgn term provides an ordering of the xs; ordered ambiguity says how separated our two y-distributions are "in the direction" given by that ordering. When U is not specified, the random variable in the CDF is understood to be $(\psi^1 - \psi^2)$ rather than $(\psi^1 - \psi^2)\,\text{sgn}[U(x^1) - U(x^2)]$. It is easy to verify that such **unordered ambiguities** are related to ordered ones by

$$A(y; U, \psi; l, x^1, x^2) = 1/2 + t_U(x^1, x^2)[A(t_U(x^1, x^2)y; \psi; l, x^1, x^2) - 1/2]$$

where $t_U(x^1, x^2) \equiv \text{sgn}[U(x^1) - U(x^2)]$.

We write just $A(U, \psi; l, x^1, x^2)$ (or $A(\psi; l, x^1, x^2)$) when we want to refer to the entire function over all y. If that entire function shrinks as we go from one n to another—if its value decreases for every value of the argument y—then intuitively, the function has been "pushed" toward more positive values of y. Taking $\lambda = v$, such a change will serve as our formalization of the concept that the distributions over U at x^1 and x^2 are "more separated" after that change in the value of v.

Expanding it in full we can write $A(y; U, \psi; n, x^1, x^2)$ as

$$\int dr^1 \, dr^2 \, ds^1 \, ds^2 \, P(r^1, s^1 \mid l) P(r^2, s^2 \mid l)$$

$$\times \Theta[y - (\psi(x^1, r^1, s^1) - \psi(x^2, r^2, s^2))\,\text{sgn}[U(x^1) - U(x^2)]],$$

or, by changing coordinates, as

$$\int dy^1 \, dy^2 \, P_\psi(y^1; l, x^1) P_\psi(y^2; l, x^2) \Theta[y - (y^1 - y^2)\,\text{sgn}[U(x^1) - U(x^2)]],$$

and similarly for unordered ambiguities. Thus, ambiguity is parameterized by the two distributions $P(\psi; l, x^i)$ as well as (for ordered ambiguities) U.[26] As a final comment, it is worth noting that there is an alternative to A, A^*, that also reflects the entire n-conditioned CDF of differences in utility values. It and our choice of A rather than A^* is discussed in Appendix G.

---

[26] Note that the ordered ambiguity does not change if we interchange x^1 and x^2, unlike the unordered ambiguity. Note also that unless $\text{sgn}[\psi(x^1, r^1, s^1) - \psi(x^2, r^2, s^2)]$ is the same

3.3 The First Premise

By considering ambiguity with $\psi = \gamma_\rho$ and $\lambda = v$, we can formalize the conclusion of reasoning about how certain changes in n affect the probability of the agent's "choosing" a particular x. We call this the **first premise**

$$A(U, \underline{\gamma}_\rho; n^a, x^1, x^2) < A(U, \underline{\gamma}_\rho; n^b, x^1, x^2) \ \forall \ x^1, x^2$$
$$\Rightarrow$$
$$\mathrm{CDF}(U \mid n^a) \leq \mathrm{CDF}(U \mid n^b),$$

where U, n^a, and n^b are arbitrary (up to the usual restrictions, that $z \in C$, that U is a function of x, etc.).[27] In other words, we presume that when the condition in the first premise holds, the distribution $P(x \mid n^a)$ must be so much better "aligned" with $U(x)$ than $P(x \mid n^b)$ is that the implication in the first premise (concerning the two associated CDFs) holds. Note that that implication does not involve a specification of r; because in general the agent knows nothing about r, the first premise, which purely concerns $P(x \mid n)$, cannot concern r.

Summarizing, U determines which of the two possible moves x^1 and x^2 by agent ρ are better; $\underline{g}_{\rho,s}$ is the (s-parameterized) private utility that agent ρ is trying to maximize, based exclusively on the value of the worldview, n (a worldview that may or may not provide the agent with the functional form of that private utility).

The first premise is, at root, the following assumption: If every one of the ambiguities $A(\underline{\gamma}_\rho; n^a, x^1, x^2)$ (one for each (x^1, x^2) pair) is superior (as far as U is concerned) to the corresponding $A(\underline{\gamma}_\rho; n^b, x^1, x^2)$, then if we replace n^b with n^a, the effect on $P(x \mid n)$ due to that superiority dominates any other characteristics of the two ns. In addition, that dominating effect pushes $P(x \mid n)$ to favor xs with high values of U. As argued earlier, this is a broadly applicable rule relating certain changes to n and associated changes to an agent's choice of x. There is no alternative we could formulate that is more conservative, i.e., that applies to more learning algorithms and only involves the distributions of the problem at hand confronting the algorithm.

To explicitly relate the first premise to intelligence, we start with the following result, which has nothing to do with learning algorithms and that holds regardless of the validity of the first premise. (Indeed, it can be seen as motivating the use of a CDF-like ambiguity to analyze properties of intelligences.)

Theorem 3. *Given any coordinates ω, κ, and λ, fixed $k \in \kappa$, and two functions V^a : $(w, k) \to \Re$ and $V^b : (w, k) \to \Re$ that are mutually factored for coordinate κ,*

$\forall \ (r^1, s^1), (r^2, s^2) \in \mathrm{supp}\, P(\cdot, \cdot \mid n)$, the associated ordered ambiguity is nonzero for some $y < 0$. More generally, to have the ambiguity be strongly weighted toward positive values of y, we need that sgn to be the same for all (r', s') in a set with measure (according to $P(r', s' \mid n)$) close to 1.

[27] Note that the functional (sic) inequality in the first premise is equivalent to $t_U(x^1, x^2)A(\underline{\gamma}_\rho; n^a, x^1, x^2) < t_U(x^1, x^2)A(\underline{\gamma}_\rho; n^b, x^1, x^2)$. In turn, this inequality implies that $U(x^1) \neq U(x^2)$, because otherwise $t_U(x^1, x^2) = 0$.

$$\mathrm{CDF}(V^a \mid l^a, k) < \mathrm{CDF}(V^b \mid l^b, k)$$

$$\Rightarrow$$

$$E(N_{\kappa, V^a} \mid l^a, k) > E(N_{\kappa, V^b} \mid l^b, k)$$

and similarly when the inequalities are both replaced by equalities.

Now take $\omega = \xi$ and for a fixed k, define $U(\cdot) \equiv V(\cdot, k)$ (so that U is a function of x). Then because $P(x \mid n, k) = P(x \mid n)$ (by definition of worldviews), assuming both $P(n^a, k)$ and $P(n^b, k)$ are nonzero, $\mathrm{CDF}(U \mid n^a) < \mathrm{CDF}(U \mid n^b)$ $\Rightarrow \mathrm{CDF}(U \mid n^a, k) < \mathrm{CDF}(U \mid n^b, k) \Rightarrow \mathrm{CDF}(V \mid n^a, k) < \mathrm{CDF}(V \mid n^b, k)$. So if we choose $\lambda = \nu$ in Theorem 3 and combine it with the first premise, we get the promised relation between ambiguities based on the x-ordering $V(x, k)$ and expected κ-intelligences of V conditioned on k and n. In turn, to relate the first premise to the problem of choosing s, use the fact that $E(N_{\kappa, V} \mid n, k, s) = E(N_{\kappa, V}(\xi, \kappa) \mid n, k, s) = E(N_{\kappa, V} \mid n, k)$ to derive the equality $E(N_{\kappa, V} \mid s) = \int dn dk P(n, k \mid s) \cdot E(N_{\kappa, V} \mid n, k)$.

3.4 Recasting the First Premise

We will need to use a more general formulation of the first premise than that given earlier. To derive this more general form, start by defining a parameterized distribution H whose parameter has redundant variables:

$$P(x \mid n) \equiv H_{\{A(\underline{\gamma}_\rho; n, x^1, x^2): x^1, x^2 \in \xi\}, n}(x).$$

Note that unordered ambiguity is used in this definition and that H implicitly carries an index identifying the agent as ρ.

In general, the complexity of $P(x \mid n)$ can be daunting, especially if ν is fine-grained enough to capture many different kinds of data that one might have the learning algorithm exploit. This complexity can make it essentially impossible to work with $P(x \mid n)$ directly. However in many situations it is reasonable to suppose that the dependence of H on its ν argument is small in comparison to associated changes in the ambiguity arguments (e.g., n's value does not set a priori biases of the learning algorithm across ξ). In such situations all aspects of $P(x \mid n)$ get reduced to the dependence of H on ambiguities. In other words, in such situations the functional dependence of $P(x \mid n)$ on the set of ambiguities can be seen as a low-dimensional parameterization of the set of all reasonable learning algorithms $P(x \mid n)$. Accordingly, in these situations one can work with the ambiguities, and thereby circumvent the difficulties of working with $P(x \mid n)$ directly.

Another advantage of reducing $P(x \mid n)$ to H is that often extremely general information concerning $P(\underline{\gamma}_\rho \mid n)$ allows us to identify ways to improve ambiguities and therefore (by the first premise) improve intelligence. Reduction to H, with its explicit dependence on those ambiguities, facilitates the associated analysis.

In particular, say that the worldview coordinate value specifies the private utility (or at least that we can assume that augmenting the worldview to contain that information would not appreciably change $P(x \mid n)$). This means that $P(\underline{\gamma}_\rho \mid n)$, which arises in calculating ambiguities, can be replaced by $P(\underline{g}_{\rho,s} \mid n)$, where $\underline{g}_{\rho,s}$ is the private utility specified by n. Assume that, in addition, $P(x \mid n)$ is not only dominated by the the set of associated ambiguities (one ambiguity for each x pair), but it can be written as a function exclusively of those ambiguities, a function whose domain is the set of all possible ambiguities. Under these two conditions we could consider the effects on $P(x \mid n)$ of replacing the actual ambiguities $\{A(\gamma_\rho; n, x^i, x^j) : x^i, x^j \in \xi\} = \{A(\underline{g}_{\rho,s}; n, x^i, x^j) : x^i, x^j \in \xi\}$, with counterfactual ambiguities $\{A(\underline{g}_{\rho,s'}; n, x^i, x^j) : x^i, x^j \in \xi\}$ that are based on the actual n at hand but are evaluated for some alternative candidate private utility $\underline{g}_{\rho,s'}$. Under certain circumstances, this approach could be used to determine what such candidate private utility to use, based on comparing the associated counterfactual ambiguities.

To use this approach in as broad a set of circumstances as possible, we must address the fact that $P(x \mid n)$ may have some dependence on n not fully captured in the associated ambiguities, e.g., when n modifies the learning algorithm by specifying biases for the learning algorithm to use. This means that the definition given earlier for H will not in general extend to parameter values whose ambiguity set does not correspond to n. Another hurdle is that often the domain of $P(x \mid n)$ need not extend to all ambiguities of the form $\{A(\underline{g}_{\rho,s'}; n, x^i, x^j) : x^i, x^j \in \xi\}$. Finally, in general, worldviews do not specify the private utility.

To circumvent these difficulties we need to introduce new notation and recast the first premise accordingly. Start by extending the domain of definition of H to write it as $H_{\{A(\psi;l,x^1,x^2):x^1,x^2\in\xi\},n}(x)$, for any coordinate value $l \in \lambda \subseteq \nu$. Here ψ is an arbitrary real-valued function of x, r, and s, not necessarily related to γ_ρ. So $H_{\{A(\psi;l,x^1,x^2):x^1,x^2\in\xi\},n}(x)$ is not necessarily related to the actual $P(x \mid n)$. Despite these freedoms, we require that for any value of its parameters $H_{\{A(\psi;l,x^1,x^2):x^1,x^2\in\xi\},n}(x)$ is a proper probability distribution over x, one that for fixed ψ and $\lambda = \nu$ is (like $P(x \mid n)$) parameterized by n. This extending of H's domain is how we circumvent the first two difficulties.

Next we introduce some succinct notation. As in the definition of worldviews, let $W \in \Omega$ refer to the set of all non-ξ coordinates we will consider in our analysis and define the distribution $P^{[\psi;\lambda]}(x, l, W) \equiv H_{\{A(\psi;l,x^1,x^2):x^1,x^2\in\xi\},n}(x)P(l, W)$, where $\lambda \subseteq \nu$. When $\psi = \gamma_\rho$, we just write $P^{[\lambda]}$. So, for example, $P^{[\nu]}(x \mid n) = P^{[\gamma_\rho;\nu]}(x \mid n) = P(x \mid n)$, $P^{[\psi;\lambda]}(x \mid l, W) = P^{[\psi;\lambda]}(x \mid l) = H_{\{A(\psi;l,x^1,x^2):x^1,x^2\in\xi\},n}(x)$, etc. Note also that $P^{[\gamma_\rho;\nu,\sigma]}(x \mid n, s) = P^{[\underline{g}_{\rho,s};\nu,\sigma]}(x \mid n, s)$. Intuitively, we view the learning algorithm as taking arbitrary set ambiguities and worldviews as input and producing a distribution over x; $P^{[\psi;\lambda]}(x \mid l)$ is the distribution over x that arises when the learning algorithm is fed the ambiguities $\{A(\psi; l, x^1, x^2) : x^1, x^2 \in \xi\}$ and worldview n specified by l.

Now consider the following elementary result.

Lemma 1. *Consider any two probability density functions over the reals, P_1 and P_2, where $P_1(u)/P_1(u') \geq P_2(u)/P_2(u') \;\forall\; u, u' \in \mathfrak{R}$ where $u > u'$. Say we also have any $\phi : \mathfrak{R} \to \mathfrak{R}$ with nowhere negative derivative. Then $\mathrm{CDF}_{P_1}(\phi) \leq \mathrm{CDF}_{P_2}(\phi)$.*

Combining this lemma with the first premise and using our new notation, we arrive at the following version of the first premise, derived in the appendix.

Theorem 4. *Given coordinate values l^a and $l^b \in \lambda \subseteq \nu$, $\exists\, H$ such that*

$$A(U, \psi^a; l^a, x^1, x^2) < A(U, \psi^b; l^b, x^1, x^2) \quad \forall\, x^1, x^2$$

$$\Rightarrow$$

$$\mathrm{CDF}^{[\psi^a;\lambda]}(U \mid l^a) \leq \mathrm{CDF}^{[\psi^b;\lambda]}(U \mid l^b),$$

where, as usual, ψ^a, ψ^b, and (the r-independent) U are arbitrary.

This theorem is illustrated geometrically in Figure 1.

Because it holds for any underlying distribution over ζ, Theorem 3 holds for CDFs and expectation values based on any $P^{[\psi;\lambda]}$, not just $P^{[\gamma_\rho;\nu]}$. Because for any ψ, $P^{[\psi;\lambda]}(x \mid l, W) = P^{[\psi;\lambda]}(x \mid l)$, the discussion following Theorem 3 holds for $P^{[\psi;\lambda]}$ conditioned on l just as well as for P conditioned on n. So Theorem 4 has the following corollary.

Corollary 1. *Given any coordinates κ and $\lambda \subseteq \nu$, fixed $k \in \kappa$, and $V : (x, k) \to \mathfrak{R}$, $\exists\, H$ such that*

$$A(V(\cdot, k), \psi^a; l^a, x^1, x^2) < A(V(\cdot, k), \psi^b; l^b, x^1, x^2) \quad \forall\, x^1, x^2$$

$$\Rightarrow$$

$$E^{[\psi^a;\lambda]}(N_{\kappa,V} \mid l^a, k) \geq E^{[\psi^b;\lambda]}(N_{\kappa,V} \mid l^b, k).$$

Summarizing, for a particular value of k, V determines which of the two possible moves x^1 and x^2 by agent ρ are better; $\underline{g}_{\rho,s}$ is the (s-parameterized) private utility that agent ρ is trying to maximize, based exclusively on the value of the worldview, n (a worldview that may provide the agent with the functional form of that private utility); ψ^a and ψ^b are two real-valued functions of x, r, and s that are used to evaluate ambiguities, and l^a and l^b are values of a conditioning variable for evaluating ambiguities, a variable that specifies n at a minimum. In addition, H is a parameterized

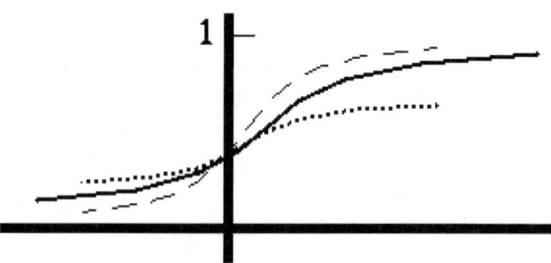

Figure 1. The solid line depicts an ambiguity $A(y; V; l, x^1, x^2)$. The dotted line depicts $A(y; KV; l, x^1, x^2) = A(y/K; V; l, x^1, x^2)$ for $K > 1$; the dashed line is $A(KV; l, x^1, x^2)$ for $0 < K < 1$. Neither of those scaled-utility ambiguities lies entirely below the original one. Accordingly, neither of those scaled utilities is recommended by the first premise.

distribution over x that is defined for any parameter value that consists of $O(\xi)$ CDFs and a worldview, a distribution that equals $P(x \mid n)$ when its parameter value is the set $\{A(\gamma_\rho; n)\}$ together with n, and more generally for any $\lambda \subseteq \nu$ is expressed as $P^{[\psi;\lambda]}(x \mid l)$ whenever the CDFs are the ambiguities $\{A(\psi; l, x^1, x^2) : x^1, x^2 \in \xi)\}$. From now on, unless explicitly stated otherwise, we will assume that we are restricting attention to an H for which Corollary 1 holds.

3.5 The Second Premise

Having rewritten the first premise, we can address the potential problem arising when the worldview does not specify the private utility. First consider any changes to s that modify the associated set of n for which $P(n \mid s)$ is substantial. Typically, any such change in the likely n fixes fairly precisely what the inducing changes in s are, as far as evaluation of ambiguities is concerned. Accordingly, when exploiting the first premise we usually restrict attention to scenarios in which $\forall\, r \in \operatorname{supp} P(r \mid s)$ we can approximate

$$\int dn\, P(n \mid s) P^{[\nu]}(x \mid n) = \int dn\, P(n \mid s) P^{[\nu,\sigma]}(x \mid n, s).$$

We refer to this approximation as the **second premise**. Note that it holds exactly if n contains a specification of $g_{\rho,s}$, and $P(x \mid n)$ only depends on the associated ambiguities, $\{A(\gamma_\rho; n, x^i, x^j)\} = \{A(g_{\rho,s}; n, x^i, x^j)\}$. If we can treat the system as if this were the case, on average, then the second premise holds.[28] A semiformal example of a more general situation where the second premise holds is presented in Appendix F.[29]

   The following corollary of the second premise is often useful.

---

[28] Conversely, if σ is "perniciously chosen" to always force n to equal n' for any s, where n' gives no information about the likely values that s is inducing of $g_{\rho,s}$ at the various r, then $\int dn\, P(n \mid s) P^{[\nu]}(x \mid n) = P(x \mid n')$ and does not reflect the ambiguities determining $\int dn\, P(n \mid s) P^{[\nu,\sigma]}(x \mid n, s) = P^{[\nu,\sigma]}(x \mid n', s)$. In such a situation the second premise will not hold. This is similar to the situation with the first premise; in both, an adversarially poor match between the learning algorithm and the learning problem at hand confounds our premise.

[29] If it weren't for the second premise, we would have to work with $P(r \mid n)$ rather than $P(r \mid n, s)$ in evaluating ambiguities. This would then require specifying a prior $P(\bar{s})$, reflecting "prior beliefs" of what the private utility is likely to be, among other aspects of s. Specifying a prior over such a space and then integrating against it can be a fraught exercise. In essence, the second premise allows us to circumvent this when averaging over n, by setting that prior to a delta function about the actual s. Nonetheless, it is important to note that we do not need a hypothesis as powerful as the second premise to do this; the second premise is only used once, in the proof of Corollary 3, and a significantly weaker version of it would suffice there. We present the "powerful" version instead for pedagogical clarity.

Corollary 2. *Where V is any utility function, $h \in \eta$ any coordinate, and $W \in \Omega$ any non-ξ coordinate,*

$$E(V \mid h, s) = \int dndW \; P(W \mid s)P(n \mid W, s) \; E^{[g_{\rho,s};v,\sigma]}(V \mid n, s, h, W).$$

Often this result can be used in conjunction with Corollary 1 to analyze the implications of various choices of s. As an example, in many situations (e.g., in very large systems) changes to ρ's private utility will have relatively little effect on the rest of the system, i.e., it will have minimal effect on the distribution over r values. Accordingly consider s^a and s^b that vary only in that choice of ρ's private utility,[30] in a situation where this implies that $P(r \mid s^a) = P(r \mid s^b) \equiv P(r \mid s^{ab})$. Let V be a utility function, so that $N_{\rho,V}$ is also. Then for both $s = s^a$ and $s = s^b$, by using Corollary 2 with $\Omega = \rho$ and $\eta = \emptyset$, we establish that

$$E(N_{\rho,V} \mid s) = \int drdn P(r \mid s^{ab})P(n \mid r, s) \; E^{[g_s;v,\sigma]}(N_{\rho,V} \mid n, r, s).$$

So by Corollary 1, taking $\lambda = v \cap \sigma$, $\kappa = \rho$, and $\psi^a = \psi^b = \underline{\gamma}_\rho$, if separately for each r for which $P(r \mid s^{ab})$ is substantial,

$$A(V(\cdot, r), \underline{\gamma}_\rho; n^a, s^a, x^1, x^2) < A(V(\cdot, r), \underline{\gamma}_\rho; n^b, s^b, x^1, x^2)$$

(for all (x^1, x^2) pairs and for all (n^a, n^b) such that both $P(n^a \mid r, s^a)$ and $P(n^b \mid r, s^b)$ are substantial) we can conclude that $E(N_{\rho,V} \mid s^a) > E(N_{\rho,V} \mid s^b)$. This approach can be used even if the coordinate utility V is factored with respect to G but the private utility is not. Note also that if we take $V = \underline{g}_{\rho,s^b}$ and have $\underline{g}_{\rho,s^a}$ be factored with respect to $\underline{g}_{\rho,s^b}$, then our reasoning implies that $E(N_{\rho,\underline{g}_{\rho,s^a}} \mid s^a) > E(N_{\rho,\underline{g}_{\rho,s^b}} \mid s^b)$.

The first two premises can also be used to analyze the effect on agent ρ of changes to the *other* agents. They can also be used to analyze changes that amount to a complete redefinition of the agent (changes we can implement by inserting commands in the value of the agent's worldview that change how it behaves), or more generally, a coordinate transformation [22]. Indeed, by those premises, H, $\underline{\gamma}_\rho$, and $P(r \mid n, s)$ parameterize $P(x \mid n)$. In particular, say $\sigma = \sigma_{\gamma_\rho} \subseteq v$, H has no direct dependence on n not arising in the ambiguities, and we take $P(r \mid s)$ to be uniform. Then for fixed H, all aspects of the learning algorithm are set by $\underline{\gamma}_\rho$, $P(n \mid r, s)$, and the associated ambiguities.

More generally, once we specify $P(r \mid s)$ in addition to these quantities, we have made all the choices available to us as designers that affect term 3 of the central equation. In principle, this allows us to solve for the optimal one of those four quantities given the others. For example, for fixed $\underline{\gamma}_\rho$, H, and $P(r \mid s)$, we could solve for which $P(n \mid r, s)$ out of a class of candidates such likelihoods optimizes expected intelligence.[31]

---

[30] Formally, our presumption is that $\forall z^a \in s^a$, $z^b \in s^b$, $\sigma_{\hat{\underline{g}}}(z^a) = \sigma_{\hat{\underline{g}}}(z^b)$.

[31] More formally, where $\sigma \subseteq \sigma_v$ sets the likelihood $P(n \mid r, s_r ho, s_v)$, we could solve for the s_v optimizing expected intelligence.

The rest of this chapter presents a few preliminary examples of such an approach, concentrating on changes to s that only alter one or more agents' private utilities, where only very broad assumptions about $P(n \mid r, s)$ are used. These are the scenarios in which the premises have been most thoroughly investigated and therefore in which confidence that H, etc., do indeed capture the totality of a learning algorithm is highest.

3.6 The Third Premise

As just illustrated, for some differences in s (namely those that only modify private utilities), we can simplify the analysis to involve only a single s-induced distribution over rs (namely $P(r \mid s^{ab})$). The analysis still involved different distributions over ns, however, one each of the two ss (in the guise of the two distributions $P(n \mid r, s)$). Moreover, to calculate expected intelligence for a given s we must average over n, and usually changes to s change $P(n \mid r, s)$ in a way difficult to predict.[32] Therefore, to exploit the first two premises to determine which of the two ss gave better expected intelligence, we had to have a desired difference in ambiguities hold for *all* pairs of ns generated from the two ss, an extremely restrictive condition.

One way around this would be to extend the analysis in a way that only involves a single s-induced distribution over ns. To see how we might do this, fix r, x^1, and x^2, and consider a pair s^a and s^b that differ only in the associated private utility for agent ρ, where those two utilities are mutually factored. Train on g_{s^b}, thereby generating an n according to $P(n \mid r, s^b)$ and thence a distribution over r', $P(r' \mid n)$, which in turn gives an ambiguity between values of the private utility at x^1 and x^2 and therefore an expected intelligence. Our choice of private utility affects this process in three ways:

1. by affecting the likely n, and therefore $P(r' \mid n)$;
2. by affecting how well distinguished utility values at x^1 and x^2 are for any associated pair of r' values generated from $P(r' \mid n)$. If $P(r' \mid n)$ is broad or the private utility is poor at distinguishing x^1 and x^2, then ambiguity will be poor; and
3. by providing one of the arguments to H, which (given the utility and the ambiguities of 2) fixes the distribution over intelligences.

In the guise of Corollary 1 (with $\lambda = \nu$, $\kappa = \Omega = \rho$, $\psi^a = g_{s^a} = V^a$, and $\psi^b = g_{s^b} = V^b$), the first premise concerns the second effect. If we combine this with the second premise (in the guise of Corollary 2, with $\Omega = \rho$), we see that the first two premises concern the last two effects of the choice of private utility on expected intelligence. However, they say nothing about the first effect of the private utility choice.

---

[32] For example, in a multistage game (see Appendix D), in general changing $g_{\rho,s}$ causes our agent to take different actions at each stage of the game, which usually then causes the behavior of the other agents at later stages to change, which in turn changes ρ's training data, contained in the value of n at those later stages.

It is typically the case that the first effect will tend to work in a correlated manner with the last two effects. That is, if for some given n generated from $\underline{g}_{\rho,s^b}$ the utility $\underline{g}_{\rho,s^a}$ results in higher intelligences (e.g., because it is better able to distinguish utility values than is $\underline{g}_{\rho,s^b}$), it is typically also the case that if one had used $\underline{g}_{\rho,s^a}$ to generate ns in the first place, it would have resulted in more informative n, and therefore $P(r' \mid n)$ would have been crisper, leading to a better ambiguity and thence expected intelligence.

We formalize this as the **third premise**.[33]

Say that s^a and s^b differ only in their associated private utilities, and that those utilities are mutually factored. Then

$$\int dn\, P(n \mid s^b) E^{[\underline{g}_{s^a};v,\sigma]}(N_\rho \mid n, s^b) \geq \int dn\, P(n \mid s^b) E^{[\underline{g}_{s^b};v,\sigma]}(N_\rho \mid n, s^b),$$

$$\Rightarrow$$

$$\int dn\, P(n \mid s^a) E^{[\underline{g}_{s^a};v,\sigma]}(N_\rho \mid n, s^a) \geq \int dn\, P(n \mid s^b) E^{[\underline{g}_{s^b};v,\sigma]}(N_\rho \mid n, s^b).$$

Together with Corollary 2 this results in the following.

Corollary 3. *Say s^a and s^b differ only in the associated private utility for agent ρ and that those utilities are mutually factored. Then*

$$\int dn dr\, P(r \mid s^b) P(n \mid r, s^b) E^{[\underline{g}_{s^a};v,\sigma]}(N_\rho \mid n, r, s^b)$$

$$\geq \int dn dr\, P(r \mid s^b) P(n \mid r, s^b) E^{[\underline{g}_{s^b};v,\sigma]}(N_\rho \mid n, r, s^b)$$

$$\Rightarrow$$

$$E(N_{\rho,\underline{g}_{s^a}} \mid s^a) \geq E(N_{\rho,\underline{g}_{s^b}} \mid s^b).$$

By Corollary 3, If, $\forall\, r$,

$$A(\underline{g}_{\rho,s^b}(\xi, r), \underline{g}_{\rho,s^b}; n, x^1, x^2, s^b) > A(\underline{g}_{\rho,s^b}(\xi, r), \underline{g}_{\rho,s^a}; n, x^1, x^2, s^b)$$

---

[33] An alternative to the version of the third premise presented here that would serve our purposes just as well would have all distributions conditioned on some $b \in \beta \subseteq \sigma$ (e.g., (r, s)), rather than just on s. One could also modify the hypothesis condition of the third premise by replacing s^b throughout with some alternative s^*, and our results would still hold under the substitution throughout of $s^b \to s^*$. Similarly one could change the integration variable $n \in v$ to some other coordinate $l \in \lambda \subseteq v$. For all such changes the results presented here—in particular Corollary 3—would still hold; the important thing for those results is that each ambiguity arising in the integrand of the left-hand side of the hypothesis condition of the third premise is evaluated with the same distribution over r^1 and r^2 as the corresponding ambiguity on the right-hand side. For pedagogical clarity, though, no such modification is considered here.

(for all (x^1, x^2), and for all n such that $P(n \mid r, s^b)$ is substantial), then by Corollary 1 the condition in Corollary 3 is met (take $\lambda = \nu \cap \sigma$ and $\kappa = \rho$, as usual). So using Corollary 3, in such a situation we can conclude that $E(N_{\rho, \underline{g}_{s^a}} \mid s^a) \geq E(N_{\rho, \underline{g}_{s^b}} \mid s^b)$, i.e., that for fixed r, s^a has better term 3 of the central equation than does s^b. This is the process that will be the central concern of the rest of this chapter: inducing improved ambiguity and then plugging the first premise (in the guise of Corollary 1) into the second and third premises (combined in Corollary 3) to infer improved expected intelligence.

In particular, again consider the situation (discussed in the section on the first premise) where $P(r \mid s^a) = P(r \mid s^b) \equiv P(r \mid s^{ab})$, and assume this also equals $P(r \mid s^b)$. If separately for each r for which $P(r \mid s^{ab})$ is substantial, and for all associated n for which $P(n \mid r, s^{ab})$ is substantial,

$$A(\underline{g}_{\rho, s^b}(\cdot, r), \underline{g}_{\rho, s^b}; n, x^1, x^2, s^b) > A(\underline{g}_{\rho, s^b}(\cdot, r), \underline{g}_{\rho, s^a}; n, x^1, x^2, s^b),$$

then we can conclude that

$$E(N_{\rho, \underline{g}_{s^a}} \mid s^a) \geq E(N_{\rho, \underline{g}_{s^b}} \mid s^b).$$

Of course, in practice this condition won't hold for all such r and n. At the same time, Corollary 3 makes it clear that it doesn't need to; we just need the associated integrals over r and n to favor s^a over s^b.

3.7 Example: The Collapsed Utility

As an example of how to use Corollary 3, consider the use of a Boltzmann learning algorithm for our agent [26], where s^b is our original s value. With such an algorithm, constructing a new private utility by scaling the original one (i.e., changing s) is equivalent to modifying the learning algorithm's temperature parameter. Now say that for any pair of moves, the ambiguity for s^b and any probable associated worldview n^b is zero for all negative y values. Then changing s by lowering the temperature will monotonically lower $A(\underline{g}_{\rho, s^b}(\xi, r), \underline{g}_{\rho, s}; n^b, x^1, x^2)$. Accordingly, doing this cannot lower expected intelligence, only increase it. (Note that the new private utility is factored with respect to the original one, so this effect of changing s also holds for expected intelligence with respect to the original private utility.)

Consider the following theorem.

Theorem 5. *Fix* $n, s^a, s^b, r \in \mathrm{supp}\, P(\cdot \mid s^b)$, *and a function* $U : x \in \xi \to \mathfrak{R}$. *Stipulate that*

(i) $\forall\, x, x' \in \xi$, $\mathrm{sgn}[U(x, r) - U(x', r)] = \mathrm{sgn}[g_{s^b}(x, r) - g_{s^b}(x', r)]$;

(ii) $\forall\, r' \in \mathrm{supp}\, P(\cdot \mid n)$, *there exists two real numbers* $A_{r'}$ *and* $B_{r'} \leq A_{r'}$ *such that* $g_{s^b}(x, r')$ *takes on both values—but no others—as one varies the* $x \in \xi$;

(iii) *for all such* r' $\underline{g}_{s^a}(x, r') = 0$ *if* $A_{r'} = B_{r'}$, *and equals* $g_{s^b}(x, r') - B_{r'}/A_{r'} - B_{r'}$ *otherwise, and* $\forall\, r' \notin \mathrm{supp}\, P(\cdot \mid n)$, g_{s^a} *is factored with respect to* g_{s^b}; *and*

(iv) *for each pair of moves, for at least one move of that pair, x^*, $\exists\, y^*$ such that*
$$P(g_{s^a}(x^*, \rho) = y \mid n) = \delta(y - y^*).$$

Then $\forall\, x^1, x^2$, $A(U, g_{s^a}; n, x^1, x^2)$ has purely nonnegative support.

(An analogous version of this result holds if instead we take $g_{s^a}(x, r') = 1$ whenever $A_{r'} = B_{r'}$.)

Condition (i) of Theorem 5 can be viewed as a weakened form of requiring that U and g_{s^b} be factored. In particular, it trivially holds for $U = g_{s^b}$, or (due to the fact that g_{s^a} is a difference utility with lead utility g_{s^b}) $U = g_{s^a}$. Conditions (ii) and (iii) mean that for each r', the values of $g_{s^a}(x, r')$ as one varies x are those of g_{s^b} "collapsed" to one of the two values 0 or 1. However, for fixed x, which of that pair of values equals $g_{s^a}(x, r')$ can differ from one r' to the next.

There are many situations in which condition (ii) of Theorem 5 holds with $g_{s^b} = G$. One example is a spin glass with G given by the Hamiltonian. Another is the simple spin system where $G(z) = \sin(\pi n(z)/2)$, $n(z)$ being defined as the total number of spins in the up configuration.

Condition (iv) means that given worldview n, context r, and a pair of moves, there is no room for uncertainty in the value of the private utility at x^*—it must equal (the typically unknown value) y^* there. (Note that which element of the pair of moves is this special x can vary with n and r.) This will often be the case if, for example, n was generated from g_{s^a}, and the agent's (n-based) "prediction" for the utility value of the particular move it actually ends up making is both unambiguous and correct. In particular, such prediction accuracy often can be induced by having all the *other* agents readily "freeze" into a static background. In turn, as an example, those other agents are likely to freeze if they all use Boltzmann learning algorithms with their temperatures set low enough, and with the windows they use to estimate the utilities of their possible moves short enough.

We call the difference utility g_{s^a} in Theorem 5 the **collapsed utility** (CU) and say that it is formed by **collapsing** g_{s^b}, because for fixed r' it is formed by collapsing all the values $g_{s^b}(x, r')$ takes on as one varies x to either 0 or 1.

When the conditions in Theorem 5 hold, the ambiguity will shrink monotonically as the CU is scaled upward. As an example, consider a Boltzmann learning algorithm in the scenario discussed at the end of the previous section, where the conditions in Theorem 5 are met for the private utility set to the CU. As the temperature parameter of that algorithm shrinks, the associated expected intelligence cannot decrease and should in particular eventually exceed that of g_{s^b}.[34] Therefore, for the choice of $g_{s^b} = G$, the value of G induced by using CU as the private utility with a low

---

[34] Formally, the fact that ambiguity for g_{s^a} has purely nonnegative support does not mean that the ambiguity for g_{s^b} has a support that extends to negative values. In practice, though, that is the case for the vast majority of $n \in \operatorname{supp} P(\cdot \mid s^b)$. Even so, we cannot conclude that the ambiguity function for g_{s^a}, extending over all y, is less than that for g_{s^b}. We can conclude that the reverse does not hold, however. Again, in practice, the discrepancy in supports usually does mean that the ambiguity function for g_{s^a} is less than that for g_{s^b}, so we can apply the first two corollaries' premises.

enough temperature should be larger than that induced using the team game at any temperature.

4 The Aristocrat and Wonderful Life Utilities

In this section we illustrate a general set of techniques for changing the private utility to monotonically lower unordered ambiguity conditioned on a particular n. As discussed earlier, when plugged into Corollary 3 such improved ambiguities can cause the new private utility to have better expected intelligence than the original one.

The analysis will be closely analogous to that behind the use of Fisher's linear discriminant in statistics. We will start by restricting the analysis to distributions obeying a linearity condition. This is essentially an extended form of assuming Gaussian distributions—such an assumption being the starting point of the derivation of Fisher's linear discriminant. We will then exploit Corollary 3 to derive "learnability" as a measure of the quality of a private utility (as far as term 3 in the central equation is concerned). Formally, learnability is identical to the Rayleigh coefficient expressed in a different setting. Completing the analogy, whereas with the Fisher discriminant one strives for coordinate transformations of a data set giving a large value of the associated Rayleigh coefficient, at the end of this section we demonstrate transformations to the private utility giving a large value of the associated learnability.

4.1 Learnability

We begin by considering the first-order expansion of the distribution of one utility in terms of the distribution of another utility.

Theorem 6. *Fix $l, l' \in \lambda \subseteq v, x^1, x^2$, an x-ordering U, and two utilities V_a and V_b, where $\exists K \in \mathfrak{R}^+$ and $h : \xi \to \mathfrak{R}$ such that*

$$P_{V_a}(y^1, y^2; l', x^1, x^2) = P_{K V_b + h}(y^1, y^2; l, x^1, x^2).$$

Then $\forall y$,

$$A[y; U, V_a; l', x^1, x^2] = A\left[\frac{y}{K} + t_U(x^1, x^2)\left(\frac{h(x^2) - h(x^1)}{K}\right); U, V_b; l, x^1, x^2\right].$$

So if in addition to the condition in Theorem 6, $\forall y$,

$$A\left[\frac{y}{K} + t_U(x^1, x^2)\left(\frac{h(x^2) - h(x^1)}{K}\right); U, V_b; l, x^1, x^2\right] < A[y; U, V_b; l, x^1, x^2],$$

then it follows that $A[U, V_a; l', x^1, x^2] < A[U, V_b; l, x^1, x^2]$.

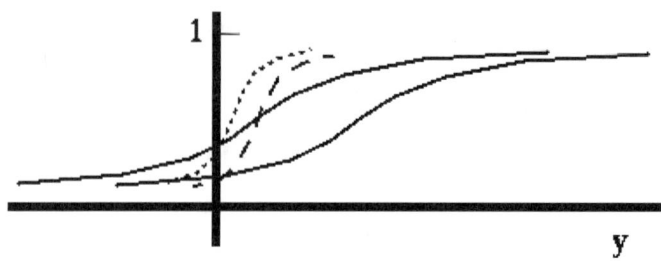

Figure 2. The leftmost solid line shows an ambiguity $A(y; V; l, x^1, x^2)$. The dotted line shows $A(y; V'; l, x^1, x^2)$ for $V' = aV$, $0 < a < 1$. $K_{V',V} = a$, and learnability of V' is the same as V's. The dashed line shows the dotted line right-shifted by $t_U(x^1, x^2)[h(x^1) - h(x^2)] > 0$, i.e., the ambiguity $A(y; U; l, x^1, x^2)$ for $U \equiv aV + h$. (Because we have not changed s, Theorem 6 must apply.) $\Lambda_f(U; l, x^1, x^2) > \Lambda_f(V'; l, x^1, x^2)$. Finally, the right most solid line depicts the dotted line expanded back to the scale of the leftmost solid line, i.e., the ambiguity of $U' \equiv \beta U$ where $\beta \equiv 1/K_{V',V}$, so that $K_{U',V} = 1$. As with the previous one, this rescaling from W to T does not affect the learnability.

We will sometimes find it convenient to put subscripts on K or h explicitly giving the values of l', V_a, l, V_b, x^1, or x^2, in that order. For example, in Figure 2 we refer to $K_{V,U}$, to mean K when $V_a = V$ and $V_b = U$.[35]

It is often the case that "to first order," changing from $V = V_b$ to $V = V_a$ doesn't change the shapes of any of the associated distribution functions $P(V(x) = v \mid l)$ (one such distribution for each x). Primarily, all the change does to those distributions is separately shift them, or contract them all by the same factor.[36,37] The condition in Theorem 6 is (a slightly weaker version of) the requirement that this property holds exactly, even if we also switch from l to l' at the same time (and therefore change the underlying probability distribution over z). The general effects of expansion or contraction of the utility on the associated ambiguity are illustrated in Figure 2.

Theorem 6 tells us in particular that when its condition is met along with the one mentioned following its presentation, then for $K = 1$ and $t_U(x^1, x^2)[h(x^2) - h(x^1)]$ negative, changing from (V_b, l) to (V_a, l') improves ambiguity. Moreover, the degree of that drop grows with increasing magnitude of $\{h(x^2) - h(x^1)\}/K$.[38] In the usual

---

[35] Note the following algebraic rules concerning such sets of distributions that are linearly related:

$$K_{l_1, V_1, l_3, V_3} = K_{l_1, V_1, l_2, V_2} K_{l_2, V_2, l_3, V_3};$$
$$K_{l_1, V_1, l_2, V_2} = 1/K_{l_2, V_2, l_1, V_1};$$
$$h_{l_1, V_1, l_3, V_3} = K_{l_1, V_1, l_2, V_2} h_{l_2, V_2, l_3, V_3} - h_{l_1, V_1, l_2, V_2};$$
$$h_{l_1, V_1, l_2, V_2} = -h_{l_2, V_2, l_1, V_1}/K_{l_2, V_2, l_1, V_1}.$$

[36] This is particularly common in situations where there are extremely many possible V values, densely packed together.

[37] Note that a linear relationship between utilities is a sufficient but not necessary condition for a linear relationship between the distributions of their values.

[38] A similar result holds if we instead consider a fixed pair (x^1, x^2) and associated K_{x^1, x^2}, so that the expansion factor can vary with moves, like the offset factor h.

way, for $l = l'$, $\lambda = \nu \cap \sigma$, $V_a = \underline{g}_{s'}$, and $V_b = \underline{g}_s$, where s and s' only differ in their private utilities, we can exploit this phenomenon in concert with Corollary 1 and then Corollary 3 to improve term 3. To that end we start with the following.

Theorem 7. *Say that the condition in Theorem 6 holds for the quadruple (l', V_a, l, V_b) with the same $K, h \; \forall \; x^1, x^2$. Then*

(i) *where f is any distribution over x,*

$$K = \sqrt{\frac{\int dx \; f(x) \, \mathrm{Var}(V_a; l', x)}{\int dx \; f(x) \, \mathrm{Var}(V_b; l, x)}}.$$

Now define

$$\Lambda_f(U; l'', x^1, x^2) \equiv \frac{E(U; l'', x^1) - E(U; l'', x^2)}{\sqrt{E_{f(x)}(\mathrm{Var}(U; l'', \xi))}},$$

where $E_{f(x)}(\mathrm{Var}(U; l'', \xi)) = \int dx \; f(x) \, \mathrm{Var}(U(x, \rho) \mid l'')$. Then

(ii)

$$\frac{h(x^2) - h(x^1)}{K} \propto \Lambda_f(V_b; l, x^1, x^2) - \Lambda_f(V_a; l', x^1, x^2),$$

where the V_a-independent proportionality constant is $\sqrt{\int dx \; f(x) \, \mathrm{Var}(V_b; l, x)}$.

We call $h(x^2) - h(x^1)/K$ the **(ambiguity) shift** and $\Lambda_f(U; l, x^1, x^2)$ the **learnability** of U for x^1, x^2, and l.[39] As a particular example, for $f(x) = (1/2)[\delta(x - x^1) + \delta(x - x^2)]$,

$$[\Lambda_f(U; l'', x^1, x^2)]^2 = 2\frac{[E(U; l'', x^1) - E(U; l'', x^2)]^2}{\mathrm{Var}(U; l'', x^1) + \mathrm{Var}(U; l'', x^2)}. \tag{2}$$

Note that $|\Lambda_f(U; l'', x^1, x^2)|$ is invariant under affine transformations of U. Typically we are interested in the case where $\mathrm{sgn}[E(V_b^1 - V_b^2; l, x^1, x^2)] = \mathrm{sgn}[E(V_a^1 - V_a^2; l, x^1, x^2)] = t_{Vb}(x^1, x^2)$, so that we can use learnability to evaluate the offset term in Theorem 6, $t_U(x^1, x^2)[h(x^2) - h(x^1)/K]$.

Intuitively, the learnability of U reflects its signal-to-noise ratio, as far as agent ρ is concerned, in that agent's process of "choosing its move." This is because the numerator term in the definition of learnability reflects how much (the expectation of) that utility varies as one changes the agent's move x with the context held fixed. In contrast, the denominator term reflects the (average over x of) how much U varies due to uncertainty in the context while keeping the move x fixed.[40]

---

[39] This latter is a slight modification from the definition used in our previous work.

[40] Low learnability is not only a problem for agents with poor learning algorithms. Even for a Bayes-optimal learning algorithm, if the "signal to noise" ratio of the private utility is poor, then the agent's intelligence for the actual r at hand can readily be far less than 1. (Bayes-optimality only means that x is set to maximize $E(\underline{g}_s \mid n, x)$, not to maximize $\underline{g}_s(x, r)$.)

The following results provide a geometric perspective on the expressions in Theorem 7:

Theorem 8. *Say that the condition in Theorem 6 holds for the quadruple* (l', V_a, l, V_b).

(i) *If both* V_a *and* V_b *are difference utilities with the same lead utility and* $\beta = 1$, *while both* $P(r'; l) = P(r'; l')$ *and* $\Lambda_f(V_b; l, x^1, x^2) < \Lambda_f(V_a; l', x^1, x^2)$, *then* $K < 1$.

(ii) *Let* $\{V_a, l'\}$ *be an equivalence class of* (V, l) *pairs all related to* (V_b, l) *as in Theorem 6. Then the learnability of those pairs multiplied by* $t_U(x^1, x^2)$ *is a shrinking function of the value of the associated ambiguities at the origin. In addition, across all pairs in that class that share some particular learnability value,* K *is inversely proportional to the slope of the ambiguity of that pair at the origin.*

(iii) *Say condition (ii) also holds for the quadruple* $(l^*, V_{a^*} \equiv \beta V_a, l, V_b)$ *(though potentially for a different* K *or* h), *where* $P(r'; l^*) = P(r'; l')$. *Then* $\Lambda_f(V_{a^*}; l^*, x^1, x^2)$ *and* $\Lambda_f(V_a; l', x^1, x^2)$ *are identical* $\forall\, x^1, x^2$, *as are the associated shifts, while* $K_{l^*, V_{a^*}, l, V_b} = \beta K_{l', V_a, l, V_b}$.[41]

(iv) *If* $K < 1$ *and* $\Lambda_f(V_a; l', x^1, x^2) > \Lambda_f(V_b; l, x^1, x^2)$ $(K > 1$ *and* $\Lambda_f(V_a; l', x^1, x^2) < \Lambda_f(V_b; l, x^1, x^2)$, *respectively), then the maximal slope of* $A(V_a; l', x^1, x)$ *is greater than (less than, resp.) the maximal slope of* $A(V_b; l, x^1, x^2)$.

To understand Theorem 7 in terms of ambiguities, for pedagogical simplicity consider making changes to a utility V without any corresponding changes to the value of λ (and therefore none to the underlying probability distribution over z). First note that such a change applied to the scale of V doesn't change how weighted the associated ambiguity is to positive y values. It doesn't change "how far" $V(x^1) - V(x^2)$ is from zero, on average. This "weight to positive y values" is reflected in the value of $|\Lambda_f|$ (which is invariant with respect to such rescalings), and therefore (by Theorem 7(ii)) is also reflected in the value of $t_U(x^1, x^2)[h(x^2) - h(x^1)/K]$. However, such a rescaling can still be useful in how it "stretches" the CDF. To see how, note by Theorem 8(iii) that if V has better learnability than some other utility U, such stretching of V may provide a new utility V' such that $K_{V', U} = 1$, which means that V' has better ambiguity than U (in light of Theorem 8(iii)).[42] In other words, to change the learnability, we must induce a rightward offset in the (potentially scaled) ambiguity of V. Having done that, a subsequent rescaling can give us an aggregate K equal to 1 (without changing learnability), and thereby provide a final utility whose ambiguity lies everywhere below that of U. The value of that offset is given by the (β-independent) ambiguity shift (see Figure 2).

---

[41] Trivially, the condition in Theorem 6 holds for (l', V_{a^*}, l, V_b) if it does for (l', V_a, l, V_b). In addition, $\Lambda_f(V_{a^*}; l', x^1, x^2) = \Lambda_f(V_a; l', x^1, x^2)$ and $K_{l', V_{a^*}, l, V_b} = \beta K_{l', V_a, l, V_b}$.

[42] Note that such rescaling amounts to changing the temperature parameter in a Boltzmann learning algorithm.

4.2 Learnability and Term 3

Plug Theorem 7 into Theorem 6, with U in Theorem 6 set to the x-ordering given by $V_b(\cdot, r)$. This shows that after appropriate rescaling of V_a, the triple (V_a, l') has better ambiguity than does (V_b, l) if it has better learnability.[43] If we plug that fact into Corollary 1, we establish the following.

Corollary 4. *Fix r, l, l', V_a, and V_b, where $\lambda \subseteq \nu$, as usual. Say $\exists\, K \in \Re^+$, $h : \xi \to \Re$, such that $\forall\, x^1, x^2$*

(i) $P_{V_a}(y^1, y^2; l', x^1, x^2) = P_{KV_b+h}(y^1, y^2; l, x^1, x^2)$; and
(ii) $t_{V_b(\cdot, r)}(x^1, x^2) \Lambda_f(V_a; l', x^1, x^2) > t_{V_b(\cdot, r)}(x^1, x^2) \Lambda_f(V_b; l, x^1, x^2)$.

Then by appropriately rescaling V_a we can assure that

$$E^{[V_a;\lambda]}(N_{\rho, V_b} \mid r, l') \geq E^{[V_b;\lambda]}(N_{\rho, V_b} \mid r, l).$$

Consider changing the private utility from V_b to a V_a, which is factored with respect to V_b. Then Corollary 4 means that if this increases the learnability (in the x-ordering preferred by $V_b(\cdot, r)$) of one's private utility, then typically it results in higher expected intelligence, for the optimal scaling of that private utility. More precisely, express Corollary 4 for $\lambda = \nu \cap \sigma$ and $l = l' \equiv (n, s)$ and then plug it into Corollary 3 with $s^b = s$, $g_{s^a} = V_a$ and $g_{s^b} = V_b$, where s^a and s^b differ only in the associated private utility for our agent, and V_a and V_b are mutually factored. Then we see that if learnability is higher with s^a than with s^b (in the x-ordering preferred by $V_b(\cdot, r)$) for enough of the n for which $P(n \mid r, s^b)$ is nonnegligible, then $s = s^a$ gives a higher expected intelligence conditioned on r and s than does $s = s^b$ (each intelligence evaluated for the associated optimal scale of the private utility).

As an added bonus, often the higher the learnability of a private utility, the more "slack" there is in setting the parameters of the associated learning algorithm while still having an ambiguity that's below that of some benchmark, a low-learnability private utility. In other words, the higher the learnability, the less careful one must be in setting such parameters to achieve expected intelligence above some threshold. In particular, the greater the ambiguity shift in Corollary 4, the broader the range of scales β for which βV_a has greater expected intelligence than does V_b. So, by using private utilities with increased learnability it often becomes less crucial that one exactly optimizes the learning algorithm's internal parameter setting the scale at which the algorithm examines utility values. This phenomenon can be amplified via "construction interference," for example, as in the following result.

Corollary 5. *Fix r and two sets of utility-(λ-value) pairs, $\{V_t, l_t\}$ and $\{V^*, l_{t^*}\}$, indexed by t and t^*, respectively. Assume all quintuples $(r, l_{t^*}, V^*, l_t, V_t)$ obey Corollary 4(i), (ii) with $V_a = V^*$, $V_b = V_t$, etc. For pedagogical simplicity, also take*

---

[43] Note that this rescaling is done before we invoke the third premise. In this way we will be able to exploit that premise to do rescaling without invoking the assumption in Theorem 8(iii).

$$\text{sgn}[V_b(x^1, r) - V_b(x^2, r)] = \text{sgn}[V_a(x^1, r) - V_a(x^2, r)] \equiv m,$$

$$\text{sgn}[E(V_b^1 - V_b^2; l, x^1, x^2)] = \text{sgn}[E(V_a^1 - V_a^2; l', x^1, x^2)] \equiv m'$$

and $m = m'$.

(i) *Define*

$$\Delta_{t,t^*x^1,x^2} \equiv \{\Lambda_f(V^*; l_{t^*}, x^1, x^2) - \Lambda_f(V_t; l_t, x^1, x^2)\}$$

$$\times \sqrt{\int dx f(x) Var(V_t; l_t, x)},$$

$$B_{t,x^1,x^2} \equiv \min(y : A(y; V_t(\cdot, r), V_t; l_t, x^1, x^2) = 1),$$

$$D_{t,x^1,x^2} \equiv \max(y : A(y; V_t(\cdot, r), V_t; l_t, x^1, x^2) = 0),$$

where, as usual, f is a fixed but arbitrary distribution over x, and we assume $\Delta_{t,t^*,x^1,x^2} \geq 0 \, \forall \, t, t^*, x^1, x^2.$

(ii) *Define $K_{t,t^*} \equiv K_{l_{t^*},V^*,l_t,V_t}$, and then define the subintervals of $\mathfrak{R}$ (one for each (t, x^1, x^2) triple)*

$$L_{t,t^*,V^*,x^1,x^2} \equiv \begin{cases} \dfrac{1}{K_{t,t^*}}\left[\dfrac{B_{t,x^1,x^2}}{B_{t,x^1,x^2} + \Delta_{t,t^*,x^1,x^2}}, \dfrac{D_{t,x^1,x^2}}{D_{t,x^1,x^2} + \Delta_{t,t^*,x^1,x^2}}\right] \\ \qquad\qquad\qquad\qquad\qquad \text{if } D_{t,x^1,x^2} < -\Delta_{t,t^*,x^1,x^2}, \\[1em] \dfrac{1}{K_{t,t^*}}\left[\dfrac{B_{t,x^1,x^2}}{B_{t,x^1,x^2} + \Delta_{t,t^*,x^1,x^2}}, \infty\right) \\ \qquad\qquad\qquad\qquad\qquad \text{if } -\Delta_{t,t^*,x^1,x^2} \leq D_{t,x^1,x^2} < 0, \\[1em] \dfrac{1}{K_{t,t^*}}\left[\dfrac{D_{t,x^1,x^2}}{D_{t,x^1,x^2} + \Delta_{t,t^*,x^1,x^2}}, \infty\right) \qquad\qquad \text{otherwise,} \end{cases}$$

and

$$L_{t,t^*,V^*} \equiv \cap_{x^1,x^2} L_{t,t^*,V^*,x^1,x^2}.$$

(iii) *Define $L_{t^*,V^*} \equiv \cup_t L_{t,t^*,V^*}.$*

Then for every t^*, $\forall \, \beta \in L_{t^*,V^*}$,

$$E^{[\beta V^*;\lambda]}(N_{V^*} \mid r, l_{t^*}) \geq \min_t E^{[V_t;\lambda]}(N_{V_t} \mid r, l_t).$$

Note that $B_{t,x^1,x^2} \geq 0$ always, because $m = m'$ for (l_t, V_t). Accordingly, L_{t^*,V^*} is never empty, always containing $\cup_t(1/K_{t,t^*})$ at least.[44,45]

---

[44] If (unlike in Corollary 4) the value of K can change with the (x^1, x^2) values, then those indices must be added to K's subscripts. In this case the conclusion of Corollary 4 need not hold; L_{t^*,V^*} can be empty.

[45] A subtle point is that in situations where $D_{t,x^1,x^2} > 0$, we can increase the scale of V_t as many times as we want and assuredly improve its ambiguity each time. (This is not

To help put Corollary 5 in context, apply Corollary 4 to the scenario of Corollary 5. This establishes that for any t^*, $\exists\, \beta \in L_{t^*,V^*}$ such that $E^{[\beta V^*;\lambda]}(N_{\beta V^*} \mid r, l_{t^*}) \geq \max_t E^{[V_t;\lambda]}(N_{\beta V_t} \mid r, l_t)$. Note also the immediate implication of Corollary 5 that $\forall\, \beta \in \cap_{t^*} L_{t^*,V^*}$,

$$\min_{t^*} E^{[\beta V^*;\lambda]}(N_{V^*} \mid r, l_{t^*}) \geq \min_t E^{[V_t;\lambda]}(N_{V_t} \mid r, l_t).$$

As an example of Corollary 5, take $\lambda = \nu \cap \sigma$, have l_{t^*} equal some fixed l^* $\forall\, t^*$, $V^* \equiv \underline{g}_{s^*}$, and $V_t \equiv \underline{g}_{s_t}$ $\forall\, t$. Have real-valued $t \in [t_1 > 0, t_2]$, where $V_t = V_{t_1}(t/t_1)$. Assuming $\Lambda_f(V^*; l^*, x^1, x^2) \geq \Lambda_f(V_t; l_t, x^1, x^2)$ $\forall\, x^1, x^2$ as usual, the range in the logarithms of β for which $E^{[\beta V^*;\lambda]}(N_{V^*} \mid r, l^*) \geq \min_t E^{[V_t;\lambda]}(N_{V_t} \mid r, l_t)$ is greater than or equal to $\ln(t_2) - \ln(t_1)$.[46]

As another example, choose $\{l_t\} = \{l_{t^*}\} = \{n \in \mathrm{supp}\, P(\nu \mid r, s^i), s^i_\rho)\}$ for some set of σ values $\{s^i_\rho\}$, with $V_t = V_{n,s^i} = \underline{g}_{s^i}$ $\forall\, i$. Also presume that $\forall\, \beta$, there is a design coordinate value s^β_ρ such that $\underline{g}_{s^\beta} = \beta V^*$. If we now plug the conclusions of Corollary 5 into Corollary 3, we establish that $\forall\, i, \beta \in \cap_{n \in \mathrm{supp}\, P(\nu \mid r, s^i)} L_{n,s^i_\rho,V^*}$,

$$E(N_{\underline{g}_{s^\beta}} \mid r, s^\beta_\rho) \geq E(N_{\underline{g}_{s'}} \mid r, s^i),$$

and therefore $\forall \beta \in \cap_{s^i, n \in \mathrm{supp}\, P(\nu \mid r, s^i)} L_{n,s^i_\rho,V^*}$,

$$E(N_{\underline{g}_{s^\beta}} \mid r, s^\beta_\rho) \geq \min_{s^i, n \in \mathrm{supp}\, P(\nu \mid r)} E(N_{\underline{g}_{s^i}} \mid r, s^i)$$

4.3 Aristocrat Utility

In general, there is no utility that is both factored with respect to the world utility that has infinite learnability.[47] The following result allows us to solve for the private

---

something we can do in the other situations.) Accordingly, if *every* instance going into L_{t^*,V^*} is such a situation, then our conclusion that rescaling V^* can assuredly give better expected intelligence than V_t is a bit irrelevant; in this scenario we can also rescale V_t to assuredly improve its expected intelligence.

[46] To see this, note that t sets the scale of V_t, just like β does for V^*. Furthermore, $K_t \equiv K_{t,t^*} = t_1 K_{t_1,t^*}/t$ if $P(r'; l^*) = P(r'; l_t)$ $\forall\, r', t$ (cf. Theorem 8(iii)). So $1/K_t$, which we know is contained in L_{t,t^*,V^*}, equals $t/t_1 K_{t_1}$. Now apply Corollary 5.

[47] As an example of when having both conditions is impossible, take $r \in \{r^1, r^2\}$, $x \in \{x^1, x^2\}$, and $G(x^1, r^1) > G(x^2, r^1)$, while $G(x^2, r^2) > G(x^1, r^2)$. Then by Theorem 1, we also must have $\gamma_\rho(x^1, r^1) > \gamma_\rho(x^2, r^1)$ and $\gamma_\rho(x^2, r^2) > \gamma_\rho(x^1, r^2)$. Also assume that $P(r'; l) = \delta(r' - r)$ $\forall\, r, s$, so $P(U = u; l, x) = \delta(u - U(x, r))$ always.

Define $A \equiv \gamma_\rho(x^1, r^2) - \gamma_\rho(x^1, r^1)$, $C \equiv \gamma_\rho(x^2, r^2) - \gamma_\rho(x^1, r^2)$, $B \equiv \gamma_\rho(x^2, r^1) - \gamma_\rho(x^2, r^2)$, and $D \equiv \gamma_\rho(x^1, r^1) - \gamma_\rho(x^2, r^1)$. So $A + B + C + D = 0$, and both $C > 0$ and $D > 0$.

Take $f(x) = 1/2$ for both x, so $\int dx\, f(x)\,\mathrm{Var}(U; r, s, x) = [A^2 + B^2]/4$, which by convexity $\geq [(A + B)/2)]^2 = [(C + D)/2)]^2$. In turn, $[E(U; l, x^1) - E(U; l, x^2)]^2 = [(D - C)/2]^2 \leq [(C + D)/2)]^2$. Combining, by the definition of learnability we see that it is bounded above by 1. **QED.**

utility that maximizes learnability and thereby find the private utility for agent ρ that should give best performance under the first three premises.

Theorem 9.

(i) *A utility U_1 is factored with respect to U_2 at z iff $\forall z' \in \rho(z) \equiv r$, with $x \equiv \xi(z')$, $U_1(x, r) = F_r(U_2(z')) - D(r)$, for some function D and some r-parameterized function F_r with positive derivative.*

(ii) *For fixed $l \in \lambda \subseteq \nu$, r, x^1, x^2, and F, the D that maximizes $\Lambda_f(U_1; l, x^1, x^2)$ is the (l, x^1, x^2)-independent quantity $E_{f(x)}(F_r(U_2(\xi, r)))$.*

(iii) *The f that maximizes the associated ambiguity shift between U_2 and U_1 is*

$$\underset{f}{\operatorname{argmin}} \left[\frac{E_{f(x)}\{\operatorname{Var}(U_2; l, \xi)\}}{E_{f(x^1), f(x^2)}\{\operatorname{Var}((F^1 - F^2)\delta(r^1 - r^2); l, \xi^1, \xi^2)\}} \right],$$

where the subscript on the denominator expectation indicates that both xs are averaged according to f, and the delta function there means that our two Fs (one for each x) are evaluated at the same r.

A particularly important example of a function F_r meeting the condition in Theorem 9 is $F_r(U_2) = U_2$. This choice results in the difference utility U_1 that takes $z = (x, r) \rightarrow U_2(x, r) - E_f(U_2(\xi, r))$. We call this the **Aristocrat Utility** (AU) for U_2 at z, $AU_{U_2, f}(z)$, reflecting the fact that it is the difference between the value of U_2 at the actual z and the average such utility.

Say a particular choice of f, f', results in conditions (i) and (ii) of Corollary 4 being met with $V_b = U_2$ and $V_a = AU_{U_2, f'}$, for the choice of λ, etc., discussed just after the presentation of Corollary 4. Then we know by that corollary that once it is appropriately rescaled, using the AU for U_2 as ρ's private utility results in an expected intelligence that is larger than is the expected intelligence that arises from using U_2 as the private utility. (Note that U_2 and $AU_{U_2, f'}$ are mutually factored.) Moreover, by Theorem 9 any other difference utility that obeys Corollary 4(i), (ii) (in concert with U_2) must have worse ambiguity than does $AU_{U_2, f'}$ and therefore worse expected intelligence.[48]

To evaluate AU for some G at some z we must be able to list all $z' \in \rho(z)$. This can be a major difficulty, for example, if one cannot observe all degrees of freedom of the system. Even if we can list all such z', we must also be able to calculate G for all those z', an often daunting task that simple observation of the actual $G(z)$ at hand cannot fulfill (in contrast to the calculational needed with a team game, for example).

Even when we cannot calculate an AU exactly, we can often use an approximate AU and thereby improve performance over a team game. For example, in an iterated game, at time step t, r for a particular player i reflects the state of the other players it is confronting. In such a situation, by observing r, often we can approximate $E_f(g_i(\xi, r))$ by an appropriate average of the value of g_i over those preceding

---

[48] Note, however, that in general there may be a utility $F_r(U_2) - D(r)$ with better learnability than AU, for example if F_r is nonlinear. Note also that whether $AU_{U_2, f'}$ obeys conditions 4(i) (ii) will depend on the choice of f' in general.

iterations when the state of the other players was r, with f being the frequency distribution of moves made by i in those iterations. In particular, consider a "bake-off" tournament of a two-player game in which each player in the tournament plays one other player in each round and keeps track of who it has played in the past and with what move and the resultant outcome. In such a situation, the expectation value for player i confronting player j that gives AU_g can often be approximated by the average payoff of player i over those previous runs where i's opponent was j.

On the other hand, even when we can evaluate AU exactly, it may be that the conditions in Corollary 4 are badly violated. In such situations, increasing learnability by using AU will not necessarily improve expected intelligence, and accordingly AU may not induce optimal performance. Indeed, it may induce *worse* performance than the team game in such situations. On the other hand, there are other modifications to the private utility that (under the first premise) may improve expected intelligence in these situations. An example of such a utility is the CU, as illustrated in [22].

4.4 Wonderful Life Utility

One technique that will often circumvent the difficulties in evaluating AU is to replace ρ with a coarser partition with poorer resolution. Although this replacement usually decreases learnability below that of AU, it still results in utilities that are far more learnable than team game utilities, while (like team games) not requiring knowledge of the set of worldpoints $\rho(z)$ in full. In this section we illustrate making such a replacement for difference utilities.

We concentrate on the case where the domain of the lead utility D_1 is all of ζ, and the secondary utility $D_2 = D_1(\phi(z))$ for some function $\phi : \zeta \to \zeta$ where $\forall z \in C, \phi$ depends only on r, i.e., $\forall r, \forall z', z'' \in r, \phi(z') = \phi(z'')$. Specifying the utility consists of choosing ϕ. While in general we can make the choice that best suits our purposes, here we will only consider a particular class of ϕ's. A more general approach might, for example, choose ϕ to maximize learnability. Intuitively, the resulting difference utility is equivalent to subtracting D_1 of a transformed z from the original $D_1(z)$, with the transform chosen to maximize the signal-to-noise ratio of the resultant function. See the discussion of Theorem 7.

Let π be a partition of ζ. Fix some subset of ζ called the **clamping element** $CL_{\hat{\pi}}$ such that $\forall p \in \pi$, D_1 is invariant across the (assumed non-empty) intersection of $CL_{\hat{\pi}}$ and p.[49] Define an associated projection operator $CL_{\hat{\pi}}(z) \equiv CL_{\hat{\pi}} \cap \pi(z)$, which for any $p \in \pi$ maps all worldpoints lying in p to the same subregion of that element, a subregion having a constant D_1 value.[50] Then the **Wonderful Life Utility** (WLU) of D_1 and π is defined by

$$\underset{D_1,\pi}{\text{WLU}}(z) \equiv D_1(z) - D_1(\underset{\hat{\pi}}{\text{CL}}(z)).\text{[51]}$$

---

[49] Note that $CL_{\hat{\pi}}$ automatically has this property, independent of D_1, if its intersection with each element of π consists of a single worldpoint.

[50] Note that both $CL_{\hat{\pi}}$ and $CL_{\hat{\pi}}(z)$ are implicitly parameterized by D_1.

[51] Note that if there is some $x' \in \xi$ such that $CL_{\hat{\pi}}(x, r) = (x', r) \forall x, r$, then WLU is a special type of AU, with a delta function f.

To state our main theorem concerning WLU, for any partition of ζ, π, and any set $B \subseteq \zeta$, define $B \cap \pi$ to be a partition of B with elements given by the intersections of B with the elements of π. Furthermore, recall from Appendix B that given two partitions π_1 and π_2, $\pi_1 \subseteq \pi_2$ iff each element of π_1 is a subset of an element of π_2. Then the following holds regardless of what subset of ζ forms C.

Theorem 10. *Let π and $\pi' \subseteq \pi$ be two partitions of ζ. Then $WLU_{D_1,\pi}$ is factored with respect to D_1 for coordinate $C \cap \pi' \ \forall z \in C$.*

As an example, with $\rho \equiv C \cap \pi$, $WLU_{G,\pi}$ is factored with respect to G for coordinate ρ.

Note that $\pi' \subseteq \pi$ means that π' is either identical to π or a "finer-resolution" version of π. So $z \to CL\hat{}_{\pi \cap \pi}(z)$, by sending all points in $\pi(z)$ to the same point, is a more severe operation, resulting in a greater loss of information, than is $z \to CL\hat{}_{\pi \cap \pi'(z)}$, which can map different points on $\pi(z)$ differently. So Theorem 10 means we can err on the side of being oversevere in our choice of clamping operator and the associated WLU is still factored.[52]

There are other advantages to WLU that hold even when $\pi = \pi'$. For example, in general $CL\hat{}_\pi(z)$ need not lie on the set C (n.b., π and $\hat{}\pi$ are partitions of ζ, not C). In such a case the function $G(CL\hat{}_\pi(z)) : C \to \Re$ is not specified by the function $G(z) : C \to \Re$. In this situation we are free to choose the values $G(CL\hat{}_\pi(z))$ to best suit our purposes, e.g., to maximize learnability.

An associated advantage is that to evaluate the WLU for coordinate $C \cap \pi$, we do *not* need to know the detailed structure of C. This is what using WLU for the coarser partition π rather than the AU for the original coordinate $C \cap \pi'$ gains us. Given a choice of clamping element, so long as we know $G(z)$ and $\pi(z)$, together with the functional form of G for the appropriate subsets of ζ, we know the value of $WLU_{G,\pi}(z)$. These advantages are borne out by the experiments reported in [17].

4.5 WLU in Repeated Games

As an example of WLU, say we have a deterministic and temporally invertible repeated game (see Appendix D). Let the $\{\omega_1, \omega_2, \ldots, \omega_J\}$ and $\{\theta_1, \theta_2, \ldots, \theta_L\}$ be two sets of generalized coordinates of C^T (not necessarily repeating coordinates). Consider a particular player or agent and presume that $\forall\ t'$ there is a single-valued mapping from $r^{t'} \to (w_1, w_2, \ldots, w_J)$ and one from $(x^{t'}, r^{t'}) \to (q_1, q_2, \ldots, q_L)$ (both implicitly set by C). So the player's context at time t' fixes the values of the

---

[52] Sometimes $WLU_{G,\pi'}(z)$ will be factored with respect to $\dot{G}$ for coordinate $C \cap \pi$ even though $\pi' \subseteq \pi$. For example, this is the case if G is independent of precisely which of the elements of π' contains z, so long as all of those elements are in $\pi(z)$. However, in general, such factoredness will not hold. Even if it doesn't, say G is *relatively* insensitive to which of the elements of π' contains z, over the set of all such elements that are in $\pi(z)$. Then $WLU_{G,\pi'}(z)$ will be quite close to factored for coordinate $C \cap \pi$. This often allows us to be "sloppy" in using WLUs, by taking π' to be only those degrees of freedom $C \cap \pi$ with "significant impact" on the value of G.

ω_i (defined for time T), and by adding in the player's move at that time we fix the values of the θ_i. Say we also have a utility U that is a single-valued function of $(w_1, w_2, \ldots, w_J, q_1, q_2, \ldots, q_L)$.

Take π to be the partition of ζ whose elements are specified by the joint values of the $\{\omega_1, \omega_2, \ldots, \omega_J\}$. Take $CL^\wedge_\pi$ to be a set of z sharing some fixed values of $\{\theta_1, \theta_2, \ldots, \theta_L\}$. Note that U is constant across the intersection of $CL^\wedge_\pi$ with any single element of π, as required for it to define a WLU.

Intuitively, $CL^\wedge_\pi(z)$ is formed by "clamping" the values of the $\{\theta_1, \theta_2, \ldots, \theta_L\}$ to their fixed value while leaving the $\{\omega_1, \omega_2, \ldots, \omega_J\}$ values unchanged. Moreover, because $r^{t'} \to (w_1, w_2, \ldots, w_J)$ is single-valued, we know that any dependency of the important aspects of z (as far as U is concerned) on our player's move at time t' is given by (a subset of) the values $\{q_1, q_2, \ldots, q_L\}$. (Recall that all values $x^{t'}$ are allowed to accompany a particular $r^{t'}$.)

By Theorem 10, we know that $WLU_{U,\pi}$ is factored with respect to U for coordinate $C \cap \pi'$ for any partition π' that is a refined version of π. In addition, $\rho^{t'} \subseteq \pi$. So $WLU_{U,\pi}$ is factored with respect to U for the coordinate given by $C \cap \rho^{t'} = \rho^{t'}$, i.e., it is factored for our player's context coordinate at time t'.

When the $\{\theta_i\}$ are minimal in that none of them is a single-valued mapping of $r^{t'}$ (i.e., none can be transferred into the set of $\{w_i\}$), we say they are our player's **effect set** [17].[53] Often a player's behavior can be modified to ensure that a particular set of $\{\theta_i\}$ contains its effect set for some particular time. When we can do this it will assure that some associated variables $\{\omega_i\}$ specify (a partition π that gives) a $WLU_{G,\pi}$ for our player's move at that time that is factored with respect to G.

4.6 WLU in Large Systems

Consider the case of very large systems, in which G typically depends significantly on many more degrees of freedom than can be varied within any single element of ρ (i.e., depends more on the value of r than on where the system is within that r).

---

[53] Sometimes the $(q_1, q_2, \ldots, q_n)$ value specifying the clamping element of an effect set can intuitively be viewed as a "null action," so that clamping can be viewed as "removing agent ρ from the system." Intuitively, in this case we can view WLU as a first-order subtraction from G of the effects on it of specifying those degrees of freedom *not* contained in the effect set (hence the name "wonderful life" utility—cf. the Frank Capra movie). More formally, in such circumstances WLU can be viewed as an extension of the Groves mechanism of traditional mechanism design, generalized to concern arbitrary (potentially time-extended) world utility functions, and to concern situations having nothing to do with valuation functions, (quasilinear) preferences, types, revelations, or the like. (See [2, 2, 7, 8, 10, 13, 14, 16, 27].) Due to its concern for signal-to-noise issues though, this extension relies crucially on rescaling of G. (Indeed, if one just subtracts the clamped term without any such rescaling, ambiguity can be badly distorted, so that performance can degrade substantially [23].) In addition, this extension allows alternative choices of the clamping operator, even clamping to illegal (i.e., not $\in C$) worldpoints. This extension can be used even in cases where there is no action that can be viewed as a "null action," equivalent to "removing the agent from the system."

So we can write $G(x, r) = G_1(x, r) + G_2(r)$, where the values of G_2 in C are far greater than those of G_1, and correspondingly the changes in the value of G_1 as one moves across C are far smaller than those of G_2. In such cases, with $\rho = C \cap \pi$ as usual, the learnability of G is far less than that of $\text{WLU}_{G,\pi}$. This is due to the following slightly more general theorem.

Theorem 11. *Let κ and $\pi \subseteq \kappa$ be two partitions of ζ. Write $H(z) = H_1(z) + H_2(\kappa(z))$, where H is defined over all ζ, and consider the agent $\rho = C \cap \pi$. Fix $l \in \lambda \subseteq \nu$, and define*

$$M \equiv \left\{ \max_{z,z'} [H_1(z) - H_1(z')] \right\}^2$$

and

$$L \equiv \int dk'\, dk''\, P(k'; l) P(k''; l) [H_2(k') - H_2(k'')]^2.$$

Then, independent of f, $\text{CL}^\wedge_\kappa$, x^1 and x^2,

$$\frac{\Lambda_f(\text{WLU}_{H,\kappa}; l, x^1, x^2)}{\Lambda_f(H; l, x^1, x^2)} \geq \frac{L}{2M} - \sqrt{\frac{L}{M}}.$$

Note that as κ becomes progressively coarser, L shrinks. So such coarsening of the clamping element will typically lead to worse learnability. In fact, in the limit of $\kappa = \emptyset$, $\text{WLU}_{H,\kappa}$ just equals H minus a constant. So in that limit, $\text{WLU}_{H,\kappa}$ and H must have the exact same learnability—in agreement with Theorem 11 and the fact that $L = 0$ in that limit.

When L greatly exceeds M, the bound in Theorem 11 is much greater than 1. So if we take $H = G$ and $\kappa = \pi$, Theorem 11 tells us that for very large systems, setting the private utility to G's WLU rather than to G may result in an extreme growth in learnability.[54] In particular, for $\lambda = \nu \cap \sigma$, in large systems it may be that $L >> M \forall l$ such that $P(l \mid s)$ is noninfinitesimal. Under the first three premises, assuming $\text{WLU}_{G,\kappa}$ and G obey the conditions in Corollary 4(i), (ii), this means that setting the private utility to WLU will result in larger expected intelligence of the agent than will setting it to G. Moreover, because that WLU is factored with respect to G, this improvement in term 3 of the central equation will not be accompanied by a degradation in term 2. This ability to scale well to large systems is one of the major advantages of WLU and AU.

4.7 WLU in Spin Glasses

As a final example, consider a spin glass with spins $\{b_i\}$. For each spin i let $\mathbf{b}_{-i}$ be the set of spins other than i, and for each i let h_i and F_i be any two functions such that

---

[54] Trivially, because learnability of AU is bounded below by that of WLU, its learnability must exceed that of a team game at least as much as WLU's does.

the Hamiltonian can be written as $\mathcal{H}(\mathbf{b}) = h_i(b_i, \mathbf{b}_{-i}) + F_i(\mathbf{b}_{-i})$. In particular, for $\mathcal{H}(\mathbf{b}) = \sum_{jk} \mathcal{H}_{jk} b_j b_k + \sum_j \mathcal{H}_j b_j$, we can have $F_i(\mathbf{b}_{-i}) = \sum_{j \neq i, k \neq i} \mathcal{H}_{jk} b_j b_k + \sum_{j \neq i} \mathcal{H}_j b_j$, and $h_i(b_i, \mathbf{b}_{-i}) = \mathcal{H}_i b_i + \mathcal{H}_{ii} b_i^2 + \sum_{j \neq i} [\mathcal{H}_{ij} + \mathcal{H}_{ji}] b_j b_i / 2$. Because at equilibrium $\mathbf{b}$ minimizes $\mathcal{H}$, and therefore given the equilibrium value of $\mathbf{b}_{-i}$, at the $\mathcal{H}$-minimizing point b_i is set to the value that minimizes $h_i(b_i, \mathbf{b}_{-i})$.

We can view this as an instance of a collective where $\mathcal{H}$ is the (negative) world utility G for a system of "agents" ρ with move b_ρ, and $g_\rho = h_\rho$. For all ρ, at the $\mathbf{b}$ that maximizes G, b_ρ is set to the value that maximizes $-h_\rho$ given $\mathbf{b}_{-\rho}$. More generally, $h_i(b_i, \mathbf{b}_{-i}) = \mathcal{H}(\mathbf{b}) - F_i(\mathbf{b}_{-i})$ is factored with respect to $G(\mathbf{b})$ (cf. Theorem 2), with the context for each agent ρ being $\mathbf{b}_{-\rho}$ and $C = \zeta$ being the set of all vectors $\mathbf{b}$. So any $\mathbf{b}$ (locally) maximizing G also simultaneously maximizes all of the $-h_i$. Frustration then is a state where all the agents' intelligences equal 1, but the system is at a local rather than global maximum of G.

Consider a particular spin or agent, ρ. Embed C, the set of all possible $\mathbf{b}$, in some larger space that allows the spin ρ to take on additional values, and redefine ζ to be that larger space. Let π be an associated ζ-partition such that $\rho \equiv C \cap \pi$. Take $\mathrm{CL}^\wedge_\pi$ to be some set off of C. Extend the domain of definition of h_ρ by setting $h_\rho(\mathrm{CL}^\wedge_\pi(\mathbf{b})) = 0 \ \forall \ b_\rho \notin C$. Then $\mathrm{WLU}_{G,\pi} = -h_\rho$, i.e., WLU is the "local Hamiltonian" perceived by spin ρ, whereas G is the Hamiltonian of the entire system.

So by Theorem 11, if the number of nonzero coupling strengths between ρ and the other spins is much smaller than the total number of nonzero coupling strengths in the system, then the learnability of ρ's local Hamiltonian far exceeds that of the global Hamiltonian. Accordingly, consider casting the evolution of the spin system as an iterated game, with each spin controlled by a learning algorithm, and each g_{ρ,s^t} set to either spin ρ's local Hamiltonian at time t or to the global Hamiltonian at that time (see Appendix D). Then, because WLU is factored with respect to G, we would expect (under the first three premises, and assuming conditions 4.1(i), (ii) hold, etc.) that at any particular time step of the game, $\mathbf{b}$ is closer to a local peak of the *global* Hamiltonian if the agents use the value at that time step of their local Hamiltonians as their private utilities, rather than use the value of the global Hamiltonian at that time step.

If we also incorporate techniques addressing term 1 in the central equation, then we can ensure that such local peaks are large compared to the global peak. Moreover, if we have the spins use a WLU with better learnability, we would expect faster convergence still. Similarly, if the spins use AU rather than their local Hamiltonians, then because this increases learnability, performance of the overall system should improve even more. (Roughly speaking, such a change in private utilities is equivalent to having the agents use mean-field approximations of their local Hamiltonians as their rewards rather than the actual values of their local Hamiltonians.) More generally, any modification of the system that induces higher learnability (while maintaining factoredness of the individual spins' private utilities with respect to the original Hamiltonian) should result in faster convergence to the minimum of the original Hamiltonian. The foregoing is borne out in experiments reported in [24].

Acknowledgments. I would like to thank Mike New, John Lawson, Joe Sill, Peter Stone, and especially Kagan Tumer and Mark Millonas for helpful discussions.

Appendix A: Intelligence, Percentiles and Generalized CDFs

A useful example of intelligence is the following:

$$N_{\rho,U}(z) \equiv \int d\mu_{\rho(z)} \, \Theta[U(z) - U(z')] \tag{3}$$

with the subscript on the (usually normalized) measure indicating it is restricted to $z' \in \rho(z)$ (usually it is also nowhere-zero in that region). For consistency with its use in expansions of CDFs, the Heaviside function is here taken to equal $0/1$ depending on if its argument is less than 0. (Having $\Theta(0) = 0$ in Equation 3 is also a valid intelligence operator.) Intuitively, this kind of intelligence quantifies the performance of z in terms of its percentile rank, exactly as is conventionally done in tests of human cognitive performance. Note that this type of intelligence is a model-free quantification of performance quality; even if z is set by an agent that wants large $N_{\rho,U}$ and $N_{\rho,U}(z)$ turns out to be large "by luck," we still give that agent credit. The analogous coordinateless expression is given by $N_U(z) \equiv \int d\mu(z') \, \Theta[U(z) - U(z')]$, where μ runs over all of C.

There is a close relationship between CDFs and intelligence in general, not just percentile-based intelligence. Theorem 3 provides an example of that relationship. For percentile-based intelligence, though, the relationship is even deeper. In particular, coordinateless percentile-based intelligence can be viewed as a generalization of cumulative distribution functions (CDFs). This generalization applies to arbitrary spaces serving as the argument of the underlying probability density function (not just $\mathfrak{R}^1$) and does not arbitrarily restrict the "sweep direction" (said direction being from $-\infty$ to $+\infty$ for the conventional case). In particular, for the special case of $z \in \mathfrak{R}^n$ and invertible $U(\cdot)$, where $|\nabla_z U(z)| = 1$ a.e., $|\nabla_z N_U(z)|$ gives the probability density $\mu(z)$ and $0 \leq N_U(z) \leq 1 \; \forall \, z$, just like with the conventional CDF for which the underlying space is $\mathfrak{R}^1$. (In fact, for $U(z \in \mathfrak{R}^1) = z + \text{constant}$, $N_U(z)$ is identical to the conventional CDF of the underlying distribution $\mu(z)$.) For the more general case, intuitively, U itself provides the flow lines of the sweep.

Percentile-type intelligence is arbitrary up to the choice of measure μ, and in a certain sense essentially any intelligence (in the sense defined in the text) can be "expressed" as a percentile-type intelligence. As an alternative to these kinds of intelligences, one might consider standardizing a utility U by simply subtracting some canonical value (like the expected value of U) from $U(z)$. This operation doesn't take into account the width of the distribution over U values, however, and therefore it doesn't tell us how significant a particular value $U(z) - E(U)$ is. To circumvent this difficulty one might "recalibrate" $U(z) - E(U)$ by dividing it by the variance of the distribution, but this can be misleading for skewed distributions; higher-order moments may be important. Formally, even such a recalibrated function runs afoul of condition (i) in the definition of intelligence.

One important property of percentile-type intelligence is that with uncountable ζ and a utility U having no plateaus in ζ, if $P(\hat{r} \mid r, s) = \mu_r(\hat{r})$ and is independent of r, then $P(N_U(z) \mid s)$ is constant, regardless of U and μ. More formally, we have the following.

Theorem 12. *Assume that for all y in some subinterval of $[0.0, 1.0]$, for all r in supp $P(\cdot \mid s)$ there exists $\hat{r}$ such that the intelligence $N_{\rho,U}(r, \hat{r}) = y$. Restrict attention to cases where the intelligence measure $\mu_r(\hat{r}) = P(\hat{r} \mid r, s)$ and is independent of r. For all such cases, $P(N_U(z) \mid s)$ is flat with value 1.0, independent of both μ and U.*

Proof. We use the complement notation discussed in Appendix B. Write

$$P(N_{\rho,U}(r, \hat{r}) = y \mid s) = \int dr \, d\hat{r}' \, P(r \mid s) P(\hat{r}' \mid r, s) P(N_{\rho,U}(r, \hat{r}') = y \mid r, s)$$

Next write the expression $P(N_{\rho,U}(r, \hat{r}) = y \mid r, s)$ as the derivative of the CDF $P(N_{\rho,U}(r, \hat{r}) \leq y \mid r, s)$ with respect to y. By assumption there exists a $\hat{r}$ such that $N_{\rho,U}(r, \hat{r}) = y$. So we can rewrite that CDF as

$$P(N_{\rho,U}(r, \hat{r}') \leq N_{\rho,U}(r, \hat{r}) \mid r, s),$$

where the probability is over $\hat{r}'$, according to the distribution $P(\hat{r}' \mid r, s)$.
We can rewrite this CDF as

$$P(U(r, \hat{r}') \leq U(r, \hat{r}) \mid r, s),$$

by property (ii) of the general definition of intelligence. In turn we can write this as

$$\int d\hat{r}' \, P(\hat{r}'' \mid r, s) \Theta(U(r, \hat{r}) - U(r, \hat{r}'))$$

$$= \int d\hat{r}' \, \mu(\hat{r}') \Theta(U(r, \hat{r}) - U(r, \hat{r}')) \qquad \text{(by assumption)}$$

$$= N_{\rho,U}(r, \hat{r}) \qquad\qquad\qquad \text{(by definition of intelligence)}$$

$$= y.$$

Therefore the derivative of our CDF $= 1$. **QED**.

Intuitively, this theorem says that the probability that a randomly sampled point has a value of $U \leq$ the yth percentile of U is just y, so its derivative $= 1$, independent of the underlying distributions. Note that both the assumption that $P(\hat{r} \mid r, s)$ is independent of r and having $\mu(\hat{r}) = P(\hat{r} \mid s)$ is "natural" in single-stage games— but not necessarily in multistage games (see Appendix D).

If the conditions in the theorem apply, then choice of U is irrelevant to term 3 in the central equation. If we choose a "reasonable" U this means that we cannot have $P(\hat{r} \mid s) = \mu(\hat{r})$ if we want to have our choice of coordinate utility make a difference.

Note, though, that the assumption about the subinterval of $[0.0, 1.0]$ will be violated if U has isoclines of nonzero probability. This will occur if μ has delta functions or if ζ is a Euclidean space and U has plateaus extending over the support of $P(z \mid s)$. A particular example of the former is when ζ is a countable space; the theorem does not apply to categorical spaces.

Appendix B: Theory of Generalized Coordinates

It can be useful to view coordinates as "subscripts" on "vectors" z. Similarly, in light of their role as partitions of C, it can be useful to view separate coordinates as separate sets, complete with analogues of the conventional operations of set theory. As explicated in this appendix, these two perspectives are intimately related.

Define $z_\rho \equiv \hat{}\rho(z)$, so $z\hat{}_\rho = \rho(z)$. Typically, we identify the elements of z_ρ not by the sets making up $\hat{}\rho(z)$, but rather by the labels of those sets. This notation is convenient when ζ is a multidimensional vector space, because it makes the natural identification of contexts with vector components consistent with the conventional subscripting of vectors. For example, say $\zeta = \Re^3$, with elements written (x, y, z). Then a context for an "agent" making "move" x, ρ_x, is most naturally taken to be the partition of $\Re^3$ that is indexed by the moves of the other players, i.e., the values of y and z. In other words, specifying y and z gives a line delineating the remaining degrees of freedom of setting $z \in \Re^3$ that are available to agent x in determining its move, and each such line is an element of the partition ρ_x. For this ρ_x, we can take the complement $\hat{}\rho_x$ to be the partition of $\Re^3$ whose elements are planes of constant x, i.e., whose elements are labeled by the value of x. We can then write $\hat{}\rho_x(z) = z_{\rho_x} \equiv z_x$. With this choice z_x is just z's x value (recall that we identify an element of z_x by its label). This is in accord with the usual notation for vector subscripts

To formulate a set theory over coordinates, first note that coordinates are not just sets, but special kinds of sets—a coordinate's elements are non-intersecting subsets of C whose union equals C. So, for example, to have $\rho_1 \cup \rho_2$ be a coordinate, it cannot be given by the set of all elements of ρ_1 and ρ_2, as it would under the conventional set-theoretic definition of the union operator. (If the union operator were defined in that conventional manner, its elements would have nonzero intersection with one another.) This means that we cannot simply view coordinates as conventional sets and define the set theory operators over coordinates accordingly; we need new definitions.

To flesh out a full "set theory" of coordinates, first note that the complement operation has already been defined. (Note that unlike in conventional set theory, here the complement operator is not single-valued.) We can also define the null set coordinate $\emptyset$ as the coordinate each of whose members is a single $z \in C$. So $\emptyset$ is bijectively related to ζ, and $\hat{}\emptyset$ can be taken to be the coordinate consisting of a single set: all of C.

To define the analogue of set inclusion, given two coordinates ρ_1 and ρ_2, we take $\rho_1 \subseteq \rho_2$ iff each element of ρ_1 is a subset of an element of ρ_2. Intuitively, ρ_1

is a finer-grained version of ρ_2 if $\rho_1 \subseteq \rho_2$, with $\rho_1(z)$ always providing at least as much information about z as does $\rho_2(z)$. So ρ_1 is a delineation of a set of degrees of freedom that includes those delineated by ρ_2. Note that $\forall \rho$, $\emptyset \subseteq \rho \subseteq \hat{} \emptyset$, just as in conventional set theory.

One special case of having $\rho_1 \subseteq \rho_2$ is where every element of ρ_1 occurs in ρ_2, as in the traditional notion of set inclusion. (For our purposes, we can broaden that special case, which is what we've done in our definition.) Note also that the $\subseteq$ relation is transitive and that both $\rho_1 \subseteq \rho_2$ and $\rho_2 \subseteq \rho_1$ iff $\rho_1 = \rho_2$, and that $\rho_1 \subseteq \rho_2$ means there are $\hat{}\rho_1$ and $\hat{}\rho_2$ such that $\hat{}\rho_2 \subseteq \hat{}\rho_1$, just as in conventional set theory.

The other set-theory-like operations over coordinates can be defined by generalizing from the special case of conventional vector subscripts. For example, $\rho_1 \cap \rho_2$ is shorthand for a coordinate whose members are given by the intersections of the members of ρ_1 and ρ_2. We make this definition to accord with the conventional vector subscript interpretation of $z_{\rho_1 \cup \rho_2}$ as having its elements be the surfaces in ζ of both constant z_{ρ_1} and constant z_{ρ_2}. (For example, when $\zeta = \mathfrak{R}^3$ and has elements written as (x, y, z), "$z_{x \cup y}$" means $z_{x,y}$, which is the set of points of constant z_x and z_y.) Given this interpretation, write $z_{\rho_1 \cup \rho_2} = \hat{}(\rho_1 \cup \rho_2) \equiv \hat{}\rho_1 \cap \hat{}\rho_2$. This then means that the elements of $\rho_1 \cap \rho_2 = z_{\hat{}\rho_1 \cup \hat{}\rho_2}$ should be surfaces of constant $z_{\hat{}\rho_1} = \rho_1(z)$ and constant $z_{\hat{}\rho_2} = \rho_2(z)$, exactly as our definition of the intersection operator stipulates.

Note that $\rho_1 \cap \rho_2 \subseteq \rho_1$, as one would like. Intuitively, the intersection operator is just the comma operator given by Cartesian products. (For example, when $\zeta = \mathfrak{R}^3$ and has elements written as (x, y), $z_x \cap z_y$ is indexed by the vector (z_x, z_y).)

Finally, the intersection operator defines the union operator as $\rho_1 \cup \rho_2 = \hat{}(\hat{}\rho_1 \cap \hat{}\rho_2) = \hat{}(z_{\rho_1} \cap z_{\rho_2})$. To illustrate this, in the example of $\mathfrak{R}^3$, where the elements of ρ_x are lines of constant (y, z), and the elements of ρ_y are lines of constant (x, z), the elements of $\rho_x \cup \rho_y$ are planes of constant z. Similarly, when $\rho_1 \subseteq \rho_2$, $\rho_2 \backslash \rho_1$ is shorthand for a particular coordinate $\rho \subseteq \rho_2$ that is disjoint from ρ_1 (i.e., such that $\rho_1 \cap \rho = \emptyset$) and $\rho_1 \cup \rho = \rho_2$. Neither operation is single-valued, in general.

Note that in analogy to set theory, any coordinate ρ_1 such that there is no $\rho_2 \subseteq \rho_1$ is equal to the null set coordinate. The analogue of a "single-element set" is a coordinate ρ that contains only itself and the null set. This is any coordinate all of whose members but one consist of a single $z \in C$, where that other member consists of two such z.

Appendix C: Miscellaneous Proofs

Proof of Theorem 1. Choose any $z', z'' \in \rho(z)$. $\text{sgn}[N_{\rho,U_1}(z') - N_{\rho,U_1}(z'')] = \text{sgn}[U_1(z') - U_1(z'')]$ for all such z' and z'', by definition of intelligence. Similarly, $\text{sgn}[N_{\rho,U_2}(z') - N_{\rho,U_2}(z'')] = \text{sgn}[U_2(z') - U_2(z'')]$ for all such points. But by hypothesis, $N_{\rho,U_2}(z'') = N_{\rho,U_1}(z'')$ and $N_{\rho,U_2}(z') = N_{\rho,U_1}(z')$. So $\text{sgn}[N_{\rho,U_1}(z') - N_{\rho,U_1}(z'')] = \text{sgn}[N_{\rho,U_2}(z') - N_{\rho,U_2}(z'')]$. Transitivity then establishes the forward direction of the theorem.

To establish the reverse direction, simply note that $sgn[U_1(z') - U_1(z'')] = sgn[U_2(z') - U_2(z'')] \; \forall \; z' \in \rho(z)$, by hypothesis, and therefore by the first part of the definition of intelligence, U_1 and U_2 have the same intelligence at z''. Because this is true for all $z'' \in \rho(z)$, U_1 and U_2 have the same intelligence throughout $\rho(z)$. **QED**

Proof of Theorem 2. Consider any $z', z'' \in \rho(z)$. We can always write $sgn[U_2(z'') - U_2(z')] = sgn[\Phi(U_2(z''), \rho(z)) - \Phi(U_2(z'), \rho(z))]$, due to the restriction on Φ. Therefore U_1 and U_2 have the same intelligence at z', by the first part of the definition of intelligence. Because this is true $\forall \; z' \in \rho(z)$, U_1 and U_2 are factored at z. This establishes the backward direction of the proof.

For the forward direction, use Theorem 1 and the fact that the system is factored to establish that $\forall \; z$ in C, $\forall \; z'', z' \in \rho(z)$, $U_1(z') = U_1(z'')$ iff $U_2(z') = U_2(z'')$. Therefore for all points in $\rho(z)$, the value of U_1 can be written as a single-valued function of the value of U_2. Because Theorem 1 also establishes that $U_1(z') > U_1(z'')$ iff $U_2(z') > U_2(z'')$, we know that that single-valued function must be strictly increasing. Identifying that function with Φ completes the proof. **QED**

Proof of Theorem 3. $CDF(V(\omega, k) \mid l^a, k) < CDF(V(\omega, k) \mid l^b, k)$ means that for any fixed z', with $y \equiv V(z')$, $P(w : V(w, k) \leq y \mid l^a, k) < P(w : V(w, k) \leq y \mid l^b, k)$. This is equivalent to $P(z : V(\omega(z), \kappa(z)) \leq y \mid l^a, k) < P(z : V(\omega(z), \kappa(z)) \leq y \mid l^b, k)$, i.e., $P(z : V(z) \leq y \mid l^a, k) < P(z : V(z) \leq y \mid l^b, k)$. Since $z \in k$ in both of these probabilities, by the second part of the definition of intelligence we get $P(z : N_{\kappa, V(\cdot, k)}(z) < N_{\kappa, V(\cdot, k)}(z') \mid l^a, k) < P(z : N_{\kappa, V(\cdot, k)}(z) \leq N_{\kappa, V(\cdot, k)}(z') \mid l^b, k) \; \forall \; z' \in k$. This, in turn, is equivalent to $CDF(N_{\kappa, V(\cdot, k)} \mid l^a, k) < CDF(N_{\kappa, V(\cdot, k)} \mid l^b, k)$.

Next write $E(N_{\kappa, V(\cdot, k)} \mid n, k) = \int_0^1 dy \; y \; P(N_{\kappa, V(\cdot, k)} = y \mid n, k)$. Integrate by parts to get

$$E(N_{\kappa, V(\cdot, k)} \mid l^a, k) - E(N_{\kappa, V(\cdot, k)} \mid l^b, k)$$
$$= \int_0^1 dy \; [CDF(N_{\kappa, V(\cdot, k)} \mid l^b, k) - CDF(N_{\kappa, V(\cdot, k)} \mid l^a, k)].$$

Because $\forall \; y$, $CDF(N_{\kappa, V(\cdot, k)} \mid l^a, k)(y) < CDF(N_{\kappa, V(\cdot, k)} \mid l^b, k)(y)$, this last integral cannot be negative. The analog for equalities of CDFs and expectations rather than inequalities follows similarly. **QED**

Proof of Lemma 1. Because both P_i are normalized and distinct (if they aren't distinct, we're done), $\exists u^*$ such that $P_1(u^*) > P_2(u^*)$. By our condition concerning the P_i, $P_1(u) > P_2(u) \; \forall \; u > u^*$. Similarly there exists a u everywhere below which P_2 exceeds P_1. Accordingly, there is a greatest lower bound on the u^*'s, T. $\forall \; y \leq T$, $P_1(u \leq y) \leq P_2(u \leq y)$, and therefore by the nonnegativity of ϕ', $\forall \; y \leq \phi(T)$, $P_1(u : \phi(u) \leq y) \leq P_2(u : \phi(u) \leq y)$. So the CDF of ϕ according to P_1 is less than that according to P_2 everywhere below T. Therefore if there is to be any y value at which the CDF of ϕ according to P_1 is greater than that according to P_2, there must be a least such y value, and therefore a corresponding least such u, u'. We know that $u' > T$. However, for all $u > T$, $P_1(u) > P_2(u)$. Therefore $P_1(u : \phi(u) \geq \phi(u')) \geq P_2(u : \phi(u) \geq \phi(u'))$. Summing the P_1 probabilities of $\phi(u)$ exceeding and being less than $\phi(u')$, and doing the same for P_2, we see that both P_i cannot be normalized, which is impossible. **QED**

Proof of Theorem 4. When the ψs both equal $\underline{\gamma}_\rho$ and $\lambda = \nu$, by its definition, H must be the actual associated n-conditioned distributions over x, $P(x \mid n^a)$ and $P(x \mid n^b)$.

To complete the proof we must demonstrate that there is at least one parametric form for H that obeys the condition in the theorem when one of the ψs does not equal $\underline{\gamma}_\rho$ or $\lambda \neq \nu$. We do this by construction. First take the derivative of each ambiguity (one for each x) to get the convolutions $\int dy^1 dy^2 P_\psi(y^1; l, x^1) P_\psi(y^2; l, x^2) \delta(y - (y^1 - y^2))$. Multiply each such convolution by y and integrate the result over all y. This gives us the differences between the means of all the distributions $P_\psi(y; l, x)$ (one distribution for each x). Translate all those means, $M(\psi, l, x)$, by the same amount so that the lowest one has value 1. Then take $P^{[\psi;\lambda]}(x^1 \mid l) \propto e^{M(\psi, l, x)}$.

Use the relation between ordered and unordered ambiguities to rewrite the condition in the theorem as $t_U(x^1, x^2) A(\psi^a; l^a, x^1, x^2) < t_U(x^1, x^2) A(\psi^b; l^b, x^1, x^2)$. Consider some particular pair x^1, x^2, where without loss of generality $t_U(x^1, x^2) = 1$. Integrate $A(y; \psi^a; l^a, x^1, x^2) - A(y; \psi^b; l^b, x^1, x^2)$ by parts. So long as

$$y[A(y; \psi^a; l^a, x^1, x^2) - A(y; \psi^b; l^b, x^1, x^2)]$$

goes to 0 as y goes to either positive or negative infinity, the result is

$$-[(M(\psi^a, l^a, x^1) - M(\psi^a, l^a, x^2)) - (M(\psi^b, l^b, x^1) - M(\psi^b, l^b, x^2))].$$

By hypothesis, $t_U(x^1, x^2)$ times this expression must be negative. Therefore

$$\frac{P^{[\psi^a;\lambda]}(x^1 \mid l^a)}{P^{[\psi^a;\lambda]}(x^2 \mid \lambda)} > \frac{P^{[\psi^b;\lambda]}(x^1 \mid l^b)}{P^{[\psi^b;\lambda]}(x^2 \mid l^b)}.$$

Now apply Lemma 1. **QED**

Proof of Corollary 2. Expand $E(U \mid r, s) = \int dn dx\, P(n \mid r, s) U(x, r) P^{[\nu]}(x \mid n)$. By the second premise we can write this integral as

$$\int dn dx\, P(n \mid r, s) U(x, r) P^{[\nu, \sigma]}(x \mid n, s)$$

$$= \int dn dx\, P(n \mid r, s) U(x, r) P^{[g_s; \nu, \sigma]}(x \mid n, s)$$

$$= \int dn dx\, P(n \mid r, s) U(x, r) P^{[g_s; \nu, \sigma]}(x \mid n, s, W)$$

$$= \int dn\, P(n \mid r, s) E^{[g_s; \nu, \sigma]}(U \mid n, s, W).$$

QED

Proof of Corollary 3. For both $\psi = \underline{g}_{s^a}$ and $\psi = \underline{g}_{s^b}$, expand

$$E^{[\psi;\nu,\sigma]}(N_\rho \mid n, s^b) \;=\; \int dr \frac{P(n \mid r, s^b) P(r \mid s^b)}{P(n \mid s^b)} E^{[\psi;\nu,\sigma]}(N_\rho \mid n, r, s^b).$$

Rearranging terms gives the hypothesis inequality of our corollary. Now apply Corollary 2 to the consequent inequality of the third premise with $\Omega = \eta = \emptyset$. **QED.**

Proof of Theorem 5. By condition (iv), the quantity y^* defined there must equal $\underline{g}_{s^a}(x^*, r)$. Now fix x^1 and x^2. By conditions (ii) and (iii), for both of those moves x^i, $\underline{g}_{s^a}(x^i, r')$ has either the value 0 or 1 for all r' arising in the expansion of $A(\underline{g}_{s^a}; n, x^1, x^2)$. Combining this with the value of y^*, we see that for any r and any pair (x^1, x^2), one of the following four cases must hold:

(I) $\underline{g}_{s^a}(x^1, r) = 0$ and
$P(\underline{g}_{s^a} = y; n, x^1)$ is a delta function about 0 and
$P(\underline{g}_{s^a} = y; n, x^2)$ is an average of two delta functions, centered about 0 and about 1;

(II) $\underline{g}_{s^a}(x^1, r) = 1$ and
$P(\underline{g}_{s^a} = y; n, x^1)$ is a delta function about 1 and
$P(\underline{g}_{s^a} = y; n, x^2)$ is an average of two delta functions, centered about 0 and about 1.

Cases III and IV are the same as I and II, but with x^1 and x^2 interchanged.

Without loss of generality assume that we're in case II. Then expand $A(y; U, \underline{g}_{s^a}; n, x^1, x^2)$ as

$$\int dy^1 \, dy^2 \, P(\underline{g}_{s^a} = y^1; n, x^1) P(\underline{g}_{s^a} = y^2; n, x^2) \Theta[y - (y^1 - y^2) \cdot$$
$$\times \text{sgn}[U(x^1, r) - U(x^2, r)]]. \tag{4}$$

This evaluates as

$$\int dy^2 \, P(\underline{g}_{s^a} = y^2; n, x^2) \Theta[y - (1 - y^2) \, \text{sgn}[U(x^1, r) - U(x^2, r)]].$$

Now $\text{sgn}[\underline{g}_{s^a}(x^1, r) - \underline{g}_{s^a}(x^2, r)]$ equals 0 or 1 for case II. So by condition (i) and the factoredness of $\underline{g}_{s^a}$ and $\underline{g}_{s^b}$, this must also be true for $\text{sgn}[U(x^1, r) - U(x^2, r)]$. Given that y^2 cannot exceed 1, this means that the theta function is nonzero only for nonnegative y. Accordingly, so is the ambiguity.

This character of the ambiguity holds for all four cases; for all of them the ambiguity $A(y; \underline{g}_{s^a}, n, x^1, x^2)$ is 0 up to $y = 0$, where it may have a jump, and then is flat up to 1, where if the first jump did not go up to 1 it now has a second jump that gets it up to 1. So its support is assuredly nonnegative. **QED.**

Proof of Theorem 6. Define $m \equiv t_U(x^1, x^2)$. Our condition means that

$$\int dy^1\, dy^2\, \Theta[y - (y^1 - y^2)m] P(V_a(x^1, \rho) = y^1 \mid l') P(V_a(x^2, \rho) = y^2 \mid l')$$

$$= \int dy^1\, dy^2\, \Theta[y - (y^1 - y^2)m]\ P(K V_b(x^1, \rho) + h(x^1) = y^1 \mid l)$$

$$\times\ P(K V_b(x^2, \rho) + h(x^2) = y^2 \mid l),$$

i.e.,

$$\int dy^1\, dy^2\, \Theta[y - (y^1 - y^2)m][P(V_a(x^1, \rho) = y^1 \mid l') P(V_a(x^2, \rho) = y^2 \mid l')]$$

$$= \int dr^1\, dr^2 \Theta[y - mK(V_b(x^1, r^1) - V_b(x^2, r^2)) - K(h(x^1) - h(x^2))]$$

$$\times\ P(r^1, r^2; l)$$

$$= \int dr^1\, dr^2\ \Theta[y/K - m(V_b(x^1, r^1) - V_b(x^2, r^2)) - m(h(x^1) - h(x^2))/K]$$

$$\times\ P(r^1, r^2; l)$$

$$= \int dy^1\, dy^2\ \Theta[\{y/K - m(h(x^1) - h(x^2))/K\} - (y^1 - y^2)m]$$

$$\times\ P(V_b(x^1, \rho) = y^1 \mid l) P(V_b(x^2, \rho) = y^2 \mid l).$$

QED

Proof of Theorem 7. To prove (i), first marginalize out y^2 from the equality relating PV_a and P_{KV_b+h} and then use the resultant equality between probability distributions to form an equality concerning the two associated variances of y^1. The resultant formula for K holds for any x^1, and therefore it holds under arbitrary averaging over the x^1.

To prove (ii), use the equality relating P_{V_a} and P_{KV_b+h} to relate the expected values of the difference $(y^1 - y^2)$, evaluated according to the two distributions P_{V_a} and P_{V_b}:

$$\int dr^1\, dr^2\ P(r^1, r^2; l', x^1, x^2)[V_a(x^1, r^1) - V_a(x^2, r^2)]$$

$$= h(x^1) - h(x^2)$$

$$+ K \int dr^1\, dr^2\ P(r^1, r^2; l', x^1, x^2)[V_b(x^1, r^1) - V_b(x^2, r^2)].$$

Next collect terms to get an expression for $[h(x^2) - h(x^1)]/K$ in terms of expected values of V_a and V_b. Finally plug in the definition of Λ_f and evaluate K to verify our equation for $[h(x^2) - h(x^1)]/K$. **QED**

Proof of Theorem 8. To prove (i), note that because $P(r'; l) = P(r'; l')$ and V_a and V_b have the same lead utility, $E(V_a; l', x^1) - E(V_a; l', x^2) = E(V_b; l, x^1) -$

$E(V_b; l, x^2)$. Therefore the drop in learnability means that $\int dx\, f(x)\, \mathrm{Var}(V_a; l', x) < \int dx\, f(x)\, \mathrm{Var}(V_b; l, x)$. Plugging this into Theorem 7(i) gives the result claimed.

To prove the second part of (ii), for pedagogical clarity define $m \equiv t_{V_A}(x^1, x^2)$ and write the derivative as

$$
\int dr^1\, dr^2\, P(r^1, r^2; l', x^1, x^2)\delta(m[V_a(x^1, r^1) - V_a(x^2, r^2)])
$$

$$
= \int dr^1\, dr^2\, P(r^1, r^2; l, x^1, x^2)
$$

$$
\times \delta(m[K\{V_b(x^1, r^1) - V_b(x^2, r^2)\} + h(x^1) - h(x^2)])
$$

$$
= K^{-1} \int dr^1\, dr^2\, P(r^1, r^2; l, x^1, x^2)
$$

$$
\times \delta\left(m[V_b(x^1, r^1) - V_b(x^2, r^2)] \right.
$$

$$
\left. - \frac{m[\Lambda_f(V_b; l, x^1, x^2) - \Lambda_f(V_a; l', x^1, x^2)]}{\sqrt{\int dx f(x) Var(V_b; l, x^1, x^2)}} \right),
$$

where Theorem 7(ii) was used in the last step. By hypothesis, the difference in learnabilities equals zero. This establishes the result claimed.

To prove the first part of (ii), use similar reasoning to write the value of the ambiguity at the origin as

$$
\int dr^1\, dr^2\, P(r^1, r^2; l', x^1, x^2)\Theta(m[V_a(x^1, r^1) - V_a(x^2, r^2)])
$$

$$
= \int dr^1\, dr^2\, P(r^1, r^2; l, x^1, x^2)
$$

$$
\times \delta\left(m[V_b(x^1, r^1) - V_b(x^2, r^2)] \right.
$$

$$
\left. - \frac{m[\Lambda_f(V_b; l, x^1, x^2) - \Lambda_f(V_a; l', x^1, x^2)]}{\sqrt{\int dx f(x) Var(V_b; l, x^1, x^2)}} \right).
$$

Part (iii) is immediate from Theorem 7(i).

Finally, to prove (iv), without loss of generality take $K < 1$ and use the trick in (ii) with $s^* = s$ to increase K to 1. Doing this reduces the maximal slope of the associated ambiguity. In addition, it results in a right-shifted version of the ambiguity $A(V_b; l, x^1, x^2)$. Therefore this reduced maximal slope is the same as the maximal slope of $A(V_b; l, x^1, x^2)$. **QED**

Proof of Collorary 5. Due to their all obeying Corollary 4(ii), all utilities share the same m, which equals all of their m's. Write

$$A(y; V^*(\cdot, r), V^*; l_{t*}, x^1, x^2)$$

$$= \int dr^1 \, dr^2 \, P(r^1, r^2; l_{t*}, x^1, x^2) \Theta[y - m(V^*(x^1, r^1) - V^*(x^2, r^2))]$$

$$= \int dr^1 \, dr^2 \, P(r^1, r^2; l_t, x^1, x^2)$$

$$\times \Theta[(\{y/K_{l_{t*}, V^*, l_t, V_t}\} - \Delta_{t, t^*, x^1, x^2}) - m(V_t(x^1, r^1) - V_t(x^2, r^2))].$$

On the other hand,

$$A(y; V_t(\cdot, r), V_t; l_t, x^1, x^2)$$

$$= \int dr^1 \, dr^2 \, P(r^1, r^2; l_t, x^1, x^2) \Theta[y - m(V_t(x^1, r^1) - V_t(x^2, r^2))].$$

By comparing our formulas for the two ambiguities, we see that as long as

$$\frac{y}{K_{t, t^*}} - \Delta_{t, t^*, x^1, x^2} \le y \qquad \forall \, y \in [D_{t, x^1, x^2}, B_{t, x^1, x^2}],$$

it follows that $A(V_t(\cdot, r), V_t; l_t, x^1, x^2) \ge A(V^*(\cdot, r), V^*; l_{t*}, x^1, x^2)$. Furthermore, by our formulas for algebraic manipulation of Ks, we know that $K_{l_{t*}, \beta K_{t, t^*}, l_t, V_t} = K_{l_{t*}, \beta K_{t, t^*}, l_{t*}, V^*} K_{l_{t*}, V^*, l_t, V_t}$. By Theorem 8(iii), this equals $\beta K_{l_{t*}, V^*, l_t, V_t} = \beta K_{t, t^*}$.

Accordingly, $L_{t, t^*, V^*, x^1, x^2}$ is the set of values β by which one could multiply K_{t, t^*} and still have the desired inequality hold, given the values of D_{t, x^1, x^2} and B_{t, x^1, x^2}. L_{t, t^*, V^*} is then defined as the set of such multiples for which we can be assured that the inequality holds for every (x^1, x^2) pair. So for every β in that set, we know that $(\beta V^*, l_{t*})$ has better ambiguity than does (V_t, l_t), for every single (x^1, x^2) pair. Accordingly, by Corollary 1, it has better expected intelligence. That means that so long as $\beta \in \cup_t L_{t, t^*, V^*}$, it follows that $(\beta V^*, l_{t*})$ has better expected intelligence than *some* (V_t, l_t). **QED**

Proof of Theorem 9. By Theorem 2, a utility U_1 is factored with respect to U_2 for agent ρ at z iff we can write it as $U_1(z') = \Phi_r(U_2(z'))$ for some r-parameterized function Φ whose first partial derivative is positive across all $z' \in \rho(z)$. Any such function can always be written as $F_r(U_2) - D$ for some function D only dependent on $\rho(z)$ and some f-parameterized function F_r whose derivative is positive. This establishes (i).

To minimize the learnability of U_1 given Φ, l, and U_2, first note that because D is independent of x, the numerator in the definition of $\Lambda_f(U_1; l, x^1, x^2)$, $E(U_1; l, x^1) - E(U_1; l, x^2)$, is independent of the choice of D. So we need only consider the denominator. Rewrite that denominator as

$$E_{f(x)}[\text{Var}(U_1; l, \xi)]$$

$$= (1/2) \int dx \, f(x) \int dr' \, dr'' \, P(r'; l) P(r''; l) [U_1(x, r') - U_1(x, r'')]^2,$$

where we have used the fact that $\text{Var}_{\{A(\tau)\}} = (1/2) \int dt_1 \, dt_2 \, P(t_1) P(t_2) [A(t_1) - A(t_2)]^2$ for any random variable τ with distribution P.

Bring the integral over x inside the other integrals, expand U_1, and introduce the shorthand $D_1(x, r) \equiv F_r(U_2(x, r))$ to get

$$\frac{1}{2} \int dr' \, dr'' \, P(r'; l) P(r''; l)$$
$$\times \int dx \, f(x)[D_1(x, r') - D_1(x, r'') - (D(r') - D(r''))]^2.$$

The innermost integral is minimized for each r' and r'' so long as for each r' and r'',

$$D(r') - D(r'') = \int dx \, f(x)[D_1(x, r') - D_1(x, r'')].$$

This can be assured by picking $D(r) = E_{f(x)}(D_1(\xi, r))$ for all r. This establishes (ii).

Because $E(U_1; r, s, x^1) - E(U_1; r, s, x^2) = E(U_2; r, s, x^1) - E(U_2; r, s, x^2)$, the ambiguity shift in going from U_2 to U_1 equals

$$(E(U_1; l, x^1) - E(U_1; l, x^2)) \left\{ 1 - \sqrt{\frac{E_f(\text{Var}(U_2; l, \xi))}{E_f(\text{Var}(U_1; l, \xi))}} \right\}.$$

So what we need to do is minimize $E_f(\text{Var}(U_2; l, \xi))/E_f(\text{Var}(U_1; l, \xi))$.

For our choice of D, by the preceding reasoning,

$$E_f(\text{Var}(U_1; l, \xi))$$
$$= \frac{1}{2} \int dr' \, dr'' \, P(r'; l,) P(r''; l) \, \text{Var}_{f(x)}(D_1(\xi, r') - D_1(\xi, r'')).$$

We again use the fact that $\text{Var}_{\{A(\tau)\}} = (1/2) \int dt_1 \, dt_2 \, P(t_1) P(t_2) [A(t_1) - A(t_2)]^2$ for any random variable τ with distribution P and associated function A to expand the Var_f into a double integral. Next rearrange terms and again use that fact, this time to reduce the integral over r' and r'' into a single variance. **QED.**

Proof of Theorem 10. Any change to z that doesn't move it out of the set $B \cap \pi'(z)$ doesn't move it out of $B \cap \pi(z)$, because all z in any element of π' lie in the same element of π. Therefore that change to z doesn't change $\pi(z)$. That means, in turn, that it does not change $D_1(\text{CL}^\wedge_\pi(z).)$ So $D_1(\text{CL}^\wedge_\pi(z).)$ can be written as a function that depends only on $B \cap \pi'(z)$. Therefore it is of the form for the secondary utility required for the difference utility to be factored with respect to agent $B \cap \pi'(z)$. **QED.**

Proof of Theorem 11. Note that $H(\text{CL}^\wedge_\kappa(z))$ can be written as a function of $\kappa(z)$, and therefore of $\rho(z)$. Accordingly, expand the numerator term in the definition of learnability in terms of r to see that that it has the same value for H and $\text{WLU}_{H,\kappa}$.

Write out $\mathrm{WLU}_{H,\kappa}(z) = H_1(z) - H_1(\mathrm{CL}_{\hat{\kappa}}(z))$ to see that the denominator term for $\Lambda_f(\mathrm{WLU}_{H,\kappa}; l, x^1, x^2)$ is bounded above by

$$\int \mathrm{d}x\, f(x) \int \mathrm{d}r'\, P(r'; l)[H_1(x, r') - H_1(\underset{\hat{\kappa}}{\mathrm{CL}}(x, r'))]^2.$$

In turn, the greatest possible value of the term in square brackets is M. So that denominator term is bounded above by M.

Write the denominator term for $\Lambda_f(H; l, x^1, x^2)$ as

$$\frac{1}{2} \int \mathrm{d}x\, f(x) \int \mathrm{d}r'\, \mathrm{d}r''\, P(r'; l) P(r''; l)$$

$$\times [\{H_2(\kappa(r')) - H_2(\kappa(r''))\} + \{H_1(x, r') - H_1(x, r'')\}]^2$$

$$= \frac{1}{2} \int \mathrm{d}x\, f(x) \int \mathrm{d}r'\, \mathrm{d}r''\, P(r'; l) P(r''; l)$$

$$\times \{[H_2(\kappa(r')) - H_2(\kappa(r''))]^2 + [H_1(x, r') - H_1(x, r'')]^2$$
$$+ 2[H_2(\kappa(r')) - H_2(\kappa(r''))][H_1(x, r') - H_1(x, r'')]\}.$$

The third of the integrals summed in this last expression is bounded below by

$$-\sqrt{M} \int \mathrm{d}x\, f(x) \int \mathrm{d}r'\, \mathrm{d}r''\, P(r'; l) P(r''; l) |H_2(\kappa(r')) - H_2(\kappa(r''))|,$$

which in turn is bounded below by $-\sqrt{ML}$, due to concavity of the squaring operator. The second of our integrals is bounded below by 0. Finally, the first of these integrals equals $L/2$ exactly. Combining, the denominator term for $\Lambda_f(H; l, x^1, x^2)$ is bounded below by $L/2 - \sqrt{ML}$. **QED.**

Appendix D: Repeating Coordinates, Multistep Games, and Constrained Optimization

Say we have a set of coordinates of ζ, indicated by $\{\zeta^1, \zeta^2, \ldots, \zeta^T\}$, with associated images of C written as $\{C^1, C^2, \ldots, C^T\}$. Conventionally the index t is called the "time" or "time step". An associated **repeating coordinate** is a set $\{\lambda^1, \lambda^2, \ldots, \lambda^T\}$ such that $\forall\, t$, $\lambda^t(z) = \lambda(\zeta^t(z))$ for some function λ whose domain is given by the union of the ranges of the coordinates $\{\zeta^i\}$, Z. For a **deterministic** set $\{\zeta^i\}$, there is a set of single-valued functions $\{E^i\}$, mapping Z to Z, such that $\zeta^{i+1} = E^i(\zeta^i)$ $\forall\, i \in \{1, \ldots, T-1\}$. The set is **time-translation-invariant** if E^i is the same for all i, and **(temporally) invertible** if the E^i are all invertible.

In close analogy to conventional game theory nomenclature, we say that we have a set of **players** $\{i\}$, each consisting of a separate triple of repeating coordinates $\{\rho_i^t\}$, $\{\xi_i^t\}$, and $\{v_i^t\}$, if for each t and i the triple $(\rho_i^t, \xi_i^t, v_i^t)$ acts as the context, move, and worldview coordinates, respectively, of an agent. If $T > 1$, we sometimes say we have a **multistep game**, and we identify each "step" with a different time.

Often we want to consider the intelligences of the players' agents with respect to some associated sequence of private utilities. We can do this if in addition to the players we have a repeating coordinate $\{\sigma^t\}$, s^1 being the design coordinate value set by the designer of the collective and $\underline{g}_{i^t}(z) \equiv \underline{g}_{i,\sigma^t(z)}(z)$ being the private utility of player i at time t.[55] In this way each player is identified with a sequence of agents.

A **multistage game** is one in which for every i, $\underline{g}_{i^t}$ is the same function of $z^T \in Z$. A **normal-form** (version of a multistage) **game** is the system ζ^1 with associated coordinates and a set of allowed points C^1, where $P(z_1)$ is set by marginalizing $P(z)$. So, in particular, $P(\underline{g}_{i^1}(z_1) = v) = \int dz \, P(z^T \mid z_1) \delta(v - \underline{g}_{i^T}(z^T))$. Intuitively, a normal-form game is the underlying multi-stage game "rolled up" into a single stage, that stage being set by the initial joint state of the players.

If for every i, $\underline{g}_{i^t}$ is the same function from $z^t \in Z$ to the reals, then we say we have an **iterated game**. More generally, if for each player i all of the $\{\underline{g}_{i^t}\}$ are the same discounted sum over $t' \in \{1, \dots, T\}$ of $R_i(z^{t'})$ for some real-valued **reward** function R_i that has domain Z, then each player's agents must try to predict the future, and we have a **repeated game**.

Note that conventional full rationality noncooperative game theory of normal-form games, involving Nash equilibria of the private utilities, is simply the analysis of scenarios in which the intelligence of z with respect to each player's private utility, given the context set by the other players' moves, equals 1. This fact suggests many extensions of conventional noncooperative game theory based on the formalism of this chapter. For example, we can consider games in which $C \neq \zeta$, i.e., not all joint moves are possible. Another modification, applicable if we use the percentile type of intelligence, is to restrict $d\mu_\rho$ to some limited "set of moves that player ρ actively considers." This provides us with the concept of an "effective Nash equilibrium" at the point z, in the sense that *over the set of moves it has considered*, each player has played a best possible move at such a point. In particular, for moves in a metric space, we could restrict each $d\mu_\rho$ to some infinitesimal neighborhood about z, and thereby define a "local Nash equilibrium" by having ρ's intelligence with respect to utility γ_ρ equal 1 for each player ρ.

More generally, as an alternative to fully rational games, one can define a bounded rational game as one in which the intelligences equal some vector ε whose components need not all equal 1. Many of the theorems of conventional game theory

---

[55] An interesting topic is whether for a particular player there is a set of functions $\{U^t(z^t)\}$ such that the values $\{x^t\}$ induce large $N_{\rho^t, U^t}(z^t)$, $\forall t \in \{1, \dots, T\}$. When there is such a set, it would seem natural to interpret the player as a set of "agents" with associated private utilities $\{U^t\}$. However, unless we can vary the private utility that the time t "agent" is supposedly trying to maximize, we have no reason to believe that the value x^t really is set by a learning algorithm trying to maximize that private utility. (We might have a coordinate akin to the explicitly nonlearning spins in Example 1 of [22].) This means that for such an interpretation to be tested, the private utility must be part of some $\{\sigma^t\}$, so we can set it. Our modifying it must then induce associated changes in the moves consistent with the supposition that a learning algorithm is controlling those moves to try to maximize those values of the private utilities, as discussed in the section on the first premise.

can be directly carried over to such bounded-rational games [19] by redefining the utility functions of the players. In other words, much of conventional full rationality game theory applies even to games with bounded rationality, under the appropriate transformation. This result has strong implications for the legitimacy of the common criticism of modern economic theory that its assumption of full rationality does not hold in the real world, implications that extend significantly beyond the Sonnenschein-Mantel-Debreu theorem equilibrium aggregate demand theorem [11].

Note also that at any point z that is a Nash equilibrium in the set of the player's utilities, every player's intelligence with respect to its utility must equal 1. Because that is the maximal value any intelligence can take on, a Nash equilibrium in those utilities is a Pareto-optimal point in the values of the associated intelligences (for the simple reason that no deviation from such a z can raise any of the intelligences). Conversely, if there exists at least one Nash equilibrium in the player utilities, then there is not a Pareto-optimal point in the values of the associated intelligences that is not a Nash equilibrium.

Note that the moves of some player i may directly set the private utility functions of the agent(s) of some other player i' in a multistep game. In particular, the private utilities of i's agents might explicitly involve inferences about the effect on $P(G \mid s^t)$ of various possible choices of $g_{(i')^t}$. Loosely speaking, when an agent of player i changes the learning algorithm, move variable, worldview variable, or private utilities of (the agents of) other players, and does so gradually based on considerations of how to improve $P(G \mid s^t)$, we refer to its learning algorithm as engaging in **macrolearning**; that agent's moves constitute online modification of s to try to improve G. We contrast this with **microlearning**, in which one agent's moves are not viewed as directly setting other agents' private utility functions, in loose analogy with the distinction between macroeconomics and microeconomics.[56]

In any kind of game, each agent only works to (try to) maximize its current private utility.[57] However g_{i^t} will not be mutually factored (with respect to moves x^t) with either the utilities $g_{i t' \neq t}$ or with G, in general. Intuitively, moves that improve the current private utility may hurt the future one, and may even (due to those future effects) hurt G. (See [1] for an example of this.) In repeated games where G is itself a discounted sum, appropriate coupling of the reward function of the player with that of G can ensure factoredness of those two reward functions. However, in iterated games—which, for example, are those that arise with the Boltzmann learning algorithms considered in [17]—there is no such assurance. And even for repeated games with discounted sum Gs, simply having each of the player's rewards be factored with

---

[56] In general, we wish to optimize G *subject to the communication restrictions at hand*. When the nodes are agents, such restrictions apply to the argument lists of their private utilities. More generally, though, the nodes can communicate with each other in ways other than via their private utilities. Indeed, part of macrolearning in the broadest sense of the term is modifying such extrautility "signaling" and "bargaining" among the nodes, to try to improve performance of the overall system. None of these "low-level" issues are addressed in this chapter.

[57] Formally, the first premise applies to moves and private utilities that share the same time, because here the full agent is defined for a single time.

respect to the associated reward of G does not ensure that the player's full private utility is factored with respect to G.[58]

Another subtlety arises if there is randomness in the dynamics of the system at times $t' > t$, and we are considering a utility function at time t that depends on components of z other than z^t (e.g., we have a multistage game). The problem is that in general we require utility functions to be expressible as a single-valued function of the move and context of any agent. So, in particular, our utility must be such a function of (x_i^t, r_i^t), despite the stochasticity at times $t' > t$.

One way around this problem is not to cast the problem as a multistep game and instead have contexts explicitly include future states of the system. We can keep the game-theoretic structure if we have z specify the state of the pseudo-random number generator underlying the stochasticity, and then have that state be included in r_i^t. This encapsulates the stochastic dynamics within a deterministic system. Another approach is to recast utilities and associated intelligences in terms of partial worldpoints $z^{t' \leq t}$ rather than full worldpoints that include time to the future of t. As an example, starting with a conventional utility U, we could define a new utility $\hat{U}(z) \equiv E(U \mid z^{t' \leq t})$. Because $\hat{U}(z') = \hat{U}(z)$ if $(z')^{t' \leq t} = z^{t' \leq t}$, $N_{\rho, \hat{U}}(z)$ only judges z by the quality of its components for times previous to the future.

There is another subtlety that can arise even in deterministic games, from the general requirement that any move can accompany any context. The problem is that this requirement is, on the face of it, incompatible with constrained optimization problems, in which typically for any moment t, C forbids some of the potential joint states of the agents at that time. The simplest way around this difficulty, when it is feasible, is simply to choose a different set of move coordinates for the agents, one in which the constraints do not restrict the agent's moves. Another way around this difficulty is to transform the problem by means of a function that maps any (unconstrained) pair (x, r) to an allowed (constrained) joint state of all agents, which in turn is what is used to determine utility values.

No such function is needed, however, if the constrained optimization problem can be cast as traversing the nodes in a graph with fixed fan-out, so that the constraints don't apply to the moves directly. To see this, first consider an iterated game with an "environment" repeating coordinate $\{\theta^t\}$. Say that the game is a Markovian control problem with N players, i.e., a multistage game where $G(z)$ only depends on the value q^T and

---

[58] In practice factoredness of reward functions often results in approximate factoredness of associated utilities if t is large enough so that the system has started to settle toward a Nash equilibrium among the players' reward functions. In turn, such settling toward a Nash equilibrium is expedited if we set s to give a good term 3 in the "reward utility version" of the central equation, in which all utilities are replaced by the associated reward functions.

For the more general scenario where factoredness of reward functions does not suffice, one can guarantee factoredness of the utilities by using reward functions set via "effect sets." As discussed in the discussion of the WLU, such reward functions can ensure factoredness by (in essence) overcompensating for all possible future effects on G of a player's current action. A more nuanced approach is investigated in [20].

$$P(q^t \mid q^{t-1}, x_1^1, x_1^2, \ldots, x_1^{t-1}, x_2^1, \ldots, x_N^{t-1})$$
$$= P(q^t \mid q^{t-1}, x_1^{t-1}, x_2^{t-1}, \ldots, x_N^{t-1})$$
$$= v(q^t, x_1^{t-1}, x_2^{t-1}, \ldots, x_N^{t-1}),$$

where v is independent of $t \in \{1, \ldots, T-1\}$.[59]

For a graph-traversal version of this problem the dynamics is single-valued, so we can write $v(q', q, x^1, \ldots, x^N) = \delta(q' - x^1 x^2 \ldots x^N(q))$ for some function of q and $(x^1, \ldots, x^N)$ that is written as $x^1 x^2 \ldots x^N(q)$. (For uncountable q, this is a continuum-limit graph.) So any constraints o on optimizing G—on finding the optimal node q in the graph—are reflected in the graph's topology.

This kind of problem is a (fixed fan-out) undirected-graph-traversal problem if the values of each ξ_i also form a group, in the following sense:

1. $\forall q \in \theta$, $\exists!(I_1, I_2, \ldots, I_N) \in \{(x^1, x^2, \ldots x^N)\}$ such that $I_1 I_2 \ldots I_N(q) = q$;
2. $\forall q \in \theta$, $\forall (x_1', x_2', \ldots x_N') \in \{(x^1, x^2, \ldots x^N)\}$, $\exists!((x')_1^{-1}, (x')_2^{-1}, \ldots (x')_N^{-1}) \in \{(x^1, x^2, \ldots x^N)\}$ such that $(x')_1^{-1}(x')_2^{-1} \ldots (x')_N^{-1} x_1' x_2' \ldots x_N'(q) = q$.

In practice, search across such a graph is easiest when the identity and inverse elements of each group of moves are independent of q and G does not vary too quickly as one traverses the graph.

Finally, as an illustration of off-equilibrium benefits of factoredness, consider the case where ζ is a Euclidean space with an iterated game structure where every $\rho^t(z)$ is a manifold and all of those manifolds are mutually orthogonal everywhere on C. Presume that all utilities are analytic. Then for small enough step sizes, having each player run a gradient ascent on its reward function must result in an increase in G, for a factored system. (However, such a gradient ascent may progressively *decrease* the values of some players' utilities.)

To see why G must increase under gradient ascent, first, as a notational matter, when M is a manifold embedded in ζ define $\nabla_M F(z)$ to be the gradient of F in some coordinate system for M, expressed as a vector in ζ. Let $\mathfrak{I}_{\rho^t}$ be the tangent plane to $\rho^t(z)$ at z. Then if G is factored with respect to $\underline{g}_{\rho^t}$, $\nabla_{\mathfrak{I}_{\rho}}(\underline{g}_{\rho^t}(z))$ must be parallel to $\nabla_{\mathfrak{I}_{\rho^t}}(G(z))$. (If there were any discrepancy between the directions of those two gradients, there would be a direction within $\rho^t(z)$ in which one could move z and in so doing end up increasing $\underline{g}_{\rho^t}$ but decreasing G.) So the dot product between those gradients is nonnegative, and therefore changing $z \to z + |\alpha| \nabla_{\mathfrak{I}_{\rho^t}}(\underline{g}_{\rho^t}(z))$ for infinitesimal α cannot decrease $G(z)$. Generalizing, note that for any utility U the gradients $\nabla_{\mathfrak{I}_{\rho^t}}(U)$ (one for each ρ^t) are mutually orthogonal, because the underlying manifolds are. Therefore having all those dot products be nonnegative means that moving z an infinitesimal amount in ζ in the direction with components in each plane $\mathfrak{I}_{\rho^t}$ given by $\nabla_{\mathfrak{I}_{\rho^t}}(\underline{g}_{\rho^t}(z))$, cannot decrease $G(z)$. So gradient ascent works for factored systems.

---

[59] Note that in this problem, G is not a direct function of the players' joint move at any time. Rather the joint move specifies the incremental change to another variable—the environment—which is what directly sets the value of G. See Appendix E on gradient ascent over categorical variables.

Similarly, fix t and consider two worldpoints z' and z'' that are infinitesimally close but potentially differ for every player. Then it may be that for no player ρ does $\rho^t(z') = \rho^t(z'')$; every player sees a different set of the moves of its opponents at z' and z''. Nonetheless, again using nonnegativity of the dot products, the system's being factored means that there must be at least one player ρ for which $\text{sgn}[G^t(z') - G^t(z'')] = \text{sgn}[g_{\rho^t}(z') - g_{\rho^t}(z'')]$. (Compare to Theorem 1.)

Appendix E: Example—Gradient Ascent for Categorical Variables

This example illustrates the many connections between traditional search techniques like gradient ascent and simulated annealing on the one hand and the use of a collective of agents to maximize a world utility on the other.

Say we have a Cartesian product space $M \equiv M^1 \times M^2 \times \cdots M^L$, where each M^i is a space of $|M^i|$ categorical (i.e., symbolic, nonnumeric) variables. Write a generic element of M as m, having components $m_i, i \in \{1, \ldots, L\}$. Consider a function $h(m) \rightarrow \Re$ that we want to maximize. Because M is not a Euclidean space, we cannot use conventional gradient ascent to do this. However, we can still use gradient ascent if we transform to a probability space.

To see how, take ζ to be the space of Euclidean vectors comprising the Cartesian product $S^{|M^1|} \times S^{|M^2|} \times \cdots S^{|M^L|}$, where each $S^{|M^i|}$ is the M^i-dimensional unit simplex. Define the function $R(z) \equiv \sum_{m \in M} (\prod_{i=1}^{L} z_{i,m_i}) \times h(m)$. The product $z_P \equiv (\prod_{i=1}^{L} z_{i,m_i})$ gives a (product) probability distribution over the space of possible $m \in M$. (Intuitively, $z_{i,j} = P(m^i = j)$.) Accordingly, $R(z)$ is the expected value of h, evaluated according to the distribution z_P.

Define $m^* \equiv \text{argmax}_m h(m)$. Then

$$\text{argmax}_z R(z) = [\quad \delta(z_{1,1} - 0), \delta(z_{1,2} - 0), \ldots, \delta(z_{1,m_1^*} - 1), \ldots, \delta(z_{1,|M^1|} - 0);$$
$$\ldots, \delta(z_{2,m_2^*} - 1), \ldots;$$
$$\ldots$$
$$\ldots, \delta(z_{L,m_L^*} - 1), \ldots \quad],$$

i.e., the z that maximizes R, z^*, is a Kronecker delta function about the m that maximizes h. However, unlike m, z lives in (a subset of) a Euclidean space. So if we make sure to always project $\nabla R(z)$ onto $S^{|M^1|} \times S^{|M^2|} \times \cdots S^{|M^L|}$, the space of allowed z, we can use gradient ascent over z values to climb G—and thereby maximize h. Intuitively, as opposed to conventional gradient ascent over the variable of direct interest (something that is meaningless for categorical variables), here we are performing gradient ascent over an auxiliary variable, and in that way maximizing the function of the variable of direct interest.[60]

---

[60] By our choice of R, here we are only considering distributions over M that have all L of the variables statistically independent. Doing so exponentially reduces the dimension

Note that R is a multilinear function over the (sub)vector spaces $\{S^{|M^i|}\}$, and its maximum must lie at a vertex of that space. There are $|M^i|$ components of the gradient of R for each variable i, giving $\sum_{i=1}^{L} |M^i|$ components all together. The value of the component corresponding to the jth possible value of M^i is given by the expected value of h conditioned on $m_i = j$. So calculating $\nabla R(z)$ means calculating $\sum_{i=1}^{L} |M^i|$ separate expectation values. Furthermore, at z^*, every component of the gradient has the same value, namely $h(m)$, and at all other z the value of every component of the gradient is bounded above by $h(m)$.[61]

Unfortunately, calculating $\nabla R(z)$ exactly is prohibitively difficult for large spaces. However, we can readily estimate the components of the gradient by recasting it as a technique for improving world utility in a collective. Define $G(z \in \zeta) \equiv R(z^T \in \zeta^T)$, where z is the history of joint states of a set of agents over a sequence of T steps in an iterated game, z^t being the state at step t of the game (see Appendix D). Define z_i^t as the vector given by projecting z^t onto the ith simplex $S^{|M^i|}$, i.e., the time t-value of the vector $(z_{i,1}, z_{i,2}, \ldots, z_{i,|M^i|})$. Have all LT of the Cartesian product variables $z_1^t \times z_2^t \times \cdots z_{i-1}^t \times z_{i+1}^t \times \cdots z_L^t$ be (the value of) a generalized agent coordinate ρ_i^t, $x_i^t = z_i^t$ being the value of the associated move. So for every agent, G is a single-valued function of that agent's move and its context, as required.[62]

The dynamical restrictions coupling all these distributions gives us C. To design that dynamics, note that even though $R(z^t)$ is in no sense a stochastic function of z^t, because of functional form of its dependence on the agents' moves we can use Monte Carlo–like techniques to estimate various aspects of $R(z^t)$. In particular, we can estimate its gradient this way and then have the dynamics use that information to increase R's value from one time step to the next, hopefully reaching the maximum by time T (in which case we have ensured that G is maximized).

More precisely, at the end of each step t, each agent (i, t) independently samples its distribution z_i^t to choose one of its actions $m_i \in M^i$. That set of L samples gives

---

of the space over which we perform the gradient ascent, compared to allowing arbitrary distributions over M. However, there may be other restrictions on the allowed distribution that results in even better performance. In the translation of the gradient ascent of $R(z)$ into a collective discussed later, such alternative stochastic forms of the distribution over m would correspond to having agents each of whose moves concerns more than one of the m_i at once.

[61] To establish the first claim, simply note that z^* is a delta function, To establish the second, note that the gradient component $E(R \mid m_i = j)$ is just the expected value of R under a different distribution, z', where z' are z are equal for all components not involving M^i, but z' has a delta function for those components. Because expected R under *any* distribution is bounded above by $R(z^*)$, it must be for z'. Accordingly, each of the components of the gradient is bounded above by $h(m)$, which establishes the claim.

[62] Strictly speaking, we need to encode in either r_i^t or x_i^t the other information specifying the full history, e.g., the values of $z^{t'}$ for $t' < t$. Otherwise that pair of coordinates do not form a complement pair. For completeness, we can choose to encapsulate all such information in r_i^t, as the current value of the seed of an invertible random-number generator used for the stochastic sampling that drives the dynamics (see later). None of the analysis presented here depends on this choice.

us a full vector m^t. Next, we evaluate a function of m^t, indexed by (i, t), whose expectation (according to z^t) is the private utility for that agent. (Note that the joint action m^t is *not* the joint move of the agents at time t; that is z^t.)

Combining that function's value with other information (e.g., the similar values for i for some times $t' < t$) provides us a training set for that agent controlling variable i. This training set constitutes the worldview for agent $(i, t+1)$, $n_i^{t+1} \in v_i^{t+1}$, and is used by the learning algorithm of agent $(i, t+1)$ to form a new z_i^{t+1}. This is done by all L agents, giving us a z^{t+1}, and the process repeats.[63]

This dynamics produces a sequence of points $\{m^t\}$ in concert with a sequence of distributions $\{z^t\}$, which (if we properly choose the private utilities, learning algorithms used to update the z_i, etc.) will settle to m^* and $\delta(m - m^*)$, respectively. As an example, for all i with the function evaluated at m^t as $h(m^t)$, so that the private utility of each agent (i, t) is $R(z^t)$. Have the associated training set for (i, t) be a set of averages of $h(m)$, one average for each of the possible m_i. Have the average for choice $j \in M^i$ be formed by summing the previously recorded $h(m)$ values that accompanied each instance where m_i equaled j, where the sum is typically weighted to reflect how long ago each of those values was recorded. So each of the $|M^i|$ components of n_i^t is nothing other than a (pseudo) Monte Carlo estimate of the components for variable M^i of the gradient of $R(z)$ at the beginning of time step t.[64] In other words, they are estimates of the components of the gradient of the private utility at the current joint move.

Accordingly, let the learning algorithm for each agent $(i, t + 1)$ be the following update rule:

$$ z_i^{t+1} = z_i^t + \alpha \left[n_i^{t+1} - \frac{\sum_j n_{i,j}^{t+1}}{|M^i|} (1, 1, \ldots) \right], $$

where the term in square brackets is the projection of $v_{i,t}$ onto its unit simplex $S^{|M^i|}$, the vector $(1, 1, \ldots)$ being normal to that simplex. To keep z in its unit simplex, have α shrink the shorter the distance along $v_{i,t}$ from z_i^t to the edge of that associated simplex, $S^{|M^i|}$. The result is that each variable in the collective performs a Monte Carlo version of gradient ascent on G and therefore on h. Moreover, the learning algorithm is a reasonable choice for an agent i trying to modify its move z_i^t to increase its private utility. Accordingly, we would expect it to obey the first premise.[65]

---

[63] A faster version of this process has all of the agents at a given time share the same m rather than each use a new sample of z^t. This can introduce extra correlations between the moves of the agents, which may violate our assumption of statistical independence among the $\{M^i\}$.

[64] It would be exactly Monte Carlo if not for the steps updating the $\{z^{t' < t}\}$. It is to account for that updating that the data going into the training set is aged.

[65] Note that the updates are invariant with respect to translations upward or downward of the function h, because such a translation of h induces an identical translation in R and therefore in n_i^t. Similarly, so long as there are at least two j for which the associated $n_{i,j}^{t+1}$

Note that maximizing G is just a problem in design of collectives. This suggests many modifications of the scheme outlined earlier. In particular, one might try many other learning algorithms besides Monte Carlo gradient ascent to try to find the z that maximizes G. For example, in a **Boltzmann learning algorithm**, each z_i^t is given by a Gibbs distribution over the $|M^i|$ possible values of its variable, with the $|M^i|$ "energies" going into that distribution given by the components of v_i^t. Using the sampling scheme with this distribution may be better than gradient ascent if the tendency of the latter to get trapped circling local maxima is a concern (say due to the inaccuracy inherent in the Monte Carlo estimating of that gradient). Similarly, one can use many private utilities besides R, in particular ones that try to exploit the first premise. Moreover, all such approaches can be used even if the G and zs are not an expected utility and associated probabilities over categorical spaces, respectively. The idea of inserting learning agents into a search problem to recast it as a problem in the design of collectives is much more general.

As an example, return to the gradient ascent learning algorithm, and consider replacing $h(m)$ with some $h^*(m)$ that is factored with respect to h for variable i. This will result in a new R, R^*. The partial derivatives of R^* with respect to the $|M^i|$ components associated with the value of variable i equal the corresponding derivatives of R, up to an overall additive term that is independent of m_i. Accordingly, if we set z_i to maximize R^* rather than R, while having all other coordinates still maximize R, we will arrive at the exact same optimizing distribution over m.

Extending this, we can have each coordinate use an associated R^* based on an h^* that is factored for that coordinate, and it will still be the case that if each z_i is set to maximize the associated R^* we end up with the same delta function over m as if all coordinates were set to maximize R. However, there is one crucial way that use of R^*s differs from uniform use of R. This arises from the fact that rather than ascending the exact gradient, we are ascending a Monte Carlo estimate of it. That estimation necessarily introduces noise into the ascent. If we can minimize that noise, the ascent should be much quicker. This is what is done when we chose the h^*s to each have the smallest ambiguity possible.[66]

---

have different values, $z_i^{t+1} \neq z_i^t$; the updating never halts. This reflects the fact that there are no local maxima.

[66] There are other ways of affecting ambiguity besides the choice of private utility, of course, and they have to be traded off other factors in general. As an example, optimizing the step sizes of the agents depends on associated ambiguities. If the step sizes used by agents other than i are too big, then the gradient estimate for coordinate i will be a poor approximation of the true direction of maximal ascent. To see this, note that if the step sizes used by agents other than i are too big, then the actual context r for agent i at time step $t + 1$ will differ significantly from the r at the time step t. However, it is that latter r that determines the value n at time step $t + 1$. Having those step sizes too large means that $P(r \mid n)$ will be broad. This, in turn, usually induces broad distributions over agent i's private utility values for each of its candidate moves. Usually, this means that the ambiguity is large.

Conversely, if the step size of agent i is too small, then it will be slow in increasing the value of its private utility. While agent i benefits from having the step sizes of other agents

From this perspective, the idea of casting a search problem as a problem in design of collectives can be motivated as a way to extend gradient ascent so it can be used with categorical variables, by transforming the search to be over a numeric space. Furthermore, even if the underlying space is numeric, casting the search problem as a problem in design of collectives has the advantage over gradient ascent that it naturally allows for large jumps in that underlying space, whether the original space is categorical or numeric, the recasting has the advantage that it allows the search to be decomposed into a set of parallel searches (one for each agent). If desired, those parallel searches can then be implemented on a parallel computer.

More generally, there is nothing about this decomposition that restricts its use to cases where the original global search algorithm is gradient ascent. So, in particular, the decomposition can be used directly over a categorical space, without first transforming the search to a numeric space. Moreover, the search and learning algorithms of the individual agents in the decomposition need not be direct analogues of the original global search procedure. In particular, those individual algorithms need not restrict their agents to changing their states by an infinitesimally small amount, as in gradient ascent. All of these extra capabilities flow from recasting the search problem as a design of collectives problem.

Another modification of vanilla gradient ascent dynamics follows from noticing we are only estimating the gradient of R, rather than evaluating it exactly, and that the estimation is a variant of Monte Carlo. These observations make it natural to modify gradient ascent dynamics by inserting a simulated-annealing-style keep or reject procedure at the end of every time step. However, we cannot do the naive thing and run that keep or reject procedure on the pair of (the value of $R(z_t)$ before time step t's modification to z_t), and (that value of R after the modification). This is because we can no more evaluate R exactly than we can its gradient. However, we *do* know what the value of h is for the starting m of time step t and for the new m generated in that time step. So we can run the keep or reject procedure based on those two values of h.

In fact, we can we can always insert such a simulated-annealing-style keep-or-reject procedure at the end of each time step, regardless of the private utility function or learning algorithm. This is exactly what is done in the technique of intelligent coordinates (IC), sometimes called "computational corporations" [25]. From the perspective of design of collectives, IC was motivated as a way to improve techniques that focus exclusively on terms 2 and 3 in the central equation (e.g., by setting the private utility). By its insertion of a keep or reject procedure, IC boosts the performance of such techniques by leveraging term 1 in the central equation while not degrading terms 2 or 3. Another way of viewing IC is as a variant of a conventional simulated-annealing-style keep or reject search algorithm. In this variation each searched variable is made "smart," its exploration values being the moves of game-playing com-

---

as small as possible, its step size cannot be too small. Because this holds for all agents, we have to trade off the two effects when determining the optimal stepsize.

puter algorithms (agents), rather than as in conventional algorithms, to random samples of a probability distribution.[67]

As a final example of an approach to optimization suggested by extending this gradient ascent example, consider replacing the gradient term with the move of a learning agent in the gradient update rule, rather than replacing the z_i^t term. There are several subtleties with implementing such an idea in practice [9]. One is that typically the value of a utility will change with t even if all the agents freeze their moves with this new approach, because such freezing means that the agents are traversing the surface, only in a constant direction. This contrasts with the typical case where the learning agents set the $\{z_i^t\}$ directly and can often result in large ambiguities. Nonetheless, especially when in constrained optimization problems like graph traversal, this alternative might be the approach of choice. (See Appendix D.)

Appendix F: General Situation Where the Second Premise Holds

We will illustrate a case where $\int dn\, P(n \mid r, s) P^{[v]}(x \mid n) = \int dn\, P(n \mid r, s) P^{[v,\sigma]}(x \mid n, s)$, and therefore the second premise holds.

Consider the integral $\int dn\, P(n \mid r, s) P^{[v]}(x \mid n)$ arising in the second premise. Expand the distribution in terms of H, and for simplicity say that H does not depend on n directly. Next suppose that $P(n \mid r, s)$ is relatively peaked for fixed r and s. This provides a scale length of the ambiguity arguments of H, given by how much they vary as n moves across that peak. Say that H is a slowly varying function of its arguments on that scale length. (This is particularly reasonable if ambiguities vary little as one traverses the peak in $P(n \mid r, s)$.) Under these circumstances we can pull the integral over n inside the H to operate directly on the vector of H's n-dependent arguments, i.e., replace

$$\int dn\, P(n \mid r, s) \mid n) H_{\{A(\underline{\gamma}_\rho; n, x^i, x^j)\}}(x) \quad \to \quad H_{\{\int dn\, P(n \mid r, s) A(\underline{\gamma}_\rho; n, x^i, x^j)\}}(x).$$

Next, consider each term $\int dn\, P(n \mid r, s) A(\underline{\gamma}_\rho; n, x^i, x^j)$ appearing inside the H. If we expand that ambiguity and pull in the integral over n, we get expressions of the form $\int dn\, P(n \mid r, s) P(\underline{g}_{\rho,\sigma}(x^1, \rho)) P(\underline{g}_{\rho,\sigma}(x^2, \rho))$. Again assume $P(n \mid r, s)$ is relatively peaked, this time on the scale of variations in $P(\underline{g}_{\rho,\sigma}(x, \rho))$. This allows us to replace

---

[67] An analogue of IC is a well-run human corporation, with G the corporation's profit, the players i identified with the employees, and the associated $\underline{g}_{it}$ given by the employees' compensation at time t. The corporation is factored if each employee's compensation directly reflects its effect on G. If each compensation package also has good ambiguity, the employees can readily discern how their behavior affects their compensation. Finally, the exploration or exploitation process is analogous to management's deciding whether to maintain or abandon a particular set of decisions by the employees. These similarities are the basis of the name "computational corporation."

$$\int dn P(n \mid r, s) P(\underline{g}_{\rho,\sigma}(x^1, \rho)) P(\underline{g}_{\rho,\sigma}(x^2, \rho))$$

$$\rightarrow \int dn P(n \mid r, s) P(\underline{g}_{\rho,\sigma}(x^1, \rho) \mid n) \int dn' P(n' \mid r, s) P(\underline{g}_{\rho,\sigma}(x^2, \rho) \mid n').$$

Expand the first integral in this product as

$$\int dr' \Big[\int dn ds'_\rho \delta(\underline{g}_{s'_\rho}(x, r') - y) P(r', s'_\rho \mid n) P(n \mid r, s) \Big]$$

(and similarly for the second).

Say that the first distribution in the integrand is peaked, in s'_ρ, about some $h(n)$, and that the second one is peaked about the n lying in the preimage $h^{-1}(s)$. (This is exactly true if n specifies s precisely.) Then we can replace

$$\int dn ds'_\rho \delta(\underline{g}_{s'_\rho}(x, r') - y) P(r', s'_\rho \mid n) P(n \mid r, s)$$

$$\rightarrow \int dn \delta(\underline{g}_s(x, r') - y) P(r', s'_\rho \mid n) P(n \mid r, s).$$

We would have arrived at the exact same expression if we had made the analogous approximations in expanding $\int dn P(n \mid r, s) P^{[\nu,\sigma]}(x \mid n, s)$ instead. Hence these approximations justify the second premise. However, the second premise can hold even if not all of those approximations of peaked distributions are valid, so long as there is sufficient cancellation among the contributions from the wings of the distributions (e.g., it will hold if $\nu \subseteq \sigma$ regardless of such peakedness). So the second premise is weaker than these approximations. In fact, under those approximations, we could always replace the ambiguities arising in H with their averages according to $P(n \mid r, s)$, something we do not do in the current analysis.

Appendix G: An Alternative Definition of Ambiguity

Note that rather than $P(y^1, y^2; \psi; l, x^1, x^2)$, the difference of the distributions of utility values at x^1 and x^2, one could consider the distribution of differences,

$$P^*(y^1, y^2; \psi; l, x^1, x^2) \equiv \int dr ds P(r, s \mid l) \delta(y^1 - \psi_s(x^1, r)) \delta(y^2 - \psi_s(x^2, r)),$$

and the associated ambiguity A^*. Now almost all of the theorems and corollaries presented here hold for ambiguities based on A^* as well as A, so we could use A^* rather than A if we wanted to. Moreover, P is P^* modified to preserve the marginals of the random variables ψ^1 and ψ^2 while making those variables be independent:

$$P(y^1, y^2; \psi; l, x^1, x^2) = P^*(y^1; \psi; l, x^1, x^2) P^*(y^2; \psi; l, x^1, x^2).$$

So A^* fixes (P^* that fixes P that fixes) A, but not vice versa, i.e., A contains less information than A^*. Furthermore, of all ambiguities based on a distribution with the same marginals as P^*, A is the "widest," having the largest region in which it is neither 0 nor 1.

However, all of this does not mean that we are just being more conservative by using A rather than A^*, i.e., that we are discarding certain predictions concerning orderings of CDFs that we would make if we used A^* while keeping other such predictions. That's because in general A can shrink in going from one l to another (i.e., its value can decrease for at least one y and not increase for any y) but A^* does not, and vice versa.[68] So either choice of ambiguity may result in predictions that would not have been made with the other choice.

In this chapter we restricted attention to learning algorithms whose behavior depends on increasing or decreasing ambiguities based on A rather than on A^*. This seems to be the case for most real-world learning algorithms, and therefore A rather than A^* seems to be the appropriate quantity to plug into our results. Only if the learning algorithm exploits information in n about the relation of utility values at the same r would changes in A^* be a better predictor of associated changes in what move the algorithm is likely to make. This is rarely the case, however. For example, training sets formed in the course of multistep games (see Appendix D) contain information about utility values for move and context pairs (one such pair for each preceding time step), rather than for multiple moves in a particular context.

However, despite this, because A^* fixes A but not vice versa, parameterizing H in terms of A^* rather than A would make H more flexible. However, because the premises only involve A, not A^*, to simplify the exposition here we will write H in terms of A.

References

1. N. I. Al-Najjar and R. Smorodinsky. Large nonanonymous repeated games. *Game and Economic Behavior*, 37(26–39), 2001.
2. R.J. Aumann and S. Hart. *Handbook of Game Theory with Economic Applications, Volumes I and II*. North-Holland Press, 1992.
3. T. Basar and G. J. Olsder. *Dynamic Noncooperative Game Theory*, second edition. Siam, Philadelphia, 1999.
4. R. H. Crites and A. G. Barto. Improving elevator performance using reinforcement learning. In D. S. Touretzky, M. C. Mozer, and M. E. Hasselmo, editors, *Advances in Neural Information Processing Systems—8*, pages 1017–23. MIT Press, 1996.
5. J. Eatwell, M. Milgate, and P. Newman. *The New Palgrave Game Theory*. Macmillan Press, 1989.
6. Y. M. Ermoliev and S. D. Flam. Learning in potential games. Technical Report IR-97-022, International Institute for Applied Systems Analysis, June 1997.
7. D. Fudenberg and J. Tirole. *Game Theory*. MIT Press, 1991.
8. V. Krishna and P. Motty. Efficient mechanism design. (Preprint), 1997.

---

[68] However, it is not possible that A can shrink while A^* increases, because if A shrinks that means the difference in the expected values of ψ at x^1 and x^2 decreases while if A^* grows that difference must increase.

9. J. Lawson and D. Wolpert. The design of collectives of agents to control non-Markovian systems. In *Transactions of American Association of Artificial Intelligence Conference 2002*, 2002.

10. R. D. Luce and H. Raiffa. *Games and Decisions*. Dover Press, 1985.

11. A. Mas-Colell, M. D. Whinston, and J. R. Green. *Microeconomic Theory*. Oxford University Press, New York, 1995.

12. D. Monderer and L. S. Sharpley. Potential games. *Games and Economic Behavior*, 14:124–43, 1996.

13. N. Nisan and A. Ronen. Algorithmic mechanism design. *Games and Economic Behavior*, 35:166–96, 2001.

14. M. Osborne and A. Rubenstein. *A Course in Game Theory*. MIT Press, Cambridge, 1994.

15. D. C. Parkes. *Iterative Combinatorial Auctions: Theory and Practice*. Ph.D. thesis, University of Pennsylvania, 2001.

16. P. Tucker and F. Berman. On market mechanisms as a software techniques. Technical Report CS96–513, University of California, San Diego, December 1996.

17. K. Tumer and D. H. Wolpert. Overview of collective intelligence. In D. H. Wolpert and K. Tumer, editors, *The Design and Analysis of Collectives*. Springer-Verlag, New York, 2002.

18. D. H. Wolpert. The lack of a priori distinctions between learning algorithms and the existence of a priori distinctions between learning algorithms. *Neural Computation*, 8:1341–90,1391–421, 1996.

19. D. H. Wolpert. A mathematics of bounded rationality. (in preparation), 1999.

20. D. H. Wolpert and J. Lawson. Designing agent collectives for systems with Markovian dynamics. In *Proceedings of the First International Joint Conference on Autonomous Agents and Multi-agent Systems*, Bologna, Italy, July 2002.

21. D. H. Wolpert and W. G. Macready. No free lunch theorems for optimization. *IEEE Transactions on Evolutionary Computation*, 1(1):67–82, 1997. Best Paper Award.

22. D. H. Wolpert and M. Millonas. Experimental tests of the theory of collectives. Available at http://ic.arc.nasa.gov/dhw, 2003.

23. D. H. Wolpert and K. Tumer. Optimal payoff functions for members of collectives. *Advances in Complex Systems*, 4(2/3):265–79, 2001.

24. D. H. Wolpert and K. Tumer. Collective intelligence, data routing and Braess' paradox. *Journal of Artificial Intelligence Research*, 16:359–87, 2002.

25. D. H. Wolpert, K. Tumer, and E. Bandari. Improving search algorithms by using intelligent coordinates. 2003, submitted.

26. D. H. Wolpert, K. Tumer, and J. Frank. Using collective intelligence to route Internet traffic. In *Advances in Neural Information Processing Systems—11*, pages 952–8. MIT Press, 1999.

27. G. Zlotkin and J. S. Rosenschein. Coalition, cryptography, and stability: Mechanisms for coalition formation in task oriented domains (Preprint), 1999.

3

On Learnable Mechanism Design

David C. Parkes*

Summary. Computation is increasingly distributed across open networks and performed by self-interested autonomous agents that represent individuals and businesses. Given that these computational agents are often in situations of strategic interaction, it is natural to turn to economics for ideas to control these systems. Mechanism design is particularly attractive in this setting, given its focus on the design of optimal rules to implement good systemwide outcomes despite individual self-interest. Yet these rich computational environments present new challenges for mechanism design, for example, because of system dynamics and because the computational cost of implementing particular equilibrium outcomes is also important. We discuss some of these challenges and provide a reinterpretation of the mathematics of collective intelligence in terms of *learnable mechanism design* for bounded-rational agents.

1 Introduction

Far from confined to a desktop machine, computation is now ubiquitous and is performed by heterogenous and networked computers, many of which are operated by and used on behalf of self-interested users. As such, computational systems increasingly exhibit the properties of economies, and it is natural to turn to incentive-based methods to construct systems with useful systemwide behaviors. Indeed, as an alternative to traditional cooperative or adversarial assumptions in computer science, a reasonable design principle for many distributed systems is that computational devices will be programmed to follow selfish, self-interested behaviors [13, 52].

The framework of *economic mechanism design* (e.g., [27]) provides a rich theoretical backdrop for an economically motivated approach to the control of decentralized computational systems. Mechanism design was first proposed as a method to implement social choices (e.g., [7, 23]). More recently, mechanism design has been adapted to implement outcomes that are individually optimal for a single agent, for example, in the setting of *optimal auction design* [41].

* Division of Engineering and Applied Sciences, Harvard University, 33 Oxford Street, Cambridge, MA 02138 parkes@eecs.harvard.edu

The key problem addressed within mechanism design is the *information problem*, in which agents have private information that the mechanism must elicit to implement a good systemwide outcome. Participants must receive appropriate incentives to reveal information truthfully. This incentive-compatibility requirement limits the outcomes that can be implemented in a game-theoretic equilibrium (e.g., [42]). However, in certain contexts it has been possible to propose *strategy-proof* mechanisms in which no participant can manipulate an outcome to their own benefit whatever the strategy of any other agent [56].

In this chapter, we introduce some of the basic methods of mechanism design, and we briefly discuss some of the new challenges in the application of ideas from mechanism design to distributed computational systems. We focus here on the particular problem of mechanism design in the presence of bounded-rational agents that employ simple learning methods to adjust toward an equilibrium. We suggest a collective-intelligence-inspired approach for mechanism design in repeated games with these simple adaptive agents. No background is assumed in mechanism design or collective intelligence.

We first review the mathematics of mechanism design and the mathematics of collective intelligence. Then we reinterpret the *factoredness* and *informative* methods of collective intelligence in the context of *incentive-compatibility* (truth revelation in equilibrium) and *learnable* mechanism design, in which payments are selected to enable computational agents to learn equilibrium strategies. In particular, we introduce a VCG-WLU mechanism, which is a hybrid of the Groves [23] family of mechanisms and the *wonderful life* local utility [58] of collective intelligence. We present simple experimental results, for a simple auction problem and a simple congestion problem, to demonstrate the advantages of this approach to mechanism design. In closing, we consider a broader agenda of *learnable mechanism design* in which mechanisms are explicitly constructed to maximize their performance with respect to a model of limited agent rationality.

2 Mechanism Design

We begin with a formal introduction to mechanism design theory, and then we outline some problems with the approach as applied to distributed and dynamic computational systems. The problems arise because of practical limits on the amount of computation and communication that is reasonable within a system. For a more complete review of mechanism design, see Jackson [27], chapter 23 of MasColell et al. [37], or chapter 2 of Parkes [46].

The mechanism design (MD) approach to solving problems in decentralized systems with self-interested agents is to formulate the design problem as an optimization problem. The parameters of the design are the kinds of strategies that will be available to agents, specified, for example, by the bidding language in an auction and the rules used to determine an outcome based on agent actions, for example, rules to determine the winning bids in an auction.

Perhaps the most successful application of MD has been to the theory of auctions. In recent years auction theory has been applied to the design of a number of real-world markets [38].

The fundamental assumption made in MD is that participants in a mechanism will follow a game-theoretic equilibrium strategy. Simply stated, each agent is expected to select actions that maximize its expected utility, given the strategies of the other agents and the rules of the game, as specified by the mechanism. As such, MD makes a strong behavioral assumption agents and the information available to agents and then selects the mechanism that will maximize some systemwide performance measure, such as seller revenue, with respect to the behavioral assumption.

As an example, suppose that a number of users are competing for access to the data-staging capabilities on a data server located in Times Square. In MD the valuations of users for different amounts of disk space are private, and the problem is to design incentives, for example, through the calculation of appropriate payments, to allocate disk space to maximize the total value across users. One cannot simply request that users report their valuations and then make an allocation based on reported valuations, because self-interested agents can be expected to overstate their values. Rather, a useful mechanism must design the rules of the game to provide incentives for agents to announce truthful information about their preferences for different outcomes.

2.1 Mechanism Design: Preliminaries

A mechanism defines a set of feasible *strategies* that restrict the kinds of messages that agents can send to the mechanism. A mechanism also fixes a particular *outcome rule*, which selects an outcome based on agent strategies.[1] Game-theoretic methods are used to analyze the properties of a mechanism under the assumption that agents are rational and will follow expected utility-maximizing strategies in equilibrium, given beliefs about the strategies of other agents and knowledge of the rules of the mechanism.

Formally, a mechanism, $\mathcal{M} = (S, x)$, defines a strategy space, S, and an *outcome rule*, $x : S^N \rightarrow \mathcal{O}$. The outcome rule selects outcome $x(s')$ in some abstract set $\mathcal{O}$, given strategy profile $s' = (s_1(\theta_1), \dots, s_N(\theta_N))$. A strategy defines an action for an agent in all possible states of the mechanism. For example, a strategy in an ascending-price auction defines when an agent will bid and what price an agent will bid, for all possible states of the auction. The outcome rule in the auction takes these strategies, and then implements the choice (an allocation and payments) based on the strategies.

An agent, $i \in \mathcal{I}$, has a *type*, $\theta_i \in \Theta$. This captures all the *private* information about an agent that is relevant to its preferences for different outcomes. Formally, a

---

[1] A mechanism must be able to make a commitment to use these rules. Without this commitment ability the equilibrium of a mechanism can quickly unravel. For example, if an auctioneer in a second-price auction cannot commit to selling the item at the second price then the auction looks more like a first-price auction [50].

type, θ_i, defines an agent's utility, $u_i(o, \theta_i)$, for outcome $o \in \mathcal{O}$. A complete strategy description, $s_i : \Theta_i \to \mathcal{S}$, defines a strategy, $s_i(\theta_i')$, for each possible type, $\theta_i' \in \Theta_i$. Given a strategy profile, $s' = (s_1', \ldots, s_N')$ and outcome rule x', then agent i's utility is $u_i(x(s'), \theta_i)$.

A mechanism is said to *implement* a social choice function, $f : \Theta^N \to \mathcal{O}$, if

$$x(s_1^*(\theta_1), \ldots, s_N^*(\theta_N)) = f(\theta), \quad \forall \theta \in \Theta^N,$$

where s^* denotes an equilibrium strategy profile, given an outcome rule, x, and strategy space, S. A number of different equilibrium solution concepts are typically considered, including *Bayesian-Nash* (BNE), *ex post Nash*, and *dominant strategy*.[2] Dominant strategy implementations are particularly robust because they do not require agents to have correct beliefs about the types of other agents or beliefs that other agents will play an equilibrium strategy. Ex post Nash equilibra also have useful robustness properties.

Two important classes of mechanisms are *direct revelation* and *indirect revelation* mechanisms. A mechanism is a direct revelation mechanism (DRM) if the strategy space available to an agent is restricted to its space of types, i.e. $S_i = \Theta_i$. In words, an agent can only make a claim to the mechanism about its preferences. An indirect mechanism is any mechanism in which the strategy space is something other than the type space of an agent. Computational concerns aside, the *revelation principle* [21, 22] states that it is possible to restrict attention to DRMs, with no loss in implementation power. In particular, anything that can be implemented in some complex mechanism $\mathcal{M}$ can also be implemented in a DRM. The intuition is that if mechanism $\mathcal{M}$ implements SCF, $f(\theta)$, in equilibrium, then we can construct a DRM, $\mathcal{M}'$, that will implement the same SCF by simulating agent equilibrium strategies and mechanism $\mathcal{M}$ within mechanism $\mathcal{M}'$. Moreover, the revelation principle states that it is sufficient to consider mechanisms in which agents will choose to announce truthful information about their preferences in equilibrium. These truthful and direct-revelation mechanisms are referred to as *incentive-compatible* mechanisms.

The revelation principle allows an analytic solution to the MD problem in a number of interesting design problems. Examples of solved MD problems include: the *bargaining problem* [6, 42] in which there is a single buyer and a single seller; the single-item *optimal auction* design problem [41] in which a seller wishes to maximize her expected revenue; and the *efficient mechanism design problem* in which the objective is to allocate resources to maximize the total value across agents.

---

[2] A strategy profile, s^*, is a Bayesian-Nash equilibrium if it maximizes the expected utility to every agent, given the strategies of the other agents and beliefs about the distribution over agent types. Every agent is assumed to have probabilistic information about the types of the other agents. All agents have the same information, and this is common knowledge. A strategy profile, s^*, is an *ex post* Nash equilibrium strategy if it is a utility-maximizing strategy for every agent given the strategies of the other agents, and *whatever* the types of the other agents. In a dominant strategy equilibrium, strategy $s_i^*(\theta_i)$, for every i, is a utility-maximizing strategy whatever the strategies and types of the other agents.

2.2 Example: Efficient Mechanism Design

It is illustrative to present the well-known Vickrey-Clarke-Groves (VCG) mechanism [7, 23, 56]. The VCG mechanism is an incentive-compatible DRM for the *efficient allocation problem*. In this setting, the outcome space, $\mathcal{O}$, is defined in terms of a choice, k, from a discrete set of possible choices, $\mathcal{K}$, and payments, $p = (p_1, \ldots, p_N)$, where p_i is the payment *by* the mechanism to each agent. Agents are assumed to have quasilinear utility functions, such that $u_i(k, p_i) = v_i(k, \theta_i) + p_i$, given choice k, payment p_i, and type θ_i. In an auction setting, an agent's type, θ_i, defines its valuation function. The systemwide objective is to implement a choice, $k^* \in \mathcal{K}$, that maximizes the total value across all agents. We can imagine that a choice, k, specifies an allocation of resources across agents. Given this, an efficient mechanism must always select the choice to maximize the total value.

By the revelation principle, we can focus on incentive-compatible DRMs. The outcome rule is defined in terms of an *allocation rule*, $g : \Theta \rightarrow \mathcal{K}$, and a *payment rule*, $p : \Theta \rightarrow \mathbb{R}^N$. Given reported types, $\hat{\theta}$, choice $g(\hat{\theta})$ is implemented and agent i makes payment $p_i(\hat{\theta})$.

The goal of efficiency, combined with incentive compatibility (IC), pins down the allocation rule:

$$g_{\text{eff}}(\theta) = \arg\max_{k \in \mathcal{K}} \sum_{i \in \mathcal{I}} v_i(k, \theta_i) \qquad \text{(EFF)}$$

for all $\theta \in \Theta$. The remaining problem is to choose a payment rule that provides incentive compatibility.

A particularly strong version of incentive compatibility is that of *strategy-proofness*, in which truth revelation is a dominant strategy, i.e. utility-maximizing whatever the strategies or preferences of other agents. Formally, strategy-proofness requires that the allocation and payment rules satisfy the following constraints:

$$v_i(g(\theta_i, \theta_{-i}), \theta_i) - p(\theta_i, \theta_{-i})$$
$$\geq v_i(g(\hat{\theta}_i, \theta_{-i}), \theta_i) - p(\hat{\theta}_i, \theta_{-i}), \qquad \forall i, \forall \theta_i, \forall \hat{\theta}_i, \forall \theta_{-i}. \qquad \text{(SP)}$$

Strategy-proofness is a useful property because agents can play their equilibrium strategy without game-theoretic modeling or counterspeculation about other agents.

The Groves [23] mechanisms completely characterize the class of efficient and strategy-proof mechanisms [22]. The payment rule in a Groves mechanism is defined as:

$$p_{\text{groves},i}(\hat{\theta}) = \sum_{j \neq i} v_j(g_{\text{eff}}(\hat{\theta}), \hat{v}_j) - h_i(\hat{\theta}_{-i}),$$

where $h_i : \Theta_{-i} \rightarrow \mathbb{R}$ is an arbitrary function on the reported types of every agent except i or simply a constant. The Groves payment rule internalizes the externality placed on the other agents in the system by the reported preferences of agent i and aligns each agent's incentives with the systemwide goal of allocative efficiency.

To understand the strategy-proofness of the Groves mechanisms, consider the utility of agent i, $u_i(\hat{\theta}_i)$, from reporting type $\hat{\theta}_i$, given g_{eff} and p_{groves}, and fix the reported types, θ_{-i}, of the other agents. Then, $u_i(\hat{\theta}_i) = v_i(g_{\text{eff}}(\hat{\theta}_i, \theta_{-i}), \theta_i) + p_{\text{groves},i}(\hat{\theta}_i, \theta_{-i})$, and substituting for p_{groves}, we have $u_i(\hat{\theta}_i) = v_i(g_{\text{eff}}(\hat{\theta}_i, \theta_{-i}), \theta_i) + \sum_{j \neq i} v_j(g_{\text{eff}}(\hat{\theta}_i, \theta_{-i}), \theta_j) - h_i(\theta_{-i})$. Truth revelation maximizes the sum of the first two terms by construction, and the final term is independent of the reported type. This holds for all reported types from other agents, and strategy-proofness follows.

From within the class of Groves mechanisms, the Vickrey-Clarke-Groves (VCG) mechanism is especially important because it minimizes the expected total payments by the mechanism to the agents, across all incentive-compatible, efficient, and *individual-rational* (IR) mechanisms [33]. An IR mechanism is one in which participation is voluntary and agents can choose not to participate. In the VCG mechanism, the payment $p_{\text{vcg},i}$ is computed as:

$$p_{\text{vcg},i}(\hat{\theta}) = \sum_{j \neq i} v_j(g_{\text{eff}}(\hat{\theta}_{-i}), \hat{\theta}_j) - \sum_{j \neq i} v_j(g_{\text{eff}}(\hat{\theta}), \hat{\theta}_j),$$

where $g_{\text{eff}}(\hat{\theta}_{-i})$ is the efficient allocation as computed with agent i removed from the system. For a single-item allocation problem, this VCG mechanism reduces to the well-known Vickrey [56] auction, which is a second-price sealed-bid auction.

The VCG mechanism has received considerable attention within computer science and operations research in recent years, in particular in application to distributed optimization problems with self-interested agents (e.g., [43, 46]). In Section 4, we will draw some connections between the payments in the VCG mechanism and the mathematics of collective intelligence.

2.3 Computational Considerations

Computational and informational considerations are largely missing from economic mechanism design. Simply stated, mechanism design assumes that *all equilibria have the same cost*. In fact, a pair of otherwise equivalent mechanisms can have equilibrium solutions with vastly different computational properties.

Briefly, some computational considerations that can impact the choice of a mechanism in practice include:

- The *computational cost*, both to agents to compute an equilibrium strategy and to the mechanism to compute the outcome based on agent strategies. Strategy-proof mechanisms are one compelling class of mechanisms that do not place an unreasonable game-theoretic burden on participants. Approximations to strategy-proof mechanisms that are intractable to implement have been suggested for some problems, where the goal is to retain strategy-proofness and simplify the problem facing the mechanism infrastructure (e.g., [35, 43]).
- The *informational cost* of computing an equilibrium. Direct revelation mechanisms require that agents submit complete and exact information about their types, to enable the mechanism to compute optimal outcomes for all possible reports from other agents. This can be unreasonable, for example, when the preference elicitation problem involves collecting information from users or solving

hard optimization problems to evaluate different outcomes, of which there can be exponentially many. In comparison, agents can often compute equilibrium strategies in indirect mechanisms with approximate information about their own types [8, 45, 49]. For example, in an ascending-price auction an agent can bid with upper and lower bounds on its value for the item. A number of recent studies consider the design of mechanisms in settings with costly preference elicitation [9, 25, 47], and the communication complexity of mechanisms [24, 44].

The basic idea in all of the aforementioned approaches to computational MD is to reduce the complexity of the proposed solution until the equilibrium of the mechanism is computable.

A fundamentally different approach is to perform MD with respect to a model of the bounded rationality of an agent. For example, to determine the optimal mechanism given a model of *satisficing* agent behavior, such as myopic best response to prices, or simple reinforcement-learning behavior. Although some studies have considered the performance of different mechanisms for models of bounded rational agents [8, 48, 49], there are currently no theories for the design of optimal mechanisms with respect to an explicit model of bounded rational agent behavior. It is an intriguing challenge, to develop an analytically tractable, yet meaningful, model of agent bounded rationality.

The mathematics of collective intelligence provides some useful insights into the challenging issues that agent bounded rationality introduced into mechanism design. In particular, the methods of collective intelligence suggest a third approach, in which mechanisms are designed to explicitly support *convergence* toward equilibrium outcomes by *simple adaptive agents*. We pick up on this in more detail in Section 4.

2.4 Dynamic Considerations

Another place where traditional MD breaks down is in its assumption that all agents are present in a system and able to reveal their type information simultaneously within the mechanism. This assumption is often unreasonable in dynamic systems, for example, in open network environments such as the Internet, where multiperiod and asynchronous interactions across anonymous and shifting agent populations is a more reasonable model [17].

It is interesting to consider the *online mechanism design problem*, in which agents are continually entering and leaving a system and the goal is to make both truth revelation of valuations and truthful announcements of arrival an equilibrium of the system (see Friedman and Parkes [18]). Online MD is interesting, for example, in the context of ad hoc network formation across peer-to-peer WiFi networks in which services maintain robust *overlay* networks as nodes enter, leave, and fail.

Once an agent's arrival and departure times are introduced into its type, the revelation principle continues to apply and reduces the problem to the space of mechanisms in which agents truthfully announce their type, and therefore also their arrival time, in equilibrium. However, standard approaches, such as the family of Groves mechanisms, only provide strategy-proof solutions in combination with optimal *on-line* algorithms that are able to make optimal sequential allocation decisions as agents arrive and announce their type. Relaxing to Bayesian-optimal online algorithms corresponds to Bayesian-Nash incentive-compatible mechanisms [18]. A simpler special case of the online MD problem occurs when it is reasonable to assume *truthful arrivals*, which can be justified if agents are myopic and react to the current state of the system as soon as they arrive. The online-truthful problem remains interesting because the sequential-decision aspect of the problem is retained.

This problem of online mechanism design with myopic agents is closely related to the problem of endogenous network and group formation in economics (e.g. [10,11,26,28]). In this work, agents arrive into a system and choose an action to maximize their myopic utility.[3] The focus is on identifying which network structures can emerge from a sequence of myopic decisions by self-interested agents. A typical setting is one of *network formation*, in which agents choose how to add a new link into a network. Recently, there has also been some attention to a *stochastic* model of network formation, in which agents arrive by some random arrival process and then take a myopic decision (e.g., [57]). Dutta and Jackson [11] identify the mechanism design approach as an important future direction for the study of network formation, where payoff division rules are imposed by a designer to promote the emergence of useful networks.

Finally, there is an interesting comparison to be drawn between the online mechanism design problem and the recent literature on utility-based models to explain the existence and generation of complex networks with particular statistical properties (see, e.g., [1]). On one hand, one can view the structure and statistics of complex networks from the perspective of solving a constrained global optimization problem [5]. On the other hand, recent models have provided local optimization-based models to explain the existence of complex networks [12]. It is interesting to ask whether there is an opportunity to leverage mechanism design in the positioning of appropriate local incentives to align local agent decisions with optimal systemwide performance, in order to encourage the emergence of complex networks with desirable topologies and statistical properties.

3 Collective Intelligence

In this section we review the mathematical theory of collectives (see "Theory of Collective Intelligence" for an introduction to collective intelligence). We provide a simple treatment that will enable a useful comparison to be drawn with the mathematics of economic mechanism design. Although there are a number of important differences between collectives and the traditional setting of mechanism design, it will be useful to draw parallels between mechanism design and collective intelligence.

The main distinction between collective intelligence (COIN) and MD is that the approach of collective intelligence is fundamentally an *indirect* paradigm. Rather

---

[3] A few studies that have considered an extensive form game model of the sequential decisions by a fixed set of agents; see, for example, Aumann & Myerson [3].

than focusing on direct-revelation mechanisms, in which agents reveal private information to the mechanism, which implements a particular outcome, the COIN approach implements an optimal systemwide outcome through the direct actions of agents.

Another distinction between COIN and MD is that in COIN it is assumed to be possible to *directly* set the utility functions of agents in order to guide their choices. In comparison, MD is more constrained because a designer can only indirectly influence agent payoffs via choice of the payment and outcome rules.

Additional distinctions between COIN and MD include:

- **No private information.** The center in COIN is assumed to have enough information about local agent preferences to compute the systemwide value for a particular state.
- **Limited rationality.** The theory of COIN allows agents to have limited rationality, including agents that follow simple best-response dynamics in response to an evolving multiagent system.

Finally, COIN has typically been implemented in *multiple-period* problems, in which agents are able to adjust their strategies across time. In comparison, MD has traditionally been applied to static environments.[4]

The ability to adjust payoffs directly, coupled with the absence of private information, would render the COIN problem trivial from an MD perspective, because there are no incentive issues to solve. However, COIN focuses instead on *computational goals*, such as providing payoffs to enable a system of bounded-rational agents to quickly adjust to good systemwide outcomes. This focus in COIN nicely complements the obsession with incentives, but has relative complacency about computational issues, within MD.

3.1 Collective Intelligence: Preliminaries

We define in this section a standard and simple COIN model. To maintain notational consistency with MD, our notation will necessarily depart from the notation in "Theory of Collective Intelligence."

Let $t \geq 1$ denote the time period and θ_i^t denote the *type* of agent i. The type in COIN is used analogously to the type in MD and is intended to capture any information that is relevant to the behavior and preferences of an agent. Because agents in COIN may be bounded-rational, and not necessarily game-theoretic, the type in COIN captures information that relates to an agent's computational and belief state, in addition to its preferences. Furthermore, the type is indexed with time period, t, and is allowed to change across periods to reflect changing preferences and changing computational state. Finally, in the standard COIN model the type can be directly controlled by the system designer.

---

[4] One exception within mechanism design is the work on repeated implementation [30], in which the center aims to implement an outcome in the long run as agent strategies converge toward a Nash equilibrium.

An agent follows a *strategy*, s_i^t, which captures information about the actions taken by the agent in period t. Taken together, the strategy and the type of an agent define its *state*, which is denoted $\xi_i^t = (s_i^t, \theta_i^t)$. Notation, $\xi_i = (\xi_i^1, \xi_i^2, \dots)$, denotes the time sequence of states for agent i, $\xi^t = (\xi_1^t, \dots, \xi_N^t)$, denotes the state of all agents in period t, and $\xi = (\xi^1, \xi^2, \dots)$ denotes the total state across all periods. The individual utility, $u_i(\theta_i^t, \xi) \geq 0$, of agent i, is defined over the total state, ξ, of the system, and is evaluated here with respect to its type at time t. Shorthand, $u_i^t(\xi)$, is used to denote the restriction to states up to and including period t.

The designer's goal is to maximize the systemwide utility across all states, denoted $G(\xi)$. Shorthand, $G^t(\xi)$, is used to denote the restriction to the social value for time periods up to and including t. The systemwide utility can depend on both the strategies and types of agents and need not be the sum over the individual agent utilities, but they can be quite general.

The central solution concept in COIN is that of a *factored system*. A system is factored if the individual utility of every agent is always aligned with the systemwide utility:

$$u_i^t(\xi) = G^t(\xi) - \Gamma_i \left(f_{-i}(\xi^1, \dots, \xi^t) \right) \qquad \text{(FAC)}$$

for all agents i and all time periods t. The function, $f_{-i}(\xi^1, \dots, \xi^t)$, takes only the components of states, $\xi^1, \dots, \xi^t$, that are *independent* of any state information related to agent i, and Γ_i is an arbitrary function over that state information. In words, a collective is factored if and only if a change at time t to the state of agent i alone, when propagated across time, will result in an increased utility to agent i if and only if it results in an increase to the systemwide utility.

The factoredness of a system is a stronger concept than the game-theoretic implementation concept in indirect MD. The main difference is that every agent should always want to select its own strategy to maximize the social value, $G(\xi)$, *whatever* the state of the system. In comparison, an incentive-compatible mechanism that implements a particular social-choice function must only ensure that an agent's incentives are aligned with the social good *when other agents also play an equilibrium strategy*. In this aspect, the factoredness solution concept of COIN is reminiscent of the strategy-proof solution concept of MD (although applied here to indirect mechanisms), in that it does not require on-equilibrium play of other agents.

We can readily verify that factoredness is sufficient to implement the choice that maximizes the systemwide utility, $G(\xi)$, in a dominant-strategy equilibrium. Let ξ^* denote the optimal social choice. Consider agent i. The states, ξ_i^*, represent a best-response choice because

$$\xi^* = \arg\max_{\xi} G(\xi) \Rightarrow \xi_i^* = \arg\max_{\xi_i'} G(\xi_i', \xi_{-i}^*) - \Gamma_i \left(f_{-i}(\xi^*) \right)$$

$$\Rightarrow \xi_i^* = \arg\max_{\xi_i'} u_i(\xi_i', \xi_i^*).$$

However, we observe that full factoredness is a strong property and is not necessary for a system of agents to maximize the value of G in equilibrium. As an example, suppose that each agent selects an action $s_i \in [0, 1]$ and that $G(s_1, s_2) = f(s_1)f(s_2)$, where $f(x)$ is a Gaussian function with mean 0.5 and variance 1. Now, suppose that the system is factored for agent 1, with $u_1(s_1, s_2) = f(s_1)f(s_2)$, but not factored for agent 2, with

$$u_2(s_1, s_2) = \begin{cases} f(s_2), & \text{if } s_1 \in [0.5 - \epsilon, 0.5 + \epsilon] \\ 1 - f(s_2), & \text{otherwise} \end{cases}$$

for some small $\epsilon > 0$. Despite this failure of factoredness, the system is factored in the neighborhood of the optimal systemwide outcome of $s^* = (0.5, 0.5)$, and this is a stable outcome.

Factoredness is a useful property for a dynamic system because it implies that a rational agent will always play to maximize the social value of the choice whatever the actions of other agents, and therefore gives useful robustness and stability properties in environments with bounded-rational, or faulty, agents.

3.2 Informative Local Utilities

The key challenge in COIN is to select factored local utilities to promote good convergence to a desired state. COIN agents are modeled as simple bounded-rational agents, rather than as traditional game-theoretic agents. In particular, the standard COIN model assumes that agents play a myopic best-response strategy as the state of a system evolves, given their current beliefs about payoffs for different strategies.

Given a particular systemwide utility, $G(\xi)$, the designer in COIN retains some flexibility in choice of factored utility functions for individual agents. Specifically, the designer can choose the functions Γ_i and f_{-i} in (FAC). The theory of collective intelligence demonstrates that utility functions that are better able to isolate the effect of an individual agent's strategy on the systemwide utility are more *informative* for simple learning agents and improve the rate of convergence to optimal systemwide agent strategies.

An example of a factoring choice with *poor* information properties is to set up a *team game* [40], with

$$u_{\text{TG},i}^t(\xi) = G^t(\xi).$$

This is clearly factored, because every agent's utility is exactly that of the overall system. However, team game utilities are not very informative because the marginal effect of an agent's own action on the system utility is likely to be masked by the effect of the actions of the other agents.

In developing a factored utility, it is important that the function, f_{-i}, leaves only components of states $(\xi^1, \ldots, \xi^t)$ that are *independent* of the states corresponding to agent i. It is not, in general, sufficient to remove only those states, $(\xi_i^1, \ldots, \xi_i^t)$, that pertain directly to agent i, because an earlier strategy of agent i can affect the strategy and beliefs of another agent in a later round. Instead, it is also necessary to remove any states for other agents that are potentially affected by the state of agent i in some earlier round. This is referred to as the *effect set* of agent i and is denoted $eff(i)$. The independent states are denoted $\xi \setminus eff(i)$, with shorthand ξ_{-i}.

Another idea for a factored local utility is presented by the *aristocratic utility* (AU), in which:

$$u^t_{AU,i}(\xi) = G^t(\xi) - E_{\xi' \in eff(i)}\left[G^t(\xi_{-i}, \xi')\right]. \tag{AU}$$

The expectation is defined with respect to current beliefs over the probability of different states in the effect set of an agent.[5] This aristocratic utility is maximally informative, with respect to a reasonable definition of the information provided by a reinforcement signal [58].

In the special case of a repeated single-stage game, the effect set of agent i is simply its own state, and the aristocratic utility simplifies to

$$u_{AU,i}(\xi) = G(\xi) - E_{s'_i \in S_i}\left[G(\xi_{-i}, s'_i)\right],$$

where the time index, t, is dropped, set S_i denotes the space of legal actions for agent i, and the expectation is taken with respect to the distribution of actions played by agent i.

Another idea for a factored local utility is presented by the *wonderful life utility* (WLU). This can be a useful approximation to AU, in particular when AU is itself difficult to compute. In WLU the states in the effect set of agent i are replaced with a single "clamped" set of states:

$$u^t_{WLU,i}(\xi) = G^t(\xi) - G^t(\xi_{-i}, CL_i), \tag{WLU}$$

where CL_i, is the *clamping factor*. This clamping defines a fixed strategy for every agent in the effect set of agent i across all periods.

In the special case of an iterated single-stage game the wonderful life utility simplifies to:

$$u_{WLU,i}(\xi) = G(\xi) - G(\xi_{-i}, CL_i),$$

where the time index, t, is dropped, and $CL_i \in S_i$ is some fixed strategy for agent i. This is factored for any choice of clamping factor.

3.3 Back to VCG Mechanisms

Interestingly, the WLU factored local utility function brings us full circle, back to the Vickrey-Clarke-Groves mechanism that was introduced in Section 2 as a canonical example of a strategy-proof solution in economic mechanism design.

Consider the special case of a WLU with clamping factor, $CL_i = \emptyset$, to represent a null move by agent i. In this case an agent's utility for some strategy ξ is equal to the marginal contribution of its own strategy to the systemwide utility. Thus, WLU with a null clamping factor implements the same equilibrium outcome as the VCG

---

[5] It is important to notice in this construction that the dynamics of the combined state (ξ_{-i}, ξ') *do not need to be consistent with the dynamical laws of the system. They are purely used as a counterfactual operator* [54].

mechanism in the special case of a revelation game in which agent strategies define the revelation of type information and the systemwide utility is the sum of individual agent utilities.

Looking at COIN, both theoretical and experimental results suggest that it is better to use a WLU with a clamping factor that is equal to an agent's *expected* move. This provides a mean-field approximation to the AU, which has provably optimal informative properties. This suggests that the informativeness of the information provided by payments in an economic mechanism will be of interest in environments in which simple but self-interested agents are learning optimal strategies through best-response dynamics and should be considered in selecting the appropriate mechanism from the class of Groves mechanisms. We pick up this theme in Section 4, where we introduce a COIN-inspired approach to MD for repeated games with simple adaptive agents.

3.4 Example: A Congestion Game

In this section, we present an example of COIN in the setting of a congestion game and review experimental results from Wolpert and Tumer [58]. Consider a simple variation on the *El Farol bar problem* [2]. Each player is deciding which night in the week to attend a bar; if too few people attend the bar is boring but if too many people attend the bar is too crowded. This is a simple *coordination game*, in which the systemwide goal is to spread the attendance evenly across the nights.

Formally, there are N players and seven nights, and every player wants to attend for the same number of nights, l. The value of l, which is selected from set $\{1, \ldots, 6\}$, defines different variations of the game. In particular, as l increases, the bar will become more crowded. In each period t, every player chooses a strategy, s_i^t. This defines a vector of 0s and 1s, e.g., (0110000), to indicate which nights the player will attend.

Given the joint strategies, $s^t = (s_1^t, \ldots, s_N^t)$, the systemwide utility for a particular week, t, is

$$G(s^t) = \sum_{k=1}^{7} \phi(x_k(s^t)),$$

where $x_k(s^t)$ is the total attendance on night k. The congestion function, $\phi(x) = x\, e^{-x/c}$ for some $c \geq 0$, and attendance x, captures the idea that the bar should not be too empty or too crowded on any single night. The function is maximized for an attendance of exactly c. The optimal systemwide outcome has players making a coordinated decision, with the same number of players attending on each night.

Notice that this problem has characteristics that are consistent with the COIN approach but different from the MD approach. First, the systemwide utility function is known to the mechanism. Second, the protocol is an indirect mechanism in which the outcome is determined directly by the strategies of the players.

Experimental results [58] compare the performance of different WLUs for different clamping factors. This is an iterated single-stage game, so the effect set for player i is simply its strategy in period t and the clamping factor defines a static strategy.

Clamping factors $CL_i = \overrightarrow{0}$, $CL_i = \overrightarrow{1}$, and $CL_i = \overrightarrow{1/7}$ are considered. Notice that it is not necessary that the clamping factors are legal moves. Let $k_i(s_i)$ denote the nights that player i chooses to attend with strategy s_i. Then, WLU for clamping factor $CL_i = (CL_{i1}, \ldots, CL_{i7})$, is defined as:

$$u_{\text{WLU},i}(s_i) = \sum_{k=1}^{7} \phi(x_k(s)) - \left[\sum_{k \notin k_i} \phi(x_k(s) + CL_{ik}) + \sum_{k \in k_i} \phi(x_k(s) - 1 + CL_{ik}) \right].$$

The mean-field approximation clamping factor, $CL_i = \overrightarrow{1/7}$ (i.e., with each player assuming that the nights are well-balanced), is shown to outperform the other WLUs, with the $\overrightarrow{0}$ clamp outperforming the $\overrightarrow{1}$ clamp except when the $\overrightarrow{1}$ clamp is a good approximation to the mean-field clamp. This can occur as congestion increases and the number of nights that a player wants to attend approaches six. The experimental results also demonstrate that all *difference* methods, with $u_i(\xi) = G(\xi) - \Gamma(f_{-i}(\xi))$, are more effective than team game methods, with $u_i(\xi) = G(\xi)$.

4 Learnable Mechanism Design for Episodic Systems

One approach to the problem of mechanism design with bounded-rational agents is to consider agents with simple learning algorithms that can adjust toward Nash equilibrium strategies [17,51]. Indeed, there is an established literature that considers the ability of agents to *learn* to play equilibria in games [19, 20, 31, 53]. The emphasis is on *simple* learners that can adjust, for example, through myopic best-response toward equilibrium strategies. A useful *learnable mechanism* would provide information, for example, via price signals, to maximize the effectiveness with which individual agents can learn equilibrium strategies.

Given the focus on methods to address agents with limited rationality in COIN, it is interesting to reinterpret the methods of COIN in terms of designing learnable mechanisms for episodic systems, such as iterated single-stage games. The methods of COIN suggest a new criteria for selecting a mechanism from within the Groves family of mechanisms, namely to provide informative signals to agents that are using simple learning methods to adjust toward equilibrium play.

4.1 The VCG-WLU Mechanism

Consider the following multiperiod MD problem. Each period, t, is a single-stage game that is repeated across periods. There is a set of choices, $\mathcal{K}$, to implement in each period, and the goal is to implement the efficient choice, k^*, which maximizes $\sum_i v_i(k, \theta_i)$, where $v_i(k, \theta_i) \geq 0$ is the value of agent i for choice k and θ_i is the type of agent i. Consider a direct-revelation mechanism, with strategy space $S_i = \Theta_i$ for each agent, and choice rule,

$$g_{\text{eff}}(\hat{\theta}) = \max_{k \in \mathcal{K}} \sum_i (v_i(k, \hat{\theta}_i)),$$

for types $\hat{\theta} = (\hat{\theta}_1, \ldots, \hat{\theta}_N)$. Given this choice rule, the systemwide utility function from COIN is

$$G(\hat{\theta}) = \sum_i v_i(g_{\text{eff}}(\hat{\theta}), \theta_i).$$

Of course, in MD, there is uncertainty about this systemwide utility because types, θ_i, are private to agents. Consider a Groves mechanism, with payment

$$p_{\text{groves},i}(\hat{\theta}) = \sum_{j \neq i} v_j(g_{\text{eff}}(\hat{\theta}), \hat{\theta}_j) - h_{-i}(\hat{\theta}_{-i}),$$

to agent i given reported types $\hat{\theta}$, and some arbitrary function, h_{-i}, on the reported types of all agents except i.

These payments, combined with outcome rule g_{eff}, *induce* individual utility functions on agents:

$$u_i(\hat{\theta}_i, \hat{\theta}_{-i}) = v_i(g_{\text{eff}}(\hat{\theta}), \theta_i) + \sum_{j \neq i} v_j(g_{\text{eff}}(\hat{\theta}), \hat{\theta}_j) - h_{-i}(\hat{\theta}_{-i}).$$

These individual agent utility functions are not always factored. However, they are factored when other agents, $j \neq i$, follow equilibrium strategies and $\hat{\theta}_{-i} = \theta_{-i}$. This follows from the incentive compatibility of Groves mechanisms:

$$u_i(\hat{\theta}_i, \hat{\theta}_{-i}) = v_i(g_{\text{eff}}(\hat{\theta}_i, \theta_{-i}), \theta_i) + \sum_{j \neq i} v_j(g_{\text{eff}}(\hat{\theta}_i, \theta_{-i}), \theta_j) - h_{-i}(\theta_{-i})$$

$$= G(\hat{\theta}_i, \hat{\theta}_{-i}) - h_{-i}(\hat{\theta}_{-i}).$$

Although the Groves payments do not make the agent utilities factored out of equilibrium, they are still sufficient to provide convergence toward equilibrium. For any strategy, $\hat{\theta}_{-i}$, from agents $j \neq i$, the best response, $s_{\text{br},i}(\hat{\theta}_{-i})$, of agent i is truth revelation:

$$s_{\text{br},i}(\hat{\theta}_{-i}) = \arg\max_{\theta_i' \in \Theta_i} u_i(\theta_i', \hat{\theta}_{-i})$$

$$= \arg\max_{\theta_i' \in \Theta_i} \left[v_i(g_{\text{eff}}(\theta_i', \hat{\theta}_{-i}), \theta_i) + \sum_{j \neq i} v_j(g_{\text{eff}}(\theta_i', \hat{\theta}_{-i}), \hat{\theta}_j) - h_{-i}(\hat{\theta}_{-i}) \right]$$

$$= \theta_i.$$

This property follows directly from the strong dominant-strategy truth-revelation properties of Groves mechanisms.

Economic MD suggests using additional properties, such as individual rationality and revenue maximizing to select the function h_{-i} and choose a particular Groves mechanism. As an example, the VCG mechanism, with $h_{-i}(\hat{\theta}_{-i}) = \sum_{j \neq i} v_j(g_{\text{eff}}(\hat{\theta}_{-i}))$, is popular because it maximizes the expected revenue across all individual rational and efficient solutions [34].

In comparison, the theory of COIN suggests that a better choice than VCG payments for a mechanism in which agents are bounded rational and adjusting toward an equilibrium is to set:

$$h_{-i}(\hat{\theta}_{-i}) = v_i(g_{\mathrm{eff}}(\bar{\theta}_i, \hat{\theta}_{-i}), \bar{\theta}_i) + \sum_{j \neq i} v_j(g_{\mathrm{eff}}(\bar{\theta}_i, \hat{\theta}_{-i}), \hat{\theta}_j), \qquad \text{(VCG-WLU)}$$

where $\bar{\theta}_i$ is the *ex ante* average type of agent i. This is analogous to setting a WLU utility, in which the clamping parameter is set to the average action of player i. We will call this hybrid the *VCG-WLU* mechanism.

This payment rule forfeits *ex post* individual rationality, because the equilibrium utility to an agent is:

$$u_i(\theta) = \sum_i v_i(g_{\mathrm{eff}}(\theta), \theta_i) - \left(v_i(g_{\mathrm{eff}}(\bar{\theta}_i, \theta_{-i}), \bar{\theta}_i) + \sum_{j \neq i} v_j(g_{\mathrm{eff}}(\bar{\theta}_i, \theta_{-i}), \theta_j) \right).$$

This equilibrium utility is negative, unless $\theta_i \geq \bar{\theta}_i$.

However, the following is sufficient to retain *ex ante* individual rationality, such that the expected utility to agent i is nonnegative:

$$\mathrm{E}_{\theta_i} \left[\sum_j v_j(g_{\mathrm{eff}}(\theta_i, \theta_{-i}), \theta_j) \right] \geq v_i(g_{\mathrm{eff}}(\bar{\theta}_i, \theta_{-i}), \bar{\theta}_i) + \sum_{j \neq i} v_j(g_{\mathrm{eff}}(\bar{\theta}_i, \theta_{-i}), \theta_j)$$

for every θ_{-i}. This requirement is explored in the following example.

Example. Consider a Vickrey auction for a single item, in which the agent type, $\theta_i \in [0, 1]$ specifies an agent's value for the item. Then *ex ante* IR requires:

$$\mathrm{E}_{\theta_i} \left[\max(\theta_i, \theta_{-i}) \right] \geq \max(\bar{\theta}_i, \theta_{-i}), \quad \forall \theta_{-i},$$

where $\bar{\theta}_i = 0.5$. Let $x(\theta_{-i}) = \max_{j \neq i} \theta_j$; then we require:

$$\mathrm{E}_{\theta_i} \left[\max(\theta_i, x) \right] \geq \max(\bar{\theta}_i, x), \quad \forall x.$$

By case analysis on x, this holds trivially when $x \geq 0.5$, and when $x < 0.5$ we have:

$$\mathrm{E}_{\theta_i} \left[\max(\theta_i, x) \right] = x + \int_{v=x}^{1} v - x \, dv = x + 1/2 - x + x^2/2 \geq 1/2 = \max(\bar{\theta}_i, x).$$

Thus, the payments suggested by the WLU clamping $\bar{\theta}_i$ satisfy *ex ante* IR in this simple example.

In the following sections we present experimental results to compare the effectiveness of the VCG-WLU mechanism with the VCG mechanism in an auction problem with simple adaptive agents, and also for a variant of the congestion game introduced in Section 3.4.

4.2 Example: Auction Game

Consider a simple allocation problem, in which there is a single item to allocate N agents each with type, θ_i, uniformly distributed between 0 and 1. The type of an agent defines its value for the item. Let $x_i = 1$ if agent i receives the item, and $x_i = 0$ otherwise, with $\sum_i x_i \leq 1$ for all feasible allocations. The utility of agent i for outcome x and payment p_i from the mechanism is

$$u_i(x, p_i, \theta_i) = \begin{cases} \theta_i + p_i, & \text{if } x_i = 1 \\ p_i, & \text{otherwise.} \end{cases}$$

The social choice function is to maximize the allocative efficiency of the outcome, with

$$G(x, \theta) = \sum_i x_i \theta_i$$

for feasible allocation x. A Groves mechanism for this single-item allocation problem first asks each agent to report its type and then implements the outcome $x(\hat{\theta})$ that maximizes $G(x, \hat{\theta})$ such that $\sum_i x_i \leq 1$, $x_i \in \{0, 1\}$. Agent i receives payment

$$p_{\text{groves},i}(\hat{\theta}) = \sum_{j \neq i} v_j(x(\hat{\theta}), \hat{\theta}_j) - h_{-i}(\hat{\theta}_{-i})$$

for some arbitrary function, h_{-i}, defined on the reported types θ_{-i} for agents $j \neq i$. We consider the following choices to complete the payment definitions:

$$h_{-i}(\hat{\theta}_{-i}) = \max_{j \neq i} \hat{\theta}_j \qquad \text{(VCG)}$$

$$h_{-i}(\hat{\theta}_{-i}) = 0 \qquad \text{(Groves-TG)}$$

$$h_{-i}(\hat{\theta}_{-i}) = \max(\bar{\theta}, \max_{j \neq i} \hat{\theta}_j) \qquad \text{(VCG-WLU)}$$

where $\bar{\theta}$ is the *average* type, in this example equal to 0.5.

Putting this together and assuming that agent 1 announces the highest type and agent 2 announces the second-highest type, the payment rules simplify to:

$$p_{\text{vcg},i} = \begin{cases} -\hat{\theta}_2, & \text{if } i = 1 \\ 0, & \text{otherwise} \end{cases}$$

$$p_{\text{TG},i} = \begin{cases} 0, & \text{if } i = 1 \\ \hat{\theta}_1, & \text{otherwise} \end{cases}$$

$$p_{\text{WLU},i} = \begin{cases} -\max(\bar{\theta}, \hat{\theta}_2), & \text{if } i = 1 \\ \hat{\theta}_1 - \max(\bar{\theta}, \hat{\theta}_1), & \text{otherwise.} \end{cases}$$

In our experiments we adopt the approach in Wolpert and Tumer [58] and use a simple reinforcement learning algorithm for individual agents. Each agent, i, considers a linear strategy $\hat{\theta}_i = k\theta_i$, for some $k \in \{0.6, 0.7, 0.8, 0.9, 1, 1.1\}$, and maintains a six-dimensional vector to estimate the utility it receives for each strategy. Let $\pi_i^t(k)$ denote the utility estimate by agent i in period t for strategy k. At the beginning of each period each agent picks the strategy to announce at random, using a Boltzmann distribution defined over the six components of the estimated utility vector. In particular, the probability of playing strategy k is proportional to $e^{(\pi_i^t(k)/temp^t)}$. The parameter, $temp^t$, controls the amount of exploration in period t.

At the end of each period the mechanism reports the allocation, x, and the payment p_i to each agent and the agent computes its utility for the outcome and updates its estimates. For example, if agent i plays strategy k in period t and receives utility π, then its new estimate for strategy k is computed as $\pi_i^{t+1}(k) = (1-\lambda^t)\pi_i^t(k)+\lambda^t\pi$. The parameter, λ^t, controls the amount of adjustment in period t.[6] An uninformative prior sets each component of the estimated utility vector to the average utility received during an initial training period in which all agents choose random strategies. Finally, the parameters, $temp^t$, and λ^t, are adjusted across periods according to decay factors $0 < \alpha < 1$ and $0 < \beta < 1$, with $temp^{t+1} = \alpha temp^t$ and $\lambda^{t+1} = \beta \lambda^t$.

In all experiments the initial temperature, $temp^1$, is equated to the average utility during the initial training period, and the decay rate, β, for the learning rate is set to fix the learning rate at the end of the final period to 0.001. We experimentally optimized the choice of the initial learning rate, λ^1, and the temperature decay rate, α, for each different choice of design with a logarithmic search in parameter space to select parameters that maximized the *average* efficiency and minimized the *average* distance to the equilibrium strategy across all periods.

Experimental Results. In the first set of experiments we considered an auction with five agents, and we set the initial training period to 200 periods and the learning period to 2000 periods. All results are averaged over 40 runs. In the second set of experiments we considered an auction with three agents, having noticed that the payments in VCG approximate those in VCG-WLU and are different only when the average value of an agent is greater than the second-highest reported value. For these experiments the initial training period was 200, and the learning period was 1000. As with five agents, the results are averaged over 40 runs.[7]

Figures 1 and 2 compare the performance of the mechanisms in the five-agent and three-agent settings. First, we plot the convergence of agent strategy to the equilibrium strategy, which is truth revelation in all auctions. Given N agents, we compute the *mean absolute error* in each period, as $1/N \sum_i |k_i - k^*|$, where k_i is the strategy selected by agent i and $k^* = 1$ is the equilibrium strategy.

Second, we plot the *efficiency* of the outcome in each period, which is the ratio of the value of the item to the agent that receives the item to the value of the agent with the maximum value. In both cases, we find it convenient to plot the *moving*

---

[6] The use of this weighted average over an exponential decay function reflects the fact that the environment is nonstationary.

[7] With five agents, the parameters (α, λ^1) were set to $(0.9973, 0.05)$, $(0.9978, 0.2)$ and $(0.9969, 0.1)$ in auctions VCG, VCG-WLU, and TG, respectively. With three agents, the parameters (α, λ^1) were set to $(0.9944, 0.2)$, $(0.9955, 0.1)$, and $(0.9932, 0.1)$.

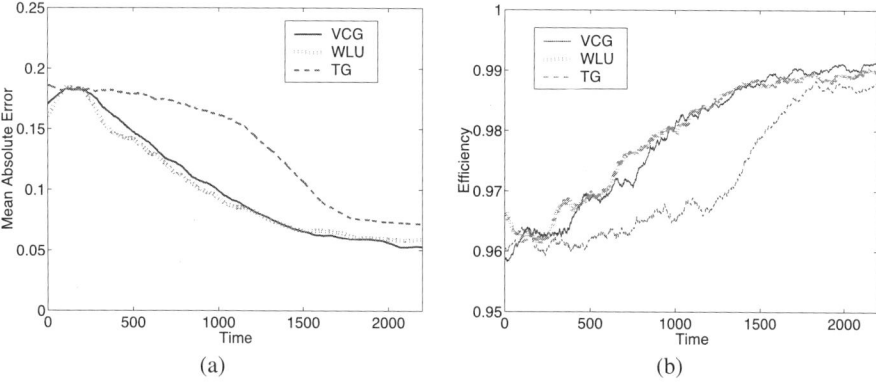

Figure 1. The auction problem with five agents, comparing the VCG, VCG-WLU, and TG payment rules. Learning begins after 200 periods: (a) Moving average of the mean absolute error between agent strategies and truth revelation; (b) moving average of the efficiency of the auction.

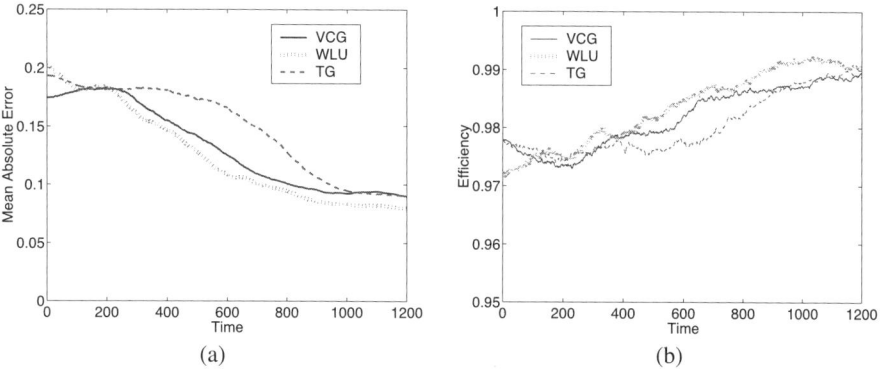

Figure 2. The auction problem with three agents, comparing the VCG, VCG-WLU, and TG payment rules. Learning begins after 200 periods: (a) Moving average of the mean absolute error between agent strategies and truth revelation; (b) moving average of the efficiency of the auction.

averages (with a window size of 100). This smooths out random fluctuations from period to period due to Boltzmann learning. Also, the first 200 periods represent the initialization period, in which agents select random strategies.

As expected, the performance of the VCG and VCG-WLU auctions dominates that of the TG auction with simple learning agents. Moreover, the VCG-WLU method appears to slightly outperform the VCG method during the early learning periods with five agents, in terms of both the accuracy of agent strategies and the average efficiency. In addition, the effect of VCG-WLU is more striking with three agents, with the COIN-inspired VCG payments providing a clear performance advantage over the regular VCG payments.

4.3 Example: Congestion Game

We illustrate the VCG-WLU mechanism on a direct-revelation variation of the congestion game. Consider a simple variation on Arthur's El Farol bar problem. There are N players, one bar, and one night. The problem is interesting because the *type* of each player defines its *tolerance* for congestion and is private to each player. Moreover, it is not certain which players will attend the bar.

On any night, the problem is to decide which players attend the bar. Let $y_i \in \{0, 1\}$ denote whether player i attends the bar (with $y_i = 1$ for attendance). Then, given a solution $y = (y_1, \ldots, y_N)$, player i with type θ_i has value:

$$v_i(y, \theta_i) = \begin{cases} x \, e^{x/\theta_i}, & \text{if } y_i = 1 \\ 0, & \text{otherwise,} \end{cases}$$

where $x = \sum_i y_i$.

Given types, $\theta = (\theta_1, \ldots, \theta_N)$, the systemwide goal is to implement a solution in which the attendance, y^*, maximizes the total value:

$$\max_y \sum_i v_i(y, \theta_i). \tag{1}$$

The problem is to strike a compromise between the different preferences of players for the level of crowdedness in the bar. For example, if enough players prefer a crowded bar then it can be beneficial from the systemwide perspective to make players attend even if that makes it more crowded than desirable for other players.

The difference from the earlier congestion game (in Section 3.4) is that the mechanism itself implements a particular attendance profile and must elicit information about player types to implement an optimal solution.

The Groves mechanism for this problem first asks players to report their type, $\hat{\theta}_i$, and then implements the outcome, $y(\hat{\theta})$, that solves Equation 1 given the reported types. Player i receives payment

$$p_{\text{groves},i}(\hat{\theta}) = \sum_{j \neq i} v_j(y(\hat{\theta}), \hat{\theta}_j) - h_{-i}(\hat{\theta}_{-i}),$$

where, as before, h_{-i} is some arbitrary function on the reported types of the other players. We again consider the particular variations that implement the VCG, VCG-WLU, and TG payments. The VCG payments require that the mechanism computes an alternative solution without each player in attendance, while the VCG-WLU payments require that the mechanism computes an alternative solution with the type of each player replaced, in turn, with the average player type.

Experimental Results. First, we consider the congestion game with eight players and possible types θ_i selected uniformly at random from $\{1, 2, 3, 4, 5, 6\}$. Second, we consider this congestion game with four players and possible types $\{1, 2, 3\}$. We use the same Boltzmann learning method as in the auction example. Each player

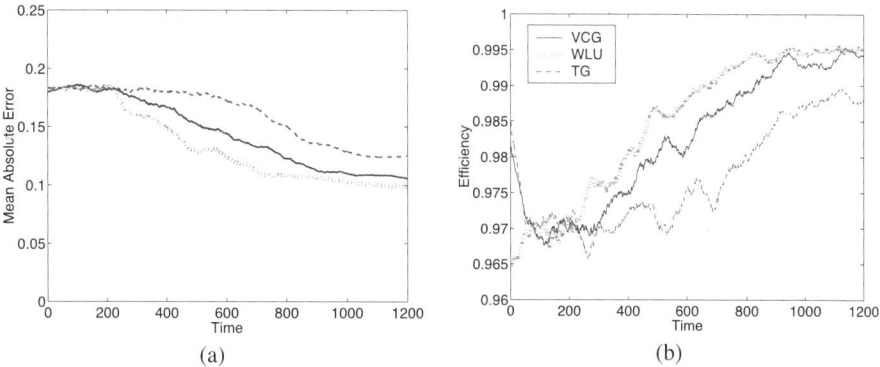

Figure 3. The congestion problem with eight players, comparing the VCG, VCG-WLU, and TG payment rules. Learning begins after 200 periods: (a) moving average of the mean absolute error between player strategies and truth revelation; (b) moving average of the efficiency of the outcome.

considers a linear strategy $\hat{\theta}_i = k\theta_i$, for some $k \in \{0.6, 0.7, 0.8, 0.9, 1, 1.1\}$ and maintains an estimate of the utility for each strategy. This induces a Boltzmann distribution to define a probability with which the player selects a particular strategy. Utility estimates are again initially set to an uninformative prior, during an initial training period in which all players follow random strategies. We experimentally optimized the choice of initial learning rate and temperature decay rate for each different choice of design.[8]

In the eight-player variation, we set the initial training period to 200 and the learning period to 1000. In the four-player variation, we set the initial training period to 100 and the learning period to 500. The eight-player results are averaged over 20 runs and the four-player results are averaged over 60 runs. Again, we were interested in comparing the eight-player and four-player variations, because we expected the VCG-WLU-to-VCG comparison to be more noticeable with fewer players.

Figures 3 and 4 compare the performance of the mechanisms in the eight-player and four-player settings. We plot the mean absolute error between the player strategies and truthful strategies in each period, and the efficiency of the outcome in each period, which in this problem is measured as the ratio between the total value of the implemented outcome to the total value of the optimal outcome. We plot the moving averages (window size of 50) to smooth out the random fluctuations due to Boltzmann learning.

As in the auction example, the performance of the TG mechanism with simple learning agents, in terms of both the speed of convergence toward an equilibrium strategy and the overall efficiency across periods, is dominated by both the VCG and the VCG-WLU mechanisms. Most striking in this congestion game example, is that

---

[8] For eight players, the parameters (α, λ^1) were set to $(0.9947, 0.2)$, $(0.9978, 0.05)$, and $(0.9932, 0.05)$ in the VCG, VCG-WLU, and TG mechanisms, respectively. For four players, the parameters were set to $(0.9865, 0.1)$, $(0.9991, 0.02)$, and $(0.9861, 0.2)$.

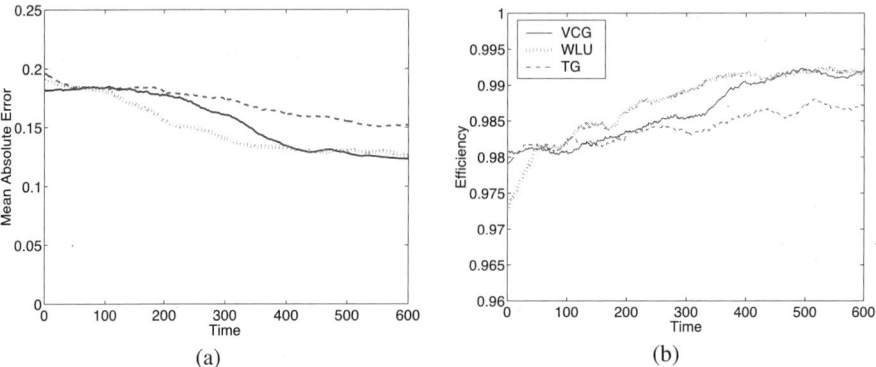

Figure 4. The congestion problem with four players, comparing the VCG, VCG-WLU, and TG payment rules. Learning begins after 100 periods: (a) moving average of the mean absolute error between player strategies and truth revelation; (b) moving average of the efficiency of the outcome.

the performance of VCG-WLU mechanism itself dominates that of the VCG mechanism, both for the eight-player and the four-player variations. This provides some experimental justification for a collective-intelligence-inspired approach to mechanism design in the presence of bounded-rational agents.

5 Summary: Toward Learnable Mechanism Design

The integration of methods from COIN into methods in mechanism design can be viewed as a first step toward learnable mechanism design. Learnable mechanism design is a natural direction to take mechanism design in complex decentralized settings. Classic mechanism design formulates an explicit *normative* model of the equilibrium behavior of an agent and selects mechanism rules that are optimal with respect to that model. In particular, the Myerson program formulates the problem as a constrained optimization problem in which one selects an outcome rule that maximizes a set of desiderata subject to incentive-compatibility constraints. In contrast, the idea presented in learnable mechanism design is to design a mechanism that is optimal with respect to a *behavioral* model of bounded-rational agents, and in particular to worry about the performance along the path toward equilibrium as well as in equilibrium itself.

The methods in this chapter assume simple Boltzmann learners and adopt the idea of informative utilities from COIN to select an instance of the Groves family of mechanisms in which payments to agents are especially informative in the feedback they provide about the effect of an agent's choice of strategy on individual utility. But this opens up many interesting questions. In particular, there has been an explosion of research into algorithms to compute Nash equilibrium (and special classes of equilibrium such as correlated equilibrium) in game-theoretic settings (e.g., [29, 32, 55]) and to identify tractable special cases of the equilibrium-computation problem (e.g., [36]). Many of the algorithms have a best-response and learning flavor (e.g., [14–16,31,39]). A natural question arises: Can we design mechanisms that induce games that have computable equilibrium or equilibria that are readily computed by simple learning agents?

In addition to identifying classes of mechanisms that induce game-theoretic situations with good computational properties, we can consider whether there is a role for *automated mechanism design* in which the rules of mechanisms are automatically adjusted *online* to provide robustness against unmodeled properties of a real system, such as those due to the limited rationality of participants.

Acknowledgments. The author has benefited from discussions with Laszlo Gulyas, Eric Friedman, Chaki Ng, Margo Seltzer, and David Wolpert. This work was supported in part by grant NCC 2-5505 from NASA Ames.

References

1. R. Albert and A.-L. Barabasi. Statistical mechanics of complex networks. *Rev. Mod. Phys.*, 74:47–97, 2002.
2. W. Brian Arthur. Inductive reasoning and bounded rationality. *AEA Papers and Proceedings*, 84(2):406–11, 1994.
3. R. Aumann and R. Myerson. Endogeneous formation of links between players and coalitions. In Al Roth, editor, *The Shapley Value*, pages 175–91. Cambridge University Press, 1988.
4. C. Boutilier. A pomdp formulation of preference elicitation problems. In *Proc. 18th National Conference on Artificial Intelligence (AAAI-02)*, July 2002. to appear.
5. J. M. Carlson and J. Doyle. Highly optimized tolerance: A mechanism for power laws in designed systems. *Physics Review E*, 60(2):1412–27, 1999.
6. K. Chatterjee and W. Samuelson. Bargaining under incomplete information. *Operations Research*, 31:835–51, 1983.
7. E. H. Clarke. Multipart pricing of public goods. *Public Choice*, 11:17–33, 1971.
8. O. Compte and P. Jehiel. Auctions and information acquisition: Sealed-bid or dynamic formats? Technical report, CERAS and UCL, 2002.
9. W. Conen and T. Sandholm. Preference elicitation in combinatorial auctions. In *Proc. 3rd ACM Conf. on Electronic Commerce (EC-01)*. ACM Press, New York, 2001.
10. B. Dutta and S. Mutuswami. Stable networks. *Journal of Economic Theory*, 76:322–44, 1997.
11. B. Dutta and M. O. Jackson. On the formation of networks and groups. In B. Dutta and M. O. Jackson, editors, *Models of the Strategic Formation of Networks and Groups*. Heidelberg: Springer-Verlag, 2002.
12. A. Fabrikant, E. Koutsoupias, and C. H. Papadimitriou. Heuristically optimized tradeoffs: A new paradigm for power laws in the Internet. In *Proc. STOC'02*, 2002.
13. J. Feigenbaum and S. Shenker. Distributed algorithmic mechanism design: Recent results and future directions. In *Proceedings of the 6th International Workshop on Discrete Algorithms and Methods for Mobile Computing and Communications*, pages 1–13, 2002.
14. D. P. Foster and R. Vohra. Calibrated learning and correlated equilibrium. *Games and Economic Behavior*, 1997.

15. D. P. Foster and R. Vohra. Regret in the on-line decision problem. *Games and Economic Behavior*, pages 7–36, 1999.
16. Y. Freund and R. E. Schapire. Adaptive game playing using multiplicative weights. *Games and Economic Behavior*, 29:79–103, 1999.
17. E. Friedman and S. Shenker. Learning and implementation in the internet. Preprint. Available at: http://www.aciri.org/shenker/decent.ps, 1997.
18. E. Friedman and D. C. Parkes. Pricing WiFi at Starbucks—Issues in online mechanism design. In *Fourth ACM Conf. on Electronic Commerce (EC'03)*, 2003 (shorter version). Extended version available at http://www.eecs.harvard.edu/~parkes/pubs/online.pdf.
19. D. Fudenberg and D. M. Kreps. Learning mixed equilibria. *Games and Economic Behavior*, 5:320–67, 1993.
20. D. Fudenberg and D. Levine. *Theory of Learning in Games*. MIT Press, 1997. forthcoming.
21. A. Gibbard. Manipulation of voting schemes: A general result. *Econometrica*, 41:587–602, 1973.
22. J. Green and J.-J. Laffont. Characterization of satisfactory mechanisms for the revelation of preferences for public goods. *Econometrica*, 45:427–38, 1977.
23. T. Groves. Incentives in teams. *Econometrica*, 41:617–31, 1973.
24. R. Holzman, N. Kfir-Dahav, D. Monderer, and M. Tennenholtz. Bundling equilibrium in combinatorial auctions. Technical report, Technion and Stanford, 2001.
25. B. Hudson and T. Sandholm. Effectiveness of preference elicitation in combinatorial auctions. In *Agent Mediated Electronic Commerce IV: Designing Mechanisms and Systems*, volume 2531 of *Lecture Notes in Artificial Intelligence*. 2002.
26. M. O. Jackson and A. Wolinsky. A strategic model of social and economic networks. *Journal of Economic Theory*, 71:44–74, 1996.
27. M. O. Jackson. Mechanism theory. In *The Encyclopedia of Life Support Systems*. EOLSS Publishers, 2000.
28. M. O. Jackson. The stability and efficiency of economic and social networks. In Murat Sertel, editor, *Advances of Economic Design*. Springer-Verlag, 2001. forthcoming.
29. S. Kakade, M. Kearns, J. Langford, and L. Ortiz. Correlated equilibria in graphical games. In *Proc. 4th ACM Conf. on Electronic Commerce*, 2003.
30. E. Kalai and J. O. Ledyard. Repeated implementation. *Journal of Economic Theory*, 83(2):308–17, 1998.
31. E. Kalai and E. Lehrer. Rational learning leads to Nash equilibrium. *Econometrica*, 61(5):1019–45, 1993.
32. M. Kearns, M. L. Littman, and S. Singh. Graphical models for game theory. In *Proc. of Conf. on Uncertainty in Artificial Intelligence*, pages 253–60, 2001.
33. V. Krishna. *Auction Theory*. Academic Press, 2002.
34. V. Krishna and Motty Perry. Efficient mechanism design. Technical report, Pennsylvania State University, 1998. Available at: http://econ.la.psu.edu/~vkrishna/vcg18.ps.
35. D. Lehmann, L. O'Callaghan, and Y. Shoham. Truth revelation in rapid, approximately efficient combinatorial auctions. In *Proc. 1st ACM Conf. on Electronic Commerce (EC-99)*, pages 96–102, 1999.
36. M. Littman, M. Kearns, and S. Singh. An efficient exact algorithm for singly connected graphical games. In *Neural Information Processing Systems*, 2002.
37. A. MasColell, M. D. Whinston, and J. R. Green. *Microeconomic Theory*. Oxford University Press, 1995.
38. P. Milgrom. *Putting Auction Theory to Work*. MIT Press, 2002.
39. M. Littman and P. Stone. A polynomial-time Nash equilibrium algorithm for repeated games. In *Proc. 4th ACM Conf. on Electronic Commerce*, 2003.

40. D. Monderer and L. S. Shapley. Potential games. *Games and Economic Behavior*, 14: 124–43, 1996.

41. R. B. Myerson. Optimal auction design. *Mathematics of Operation Research*, 6:58–73, 1981.

42. R. B. Myerson and Mark A Satterthwaite. Efficient mechanisms for bilateral trading. *Journal of Economic Theory*, 28:265–81, 1983.

43. N. Nisan and A. Ronen. Algorithmic mechanism design. *Games and Economic Behavior*, 35:166–96, 2001.

44. N. Nisan and I. Segal. The communication complexity of efficient allocation problems. Technical report, Hebrew University and Stanford University, 2002.

45. D. C. Parkes. Optimal auction design for agents with hard valuation problems. In *Proc. IJCAI-99 Workshop on Agent Mediated Electronic Commerce*, pages 206–19, July 1999. Stockholm.

46. D. C. Parkes. *Iterative Combinatorial Auctions: Achieving Economic and Computational Efficiency*. Ph.D. thesis, Department of Computer and Information Science, University of Pennsylvania, May 2001. Available at: http://www.cis.upenn.edu/~dparkes/diss.html.

47. D. C. Parkes. Price-based information certificates for minimal-revelation combinatorial auctions. In *Agent Mediated Electronic Commerce IV: Designing Mechanisms and Systems*, volume 2531 of *Lecture Notes in Artificial Intelligence*. 2002.

48. D. C. Parkes, J. R. Kalagnanam, and M. Eso. Vickrey-based surplus distribution in combinatorial exchanges. In *Proc. 17th International Joint Conference on Artificial Intelligence (IJCAI-01)*, 2001.

49. D. C. Parkes and L. H. Ungar. Iterative combinatorial auctions: Theory and practice. In *Proc. 17th National Conference on Artificial Intelligence (AAAI-00)*, pages 74–81, July 2000.

50. R. P. McAfee and J. McMillan. Auctions and bidding. *Journal of Economic Literature*, 25:699–738, June 1987.

51. S. Shenker. Making greed work in networks: A game-theoretic analysis of switch service disciplines. In *SIGCOMM Symposium on Communications Architectures and Protocols*, pages 47–57, 1994.

52. J. Shneidman and D. C. Parkes. Rationality and self-interest in peer to peer networks. In *2nd Int. Workshop on Peer-to-Peer Systems (IPTPS'03)*, 2003.

53. S. Singh, M. Kearns, and Y. Mansour. Nash convergence of gradient dynamics in general-sum games. In *Proc. UAI'00*, 2000.

54. K. Tumer and D. H. Wolpert. Collective intelligence and Braess' paradox. In *Proc. 17th National Conference on Artificial Intelligence (AAAI-00)*, pages 104–9, 2000.

55. D. Vickrey and D. Koller. Multi-agent algorithms for solving graphical games. In *Proc. National Conf. on Artificial Intelligence (AAAI'02)*, 2002.

56. W. Vickrey. Counterspeculation, auctions, and competitive sealed tenders. *Journal of Finance*, 16:8–37, 1961.

57. A. Watts. A dynamic model of network formation. *Games and Economic Behavior*, 34: 331–41, 2001.

58. D. H. Wolpert and K. Tumer. Optimal payoff functions for members of collectives. In *Advances in Complex Systems*. 2001.

Asynchronous Learning in Decentralized Environments: A Game-Theoretic Approach

Eric J. Friedman*

1 Introduction

Many of the chapters in this book consider collectives that are cooperative; all agents work together to achieve a common goal—maximizing the "world utility function." Often this is achieved by allowing agents to behave selfishly according to some "personal utility function," although this utility function is explicitly imposed by the designer so is not truly "selfish." In this chapter we consider the problems that arise when agents are truly selfish and their personal utility functions are intrinsic to their behavior. As designers we cannot directly alter these utility functions arbitrarily; all we can do is to adjust the ways in which the agents interact with each other and the system in order to achieve our own design goals. In game theory, this is the mechanism design problem, and the design goal is denoted the "social choice function" (SCF).[1]

Note that these design goals may be distinct from the agents' goals. For example, the most common SCFs to keep in mind are the utilitarian (or maximizing) SCF, which simply maximizes the sum of all the agents' personal utility functions, or the egalitarian (or fair) SCF, which maximizes the value of the smallest personal utility function or some combination of these two, combining maximization and fairness. However, the designer's SCF might be unrelated to the agents' personal utility functions. This commonly occurs in auctions, where the designer's goal is to maximize revenue.

Our main interest in this problem arises from problems on the Internet, in which agents may be either users or autonomous agents (bots). While, in the not-so-distant past agents could, with some level of accuracy, be assumed to be cooperative, this is no longer a reasonable assumption for a modern analysis of the Internet. This is clearly true at the user level, where users may behave selfishly but is probably even

* School of Operations Research and Industrial Engineering, Cornell University, Ithaca, NY 14853 friedman@orie.cornell.edu

[1] This chapter is meant to be self-contained (but telescopic) at an informal level. For a more complete introduction to mechanism design, see [10, 14].

necessary at lower levels such as network protocols, because the Internet is made up of many profit-maximizing autonomous systems.[2]

For example, the current stability of the Internet can be attributed to the fact that most traffic uses the standard TCP protocol, which reacts to congestion on the network by reducing its transmission rate. This is necessary to avoid "congestive collapses," which plagued the Internet in the mid-1980s and led to many crashes of significant parts of the Internet. This is no longer a significant problem due to the near universal adoption of congestion control.[3]

However, from a selfish point of view, congestion control is detrimental to an individual agent, because if everyone else is using it, then an agent can unilaterally increase their utility by disabling it on their own TCP connection. A single user disabling congestion control is obviously not a threat to the stability of the Internet; however, if everyone did it then one could expect frequent congestive collapses and everyone would suffer. Thus, the design of protocols, for which agents do not have strong incentives to circumvent, is, we believe, one of the fundamental tasks for the continued development and health of the Internet.

In this chapter we will provide an intuitive introduction to our work on this subject. The formal analysis can be found in [8]; details of the simulations are in [11], and the experiments are discussed in [9].

2 Mechanism Design

It is useful to formulate our problems according to the mechanism design paradigm. We assume that there is a set of feasible outcomes $p \in P$. For example, in a simplified version of the TCP example discussed earlier, p describes the complete state of the system, which includes every agent's transmission rate and delays. Clearly, by adjusting priorities in the network (such as in routers) one can feasibly redistribute delays; however, it is not possible to eliminate such delays completely, and this restricts the choice of the set P.

Next we assume that agents have utilities over outcomes, $U(p) \in \mathcal{U}^n$, where $\mathcal{U}$ is the set of possible utility functions. For example, it would be natural to assume that agents' utilities are nondecreasing in their transmission rates and nonincreasing in their delays.

As discussed in the introduction, we allow for a wide range of world utilities, which are commonly called the social choice functions, $\mathcal{F}: F | \mathcal{U}^n \to P$. Symbolically the utilitarian SCF is given by maximizing the utilitarian objective function,[4] $\sum_i U_i(F(U))$ while the egalitarian objective function is (essentially) given by $\min_i U_i(F(U))$.[5]

---

[2] See [4] for an interesting example of this relating to the BGP routing protocol.

[3] One notable exception to this is streaming media, for which reliable congestion controls have only recently been developed and are expected to be adopted in the near future [5].

[4] Note the definition of social choice function is standard, but the "social objective function" is not in the literature on mechanism design.

[5] Actually, the egalitarian social choice function is usually defined in terms of a lexicographic

The system we design that determines the interactions among the agents is known as a *mechanism*. Abstractly a mechanism consists of message spaces, A_i, and a mechanism function $M|A \rightarrow P$. We interpret this as a two-stage process in which each agent chooses a message to send $a_i \in A_i$ and then the mechanism chooses the outcome $M(a)$. For this mechanism we get an induced utility for message vectors, $G_i(a) = U_i(M(a))$. This is the utility to the agent for choosing message a_i when the other agents choose a_{-i}, and thus the vector or messages is $a = (a_i, a_{-i})$.

We can now interpret this as a game in which agents are attempting to choose a_i so as to maximize their own utility. In this view the forward problem is that of finding the solution concept, $S(U)$, for this game, that is, the set of vectors a that could arise when a group of agents play this game, while the reverse problem is that of choosing A and $M(\cdot)$ to maximize the social objective function.

3 Game-Theoretic Analysis: The Forward Problem

In this section we discuss the so-called "forward problem" or that of finding the relevant solution concept. In the standard mechanism design literature the solution concept is typically assumed to be either the Nash equilibrium of the game or the dominant strategy outcome (both defined later). Our claim, based on theoretical analyses, simulations, and experiments with human subjects, is that these are not adequate in the noisy, asynchronous setting of the Internet where information about the underlying network and the behavior of other agents is extremely limited. In the following we will provide a simplified outline of this argument.

First consider the well-known prisoner's dilemma:[6]

	C	D
C	1, 1	−1, 2
D	2, −1	0, 0

This table represents the game (mechanism). Both the row agent and the column agent can choose actions C (cooperate) or D (defect), which determine the vector of payoffs. For example, if both agents cooperate, then both receive 1 unit of utility, and if one cooperates and the other defects, then the defector gets 2 and the cooperator only gets −1.

It is well known that the rational outcome of this game is for both agents to defect, because defecting is always optimal (gets more utility), no matter what strategy your opponent chooses. In the language of mechanism design, we say that D strictly

---

ordering of the sorted vector of U_is and in the continuous setting cannot be computed as the maximum of a continuous objective function.

[6] We consider the prisoner's dilemma for simplicity, but note that there are many applications of the following ideas. See [8] for a detailed bibliography and [6] for a recent application to routing and TCP.

dominates C. Thus, we can construct a solution concept for which $S^{Dom}(U)$ only contains strategies that are not dominated, and for the prisoners' dilemma, this set would contain a single strategy vector (D, D).

Next consider a slightly more complicated game, the prisoner and the altruist, in which the column agent develops a conscience. Now, if one player defects but the other doesn't, the defector feels guilty, which reduces utility in this outcome:

	C	D
C	1, 1	−1, 0
D	2, −1	0, 0

In this game one can easily check that $S^{Dom}(U) = \{(D, D), (D, C)\}$; however, because the row agent never chooses C it is irrational for the column agent to choose C because it really faces the following game:

	C	D
D	2, −1	0, 0

In this "reduced game" C is strictly dominated by D. Thus, we consider the solution concept induced by "iterated dominance" in which we iteratively remove dominated strategies. This procedure is well defined (and independent of the order of removals) and yields $S^{ItDom}(U) = \{(D, D)\}$.

The solution concept S^{ItDom} is quite common in mechanism design and is larger than most others typically studied, such as the set of Nash equilibria, e.g., $S^{ItDom} \supset S^{Nash}$. When learners know their own utility function, it is easy to see that most reasonable models of learning will converge to S^{ItDom}, as shown quite generally in [15].

The intuition behind this result is quite straightforward. Initially, agents would never play dominated strategies. After a reasonable period of time agents notice that their opponents are not playing these strategies and thus stop playing strategies that are dominated with respect to this smaller set of opposing strategies. This process iterates until play is within S^{ItDom}. Note that knowledge of one's own payoffs and observation of other agents' strategies are crucial to this argument.[7]

3.1 Decentralized Learning with Limited Information

In many settings an individual may not know its own utility function explicitly. For example, when I adjust the controls on my TV set (such as brightness or contrast) I am unable to optimize the picture without trial. Additionally, on the Internet I do

---

[7] Note that this is the author's interpretation of Milgrom and Robert's results and differs somewhat from the interpretation given in their paper [15].

not know the effect of an increase in transmission rate on congestion-related delays, because I do not know the details of the transport layer of the network. Interestingly, even if agents do not know their own utility functions but are "reasonable learners"[8] and play is synchronous, such that every agent simultaneously updates its strategy at discrete intervals, then play (approximately) converges to S^{ItDom} as shown in [8].[9] The intuition behind this result is based on the idea that dominated strategies have a lower expected payoff under any probability distribution of opponents' strategies and if an agent "experiments" sufficiently often and randomly then it will be able to detect dominated strategies.

3.2 Asynchronous Play

Interestingly, when play is asynchronous (as is typical on the Internet and in many other "real-time" settings), play need not converge to S^{ItDom}, and thus we should consider a weaker (larger) solution concept if we want to guarantee that our mechanism will work as desired.

To gain some intuition, consider the prisoner and the altruist, but this time assume that the prisoner gets to choose first and then the altruist chooses a strategy *based on the knowledge of the strategy chosen by the prisoner*. In this case, if the prisoner chooses D then so will the altruist, and if the prisoner chooses C then the altruist will also choose C, and this will result in a higher payoff to the prisoner. Thus the prisoner will choose C and the outcome will be (C, C), which is not in S^{ItDom}. This is known as the Stackelberg outcome [20].

Although we are not actually considering Stackelberg's model as just described, we claim that such outcomes can naturally arise in asynchronous learning. First we describe a simple model of asynchronous play, motivated by the Internet.

Consider an agent trying to decide the rate at which to transmit data over a network. The agent's choice of how often to update the transmission rate should depend on both the round-trip time between the computer and the one it is communicating with and the amount of "noise" in the congestion observed. This is because the only information that the agent receives is packet acknowledgments (ACKs) or lack of them. These ACKs are only received after a packet reaches the destination successfully and the ACK travels back to the origin. Thus, new information is received with a delay of at least the round-trip time. In addition, the variance of the round-trip times can be quite large; thus it would be sensible to average some reasonable number of round-trip times before significantly altering the transmission rate.

Thus, we model agents as maintaining a specific strategy for a fixed period of time and then choosing a new strategy based on some average of the performance in the previous period. There is no reason to assume that these periods are synchronized or even similar between different agents. For example, the round-trip time can range from several milliseconds on a local network to half a second (or longer) when transmitting internationally.

---

[8] The technical definition of a reasonable learner is fairly complicated [8], but most adaptive learning algorithms, such as those used on the Internet, are reasonable in this sense.

[9] Note that convergence is in the sense of PAC learning [19].

Consider a situation in which a very slow agent is in a game with a much faster agent. In this case, it is as if the slower agent were the Stackelberg leader, because during a single period of the slow agent, the fast agent will converge to and mostly play the best response to the slow agent's strategy. Then the slow agent will learn the action that yields the highest payoff, *based on the opponent's optimal responses*. It is straightforward to see that this will yield the Stackelberg outcome.

Thus, for asynchronous games our solution concept S^{Async} should at least contain all Stackelberg outcomes S^{Stack} and thus will not be contained within S^{ItDom}.

In [8] we propose a Stackelberg solution concept constructed from any synchronous solution concept that takes into account all possible "extremely asynchronous games" and constructs a minimal solution concept such that no smaller solution concept would be useful. For example, if we believed that synchronous play converged to Nash equilibria (which we don't!) then for asynchronous play the smallest reasonable solution concept would contain all (generalized) Stackelberg equilibria.

Note that this leads to a counterintuitive result for learning in these settings, because for many of the most common problems on the Internet, such as adjusting transmission rate with FIFO queuing, the slower agent may get a higher payoff than the fast one! Thus, less sophisticated (slower) algorithms may be preferred for game-theoretic reasons.[10]

3.3 Guaranteed Convergence

The results in the previous section provide lower bounds for the relevant solution concept in asynchronous decentralized environments. Although we don't know the relevant solution concept S^{Async} precisely, we can prove an upper bound on this set, i.e., a set S^O such that $S^O \supset S^{AsyncDec}$.

Consider the payoff matrix for the prisoner in the prisoner and the altruist game:

	C	D
C	1	−1
D	2	0

In an asynchronous decentralized setting, the reason the prisoner may not realize that C is dominated is because based on the information there is no reason that the payoff matrix couldn't be:

	C	D
C	−1	1
D	2	0

---

[10] Note that it is quite common in game theory for less sophisticated agents to outplay extremely sophisticated ones. One particularly interesting and important example is the well-known tit-for-tat strategy, which outperformed many significantly sophisticated strategies in computational tournaments [2].

This is the matrix obtained by swapping the payoffs when C is played, and in this game C is not dominated.

This could not arise if all the payoffs for playing D were larger than all the payoffs for playing C because then for any permutation of the payoffs, D would dominate C. In general, we call such a strategy "overwhelmed." Because agents will clearly learn not to play overwhelmed strategies, an iteration of this argument shows that they will converge to the set S^{ItOver}, which is obtained by the iterated elimination of overwhelmed strategies. In [8] we prove that reasonable learners will (approximately) converge to S^{ItOver}, and thus we have shown that $S^{Stack} \subseteq S^{Async} \subseteq S^{ItOver}$.

Notice that for both the prisoners' dilemma and the prisoner and the altruist game the set S^{ItOver} contains all of the strategies and thus provides an uninteresting result for the forward problem in asynchronous settings. Indeed, for typical games this is true. For example, in standard network congestion models no strategies are overwhelmed.

However, as we will discuss, our main interest here is whether we can construct mechanisms that have nice properties, such as having guaranteed convergence, i.e., $|S^{ItOver}(U)| = 1$ for all $U \in \mathcal{U}^n$. One interesting example of such a mechanism arises on a network in which all servers use the "fair-share" protocol [7, 18], as discussed later.

3.4 Numerical and Experimental Support

Because our goal in this analysis is to develop useful tools to apply to the Internet and other decentralized environments we should validate our results as a theorem is only as good as the axioms on which it is based.

One validation is based on a set of numerical simulations. This work ([11]) studied a wide variety of common learning algorithms in a variety of settings. It showed rapid convergence to S^{ItOver} but slow or nonconvergence to S^{ItDom} and provided clear evidence of convergence to Stackelberg outcomes in highly asynchronous settings. However, it did raise issues about when asynchrony is relevant, for example, under small amounts of asynchrony, play often converged to S^{ItDom}.

A second validation is based on a set of experiments with human subjects. In that work ([9]) we studied the convergence of people adjusting a data-rate slider on a Web browser. The data clearly shows nonconvergence to S^{ItDom} and approximate convergence to S^{ItOver} for a small number of agents (0–5). It also showed (approximate) Stackelberg behavior. However, for a larger number of agents (8) play did not even converge to S^{ItOver}. Thus, when designing mechanisms for real people in decentralized settings, one needs to be very careful!

4 Mechanism Design: The Inverse Problem

Although finding the correct solution concept and solving the forward problem is interesting in its own right, the inverse problem, that of constructing a mechanism that "implements" the social choice function is of great practical importance, especially in engineering settings. For example, our main interest in the forward problem for networks is to assist in the designs of network protocols that lead to stable and efficient networks.

Clearly, this problem depends crucially on the solution concept. For example, implementation for both S^{Nash} and S^{ItDom} has been well studied and the condition under which a social choice function can be implemented in these solution concepts is well understood. In particular, many important social choice functions can be implemented and almost any social choice function can be approximately implemented to any degree of accuracy [12] for either of these.[11]

However, in the asynchronous decentralized setting the problem appears to be much more difficult, because the solution concepts are much weaker. Although our work here is preliminary, the following results demonstrate the difficulty of implementing social choice functions in these settings.

Given a social choice function, $F|U \rightarrow P$, we consider the so-called direct mechanism, in which agents simply reveal their type or utility function U_i, and the mechanism chooses the outcome defined by the social choice function, i.e., $A_i = \mathcal{U}_i$ and $G_i(a) = F(a)$. Clearly, in a direct mechanism an agent may have incentives to misstate their type. For example, in a salary mechanism, typically the firm states that it is on the verge of bankruptcy, while the employee usually has a large and underfed family.

We say that a direct mechanism is strictly strategy-proof, if reporting truthfully is always a dominant strategy for every agent. It is proven in [8] that for any solution concept $S^{AsynDec}$ that contains S^{Stack} only social choice functions that are strictly strategy-proof can be implemented in $S^{AsynDec}$. Thus, in an asynchronous decentralized setting the restriction on implementable social choice functions is quite severe. Furthermore, under reasonable assumptions on the set $\mathcal{U}$ there are more severe restrictions.

In fact, although we don't know the precise restrictions for implementing under $S^{AsynDec}$, we have proven that in order for a mechanism to implement a social choice function under S^{ItOver} the social choice function must be strictly coalitionally strategy-proof. That implies that not only is it in the best interest of every agent to report its utility function truthfully in the direct mechanism, but even for groups of colluding agents the best strategy is for all to report truthfully. If this were also true for implementation under $S^{AsynDec}$, then this constraint of the set of implementable social choice functions would be extremely severe.

It is possible that one can approximately implement a significantly larger class of social choice functions to a high degree of accuracy; however, we do not know of any results of this type for asynchronous decentralized systems. Some interesting results in this direction have been shown by several authors [1, 13, 16].

---

[11] However, even for these solution concepts the mechanisms that implement various social choice functions seem quite fragile and unrealistic.

5 Example: Sharing a Congested Link

In this section we consider an important example: a group of users sharing a congested data network. For simplicity, we will focus on a simple network with a single link, but most of our analysis generalizes directly to arbitrary network structures. This model was first studied in [17], and our presentation follows that paper.

Consider n users sharing a single congested data link. Each user has a utility function $U_i \in \mathcal{U}$ that is a function of $p_i = (l_i, d_i)$ where l_i is the transmission rate and d_i is the average delay faced by user i's packets. The set $\mathcal{U}$ is the set of all concave functions that are nondecreasing in l_i and nonincreasing in d_i.

Clearly $P \subset \Re_+^{2n}$, but the precise characterization of P is complex and depends critically on the technology. For example, if we assume that users' packets are generated according to a Poisson process and that the transmission times (or packet sizes) follows an exponential distribution, then the set P is characterized by the following set of constraints :

$$\forall S \subset \{1, 2, \ldots, n\}, \qquad \sum_{i \in S} l_i d_i \geq C\left(\sum_{i \in S} l_i\right),$$

where $C(x) = x/(\mu - x)$ and μ is the capacity of the link.

First we consider the forward problem for some well-known protocols. For example, the most common mechanism arises from first-in–first-out (FIFO) queuing, in which the packets are served in order of their arrival. Under this protocol we get a game in which users choose their transmission rate, l_i, and obtain a delay from the system of $d_i = C(\sum_i l_i)/l_i$.

While FIFO is commonly used, it is easy to see for this mechanism that $|S^{Stack}| \neq 1$ for most choices of utility functions by considering the first-order conditions. Thus, the outcome need not be unique under FIFO. In fact, when people play this game, play does not seem to converge [9].

A second interesting protocol is the fair-share mechanism introduced in [18], which is closely related to fair queuing [3], a well-known protocol. Under fair share we can recursively compute the delays, as follows. First, reorder the agents so that $l_1 \leq l_2 \leq \cdots \leq l_n$. Then define $v_i = C(l_1 + \cdots + l_i + (n - i)l_i)/(n - i + 1)$. The fair-share mechanism is defined by $d_i = \sum_{j=1}^{i} v_j/l_i$. The key characteristic of this mechanism is the fact that a user's delay is not affected by small changes in transmission rates of users with higher transmission rates.

Interestingly, for any realization of utility functions and any number of users, $|S^{ItOver}| = 1$ and thus play is guaranteed to converge (to the Nash equilibrium) under the fair-share mechanism. Thus, networks with fair-share mechanisms are more stable than those using FIFO. This is seen empirically in [9].

Lastly, we note that the mechanism design problem (or inverse problem) is easy to solve for the standard social choice functions when the solution concept is S^{Nash} or S^{ItDom}, and we are interested in approximate optimization. (See [17] for the former and [12] for the latter.) However, for the case of S^{Async} there does not exist a mechanism that implements the utilitarian social choice function. This and other negative results are proven in [8].

One important open question is whether one can circumvent these negative results using ideas such as pricing or by providing additional information that would allow users to learn more efficiently. (See [8] for further discussion.) Another interesting approach is to design mechanisms that are within a constant factor of optimality, such as in [1, 16].

These are among many open questions still to be resolved in the application of mechanism design to decentralized settings, such as the Internet.

Acknowledgments. This paper is based directly on joint work with Scott Shenker, Mike Shor, Amy Greenwald, Adam Landsberg, and Barry Sopher and indirectly on conversations with many others.

References

1. A. Archer and É. Tardos. Truthful mechanisms for one-parameter agents. In *Proceedings of the 42nd Annual Symposium on Foundations of Computer Science*, 2001.
2. R. Axelrod. *The Evolution of Cooperation*. Basic Books, New York, 1984.
3. A. Demers, S. Keshav, and S. Shenker. Analysis and simulation of a fair queueing algorithm. *Journal of Internetworking*, 1(1):3–26, January 1990.
4. J. Feigenbaum, C. Papadimitriou, R. Sami, and S. Shenker. A bgp-based mechanism for lowest-cost routing. In *Proceedings of the 2002 ACM Symposium on Principles of Distributed Computing*, 2002.
5. S. Floyd, M. Handley, J. Padhye, and J. Widmer. Equation-based congestion control for unicast applications. In *Proc. ACM Sigcomm 2000*, 2000.
6. E. Friedman. Selfish routing on data networks isn't too bad: Genericity, tcp and ospf. Cornell University, 2002.
7. E. J. Friedman. Strategic properties of heterogeneous serial cost sharing. Mathematical Social Sciences (forthcoming), 2000.
8. E. J. Friedman and S. Shenker. Learning and implementation in the Internet. 2002. Available from www.orie.cornell.edu/~friedman.
9. E. J. Friedman, M. Shor, S. Shenker, and B. Sopher. Asynchronous learning with limited information: An experimental analysis. 2001. Available from www.orie.cornell.edu/~friedman.
10. D. Fudenberg and J. Tirole. *Game Theory*. MIT Press, 1991.
11. A. Greenwald, E. Friedman, and S. Shenker. Learning in network contexts: Experimental results from simulations. *Games and Economic Behavior*, 35(1):80–123, 1999.
12. Matthew Jackson. A crash course in implementation theory. *Social Choice and Welfare*, 2001.
13. K. Jain and V. Vazirani. Applications of approximation algorithms to cooperative games. In *Proceedings of the 33rd Annual ACM Symposium on the Theory of Computing*, pages 364–72, 2001.
14. A. Mas-Colell, M. Whinston, and J. Green. *Microeconomic Theory*. Oxford University Press, 1995.
15. P. Milgrom and J. Roberts. Rationalizability, learning and equilibrium in games with strategic complementarities. *Econometrica*, 58:1255–78, 1990.
16. N. Nisan and A. Ronen. Algorithmic mechanism design. In *Proceedings of the 31st Annual ACM Symposium on the Theory of Computing*, pages 129–40, 1999.

17. S. Shenker. Efficient network allocations with selfish users. In P. J. B. King, I. Mitrani, and R. J. Pooley, editors, *Performance '90*, pages 279–85. North-Holland, New York, 1990.

18. S. Shenker. Making greed work in networks: A game-theoretic analysis of switch service disciplines. *IEEE/ACM Transactions on Networking*, 3:819–31, 1995.

19. L. Valiant. A theory of the learnable. In *Proceedings of the Sixteenth Annual ACM Symposium on Theory of Computing*, Washington, D.C., 1984.

20. H. von Stackelberg. *Marktform und Gleichgewicht*. Springer-Verlag, 1934. English translation, *The Theory of the Market Economy*, Oxford University Press, 1952.

5

Competition between Adaptive Agents: Learning and Collective Efficiency

Damien Challet*

Summary. We use the minority game and some of its variants to show how efficiency depends on learning in models of agents competing for limited resources. Exact results from statistical physics give a clear understanding of the phenomenology and open the way to the study of inverse problems. What agents can optimize and how well are discussed in detail.

Designed as a simplification of Arthur's El Farol bar problem [1], the minority game [2, 3] provides a natural framework for studying how selfish adaptive agents can cope with competition. The major contribution of the minority game is not only to symmetrize the problem, which physicists like very much, but also to introduce a well parameterized set of strategies, and more generally to provide a well-defined and workable family of models.

In this game, N agents have to choose between two choices at each time step; those in the minority win, the others lose. Obviously, it is easier to lose than to win, as the number of winners cannot exceed that of losers. If the game is played once, only a random choice is reasonable, according to game theory [4]. When the game is repeated, it is sensible to suppose that agents will try to learn from the past in order to outperform the other agents, hence, the question of learning arises, as the minority mechanism entails a never-ending competition.

Let me first introduce the game and the needed formalism. There are N agents, agent i taking action $a_i \in \{-1, +1\}$. A game master aggregates the individual actions into $A = \sum_{i=1}^{N} a_i$ and gives private payoffs $-a_i g(A)$ to each agent $i = 1, \ldots, N$. The minority structure of the game implies that g must be an odd function of A. The simplest choice for g may seem to be $g(A) = \mathrm{sgn}(A)$, but a linear function is better suited to mathematical analysis. The MG is a negative-sum game, as the total payoff given to the agents is $-\sum_{i=1}^{N} a_i g(A) = -g(A)A < 0$, because g is an odd function. In particular, the linear payoff function gives a total

* Theoretical Physics, Oxford University, 1 Keble Road, Oxford OX1 3NP, United Kingdom
  challet@thphys.ox.ac.uk

loss of A^2; when the game is repeated, the average total loss is the fluctuations of the attendance $\sigma^2 = \langle A^2 \rangle$ where the average is over time.

From the point of view of the agents, it is a measure of payoff waste. That is why many papers on the MG consider it the global utility of the system (world utility hereafter), and try, of course to minimize it (forward problem). I shall review the quest for small σ^2, focusing on exact results, and show that all proposed mechanisms lead essentially to the same results.[1] A particular emphasis will be put on inductive behavior, as it gives rise to particularly rich phenomenology and is well understood. Finally, the inverse problem is addressed, by deriving what private payoff function g to use given a world utility W to minimize.

1 No Public Information

1.1 "If It Ain't Broken, Don't Fix It"

The arguably simplest behavior is the following [8]: If agent i wins at time t, it sticks to its choice $a_i(t)$ until it loses, when it takes the opposite choice with probability p. The dynamics is Markovian and thus can be solved exactly [8]. When N is large, the fluctuations σ^2 are of order $(pN)^2$; indeed, as the number of losers is $\sim N$, the average number of agents changing their minds at time t is $\sim pN$. Therefore, one can distinguish three regimes:

- $pN = x = cst$—this leads to small fluctuations $\sigma^2 = 1 + 4x(1 + x/3)$, which tend to the absolute minimum $\sigma^2 = 1$ when $x \to 0$. The time needed to reach the stationary state is typically of order $\sqrt{N}$;
- $p \sim 1/\sqrt{N}$—this yields $\sigma^2 \sim N$, which is the order of magnitude produced by agents making independent choices;
- $pN \gg 1$—In this case, a finite fraction of agents change their mind at each time step and $\sigma^2 = N(Np^2 + 4(1 - p))/(2 - p)^2 \sim N^2$.

The major problem here is that p needs to be tuned in order to reach high efficiency. But it is very easy to design a feedback from the fluctuations on p [9] that lowers p as long as the fluctuations are too high and to use the results to relate the fluctuations to $p(t \to \infty)$. Mathematically, this amounts to taking $p(t = 0) = 1$, $dp/dt = -f(p, N, t)$. For instance, $f(t) = t^{-\beta}$ seems appropriate as long as β is small enough. Note that $p(t) \to 0$ as $t \to \infty$; in words, the system eventually freezes. From the optimization point of view, this is welcome, but for agents complete freezing, although being a Nash equilibrium [4], is not satisfactory, as it may be better for an agent sitting on the losing side to provoke a game quake and to profit from a rearrangement of the winners and losers. Therefore, an unanswered question is where to stop the time evolution of p.

---

[1] Evolutionary models (see, for instance, [2, 5–7]) are very different in nature and are not reviewed here, mostly because they are not exactly solvable.

Nevertheless, this simple example illustrates what happens in MGs: The efficiency essentially depends on the opinion switching rate, which depends on the learning rate. It has to be small to reach a good level of efficiency.

1.2 Inductive Behavior

Inductive behavior can remedy the problems of the previous learning scheme if, as we shall see, agents know the nature of the game they are playing. This section is a simplified version of the simplest setting for inductive agents of [10]. At time t, each agent $i = 1, \ldots, N$ plays $+1$ with probability $\pi_i(t)$, and -1 with probability $1 - \pi_i(t)$. Learning consists in changing π_i given the outcome of the game at time t. For this purpose, each agent i has a numerical register $\Delta_i(t)$ that reflects its *perception* at time t of the relative success of action $+1$ versus action -1. In other words, $\Delta_i(t) > 0$ means that the agent believes that action $+1$ has been more successful than -1. The idea is the following: If agent i observes $A(t) < 0$, it will increase Δ_i and hence its probability of playing $a_i = +1$ at the next time step. Reinforcement here means that π_i is an increasing function of Δ_i. For reasons that will become obvious later, it is advisable to take $\pi_i = (1 + m_i)/2$ and $m_i = \chi(\Delta_i)/2$, where χ is an increasing function and $\chi(\pm\infty) = \pm 1$. The way in which $\Delta_i(t)$ is updated is the last and most crucial element of the learning dynamics to be specified:

$$\Delta_i(t+1) = \Delta_i(t) - \frac{1}{N}[A(t) - \eta a_i(t)]. \tag{1}$$

The η term describes the fact that agent i may account for its own contribution to $A(t)$. When $\eta = 0$, the agent believes that $A(t)$ is an *external process* on which it has no influence or does not know what kind of game it is playing. It may be called *naive* in this respect. For $\eta = 1$, agent i considers only the behavior of other agents $A_{-i}(t) = A(t) - a_i(t)$ and does not react to its own action $a_i(t)$. As we shall see, this subtlety is the key to high efficiency. The private utility of sophisticated agents corresponds more or less to what is called aristocrat utility (AU) in COIN's nomenclature [11].

1.2.1 Naive Agents $\eta = 0$

It is possible to show that agents minimize the *predictability* $H = \langle A \rangle^2$. As a consequence H vanishes in the $t \to \infty$ limit. There are, of course, many states with $H = 0$, and the dynamics selects that which is "closest" to the initial condition. To be more precise, let $\Delta_i(0)$ be the initial condition (which encodes the a priori beliefs of agent i on which action is the best). As $t \to \infty$, $\langle A \rangle_t = \sum_i m_i(t) \to 0$ and Δ_i converges to

$$\Delta_i(\infty) = \Delta_i(0) + \delta A, \qquad \text{with } \delta A = \int_0^\infty dt \langle A \rangle_t. \tag{2}$$

The condition $\langle A \rangle_\infty = 0$ provides an equation for δA

$$0 = \sum_{i=1}^{N} \chi \left(\Delta_i(0) + \delta A \right). \tag{3}$$

By the monotonicity property of χ, this equation has one and only one solution.

The asymptotic state of this dynamics is information-efficient ($H = 0$), but it is not optimal, as, in general, this state *is not* a Nash equilibrium. The fluctuations are indeed determined by the behavior of $\chi(x)$. This is best seen with a particular example: assume that the agents behave according to a Logit model of discrete choice [12] where the probability of choice a is proportional to the exponential of the "score" U_a of that choice: $\pi(a) \propto e^{\Gamma U_a/2}$. With only two choices $a = \pm 1$, $\pi(a) = (1 + am)/2$ and $\Delta = U_+ - U_-$, we obtain[2]

$$\chi(\Delta) = \tanh(\Gamma \Delta), \qquad \forall i. \tag{4}$$

Here Γ is the learning rate, which measures the scale of the reaction in the agent's behavior (i.e. in m_i) to a change in Δ_i [14]. We also assume that agents have no prior beliefs: $\Delta_i(0) = 0$. Hence $\Delta_i(t) \equiv y(t)/\Gamma$ is the same for all agents. From the results discussed earlier, we expect, in this case, the system to converge to the symmetric Nash equilibrium $m_i = 0$ for all i. This is not going to be true if agents are too reactive, i.e., if $\Gamma > \Gamma_c$. Indeed, $y(t) = \Gamma \Delta_i(t)$ satisfies the equation

$$y(t+1) = y(t) - \frac{\Gamma}{N} \sum_{i=1}^{N} a_i(t)$$
$$\simeq y(t) - \Gamma \tanh[y(t)], \tag{5}$$

where the approximation in the last equation relies on the law of large numbers for $N \gg 1$. Equation 5 is a dynamical system. The point $y^0 = 0$ is stationary, but it is easy to see that it is only stable for $\Gamma < \Gamma_c = 2$. For $\Gamma > 2$, a cycle of period 2 arises, as shown in Figure 1. This has dramatic effects on the optimality of the system. Indeed, let $\pm y^*$ be the two values taken by $y(t)$ in this cycle.[3] Because $y(t+1) = -y(t) = \pm y^*$ we still have $\langle A \rangle = 0$ and hence $H = 0$. On the other hand $\sigma^2 = N^2 y^{*2}$ is of order N^2, which is even worse than the symmetric Nash equilibrium $\pi_i = 1/2$ for all i, where $\sigma^2 = N$.

Hence, one again finds a transition from $\sigma^2 \propto N$ to $\sigma^2 \propto N^2$ when the learning rate is too large.

1.2.2 Sophisticated Agents $\eta > 0$

It is easy to check that with $\eta > 0$, following the same steps as in the previous section, the learning dynamics of agents minimize the function

$$H_\eta = \langle A \rangle^2 - \eta \sum_{i=1}^{N} m_i^2. \tag{6}$$

---

[2] This learning model was introduced by [13] in the context of the MG.
[3] $\pm y^*$ are the two nonzero solutions of $2y = \Gamma \tanh(y)$.

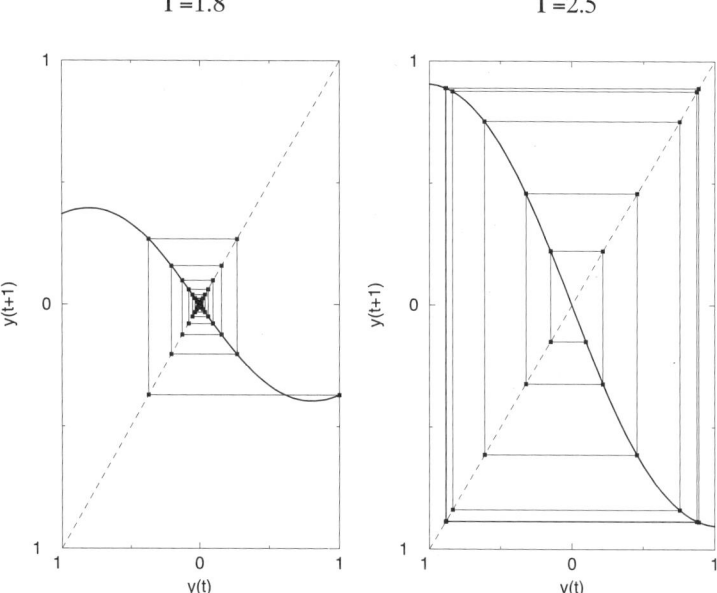

Figure 1. Graphical iteration of the map $y(t)$ for $\Gamma = 1.8 < \Gamma_c$ and $\Gamma = 2.5 > \Gamma_c$.

Because H_η is a harmonic function, H_η attains its minima on the boundary of the domain $[-1, 1]^N$. In other words, $m_i = \pm 1$ for all i, which means that agents play pure strategies $a_i = m_i$. The stable states are optimal Nash equilibria for N even. By playing pure strategies, agents minimize the second term of H_η. Of all corner states where $m_i^2 = 1$ for all i, agents select those with $\langle A \rangle = 0$ by dividing into two equal groups playing opposite actions. All these states have minimal "energy" $H_\eta = -N\eta$. Which of these states is selected depends on the initial conditions $\Delta_i(0)$, but this has no influence on the outcome, because $\langle A \rangle = 0$.

Note that the set of stable states is *disconnected*. Each state has its basin of attraction in the space of $\Delta_i(0)$. The stable state changes discontinuously as $\Delta_i(0)$ is varied. This contrasts with the case $\eta = 0$, where Equation 3 implies that the stationary state changes continuously with $\Delta_i(0)$ and the set of stationary states is connected.

For N odd, similar conclusions can be found. This can be understood by adding a further agent to a state with $N - 1$ (even) agents in a Nash equilibrium. Then $H_\eta = (1 - \eta)m_N^2$, so for $\eta < 1$ the new agent will play a mixed strategy $m_i = 0$, whereas for $\eta > 1$ it will play a pure strategy. In both cases other agents have no incentive to change their position. In this case we find $\sigma^2 \leq 1$.

It is remarkable how the addition of the parameter η radically changes the nature of the stationary state. Most strikingly, fluctuations are reduced by a factor N. From a design point of view, this means that one has either to give personalized feedback to autonomous agents or to make them more sophisticated, for instance, because they need to know the functional form of the payoff.

2 Public Information

As each agent has an influence on the outcome of the game, the behavior of a particular agent may introduce patterns that the other agents will try to exploit. For instance, if only one agent begins to think that the outcome of the next game depends on some external state, such as the present weather of Oxford, and behave accordingly, then indeed, the outcome will depend on it.[4] But this means that other agents can exploit this new pattern by behaving conditionally on the same state. One example of the public information state family that agents may consider as relevant is the past winning choices, for instance, a window of size M of past outcomes [2]. Each such state can be represented by a bit string of size M, hence there are 2^M possible states of the world. This kind of state has a dynamics of its own: It diffuses on a so-called De Bruijn graph [15]. Another state dynamics consists simply in drawing at random the state at time t from some ensemble [16] of size P (e.g., $P = 2^M$). All exact results in the following are obtained with this setup.

2.1 Neural Networks

Two types of neural networks have been studied in the context of the MG [17–19]. Beyond the mere academic question of how well or badly they can perform, it is worth noting that these papers were interested for the first time in *interacting* neural networks.

References [17, 18] introduced simple perceptrons playing the minority game. Each perceptron $i = 1, \ldots, N$ is made up of M weights $\mathbf{w}_i = (w_1^1, \ldots, w_1^M)$, which are drawn at random before the game begins. The decision of network i is $a_i = \text{sgn}(\mathbf{w}.\mu)$, where μ is the vector containing the M last minority signs. The payoff was chosen to be $-a_i \, \text{sgn}(A)$. Neural networks are trained following the usual Hebbian rule, that is,

$$\mathbf{w}_i(t+1) = \mathbf{w}_i(t) - \frac{\eta}{M} \mu_t \, \text{sgn}(A_t). \tag{7}$$

Under some simplifying assumptions, it is possible to find that the fluctuations are given by [17, 18]:

$$\sigma^2 = N + N(N-1)\left(1 - \frac{2}{\pi} \arccos \frac{K - 1/(N-1)}{K+1}\right), \tag{8}$$

where

$$K = \frac{\eta^2 \pi}{16}\left(1 + \sqrt{1 + \frac{16(\pi - 2)}{\eta^2 \pi N}}\right).$$

The best efficiency, obtained in the limit $\eta \to 0$, is given by

---

[4] This kind of self-fulfilled prophecy is found, for instance, in financial markets, where it is called "sunspot effect."

$$\sigma^2 = N\left(1 - \frac{2}{\pi}\right). \tag{9}$$

This means that the fluctuations are at best of order N and at worst of order N^2 when the learning rate is too high. This is likely to be corrected for neural networks with sophisticated private utility.

2.2 Inductive behavior

El Farol's problem was introduced with public information and inductive behavior [1], but with no precise characterization of the strategy space. In most MG-inspired models, a strategy is a lookup table a, or a map, or a function, which predicts the next outcome a^μ for each state μ and whose entries are fixed for the whole duration of the game. Each agent i has a set of S strategies, say $S = 2$ ($a_{i,1}$ and $a_{i,2}$), and uses them essentially in the same way as before [2].

Naive Agents

To each strategy, agent i associates a score $U_{i,s}$ that evolves according to

$$U_{i,s}(t+1) = U_{i,s}(t) - a_{i,s}^{\mu(t)} g[A(t)]. \tag{10}$$

Because we consider $S = 2$, only the difference between $\Delta_i = U_{i,2} - U_{i,1}$ matters, and

$$\Delta_i(t+1) = \Delta_i(t) - (a_{i,2}^{\mu(t)} - a_{i,1}^{\mu(t)})g[A(t)]. \tag{11}$$

Note that now Δ_i encodes the perception of the relative performance of the two strategies of agent i, $\Delta_i > 0$, meaning that the agent i thinks that strategy 2 is better than strategy 1, and m_i is the frequency of use of strategy 2. As before, we consider $\chi(x) = \tanh(\Gamma x)$. This kind of agent minimizes the predictability, which now has to be averaged over the public information states

$$H = \frac{1}{P}\sum_{\mu=1}^{P}\langle A \mid \mu\rangle^2 = \overline{\langle A\rangle^2}, \tag{12}$$

where $\overline{Q} = \sum_{\mu=1}^{P} Q^\mu$ is a useful shortcut for the average over the states of the world. In contrast with the case with no information, H is not always canceled by the agents. This is due to the fact that the agents are faced to P possible states, but their control over their behavior is limited: when they switch from one strategy to another, they change their behavior potentially for all states. In fact all macroscopic quantities such as H/N and σ^2/N depend on the ratio $\alpha = P/N$ [20–22], which is therefore the control parameter of the system. Solving this model is much more complex and requires tools of statistical physics of disordered systems [23]. The resulting picture is that for infinite system size ($P, N \to \infty$ with $P/N = \alpha = $ cst) [22] (see also Figure 2),

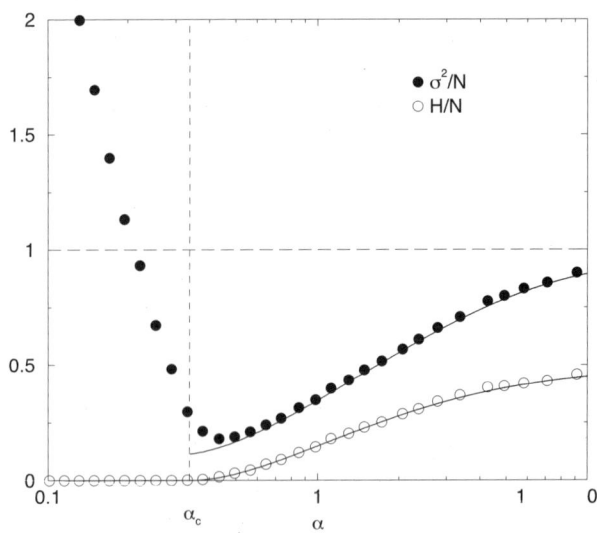

Figure 2. Fluctuations and predictability produced by naive agents $P = 64$, $300P$ iterations, average over 100 realizations. This kind of figure is first found in [20].

- $H > 0$ if $\alpha = N/P > \alpha_c = 0.3374\ldots$. In this region, the system is not informationally efficient. It tends to a stationary state that is unique and stable and does not depend on either Γ or initial conditions. Γ is a time scale [14].
- $H = 0$ when $\alpha < \alpha_c$. Because agents succeed in minimizing H, the question for them is what should they do? They do not know, and as a result, the dynamics of the system is very complex: It depends on initial conditions [10, 24–26][5] and on Γ [13, 25, 26]. Any value of the fluctuations can be obtained, from $\sigma^2 = 1$ for very heterogeneous initial conditions $\Delta_i(t = 0)$ to $\sigma^2 \sim N^2$ for $\Gamma = \infty$ and homogeneous initial conditions, including $\sigma^2 \sim N$ for $\Gamma = 0$ and any initial conditions. Two alternative theories have been proposed, one that is exact but has to be iterated [25] and another that rests on a closed form for the fluctuations [26]. Iterating the exact theory is hard, because the tth iteration is obtained by inverting $t \times t$ matrices, and one has to average of several realizations. Nevertheless, a hundred numerical iterations bring promising results [27].

The origin of the phase transition can easily be understood in terms of linear algebra: Canceling $H = 0$ means that $\langle A \mid \mu \rangle = 0$ for all μ. This is nothing other than a set of P linear equations of N variables $\{m_i\}$. As the variables are bounded ($0 \leq m_i^2 \leq 1$), one needs more than P of them, $N = P/\alpha_c > P$ to be precise [28].

In fact, the transition from low to high (anomalous) fluctuations does not occur at α_c for finite system size as clearly appears on Figure 2. This can be traced back to a signal-to-noise ratio transition [29]: The system is dynamically stable in the phase of $H > 0$ as long as the signal-to-noise ratio H/σ^2 is larger than $K/\sqrt{P}$ for

---

[5] Physicists say that it is not ergodic.

some constant K. This transition is universal for naive competing agents. Hence in this kind of interacting agent system, the ultimate cause of large fluctuations is this signal-to-noise transition and high learning rate. Sophisticated agents are not affected by this problem, as explained later.

Sophisticated Agents

As before, a sophisticated agent is able to disentangle its own contribution from $g(A)$. Equation 10 becomes [22, 30]:

$$\Delta_i(t+1) = \Delta_i(t) - (a_{i,1}^{\mu(t)} - a_{i,2}^{\mu(t)})g(A(t) - a_i(t)). \tag{13}$$

When the payoff is linear, $g(A) = A$, the agents also minimize the fluctuations $\sigma^2 = \langle A^2 \rangle$. Similarly, they end up using only one strategy, which implies that $H = \sigma^2$. In this case, they cannot cancel A for all μ at the same time, hence $\sigma^2/N > 0$. How to solve this case exactly is known in principle [22, 30]. "In principle" here means that the minimization of σ^2 is hard from a technical point of view; how much harder is also a difficult question to answer. A first step was done in [31], which is able to describe reasonably well the behavior of the system. Interestingly, in this case the signal-to-noise ratio transition does not exist, as the signal is also the noise ($H = \sigma^2$); hence, there is no high volatility region (see Figure 3). Therefore, the fluctuations are again considerably reduced by introducing sophisticated agents. An important point here is that the number of stable final states $\{m_i\}$ [31] grows exponentially when N increases. Which is selected depends on the initial conditions, but the efficiency of the final state greatly fluctuates. As the agents (and the programmer) have no clue which to select, the system ends up having nonoptimal fluctuations of order N, as seen in Figure 3.

3 Forward and Inverse Problems

Inductive agents minimize a world utility whose determination is the first step in solving the forward problem. Finding analytically its minimum is then possible *in principle* thanks to methods of statistical physics [23]. The inverse problem consists in starting from a world utility W and finding the appropriate private payoff.

3.1 Naive Agents

The case with no information ($P = 1$) is trivial, because $\langle A \rangle = 0$ in the stationary state; hence all functions $H_{2n} = \langle A \rangle^{2n}$ (n integer) are minimized by a linear payoff. When the agents have access to public information ($P > 1$), the world utility W, given any private payoff function $g(A)$, is [26]:

$$W_{\text{naive}}(\{m_i\}) = \frac{1}{P} \sum_{\mu=1}^{P} \int_{-\infty}^{\infty} \frac{dx}{\sqrt{2\pi}} e^{-x^2/2} G\left(\langle A \mid \mu \rangle(\{m_i\}) + x\sqrt{D}\right), \tag{14}$$

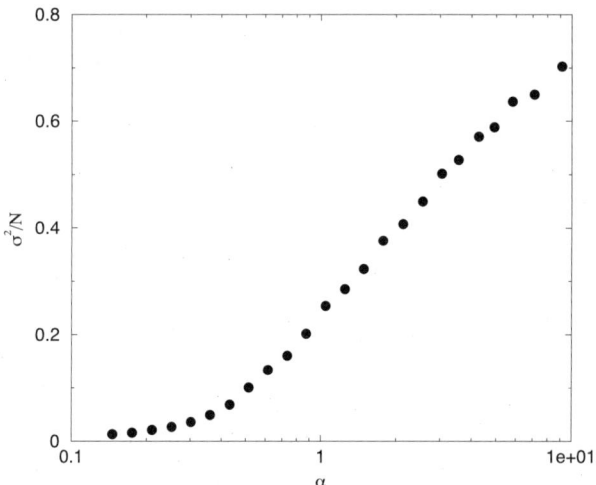

Figure 3. Fluctuations produced by sophisticated agents $P = 64$, $NIT = 100P$, average over 100 realizations.

where $g(x) = dG(x)/dx$ and $D = \sigma^2 - H = (N - \sum_i m_i^2)/2$. In other words, the agents select the set of strategy usage frequencies $\{m_i\}$ that minimizes U. The final state is unique and does not depend on the initial conditions. Note that in Equation 14, only powers of $\langle A \mid \mu \rangle$ $(\mu = 1, \dots, P)$ appear, which means that naive agents are only able to minimize world utility functions that depend on these quantities. This implies that a phase transition always happens if the agents are naive, and even more, that it always happen at the same $\alpha_c = 0.3374\dots$, as seen conjecture from numerical simulations in [32]. As explained above, α_c is the point where it is algebraically possible to cancel all $\langle A \mid \mu \rangle$ [28]. This theory also means that the stationary state depends only weakly on the payoff, which can be seen numerically by comparing the m_i of a given set of agents for different payoffs.

The inverse problem is to find g given W. Let us focus on the particular example $W = \overline{\langle A \rangle^{2n}}$, ($n$ integer). First, one determines the world utility $W^{(2k)}$ associated with $g(x) = 2kx^{2k-1}$, where k is an integer and

$$W^{(2k)} = \sum_{l=0}^{k} \binom{2k}{2l} D^{k-l} X_{2(k-l)} H_{2l}, \tag{15}$$

where $X_l = \int \exp(-x^2/2)x^l/\sqrt{2\pi}$ is the lth moment of a Gaussian distribution of unitary variance and zero average, and $H_{2l} = \overline{\langle A \rangle^{2l}}$ is the $2l$ norm of the vector $(\langle A \mid \mu \rangle)$. Suppose that one wishes to minimize $W = H_{2n}$. This can be done *in principle* with a linear combination of the $W^{(2k)}$:

$$W = \overline{\langle A \mid \mu \rangle^{2n}} = \sum_{k=0}^{n} a_k W^{(2k)} = \sum_{k=0}^{n} a_k \sum_{l=0}^{k} \binom{2k}{2l} D^{k-l} X_{2(k-l)} H_{2l}. \tag{16}$$

The condition on the $\{a_k\}$ is that the coefficient of H_{2k} be 0 for $k = 0, \ldots, n - 1$, and the coefficient of H_{2n} is 1, that is,

$$\sum_{m=k}^{n} a_m \binom{2m}{2k} D^{m-k} X_{2(m-k)} = 0 \qquad 1 \le k \le n - 1, \tag{17}$$

and $a_n = 1$. Then the problem is solved by finding the solution of these $n - 1$ linear equations of $a_k, k = 1, \ldots, n-1$, and taking $g(x) = \sum_{k=1}^{n} a_k x^{2k-1}$. Note, however, that the set of problems that naive agents can solve is of limited practical interest.

3.2 Sophisticated Agents

Sophisticated agents instead have

$$W_{\text{naive}}(\{m_i\}) = \frac{1}{PN} \sum_{\mu=1}^{P} \int_{-\infty}^{\infty} \frac{dx}{\sqrt{2\pi}} e^{-x^2/2} \sum_i G\left(\langle A_{-i}^{\mu}(\{m_i\})\rangle + x\sqrt{D_{-i}}\right), \tag{18}$$

where $D_{-i} = [(N - 1) - \sum_{j \ne i} m_j^2]/2$. This case is much simpler than the previous one, as all agents end up playing only one strategy [22], that is, $D_{-i} = 0$. Therefore, in this case, if $g(A) = 2kA^{2k+1}$,

$$W^{(2k)} = \langle A^{2k} \rangle. \tag{19}$$

Interestingly, similar functions are well studied in statistical physics, where they usually represent the energy of interacting magnetic moments called "spins" [33]; a (classical) spin can have two values -1 or $+1$, which is the equivalent of choosing strategy 1 or 2. A well-known qualitative change occurs between $k = 2$ and $k > 2$, where the mathematical minimization of W is somehow less problematic; this may also be the case in such MGs. The final state is not unique and depends on initial conditions, implying that agents are not particularly good at minimizing such functions.

3.3 Example: Agent-Based Optimization

Some optimization problems are so hard to solve that they have a name: NP-hard [34]. There is no algorithm that can find the optimum of this kind of problem in polynomial time. One of them consists in finding among N either analogic or binary components whose combination is the least defective [35]: In the problem with analogic components, one has a set of N measuring devices; instead of A, each of them records the wrong value $A + a_i$ with a constant bias $a_i, i = 1, \ldots, N$, drawn from a given probability function. The problem is to find a subset such that the average bias

$$\epsilon\{n_i\} = \frac{|\sum_{i=1}^{N} n_i a_i|}{\sum_{j=1}^{N} n_j} \tag{20}$$

is minimal. Here $n_i = 0, 1$ depending on whether component i is included in the sub-set. Statistical physics shows that $\langle \epsilon_{opt} \rangle \sim C\, 2^{-N}/\sqrt{N}$ for large N, with $C \simeq 4.6$ (the average is over the samples). In order to find the optimal subset, one cannot do better than enumerating all the 2^N possibilities. This makes it hard to tackle such problems for N larger than 40 with current computers. Agent-based optimization, on the other hand, typically needs $O(N)$ iterations and can be used with much larger samples. It is clear that one cannot expect this method to perform as well as enu-meration; how well it performs as a function of the setup is a valuable question. Reference [37] compares a set of private payoffs and concludes that agent-based optimization is better than simulated annealing for short times and large samples, provided the agents' private utility is "aristocratic."

Optimizing $h = |\sum_{i=1}^{N} n_i a_i|$ and then dividing by the number of components used in the chosen subset leads to almost optimal subsets [35]. Hence, we can use sophisticated MG agents to optimize h^2 [38], which plays the role of fluctuations in the MG. The most straightforward application of the MG is to give two devices to each agent, which are their strategies. Each agent ends up playing with only one strategy. This setup constrains the use of $N/2$ devices in the optimal subset and gives an error of order $N^{-1.5}$, to be compared with the exponential decay of the optimal average error ϵ_{opt}. One can unconstrain the agents by giving only one component to each agent and letting them decide whether to include their components or not into ϵ, making the game "grand canonical" [39, 40]. This is achieved by the following score evolution

$$U_i(t+1) = U_i(t) - a_i[A - n_i(t)a_i] \qquad (21)$$

and $n_i(t) = \Theta[U_i(t)]$. The $-n_i a_i$ term makes the agents sophisticated. This gives similar results as in [37], as indeed the aristocrat utility is essentially the same con-cept as sophisticated agents. But in any case, it minimizes the fluctuations but does not optimize them. The resulting error ϵ is much better with $S = 1$ than with $S = 2$: It decays $\sim N^{-2}$ (Figure 4). Therefore, as in the optimal case, unconstraining the problem by not fixing the number of selected components leads to much better effi-ciency.

At this stage, one can substantially improve the error, remaining in the $O(N)$ complexity regime. First, because the agents update their behavior simultaneously, they may be unable to distinguish whether removing only one component improves the error. We can do it by hand at the end of the simulations, repeatedly. This is a kind of greedy algorithm. On average, about 1.5 component are removed. In both the $S = 2$ and $S = 1$ cases, this results in a large improvement (see Figure 4) and curiously produces the same error with a decay $\sim N^{-2.3}$. Nevertheless, the final error is still far from optimality. This illustrates how hard this optimization problem is. Much better results can be obtained by removing a group of two or three components, *ad libitum*, but of course, this needs more computing resources $(O(N^2), O(N^3), \dots)$, and it eventually amounts to enumerating all possibilities.

Here is the second trick that keeps the complexity with the $O(N)$ regime. As mentioned, the final state depends on the initial conditions and is often not optimal or even near optimal. But it is still a local minimum of h^2. Therefore the idea is

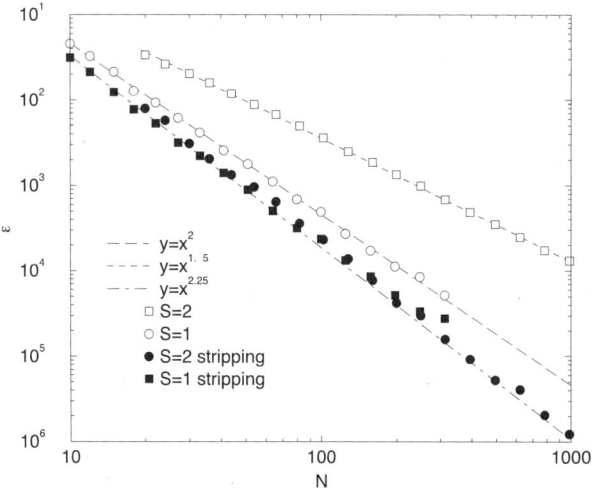

Figure 4. Average error ϵ versus the size N of the defective component set for MG with $S = 2$ (circles), and $S = 1$ (squares), $S = 2$ with removal (stars) and $S = 1$ with removal (full squares). $500N$ iterations per run, averages over 1000 samples.

to do T runs with the same set of defective devices, changing the initial condition $U_i(t = 0)$ and selecting the best run. It is a kind of simulated annealing [36] with zero temperature or partial enumeration where repetition would be allowed. Interestingly, Figure 5 reports that the decay is apparently a power law first and then begins to saturate. For $S = 1$, the exponent is about -0.5 and 0.4 for $S = 2$; it depends weakly on N. Remarkably, the error decreases faster with $S = 1$ agents than with $S = 2$. Note that the optimal value is about 10^{-6}, hence, agents are far from it. This is due to the fact that the agents use too many components. Nevertheless, the improvement brought by this method is impressive and increases as N increases but cannot keep up with the exponential decay of ϵ_{opt}: The difference becomes more abysmal. The component removal further lowers the error (Figure 5), and more in the $S = 2$ than in the $S = 1$ case. This advantage is reversed for T large enough when N is larger, as reported by the right panel of Figure 5).

The other optimization problem recycles binary components [35]: One has a set of N partially defective processors, each able to perform P different operations. The manufacturing process is supposed to be fault with probability f for each operation of each component. Mathematically, the operation μ of processor a is permanently defective ($a^\mu = -1$) with probability f and works permanently with probability $1 - f$ ($a^\mu = 1$). The probability that a component is working becomes vanishingly small when P grows at fixed f. The task consists in finding a subset such that the majority of its components gives the right answer, that is,

$$\sum_{i=1}^{N} n_i a_i^\mu > 0 \qquad \text{for all } \mu = 1, \ldots, P. \tag{22}$$

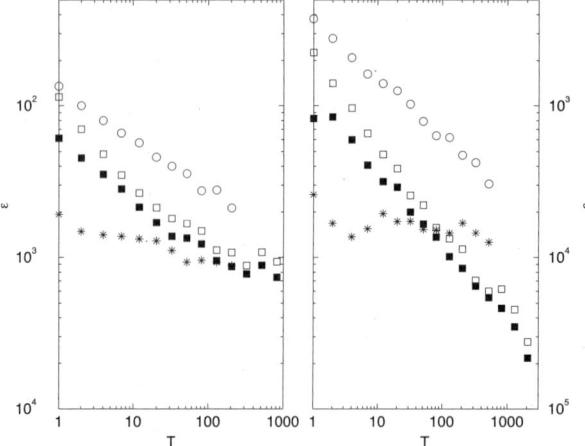

Figure 5. Average error ϵ versus the number of runs for each sample of the defective compo-nent set for MG with $S = 2$ (circles), and $S = 1$ (squares), $S = 2$ with removal (stars) and $S = 1$ with removal (full squares). Left panel: $N = 20$, averages over 1000 samples; right panel: $N = 50$, average over 200 samples.

Surprisingly, the fraction ϕ of samples in which a perfectly working subset of com-ponents can be found increases very quickly as N grows at fixed P and f [35] (see also Figure 6). Finding a subset that works perfectly is an easy problem when it is possible, but finding the one with the fewest components is hard [35]. By contrast

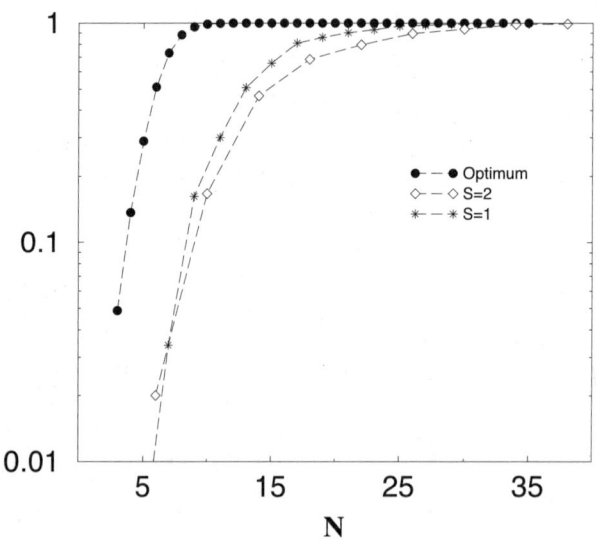

Figure 6. Fraction of samples for which a perfectly working subset of components can be found. $f = 0.2$, average over 1000 runs.

with the minimization of fluctuations, here one wishes to maximize A given μ, that is, the predictability H. Because all the agents eventually use only one strategy in majority games [21], $H = \sigma^2$, hence, the fluctuations σ^2 are also maximized: Naive agents are also sophisticated in this case. A simple majority game does not favor any particular sign of A^μ a priori. However, if $f \ll 1/2$ the sign $+$, hence mostly working combinations, are favored. In practice, a majority game payoff increase is $ag(A)$ instead of $-ag(A)$ as in minority games, which means that here one has

$$U_i(t + 1) = U_i(t) + a_i^{\mu(t)} A(t). \tag{23}$$

Majority games with $S = 1$ turn out to be better than those agents with $S = 2$, as shown in Figure 6, where the results of enumeration are also displayed. As the problem to find a working subset is easy for N large enough, the agents are successful.

4 Conclusions

The efficiency of minority games seems to be universal with respect to agents' learning rate: If the latter is too high, anomalous fluctuations, hence small efficiency, arise. However, these are totally suppressed if the agents are sophisticated and can optimally coordinate if there is no public information. An unexplored issue is what happens with neural networks, taking into account their impact on the game. Based on the universality, it would be tempting to study neural networks with the payoff of sophisticated agents.

The study of forward and inverse problems showed the limitations of agent-based optimization in hard cases, which leaves the interesting open question of how to improve the overall performance and how the setup of agent-based models can and must be tuned for individual cases.

I am grateful to J.-P. Garrahan, N. F. Johnson, M. Marsili, and D. Sherrington for numerous discussions. This work has been supported by EPSRC.

References

1. W. B. Arthur, *Am. Econ. Assoc. Papers and Proc.* **84**, 406, 1994.
2. D. Challet and Y.-C. Zhang, *Physica A*, **246**, 407 (1997) Preprint adap-org/9708006.
3. D. Challet, the minority game's Web page: http://www.unifr.ch/econophysics/minority.
4. J. W. Weibull, *Evolutionary Game Theory*, MIT Press, Cambridge, Mass. (1995).
5. D. Challet and Y.-C. Zhang, *Physica A*, **256**, 514 (1998). Preprint cond-mat/9805084.
6. Y. Li, R. Riolo, and R. Savit, *Physica A*, **276**, 234 (2000). Preprint cond-mat/9903415.
7. Y. Li, R. Riolo, and R. Savit, *Physica A*, **276**, 265 (2000). Preprint cond-mat/9906001.
8. G. Reents, R. Metlzer, and W. Kinzel. Preprint cond-mat/0007351.
9. D. Challet, unpublished.
10. M. Marsili and D. Challet, *Adv. Complex Systems*, **3**-I (2001). Preprint cond-mat/0004376.
11. D. H. Wolpert and K. Tumer, Technical Report NASA-ARC-IC-99-63, NASA, 1999.
12. D. Fudenberg and D. K. Levine, *The Theory of Learning in Games*, MIT Press, Cambridge, Mass., 1998.

13. A. Cavagna, J. P. Garrahan, I. Giardina, and D. Sherrington, *Phys. Rev. Lett.*, **83**, 4429 (1999).
14. D. Challet, M. Marsili, and R. Zecchina, *Phys. Rev. Lett.* **85**, 5008 (2000). E-print cond-mat/0004308.
15. D. Challet and M. Marsili, *Phys. Rev. E*, **62**, 1862 (2000). Preprint cond-mat/0004196.
16. A. Cavagna, *Phys. Rev. E*, **59**, R3783 (1999).
17. W. Kinzel, R. Metzler, and I. Kanter, "Dynamics of interacting neural networks," *J. Phys. A*, 33 (2000), L141-L147. Preprint cond-mat/9906058.
18. W. Kinzel, R. Metzler, and I. Kanter, "Interacting neural networks," (2000). Preprint cond-mat/0003051.
19. J. Wakeling and P. Bak, *Phys. Rev. E*, **64**, 051920 (2001).
20. R. Savit, R. Manuca, and R. Riolo, *Phys. Rev. Lett.*, **82**, 2203 (1999).
21. D. Challet and M. Marsili, *Phys. Rev. E*, **60**, R6271 (1999). Preprint cond-mat/9904071.
22. D. Challet, M. Marsili, and R. Zecchina, *Phys. Rev. Lett.*, **84**, 1824 (2000). Preprint cond-mat/9904392.
23. V. Dotsenko, *An Introduction to the Theory of Spin Glasses and Neural Networks*, World Scientific Publishing (1995).
24. J. P. Garrahan, E. Moro, and D. Sherrington, *Phys. Rev. E*, **62**, R9 (2000).
25. J. A. F. Heimel and A. C. C. Coolen, *Phys. Rev. E*, **63**, 056121 (2001). E-print cond-mat/0012045.
26. M. Marsili and D. Challet, *Phys. Rev. E*, **64**, 056138 (2001). Preprint cond-mat/0102257.
27. T. Galla and D. Sherrington, preprint.
28. D. Challet, M. Marsili, and Y.-C. Zhang, *Physica A*, **276**, 284 (2000). Preprint cond-mat/9909265.
29. D. Challet and M. Marsili, submitted to *Phys. Rev. Lett.* (2002).
30. M. Marsili, D. Challet, and R. Zecchina, *Physica A*, **280**, 522 (2000). Preprint cond-mat/9908480.
31. A. De Martino and M. Marsili, *J. Phys. A*, **34**, 2525 (2001). Preprint cond-mat/0007397.
32. Y. Li, A. VanDeemen, and R. Savit, *Physica A*, **284**, 461 (2000). Preprint nlin/0002004.
33. M. Mezard, G. Parisi, and M. A. Virasoro, *Spin Glass Theory and Beyond*, World Scientific, 1987.
34. M. R. Garey and D. S. Johnson, *Computers and Intractability: A Guide to the Theory of NP-Completeness*, W. H. Freeman, New York, 1997.
35. D. Challet and N. F. Johnson, *Phys. Rev. Lett.*, **89**, 028701(2002). Preprint cond-mat/0203028.
36. J. Kirkpatrick, et al., *Science*, **220**, 671 (1983).
37. D. Wolpert and K. Tumer, preprint (2002).
38. D. Challet and N. F. Johnson, unpublished (2002).
39. F. Slanina and Y.-C. Zhang, *Physica A*, **272**, 257 (1999). E-print cond-mat/9906249.
40. P. Jefferies, M. L. Hart, P. M. Hui, and N. F. Johnson, *Int. J. Th and Appl. Fin.*, **3**-3 (2000). E-print cond-mat/9910072.
41. T. S. Lo, P. M. Hui, and N. F. Johnson. E-print cond-mat/0008387.

6

Managing Catastrophic Changes in a Collective

David Lamper*, Paul Jefferies*, Michael Hart*, and Neil F. Johnson*

Summary. We address the important practical issue of understanding, predicting, and eventually controlling catastrophic endogenous changes in a collective. Such large internal changes arise as macroscopic manifestations of the microscopic dynamics, and their presence can be regarded as one of the defining features of an evolving complex system. We consider the specific case of a multiagent system related to the El Farol Bar model and show explicitly how the information concerning such large macroscopic changes becomes encoded in the microscopic dynamics. Our findings suggest that these large endogenous changes can be avoided either by pre-design of the collective machinery itself or in the postdesign stage via continual monitoring and occasional "vaccinations."

1 Introduction

Understanding the relationship between the overall macroscopic performance of a collective and its design at the microscopic level is a high priority for the collectives field (see, for example, [29]). Typically such performance can be measured in terms of a macroscopic variable of the system that fluctuates in time, for example, the level of waste of a global resource. An example that can be seen in other chapters of this book is the discussion of the fluctuations in attendance in the El Farol Bar game and related multiagent models such as the minority game. In those cases, one is particularly interested in understanding how to minimize the typical size of such fluctuations and hence "optimize" performance by minimizing the average waste. In practice, however, such optimization is not necessarily the key issue. Biology is a wonderful example of a nonoptimal system, yet one that does a fantastic job of avoiding catastrophic large changes. The human body, for example, has a complex network of feedback loops in place in order to "survive." While very few of us exist at our peak level, and even fewer of us hold world records in athletics, we do a pretty good job of coping with everything our changing bodies and the changing

* Oxford University, Parks Road, Oxford OX1 3PU, U.K.
  d.lamper@physics.ox.ac.uk; p.jefferies@physics.ox.ac.uk;
  m.hart@physics.ox.ac.uk; n.johnson@physics.ox.ac.uk

environment throw at us. Moreover, the human system can self-manage this difficult situation for up to 100 years, an unimaginable feat for any computer-based system. In short, we may not be optimal in the sense of minimizing waste, but our system can handle sudden changes in the environment (i.e., *exogenous* changes) and typically manages to resist the tendency to self-generate large unexpected (*endogenous*) changes or "system crashes."

Large unexpected changes, or so-called extreme events, happen infrequently, yet tend to dictate the long-term dynamical behavior of real-world systems in disciplines as diverse as biology and economics, ecology and evolution. Their consequences are often catastrophic; for example, the sudden jamming of traffic in an information system or on a highway; a fatal change within the human immune system; so-called punctuated equilibria in evolution leading to the sudden extinction of an entire species; and crashes in a financial market [2, 18, 24]. The ability to generate large internal, endogenous changes is a defining characteristic of complex systems and arguably of nature and life itself because it leads to evolution through innovation. Thinking through to the management of real-world complex systems and collectives, in particular the risk associated with such catastrophic changes, one wonders whether these large events could eventually be controlled or avoided altogether?

Here we take the first few steps in the direction of "risk management" in collectives. We consider the specific problem of a complex adaptive multiagent population competing for some limited resource. The system is a variant of Arthur's famous El Farol Bar model [1] and exhibits large, self-generated changes. We show that information about the large endogenous changes becomes encoded in the system ahead of the large change itself. The implication is that with a reasonable amount of information, the large change would cease to be a "surprise." This work therefore has relevance to both the forward and reverse problems in collectives. In predesign collectives, i.e., collectives in which the individual components can be tailor-made to have certain fixed properties, such knowledge could help in the design of "safe" agents whose collective behavior is such that large changes are avoided altogether. In postdesign collectives, i.e., collectives for which a designer has no control over the properties of the individual components, one could nevertheless hope to control such large changes in order to minimize the potential damage. In particular, one could imagine some form of soft monitoring, whereby an external regulator monitored the system output, detected certain precursors suggesting a dangerous buildup to a large change, and then intervened to divert it. Going further, we have recently shown [12] that such systems can actually be "vaccinated" ahead of such large changes, thereby affording the system a degree of temporary immunity.

The science of complex systems, as befits its name, lacks a simple definition [25,30]. It has been used to refer to systems that are intermediate between perfect order and perfect disorder; or even as a simple restatement of the cliché that the behavior of some systems as a whole can be more than the sum of their parts. Formal definitions of complexity do exist in the computational and information sciences, but they apply to specific systems [3]. Here we focus on systems where both the properties of the individual components and the nature of their interactions are reasonably well understood. The constituents themselves can be rather simple, and the relation between any two may also be well understood, yet the collective behavior of the ensemble still manages to escape any simple explanation. A simple example that captures the idea of (co-)evolution and bounded rationality is Arthur's El Farol Bar problem [1]. At its most basic level, this is an example of a game involving a fixed population of players (agents) N_{tot} competing for a limited resource L. No more than $L < N_{tot}$ agents can win at each time step. The agents are adaptive and try to predict the next winning outcome, which is determined only by their own choices. Each agent is equipped with a number of strategies from which to choose and can do so adaptively based on its present environment. Recent experiments confirm that humans indeed possess such different strategies, despite being faced with the same history [13]. In short, the El Farol Bar problem contains the following key "complex" elements:

- a population of heterogeneous agents with bounded rationality;
- agents who use history-based strategies on which they base their actions; and
- a method of aggregating agents' behavior into a global outcome, which introduces feedback into the system.

Our study focuses on a generic multiagent system, based on the El Farol Bar problem, which has already been shown to reproduce statistical and dynamical features similar to those of a real-world complex adaptive system: a financial market. (See www.unifr.ch/econophysics for a detailed account of the extent to which financial markets represent complex systems and their associated statistical and dynamical properties.) Our model also exhibits the crucial feature of seemingly spontaneous large changes of variable duration [20, 21]. Although our study is therefore specific to a particular model, we believe that *any* multiagent model that shares these elements would benefit from the techniques described in this chapter. Recently the concept of an *agent* has become increasingly important in both artificial intelligence and mainstream computer science [28]. In contrast to the agents considered within El Farol–like complex systems as in this chapter, the agents in these other fields are typically more sophisticated and are often used to perform specific tasks in a wide range of different areas, e.g., e-commerce, classification, information retrieval, and management of networks [8, 17]. By studying complex systems involving more basic agents but that retain the ability to react to their present environment, we aim to develop approaches that may be useful in more complicated collectives comprising richer components.

The chapter is arranged as follows. In Section 2 we introduce our generic complex system, and in Section 3 demonstrate its ability to generate time series that include occasional large movements. In Section 4 we investigate the game dynamics during these large changes and determine what is occurring microscopically within the model system. In Section 4.1 we introduce a method of understanding when a large change is possible within the system and obtain approximate expressions for its duration in Section 4.2. This leads to an understanding of how such large changes may be avoided.

2 The Grand Canonical Bar Game

We consider a generic complex system in which a population of N_{tot} heterogeneous agents with limited capabilities and information repeatedly compete for a limited global resource. The model is a generalization of Arthur's bar model where agents will only take part, or play, if they are sufficiently confident of the strategies they hold. A strategy is a forecasting rule that generates a prediction of the next winning outcome based on knowledge of the recent history of winning choices. This is the grand canonical bar game (GCBG),[1] It captures some of the key behavioral phenomena that are important in collectives and complex systems: those of competition, frustration, and adaptability. It is also a "minimal" system of only a few parameters.

The GCBG comprises a number of agents N_{tot} who repeatedly decide whether to enter a game where the choices are A or B. Because of the limited global resource, only agents who are sufficiently confident of winning will participate at each time step. The outcome at each time step represents the winning decision, A or B. The agents are adaptive in their strategy choices, but not evolutionary; there is no discovery of new strategies by the agents. A maximum of $L(t)$ agents can win at each time step. Changing $L(t)$ affects the system's quasiequilibrium; hence $L(t)$ can be used to mimic the changing external environment. In the limit that $L(t)$ is time-independent and all agents are forced to play at each time step, our model reverts to Arthur's El Farol Bar model. A schematic of the game structure is shown in Figure 1, clearly indicating the feedback present within the system. The method of encoding the outcomes in the game via a binary alphabet and the associated strategy space, were introduced by Challet and Zhang [5]. However, the GCBG differs from the basic minority game in its use of an external resource level and a variable number of participating agents per time step as a result of the finite confidence level. The agents are of limited yet similar capabilities. Each agent is assigned a "brain-size" m; this is the length of the past history bit string that an agent can use when making its next decision. A common bit string of the m most recent outcomes is made available to the agents at each time step. This is the only information they can use to decide which option to choose in subsequent time steps. Each agent randomly picks q strategies at the beginning of the game, with repetitions allowed. A strategy uses information from the historical record of winning options to generate a prediction [5]. After each turn, the agent assigns one (virtual) point to each strategy that would have predicted the correct outcome and minus one for an incorrect prediction. The resulting time series appears random yet is non-Markovian, with subtle temporal correlations that put it beyond any random walk–based description. Multiagent games such as the present GCBG may be simulated on a computer but can also be expressed in analytic form. In the next section we introduce some notation used in the remainder of this chapter.

---

[1] Grand canonical is a term used in statistical physics to describe a system with a variable number of particles.

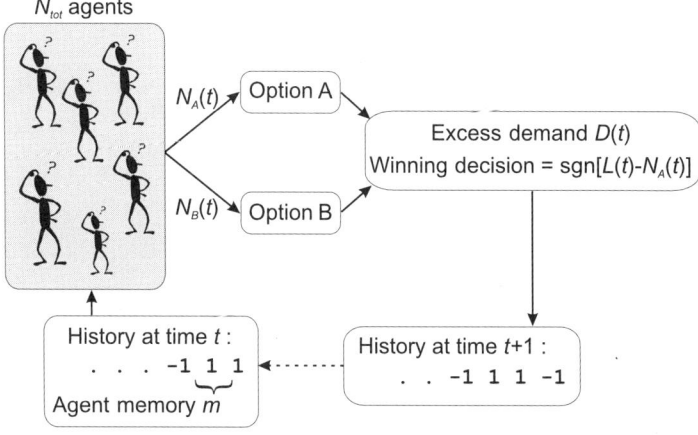

Figure 1. Schematic of game structure.

2.1 Notation

A subset of the agent population that are sufficiently confident of winning are active at each time step. At each time step t we denote the number of agents choosing option A as $N_A(t)$ and the number choosing B as $N_B(t)$. If $L(t) - N_A(t) > 0$ the winning decision is A and vice versa. The winning decision is thus given by

$$w(t) = \text{sgn}\left[L(t) - N_A(t)\right],$$

where sgn$[x]$ is the sign function defined by

$$\text{sgn}[x] = \begin{cases} -1 & \text{for } x < 0, \\ 0 & \text{for } x = 0, \\ 1 & \text{for } x > 0. \end{cases}$$

We denote by $w(t)$ the winning option at time t, where a value of $1 \Rightarrow$ option A, and $-1 \Rightarrow$ option B. We frequently have to represent the two possible choices, A and B, in numerical form; 1 always implies option A and -1 implies option B. If $w(t) = 0$, indicating no clear winning option, this value is replaced with a random coin toss.

The "excess demand" $D(t) = N_A(t) - N_B(t)$ (which mimics price change in a market) and number $V(t) = N_A(t) + N_B(t)$ of active agents (which mimics volume) represent output variables. These two quantities fluctuate with time and can be combined to construct other global quantities of interest for the complex system studied. We define the cumulative excess demand as $P(t)$. In the context of a financial market, this can be regarded as a pseudoprice. Typically we use the example of a financial market, but the excess demand can be interpreted in many different circumstances, e.g., as a measure of resource use within a system. If we define $L(t) = \phi V(t)$, where $0 \leq \phi \leq 1$, then only a fraction ϕ of the active population can win. By varying the value of ϕ, it is possible to change the equilibrium value of $D(t)$; see Figure 2.

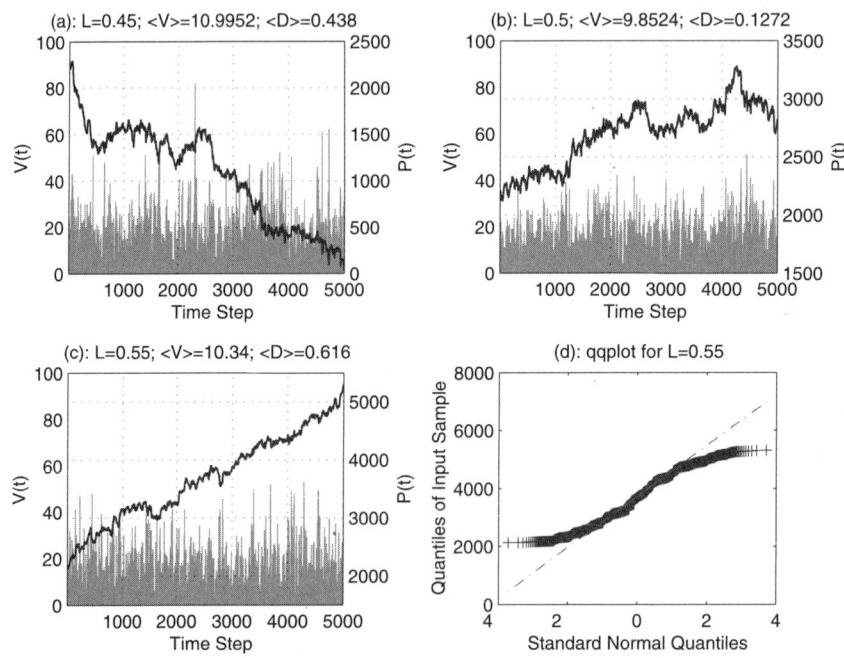

Figure 2. Typical time evolution of the complex adaptive system for differing values of the global resource level: (a) $L = 0.45V(t)$, (b) $L = 0.5V(t)$, and (c) $L = 0.55V(t)$. In each case, the thick line $P(t)$ represents the cumulative excess demand. For L greater (less) than $0.5N_{tot}$, $P(t)$ has an upward (downward) trend. (d) Corresponding qq-plot for $L = 0.55V(t)$ series illustrating the presence of power-law-like fat tails. The result for a normal distribution would be a diagonal line, as indicated.

The only global information available to the agents is a common bit string memory of the m most recent outcomes. Consider $m = 2$; the $P = 2^m = 4$ possible history bit strings are AA, AB, BA, and BB, with the rightmost letter representing the winning choice at the last time step. The history, or equivalently the global information available to the agents, can be represented in decimal form $\mu \in \{0, 1, \ldots, P - 1\}$:

$$\mu(t) = \sum_{i=1}^{m} 2^{i-1} [w(t - i) + 1].$$

The global information $\mu(t)$ is updated by dropping the first bit and concatenating the latest outcome to the end of the string.

At the beginning of the game, each agent randomly picks q (> 1) strategies, making the agents heterogeneous in their strategy sets.[2] This initial strategy assignment is fixed from the outset of each simulation and provides a systematic disorder that

---

[2] Agents are only adaptive if they have more than one strategy to play with; for $q = 1$ the game has a trivial periodic structure.

is built into each run. This is referred to as the *quenched disorder* in the game. An agent decides which option to choose at a given time step based on the prediction of a strategy, which consists of a response, $a^{\mu(t)} \in \{-1, 1\}$, to the global information $\mu(t)$. For its current play, an agent chooses its strategy that would have performed best over the history of the game until that time, i.e., has the most virtual points.

Agents have a time horizon T over which virtual points are collected and a threshold probability level τ that mimics a "confidence." Only strategies having more than r points are used, where

$$r = T(2\tau - 1).$$

We call these *active* strategies. Agents with no active strategies within their individual set of q strategies do not play at that time step and become temporarily inactive. Agents with one or more active strategies play the one with the highest virtual point score; any ties between active strategies are resolved using a coin toss. If an agent's threshold to play is low, we would expect the agent to play a large proportion of the time as their best strategy will have invariably scored higher than this threshold. Conversely, for high τ, the agent will hardly play at all. The coin tosses used to resolve ties in decisions (i.e., $N_A = N_B$) and active-strategy scores inject stochasticity into the game's evolution. The implementation of the strategies is discussed in Section 2.2.

After each turn, agents update the scores of their strategies with the reward function

$$\chi[N_A(t), L(t)] = \text{sgn}\,[N_A(t) - L(t)], \tag{1}$$

namely $+1$ for choosing the correct, winning, outcome and -1 for choosing the incorrect outcome. The virtual points for strategy R are updated via

$$S_R(t) = \sum_{i=t-T}^{t-1} a_R^{\mu(i)}\, \chi\Big[N_A(i), L(i)\Big],$$

where $a_R^{\mu(t)}$ is the response of strategy R to global information $\mu(t)$, and the summation is taken over a rolling window of fixed length T.[3] To start the simulation, we set the initial strategy scores to be zero: $S_R(0) = 0$. Because of the feedback in the game, any particular strategy's success is shortlived. If all the agents begin to

---

[3] It is also possible to construct an exponentially weighted window of characteristic length T, with a decay parameter $\lambda = 1 - 1/T$. The strategy score updating Equation 4 becomes $\mathbf{S}(t+1) = \mathbf{a}^{\mu(t)}w(t) + \lambda\mathbf{S}(t)$. This has the advantage of removing the hard cut off from the rolling window (a Fourier transform of the demand can show the effect of this periodicity in the time series) and is a rapid recursive calculation. But strategy scores are no longer integers, and the probability of a strategy score tie is now very low. Because one source of stochasticity has now been effectively removed, there must be occasional periods of inactivity to inject stochasticity, which helps to prevent group, or cyclic, behavior when the game traces out a deterministic path.

use similar strategies and hence make the same decision, such a strategy ceases to be profitable and is subsequently dropped. This encourages heterogeneity among the agent population.

The demand $D(t)$ and volume $V(t)$, which can be identified as the output from the model system, are given by

$$D(t) = \mathbf{n}(t) \cdot \left(\mathbf{a}^{\mu(t)} \mathcal{H} \big[\mathbf{S}(t) - r \big] \right) = \sum_{R=1}^{Q} n_R(t) a_R^{\mu(t)} \mathcal{H} \big[S_R(t) - r \big], \quad \text{(2a)}$$

$$V(t) = \mathbf{n}(t) \cdot \mathcal{H} \big[\mathbf{S}(t) - r \big] = \sum_{R=1}^{Q} n_R(t) \mathcal{H} \big[S_R(t) - r \big], \quad \text{(2b)}$$

where $n_R(t)$ represents the number of agents playing strategy R at time step t.

The demand $D(t)$ is made up of two groups of agents at each time step: $D_D(t)$ agents who act in a deterministic manner, i.e., do not require a coin toss to decide which choice to make (because either they have one strategy that is better than their others or their highest-scoring strategies are tied but give the same response to the history $\mu(t)$), and $D_U(t)$ agents that act in an undecided way, i.e., they require the toss of a coin to decide which choice to make (because they have two (or more) highest-scoring tied strategies that give different responses at that turn of the game). Inactive agents do not contribute to the demand. Hence we can rewrite Equation 2a as

$$D(t) = D_D(t) + D_U(t). \quad \text{(3)}$$

Without the stochastic influence of the undecided agents the game will tend to exhibit group or cyclic behavior, where the game eventually traces out a deterministic path. The period of this cyclic behavior is dependent on the quenched disorder present in the simulation and could be very long.

The number of agents holding a particular combination of strategies can also be expressed as a q-dimensional tensor Ω [11], where the entry $\Omega_{R1,R2,...}$ represents the number of agents holding strategies $\{R1, R2, \ldots\}$. This quenched disorder is fixed at the beginning of the game. It is useful to construct a symmetric configuration Ψ in the sense that $\Psi_{R1,R2,...} = \Psi_{p\{R1,R2,...\}}$ where $p\{R1, R2, \ldots\}$ is any permutation of the strategies $R1, R2, \ldots$; for $q = 2$ we let $\Psi = (1/2)(\Omega + \Omega^T)$. Elements $\Psi_{R,R'}$ enumerate the number of agents holding both strategy R and R'. We focus on $q = 2$ strategies per agent, although the formalism can be generalized. At time step t, $D_D(t)$ can now be expressed as

$$D_D(t) = \sum_{R=1}^{Q} a_R^{\mu(t)} \mathcal{H}[S_R(t) - r] \sum_{R'=1}^{Q} (1 + \text{sgn}\,[S_R(t) - S_{R'}(t)])\, \Psi_{R,R'}.$$

The number of undecided agents N_U is given by

$$N_U(t) = \sum_{R,R'} \mathcal{H}[S_R(t) - r]\delta(S_R(t) - S_{R'}(t))[1 - \delta(a_R^{\mu(t)} - a_{R'}^{\mu(t)})]\Psi_{R,R'},$$

and hence the demand of the undecided agents $D_U(t)$ is distributed binomially:

$$D_U(t) = 2 \, \text{Bin}\left(N_U(t), \frac{1}{2}\right) - N_U(t),$$

where $\text{Bin}(n, p)$ is a sample from a binomial distribution of n trials with probability of success p.

2.2 The Strategy Space

The strategy space analysis was inspired by the work of Challet and Zhang [5,6]. A strategy consists of a response, $a^\mu \in \{-1, 1\}$, to each possible bit string μ, $a^\mu = 1 \Rightarrow$ option A, and $a^\mu = -1 \Rightarrow$ option B. Consider $m = 2$, each strategy can be represented by a string of $P = 4$ bits [i j k l] with $i, j, k, l = -1$ or $+1$ corresponding to the decisions based on the histories AA, AB, BA, and BB, respectively. For example, strategy [−1 −1 −1 −1] corresponds to deciding to pick option B irrespective of the $m = 2$ bit string. [1 1 1 1] corresponds to deciding to pick option A irrespective of the $m = 2$ bit string. [1 −1 1 −1] corresponds to deciding to pick option A given the histories AA and BA, and pick option B given histories AB and BB. A subset of strategies can further be classed as one of the following:

- *Anticorrelated*: for example, any two agents using the strategies [−1−1−1−1] and [1 1 1 1] would take the opposite action irrespective of the sequence of previous outcomes. Hence one agent will always do the opposite of the other agent, and their net effect on the excess demand $D(t)$ will be zero.
- *Uncorrelated*: for example, any two agents using the strategies [−1 −1 −1 −1] and [1 −1 1 −1] would take the opposite action for two of the four histories and take the same action for the remaining two histories. Assuming that the $m = 2$ histories occur equally often, the actions of the two agents will be uncorrelated on average.

A convenient measure of the distance of any two strategies is the relative Hamming distance, defined as the number of bits that need to be changed in going from one strategy to another. For example, the Hamming distance between [−1 −1 −1 −1] and [1 1 1 1] is 4, while the Hamming distance between [−1 −1 −1 −1] and [1 −1 1 −1] is just 2.

The collection of all possible strategies (and their associated virtual points) is hereafter referred to as the *strategy space*, see, e.g., Figure 3. This object can be thought of as a common property of the game itself, being updated centrally after each time step. Each individual agent monitors only a fixed subset q of the Q possible strategies (with the small caveat that a repeated strategy choice is possible). After each turn, an agent assigns one (virtual) point to each of its strategies, which would have predicted the correct outcome. The virtual points for each strategy can be represented by the strategy score vector $\mathbf{S}(t)$ and are given by

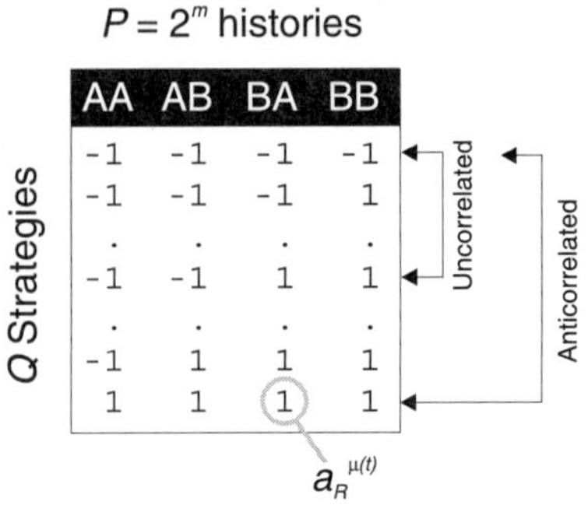

$$P = 2^m \text{ histories}$$

Figure 3. Stylistic example of the $m = 2$ strategy space.

$$\mathbf{S}(t) = \sum_{i=t-T}^{t-1} \mathbf{a}^{\mu(i)} \chi \Big[N_A(i), L(i) \Big]. \tag{4}$$

In total, there are $Q = 2^P$ possible strategies that define the decisions in response to all possible m history bit strings. This is referred to as the full strategy space (FSS). However, the principal features of the system are reproduced in a smaller reduced strategy space (RSS) of $Q = 2^{m+1}$ strategies, wherein any two strategies are either uncorrelated or anticorrelated [6], i.e., separated by a Hamming distance of either 2^m or 2^{m-1}. The full and reduced strategy space $\mathbf{a}$ for $m = 2$ has been reproduced in Figure 4. Each row represents a strategy, each column is assigned to a particular history, giving the strategy space a dimension of $P \times Q$. The prediction of strategy

$$
\mathbf{a} = \begin{pmatrix}
-1 & -1 & -1 & -1 \\
-1 & -1 & -1 & 1 \\
-1 & -1 & 1 & -1 \\
-1 & -1 & 1 & 1 \\
-1 & 1 & -1 & -1 \\
-1 & 1 & -1 & 1 \\
-1 & 1 & 1 & -1 \\
-1 & 1 & 1 & 1 \\
1 & -1 & -1 & -1 \\
1 & -1 & -1 & 1 \\
1 & -1 & 1 & -1 \\
1 & -1 & 1 & 1 \\
1 & 1 & -1 & -1 \\
1 & 1 & -1 & 1 \\
1 & 1 & 1 & -1 \\
1 & 1 & 1 & 1
\end{pmatrix}
\qquad
\mathbf{a} = \begin{pmatrix}
-1 & -1 & -1 & -1 \\
-1 & 1 & -1 & 1 \\
1 & 1 & -1 & -1 \\
1 & -1 & -1 & 1 \\
1 & 1 & 1 & 1 \\
1 & -1 & 1 & -1 \\
-1 & -1 & 1 & 1 \\
-1 & 1 & 1 & -1
\end{pmatrix}
$$

Figure 4. Example of an $m = 2$ strategy space. The full strategy space containing 16 strategies is reproduced on the left, with the reduced strategy space of 8 strategies on the right.

R to information μ is a_R^{μ} and corresponds to the (R, μ) element of **a**. The ordering of the rows is unimportant.

Within the strategy space, each strategy R has an anticorrelated strategy $\bar{R}$. We note that the anticorrelated strategies are effectively redundant, as their predictions and strategy scores can be recovered from their anticorrelated pair:

$$\mathbf{a}_{\bar{R}}^{\mu} = -\mathbf{a}_{R}^{\mu}, \tag{5a}$$

$$\mathbf{S}_{\bar{R}}(t) = -\mathbf{S}_{R}(t). \tag{5b}$$

Equation 5a is true by definition, i.e., a strategy and its anticorrelated pair always give the opposite prediction. However, Equation 5b requires a symmetric scoring rule to be used, which is satisfied by Equation 1. Thus we can reproduce the dynamics using a space of just P strategies, in which agents choose both a strategy and whether to agree or disagree with its prediction. Reducing the size of the strategy space is advantageous as it reduces memory requirements and increases the speed of the simulation. For a more detailed description of how to implement such a system, see [22].

3 Demonstration of Large Changes

A ubiquitous feature of complex systems is that large changes, or "extreme events," arise far more often than would be expected if the individual agents acted independently. We frequently refer to crashes but are interested in large moves in either direction. With a suitable choice of parameters the GCBG is able to generate time series that include occasional large movements, see, e.g., Figure 5.

The game can be broadly classified into three regimes:

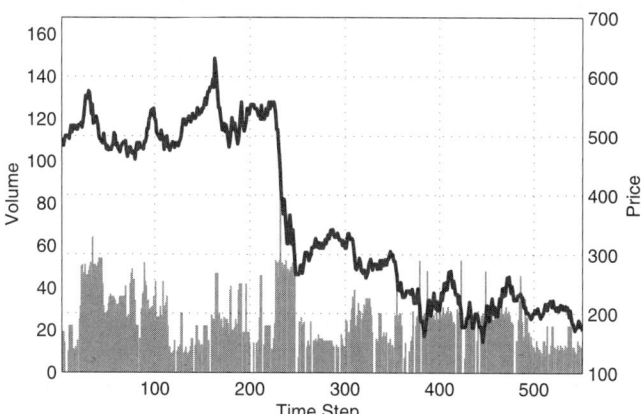

Figure 5. Example of a time series exhibiting large changes. The model parameters were $N_{tot} = 101$, $T = 60$, $\tau = 0.53$, $m = 3$, and $q = 2$.

1. The number of strategies in play is much greater than the total available: Groups of traders will play using the same strategy and therefore crowds should dominate the game [19].
2. The number of strategies in play is much smaller than the total available: Grouping behavior is therefore minimal.
3. The number of strategies in play is comparable to the total number available.

We focus on the third regime, because this yields seemingly random dynamics with occasional large movements.

Large changes seem to exhibit a wide range of possible durations and magnitudes, making them difficult to capture using traditional statistical techniques based on one- or two-point probability distributions. A common feature, however, is an obvious trend (i.e., to the eye) in one direction over a reasonably short time window: We use this as a working definition of a large change. (In fact, all the large changes discussed here represent $> 3\sigma$ events.) In both our model and the real-world system, these large changes arise more frequently than would be expected from a random walk model [18].

In Section 3.1 we consider the distribution of the excess demand created by our generic system and perform a simple analysis to discuss the statistics of extreme events. To determine whether large movements occur due to a single random event, we examine the stochastic influence within the model in Section 3.2 and find that they arise through a global cooperation occurring over the whole system.

3.1 Tail Estimation

Traditional parametric statistical methods are ill-suited for dealing with extreme events, which have little historical data associated with them. Provided the distribution has a finite variance and the increments are independent, the central limit theorem will apply near the center of the distribution but does not tell us anything about the tails [4].[4] In recent years extreme value theory (EVT), a branch of probability theory that focuses explicitly on extreme outcomes, has received increasing attention [10]. EVT considers the distribution of extreme returns rather than the distribution of all returns. It can be shown that the limiting distribution of extreme returns observed over a long time period is largely independent of the distribution of returns itself. The upper tail of a fat-tailed cumulative distribution function F behaves asymptotically like the tail of the Pareto distribution given by $1 - F(x) \approx cx^{-\alpha}$, for $c > 0, \alpha > 0$, and $x \geq C$, where C is a threshold above which the assumed algebraic form is valid, and c is a normalizing constant. The tail index α determines the heaviness of the tail of a distribution and plays a key role in tail-related risk measures, representing the maximal order of finite moments. Only the first k moments, where $k < \alpha$, are bounded. The greater the tail index, the "fatter" the tail and the greater the incidence of extreme events.

---

[4] The speed at which the distribution will converge to a Gaussian is given by the Berry-Esseen theorem; a finite second moment ensures Gaussian behavior, and the speed of convergence is controlled by the size of the third moment of $|x|$ [26].

An important issue in the study of fat-tailed distributions is the estimation of the tail index α. There are a number of methods to estimate the tail index, some using asymptotic results from EVT, from which values can be estimated using maximum likelihood techniques. However, the Hill estimator is commonly used, as it is suitable for tail estimation of fat-tailed distributions and is relatively easy to implement [14]. Consider a sample $X_1, X_2, \ldots, X_n$ of n observations drawn from a stationary iid process, and let $X_{(1)} \geq X_{(2)} \geq \cdots \geq X_{(n)}$ be the descending-order statistics. The Hill estimator is based on the difference between the mth largest observation and the average of the m largest observations:

$$\hat{\xi}_m = \frac{1}{m} \sum_{i=1}^{m} \log X_{(i)} - \log X_{(m)},$$

where $\xi = 1/\alpha$ is the shape parameter and m is the number of order statistics used in the tail estimation. The appropriate choice of value m is a nontrivial problem, because this requires us to decide where the tail begins. There is a trade-off between the bias and variance of the estimator in choosing m. If we choose a large value of m, the number of order statistics used increases and the variance of the estimator will decrease. However, choosing a high m also introduces some observations from the center of the distribution and the estimation becomes biased. But if it is too small, the estimate will be based on just a few of the largest observations and the estimator will lack precision. Several methods for the determination of an optimal sample fraction for the Hill estimator have been proposed [7, 9]. In Figure 6 a Hill plot is constructed from the simulation data used to create Figure 5. A threshold is selected from the plot where the shape parameter is fairly stable, giving an estimate of the tail index $\alpha \approx 3.7$. To obtain the most accurate tail estimate, a combination of several techniques should be considered.

3.2 The Effect of Stochasticity

To investigate the stochastic influence due to the effect of coin tosses, we have studied their occurrence during the simulation. We define two types of coin toss: type (i), which occurs when an agent has a tie between active strategy options that predict differing outcomes, and type (ii), which occurs when the number of agents choosing option A is equal to the number choosing option B. The main conclusion is that there is no single coin toss that immediately causes a large change within the system. The large movements observed as arising endogenously in the system result from the organization of temporal and spatial (i.e., strategy space) correlations. In common with other complex adaptive systems, this organization does not arise in general from a nucleation phase diffusing across the system, e.g., it cannot be traced to a particular coin toss by a particular agent that triggers the "avalanche." Rather, it results from a progressive and more global cooperation occurring over the whole system via repetitive interactions [27].

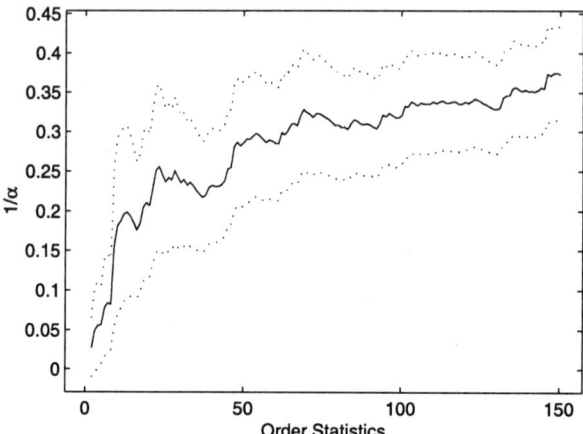

Figure 6. Hill plot with a 0.95 confidence interval. The estimated value of the shape parameter ξ is plotted against the number of upper-order statistics m used in the estimation. A value of ξ is selected from the plot where the shape parameter is fairly stable.

4 A Study of Extreme Events

In this section we consider the generic complex system introduced in Section 2 in which a population of N_{tot} heterogeneous agents with limited capabilities and information repeatedly compete for a limited global resource. We focus on extreme events that are endogenous (i.e., internally produced by the agents themselves) and provide a microscopic understanding as to their buildup and likely duration.

4.1 Nodal weight decomposition

The dynamics of the game history can be usefully represented on a directed De Bruijn graph [23]. This is a graph whose nodes are sequences of symbols from some alphabet and whose edges represent possible transitions between these nodes. It has numerous interesting properties and is frequently discussed in the context of parallel algorithms and communication networks. This is an effective method of representing the evolution of the system, and in Figure 7 we plot the De Bruijn graph for an $m = 3$ game.

Large changes occur when connected nodes become persistent and the game makes successive moves in the same direction. Only nodes 0 and 7 can exhibit perfect nodal persistence, where an allowed transition can return the system to exactly the same node. This is the simplest type of large change, e.g., $\mu(t) = 0, 0, 0, 0, \ldots$, where all successive price changes are in the *same* direction. We call this a "fixed-node crash" (or rally). There are many other possibilities reflecting the wide range of forms and durations that a large change can undertake. For example, on the $m = 3$ De Bruijn graph in Figure 7 the cycle $\mu = 0, 0, 1, 2, 4, 0, \ldots$ has four out of the five transitions producing price changes of the same sign (it is persistent on nodes 1, 2, 4, and antipersistent on node 0). We call this a "cyclic-node

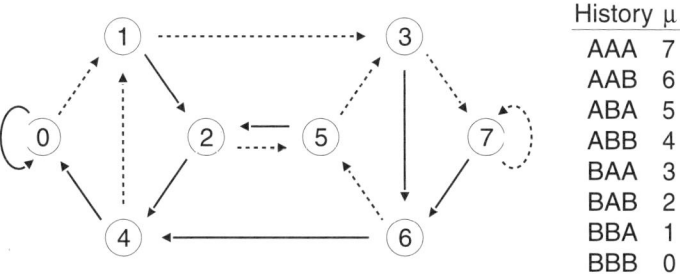

Figure 7. Dynamical behavior of the global information is described by transitions on the De Bruijn graph. Graph for population of $m = 3$ agents. Dashed transitions represent positive demand D, solid transitions represent negative demand, with each transition incurring an increment to the score vector **S**.

crash." Stable behavior occurs on a path where all transitions are equally visited, e.g., $\mu(t) = 0, 0, 1, 3, 6, 5, 3, 7, 7, 6, 4, 1, 2, 5, 4, \ldots$.

To identify moments when large changes occur, we need to recognize when history nodes are likely to become persistent. Whether a node is persistent or not will depend on the action of the agents at that time step, which is determined by the predictions of the strategies they hold. If the majority of active strategies generate a prediction of the same outcome, then the demand at that time step is likely to continue in that direction. Thus a suitable condition for a large movement is when there is a consensus of opinion regarding the next outcome among the active strategies. This occurs when the pattern of active strategies within the strategy space matches up with the pattern of strategy predictions for a history node μ; see Figure 8.

The strategy predictions will depend on the global information $\mu(t)$, and the distribution of active strategies depends on the strategy score vector $\mathbf{S}(t)$. At each time step $\mathbf{S}(t)$ is updated according to whether a strategy predicted the winning outcome $w(t)$; the incremental strategy score is given by a column of the strategy matrix **a** determined by $\mu(t)$. In total there are P orthogonal increment vectors $\mathbf{a}^\mu$, one for each value of μ. We can express the strategy score Equation 4 as

(a)

R	Active	Prediction: a^0
1	1	A
2	1	B
3	0	A
4	0	B

(b)

R	Active	Prediction: a^0
1	1	A
2	0	B
3	1	A
4	0	B

Figure 8. Two different configurations of the strategy space for $\mu(t) = 0$. The columns represent: R = strategy index; Active = where 1 represents an active strategy and 0 an inactive strategy, i.e., $\mathcal{H}[S_R(t) - r]$; Prediction = the prediction of the strategy, which is given by a_R^0. In (a) there is no consensus in the predictions of the active strategies; the active strategies do not share the same pattern as $\mathbf{a}^0$. In (b) there is a consensus of opinion. All the active strategies predict option A because the pattern of active strategies is similar to the pattern of strategy predictions.

$$\mathbf{S}(t) = c_0\mathbf{a}^0 + c_1\mathbf{a}^1 + \ldots + c_{P-1}\mathbf{a}^{P-1} = \sum_{j=0}^{P-1} c_j\mathbf{a}^j, \tag{6}$$

where c_j represents the *nodal weight* for history node $\mu = j$. The nodal weights represent the number of negative return transitions from node μ minus the number of positive return transitions, in the time window $t - T \rightarrow t - 1$. The values of these nodal weights are important in identifying periods in which large changes can occur. If the value of a nodal weight is near zero, this implies that the number of active strategies predicting outcome A will be similar to the number predicting outcome B when that node is reached. The excess demand will then depend on the quenched disorder and the undecided agents but is likely to be small. Conversely, if the value of a nodal weight is significantly different from zero, this indicates a bias in the strategy space, i.e., the same pattern is evident in the active strategies and the strategy predictions. When the game trajectory hits this node, the majority of active strategies will predict the same outcome, and there will be a consensus among the agents. This is likely to lead to a large excess demand and therefore a large change. Thus high absolute nodal weight implies persistence in transitions from that node, i.e., persistence in $D|\mu$.

The mean of the strategy scores predicting an A or B at node μ are linked to their nodal weight:

$$E\left[S_{R \ni a_R^\mu = 1}(t)\right] = c_\mu(t), \tag{7a}$$

$$E\left[S_{R \ni a_R^\mu = -1}(t)\right] = -c_\mu(t). \tag{7b}$$

This symmetry occurs because each strategy has an anticorrelated strategy in the strategy space.

The nodal weight decomposition provides a succinct method of describing the state of the strategy space. We are concerned with high nodal weights on game cycles that can become persistent. When a nodal weight value becomes large, this is a warning sign that the system is in a suitable state to undergo a large change. Figure 9 illustrates a large change that starts as a fixed-node crash and then subsequently becomes a cyclic-node crash.

4.2 Estimating the Crash Length

We are interested in the dynamics of large changes and use a simplified version of the system to obtain an analytic expression for the expected crash length. Reference [15] showed that the GCBG can be usefully described as a stochastically disturbed deterministic system. As stated in Equation 3, the demand can be divided into contributions arising from agents acting on a definite strategy $D_D(t)$ and that from the undecided agents D_U. The average contribution of the undecided agents to the net demand will be zero, i.e., $E[D_U(t)] = 0$. Averaging over our model's stochasticity in this way yields a description of the game's deterministic dynamics. By examining these dynamics, we can determine when a large change is likely. For $q = 2$ the demand function can be expressed as

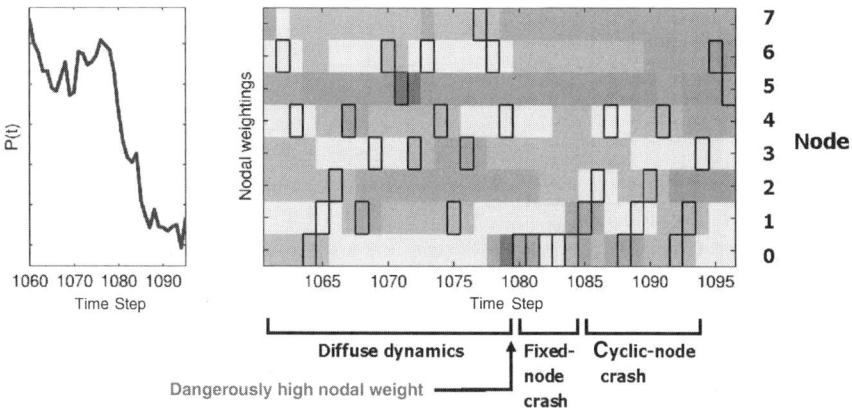

Figure 9. Dynamical behavior of complex system (e.g. price $P(t)$ in financial market) described by evolution of nodal weights c_μ. History at each time step indicated by black square. Large change preceded by abnormally high nodal weight. Large change incorporates fixed-node and cyclic-node crashes.

$$D(t) = \sum_{R=1}^{Q} a_R^{\mu(t)} \mathcal{H}[S_R(t) - r] \sum_{R'=1}^{Q} (1 + \mathrm{sgn}\,[S_R(t) - S_{R'}(t)])\,\Psi_{R,R'}, \quad (8)$$

where Ψ is the symmetrized strategy allocation matrix, which constitutes the quenched disorder present during the system's evolution. The volume $V(t)$ is given by the same expression as $D(t)$ replacing $a_R^{\mu(t)}$ by unity.

For the parameter ranges of interest, the choice about whether a strategy is played by an agent is more determined by whether that strategy's score is above the threshold than whether it is their highest-scoring strategy. This is because agents are only likely to have at most one strategy whose score lies above the threshold for confidence levels $r \geq 0$. Making the additional numerically justified approximation of small quenched disorder (i.e., the variance of the entries in the strategy-allocation matrix Ψ is smaller than their mean for the parameter range of interest [15]), the demand and volume become

$$D(t) = \sum_{R=1}^{Q} a_R^{\mu(t)} \mathcal{H}[S_R(t) - r] \sum_{R'=1}^{Q} \frac{N}{Q^2}$$

$$= \frac{N}{Q} \sum_{R=1}^{Q} a_R^{\mu(t)} \mathcal{H}[S_R(t) - r]$$

$$= \frac{N}{Q} \sum_{R=1}^{Q} a_R^{\mu(t)} \frac{1}{2}\left(1 + \mathrm{sgn}\,[S_R(t) - r]\right)$$

$$= \frac{N}{2Q} \sum_{R=1}^{Q} a_R^{\mu(t)} \operatorname{sgn}[S_R(t) - r], \tag{9a}$$

$$V(t) = \frac{N}{Q} \sum_{R=1}^{Q} \mathcal{H}[S_R(t) - r] = \frac{N}{2} + \frac{N}{2Q} \sum_{R=1}^{Q} \operatorname{sgn}[S_R(t) - r]. \tag{9b}$$

Let us suppose persistence on node $\mu = 0$ starts at time t_0. How long will the resulting large change last? To answer this, we decompose Equation 9a into strategies that predict option A at $\mu = 0$ and those that predict B. We first consider the particular case where the node $\mu = 0$ was not visited during the previous T time steps, hence the loss of score increment from time step $t - T$ will not affect $\mathbf{S}(t)$ on average. At any later time $t_0 + \tau$ during the large change, Equations 9a and 9b are given by

$D(t_0 + \tau)$

$$= -\frac{N}{2Q} \left\{ \sum_{R \ni a_R^\mu = -1} \operatorname{sgn}[S_R(t_0) - r - \tau] - \sum_{R \ni a_R^\mu = 1} \operatorname{sgn}[S_R(t_0) - r + \tau] \right\}, \tag{10}$$

$V(t_0 + \tau)$

$$= \frac{N}{2} + \frac{N}{2Q} \left\{ \sum_{R \ni a_R^\mu = -1} \operatorname{sgn}[S_R(t_0) - r - \tau] + \sum_{R \ni a_R^\mu = 1} \operatorname{sgn}[S_R(t_0) - r + \tau] \right\}.$$

The magnitude of the demand $|D(t_0 + \tau)|$ decreases as the persistence time τ increases, and the large change will end at time $t_0 + \tau_c$ when the right-hand side of Equation 10 becomes zero. We denote the persistence time or "crash length" by τ_c. It is easy to obtain an upper limit for the duration of a large change by determining when the demand D changes sign. This occurs when the mean of the scores of the strategies predicting A return to 0, i.e.,

$$\tau_c = \mathrm{E}\left[S_{R \ni a_R^\mu = -1}(t_0)\right]$$
$$= -c_0(t_0)$$

from Equation 7b. Thus the crash length will depend on the score difference between strategies predicting option A and those predicting B. In the more general case, where the node $\mu = 0$ was visited during the previous T time steps, τ_c is given by the largest τ value, which satisfies

$$\tau = -\left(c_0(t_0) + \sum_{\{t'\}} \operatorname{sgn}[D(t')] \right), \tag{11}$$

where $\{t'\} \ni (\mu(t') = 0 \cap t_0 - T \le t' \le t_0 - T + \tau)$. The summation accounts for any $\mu = 0$ transitions in the period $t_0 - T$ to $t_0 - T + \tau$.

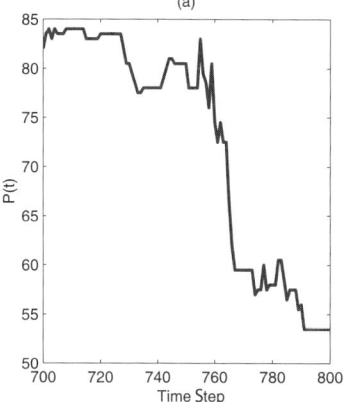
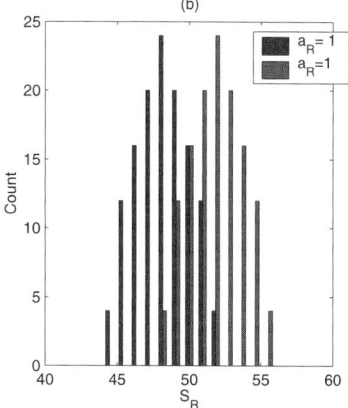

Figure 10. Empirical strategy score distribution. (b) is the strategy score distribution at time step 760 from the series depicted in (a).

To obtain an improved estimate of τ_c and investigate the behavior of the demand and volume, it is necessary to assume a distribution for the strategy scores. In Figure 10 we plot an example of the strategy score distribution prior to a large change. We assume that the scores have a near-normal distribution, i.e., $S_{R \ni a_R^\mu = -1}(t_0) \sim N[-c_0(t_0), \sigma]$, as shown Figure 11.[5] Consequently, prior to a large change, the score distribution tends to split into two halves. Substitution into Equation 10 gives the expected demand and volume during the crash:

$$D(t_0 + \tau) \propto \Phi\left[\frac{c_0(t_0) - r + \tau}{\sigma}\right] - \Phi\left[\frac{-c_0(t_0) - r - \tau}{\sigma}\right],$$

$$V(t_0 + \tau) \propto \Phi\left[\frac{c_0(t_0) - r + \tau}{\sigma}\right] + \Phi\left[\frac{-c_0(t_0) - r - \tau}{\sigma}\right].$$

These forms are illustrated in Figure 12. As the spread in the strategy score distribution is increased, the dependence of D and V on the parameters τ and r becomes weaker and the surfaces flatten out, leading to a smoother drawdown, as opposed to a sudden severe crash. In the limit $\sigma \to 0$, the crash length $\tau_c = -c_0(t_0) - |r|$. As the parameters c_0, σ, r are varied, it can be seen that the behavior of the demand and volume during the large change can exhibit markedly different qualitative forms.

4.3 Repeated Occurrence of Large Changes

We now turn to the important practical question of whether history will repeat itself, i.e., given that a large change has recently happened, is it likely to happen again? If so, is it likely to be even bigger? Suppose the system has built up a negative nodal

---

[5] At some points during the simulation the distribution can be more complex, e.g., multimodal behavior.

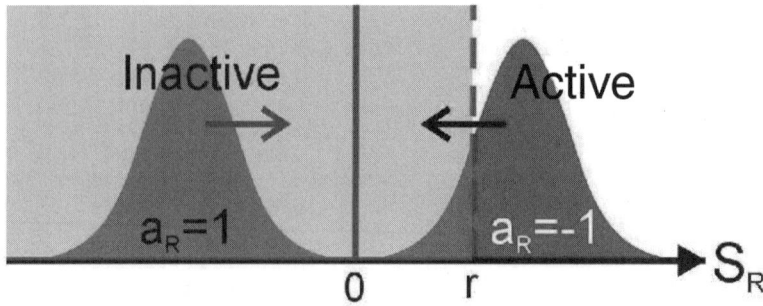

Figure 11. Schematic representation of strategy score distribution prior to crash. Arrows indicate subsequent motion during crash period.

weight for $\mu = 0$ at some point in the game (see Figure 13a). It then hits node $\mu = 0$ at time t_0 producing a large change (Figure 13b). The nodal weight c_0 is hence restored to zero (Figure 13c). In this model the previous buildup is then forgotten because of the finite T score window, hence c_0 becomes positive (Figure 13d). The system then corrects this imbalance (Figure 13e), restoring c_0 to 0. The large change is then forgotten, hence c_0 becomes negative (Figure 13f). The system should therefore crash again; however, a crash will *only* reappear if the system's trajectory subsequently returns to node $\mu = 0$. Interestingly, we find that the *disorder* in the initial distribution of strategies among agents (i.e., the quenched disorder in Ψ) can play a deciding role in the issue of "births and revivals" of large changes because it leads

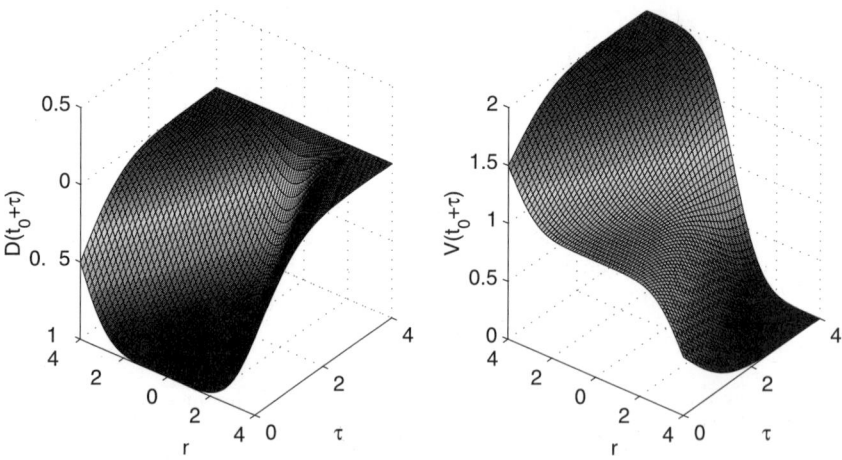

Figure 12. Plots of expected demand $D(t)$ and volume $V(t)$ during crash period showing range of different possible behavior as system parameters are varied.

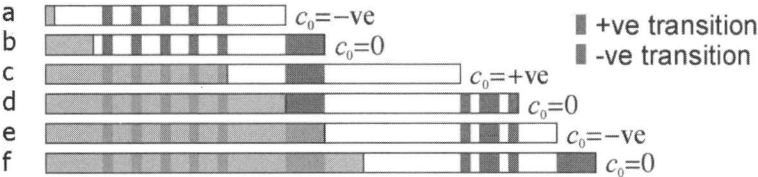

Figure 13. Representation of how large changes can recur due to finite memory of agents. Gray area shows history period outside agents' memory. Example shows recurring fixed-node crash at node $\mu = 0$.

to a slight bias in the outcome, and hence the subsequent transition, at each node. In certain configurations, this system may demonstrate repeated instabilities, leading to large changes. When $c_{\mu(t)} = 0$ (see Figure 13c), it follows that sgn$[D(t)]$ is more likely to be equal to sgn$[\mathbf{a}^{\mu(t)} \cdot \mathbf{x}]$, where $x_R = \sum_{R'} \Psi_{R,R'}$ is a strategy weight vector with x_R corresponding to the number of agents who hold strategy R [16]. The quenched disorder therefore provides a crucial bias for determining the future trajectory on the De Bruijn graph when the nodal weight is small and hence can decide whether a given large change recurs or simply disappears. The quenched disorder also provides a *catalyst* for building up a very large change [16].

5 Concluding Remarks

We have addressed the issue of understanding, predicting, and eventually controlling catastrophic endogenous changes in a collective. By using information about the strategy weights within the model, we have developed a method for determining when a large change is likely within a generic complex system, the so-called GCBG, and obtained an analytic expression for its expected duration. Our work opens up the study of how a complex systems manager might use this information to control the long-term evolution of a complex system by introducing, or manipulating, such large changes [16]. As an example, we give a quick three-step solution to prevent large changes: (1) Use the past history of outcomes to build up an estimate of the score vector $S(t)$ and the nodal weights $\{c_{\mu(t)}\}$ on the various critical nodes, such as $\mu = 0$ in the case of the fixed-node crash. (2) Monitor these weights to check for any large buildup. (3) If such a buildup occurs, step in to prevent the system hitting that node until the weights have decreased. Finally we note that it can sometimes be beneficial to induce small changes ahead of time, in order to avoid larger changes in the future. We call this process "immunization" and refer to [12] for more details.

References

1. W. B. Arthur. Inductive reasoning and bounded rationality. *AEA Papers and Proceedings*, **84**(2):406–11, 1994.

2. P. Bak. *How Nature Works: The Science of Self-Organised Criticality.* Oxford University Press, Oxford, 1997.

3. G. Boffetta, M. Cencini, M. Falcioni, and A. Vulpiani. Predictability: A way to characterize complexity. *Physics Reports*, **356**:367–474, 2002.

4. J.-P. Bouchaud and M. Potters. *Theory of Financial Risks.* Cambridge University Press, Cambridge, 2000.

5. D. Challet and Y.-C. Zhang. Emergence of cooperation and organization in an evolutionary game. *Physica A*, **246**(3–4):407–18, 1997.

6. D. Challet and Y.-C. Zhang. On the minority game: Analytical and numerical studies. *Physica A*, **256**(3–4):514–32, 1998.

7. J. Danielsson, L. de Haan, L. Peng, and C. G. de Vries. Using a bootstrap method to choose the sample fraction in tail index estimation. *Journal of Multivariate Analysis*, **76**:226–48, 2001.

8. M. D'Inverno and M. Luck, editors. *The Fourth UK Workshop on Multi-agent Systems*, December 2001.

9. H. Drees and E. Kaufmann. Selecting the optimal sample fraction in univariate extreme value estimation. *Stochastic Processes and Their Applications*, **75**:149–72, 1998.

10. P. Embrechts, C. Klüppelberg, and T. Mikosch. *Modelling Extremal Events for Insurance and Finance.* Springer, London, 1999.

11. M. L. Hart, P. Jefferies, and N. F. Johnson. Dynamics of the time horizon minority game. `cond-mat/0102384`, December 2001.

12. M. L. Hart, D. Lamper, and N. F. Johnson. An investigation of crash avoidance in a complex system. `cond-mat/0207588`. See also *Physica A*, in press (2002).

13. R. A. Heath. Can people predict chaotic sequences. *Nonlinear Dynamics, Psychology, & Life Sciences*, **6**:37–54, 2002.

14. B. M. Hill. A simple general approach to inference about the tail of a distribution. *Annals of Statistics*, **46**:1163–73, 1975.

15. P. Jefferies, M. L. Hart, and N. F. Johnson. Deterministic dynamics in the minority game. *Physical Review E*, **65**(016105), 2002.

16. P. Jefferies, D. Lamper, and N. F. Johnson. Anatomy of extreme events in a complex adaptive system. `cond-mat/0201540`.

17. N. R. Jennings and Y. Lespérance, editors. *Intelligent Agents VI*, number 1757 in Lecture Notes in Computer Science. Springer, 2000.

18. A. Johansen and D. Sornette. Large stock market price drawdowns are outliers. *Journal of Risk*, **4**(2), 2002.

19. N. F. Johnson, M. L. Hart, and P. M. Hui. Crowd effects and volatility in markets with competing agents. *Physica A*, **269**(1):1–8, 2000.

20. N. F. Johnson, M. L. Hart, P. M. Hui, and D. Zheng. Trader dynamics in a model market. *International Journal of Theoretical and Applied Finance*, **3**(4):443–50, 2000.

21. D. Lamper, S. H. Howison, and N. F. Johnson. Predictability of large future changes in a competitive evolving population. *Physical Review Letters*, **88**(017902), 2002.

22. D. Lamper and N. F. Johnson. Complexity. forthcoming in *Dr Dobb's Journal*, 2002.

23. R. Metzler. Antipersistant binary time series. *Journal of Physics A*, **35**(3):721–30, 2002.

24. P. Ormerod. Surprised by depression. *Financial Times*, p. 25, February 19, 2001.

25. Complex systems. *Science*, **284**(5411), 1999.

26. M. F. Shlesinger. Comment on "Stochastic process with ultraslow convergence to a Gaussian: The truncated Levy flight." *Physical Review Letters*, **74**(24):4959, 1995.

27. D. Sornette. *Critical Phenomena in Natural Sciences.* Springer, New York, 2000.

28. M. Wooldridge and N. R. Jennings. Intelligent agents: Theory and practice. *Knowledge Engineering Review*, **10**(2), June 1995.

29. D. H. Wolpert, K. Wheeler, and K. Tumer. Collective intelligence for control of distributed dynamical systems). *Europhysics Letters*, **49**:March 2000.
30. K. Ziemelis. Complex systems. *Nature*, **410**, March 2001.

7

Effects of Interagent Communications on the Collective

Zoltán Toroczkai,[1] Marian Anghel,[2] György Korniss,[3] and Kevin E. Bassler[4]

Summary. Based on a recently introduced networked multiagent game [2], we study how agent-agent communications across a complex social network can affect the evolution of the collective during multiple iterations of the game. We show that the information obtained from the social network local to the agent can override the global information source and thus completely change the evolution of the collective compared to the nonnetworked situation. In addition, we show that when trait diversity is low, namely when the agents' action space is severely limited, the overall stability of "leader agents" is improved.

1 General Considerations and Introduction

Agent-based systems constitute a novel class of paradigm systems that have a rather wide range of applicability from social science, economics, designer systems, robotics, and critical infrastructure modeling, to defense applications and intelligence. The individual or agent is described by a number of fundamental components including: (1) a set of *local* (to the agent) *utility functions*, (2) the drive to *optimize* these utilities (for example, agents on a highway try to maximize their speed while minimizing the chance of collisions), (3) a set of possible *actions* (accelerate, brake, swerve) from which the agent chooses its ultimate response, and (4) an *information pool* which is information obtained from the environment in the present and the past, such as the sequence of responses from the environment following the agent's actions. Here, by environment, we mean the "rest of the world" for the agent, which includes other agents, and (5) a set of *strategies*, which are functions (not necessarily

[1] Complex Systems Group and Center for Nonlinear Studies, Los Alamos National Laboratory, Los Alamos, NM 87545 `toro@lanl.gov`

[2] Computer and Computational Sciences Division, Los Alamos National Laboratory, Los Alamos, NM 87545

[3] Department of Physics, Applied Physics, and Astronomy, Rensselaer Polytechnic Institute, 110 8th Street, Troy, NY 12180

[4] Department of Physics, 617 Science and Research Bldg. I, University of Houston, Houston, TX, 77204

deterministic) that generate an action in an attempt to optimize its utilities ("what I want") based on the information pool ("what I know") of the agent. Strategies can also be formulated as ways of "thinking" of an agent.

These systems are situated between classical, deductive, few-player game-theoretic systems and the typical many-particle systems of statistical mechanics. The players or agents of a classical deductive (or fully rational) few-player (two- or three-player) game can have the possibility of performing a rather exhaustive search of the choice tree (or state space) and look for the next best action *given* the actions of other players. The player that is able to evaluate deeper and for longer the choice tree will, typically, be the winner of the game (such as chess). This type of *long-term planning*, however, is impossible when the number of players is large. Because of this hardship in strategy evaluation, the players will not act in a deductive fashion but rather inductively, the game essentially being defined by a series of *bounded rationality* choices from the part of the players (especially human players); see Brian Arthur's seminal work on bounded rationality [3]. This in some sense constitutes good news for the modeler, because it considerably lessens the memory effects in the game in contrast to the case of purely deductive games, and thus raises the hope of a probabilistic or statistical analysis. As a matter of fact, it introduces some degree of "markovianity" into the game. On the other hand these systems are fundamentally different from classical many-particle systems (which are studied using statistical methods) through several aspects, the most important being the fact that agents have the possibility of *choice* in their response function to external stimulus, in contrast to classical particle systems, where there is only one force law that generates the response (for example, a spin in a magnetic system will always flip according to the same, e.g., Ising, Hamiltonian). In addition, agents may be *adaptive*, namely, they can generate new response functions into their strategy space. Another important characteristic of agent systems or *collectives* is the fact that the number of agents is still much smaller than what one finds in classical statistical mechanics systems in which the thermodynamic limit is well justified. In contrast to the 10^{23} order of particle numbers in a mol of gas, in agent systems one never expects to see more than 10^8 agents. This introduces another important difficulty for the theory of collectives: the existence of large fluctuations.

So far, the only good news is the bounded rationality effect generated by the impossibility of an agent to traverse the choice tree in a multiagent game and to make deductive choices, and thus it is due to *incomplete information*. Instead, the agents will tend to use inductive mechanisms based on pattern recognition in the information pool. One such ubiquitous mechanism is **reinforcement learning** (RL) [11]. Reinforcement learning is a mechanism for statistical inference created through repeated interactions with the environment. In particular, RL will generate weights, rating the correlation level between the input, which is the (information, strategy, action) triple, and the output, which is the response from the environment. For example, given a busy highway with cars driving at high speed, a sudden brake will almost always lead to an accident. Due to incomplete information, however, these weights might be time-dependent. In this naive example, if the agent receives the information that other cars are suddenly braking (there is an accident ahead) then a sudden braking will most likely avoid an accident for the agent.

As formulated by Wolpert and Tumer, there are two fundamental problem classes in agent-based systems: (1) the **analysis** class of problems, where the composition of the collective is part of the problem specification, and one's goal is to map out collective behavior from the study of the interactions on the individual level (micro to macro approach), and (2) the **design** class of problems, where the challenge is to design the local utility functions for the agents such that while every agent tries to optimize its own utilities in a selfish manner, it will ultimately contribute at the same time to the improvement or optimization of a global measure, "world utility," which is a characteristic of the collective and which ultimately is the utility function for the designer.

For the sake of clarity in the following, we adopt and reiterate the definition of a multiagent system or collective, as introduced recently by Wolpert and Tumer [23], which we will then extend to include interagent communications.

An agent-collective is defined [23] by:

1. a set of discrete, autonomous entities (individuals, agents, players) with a certain degree of intelligence, adaptability, and flexibility in the choice of their actions in response to external stimulus or to follow personal goals (maximize or minimize a set of utility functions).
2. there is no (or very little) centralized control.
3. there is a globally available world utility function that rates the past performance of the collective (world history function).
4. the choice of response function of an agent couples to the world utility function via *reinforcement learning*.

One aspect this definition does not include is the fact that agents in reality are not only coupled to the world history function, which is common and global information, but they may exchange information among themselves or give advice, which can *influence* their actions and thus possibly the evolution of the game or collective. One could also say that the information pool available to the agent (as defined in the very first paragraph) has two components: globally available information (world utilities) and local information generated by the collective in proximity of the respective agent. This interagent exchange is happening on the backbone of a network, which we shall term (for natural reasons) the *social network*.

In a previous paper [2] we addressed the following questions: Can the effects of interagent communication aggregate up to the global level and considerably affect the global behavior of the collective? If so, is it possible to design interagent communication *rules* on the agent level so that when those are enforced it will improve the global utility function and make the collective (such as a market), e.g., more efficient? We have found an affirmative answer for both questions, using a simple model, namely a networked version of the well-known minority game (MG), a model we also present here in detail. We will present further results pertinent to the networked MG, namely how the information content of the global information source is being affected by the presence of the communication network and, a result about the stability of a leader agent, where leadership level of a given agent is defined by the number of other agents acting on (or following the) advice obtained from that agent.

Thus the class of agent-based systems that we consider will have another clause:

4. the choice of response function of an agent couples to: (a) the world utility function *and* (b) the information gathered from neighboring agents on the social network, via RL.

2 Collectives on Networks

In order to study such systems we recall a networked multiagent model that we recently introduced in [2]. For the sake of completeness we will reiterate here the definition of the model.

A simple model that naturally fits the definition given by Wolpert and Tumer for a collective is the well-known minority game (MG) [6, 10, 18], which is a computer-friendly version introduced by Challet and Zhang of the original El Farol Bar problem of Brian Arthur [3]. We then modify this model to include interagent interactions on a social network.

In the MG, which is an iterated game, at every step, N agents have to choose between two different options, symbolized by A and B (e.g., "buy" or "sell"). Only agents in the minority group get a reward. The agents have access to global information, which is the identity of the minority group for the past m rounds, and a set of S strategies available to them. A strategy is a prediction [3] for outcome A or B, in response to *all* possible histories of length m. The strategies are distributed randomly among agents, and thus in general the agents have different sets of S strategies. They make their next choice in the game using reinforcement learning: Every agent keeps a score for each of the S strategies, which he then increments by unity (in each round) if that strategy predicted the minority outcome, independent of whether it was actually used. The strategy used to make the new choice is the one with the best score up to that time. If two or more strategies share the best score, then one of those strategies is picked randomly.

The agent-agent interactions are modeled on a social network represented by a graph with vertices representing the agents and edges representing acquaintanceship between pairs of agents. This network of acquaintances forms the substrate network (**G**), or skeleton for interagent communications [8, 12, 16, 17, 19, 20]. An edge ab in **G** means that agents a and b may exchange game-relevant information. However, it does not indicate whether the exchanges influence the action by any of the involved agents. That information is modeled by a second network, the *action network* (**F**), which is a directed subset of **G**, and in which an edge ab means that agent a *acts* on the advice of agent b (for example, when buying or selling), and thus material values are being moved based on advice passing through a social link. Just as in the standard MG, in order to make its next decision, every agent uses the best strategy to predict what the next minority choice will be. However, it does not act on it just yet.

This prediction constitutes an opinion, which is then shared with all first neighbors on the substrate network **G**. This is done by all agents, and thus our agent will also obtain as information the predictions of all the first neighbors. The agent then uses this information to make its final choice via reinforcement learning: it keeps score for the prediction performance of all its first neighbors and itself, which it updates after every round by incrementing the scores of the agents whose prediction was correct. Then the agent uses and acts on the prediction or opinion of the neighboring agent with the highest score. Of course, if the agent has a better score than any of its neighbors, then it acts on its own prediction.

We now give a mathematical formulation of the minority game on an arbitrary substrate network, **G**. An agent has two types of information available before making a decision: (a) global information that rates the past histories of the collective in form of a string of m bits and (b) local information obtained as predictions from its neighbors on the social network **G**. The global information serves as feedback on the predictive power of the neighbors' strategies and its own strategies. Let us denote by $\mu = (\mu_1 \mu_2 \ldots \mu_m)$ the history string at time t. There are in total $P = 2^m$ such strings, and they form the history space $\mathbb{P}$. If $\lambda(t+1)$ denotes the new bit at time $t+1$, then $\mu_i(t+1) = \mu_{i+1}(t)$ for $i = 1, \ldots, m-1$ and $\mu_m(t+1) = \lambda(t+1)$. The new bit is given by

$$\lambda(t+1) = \theta(A(t+1) - N/2) , \tag{1}$$

where $\theta(x)$ is the Heaviside step function ($\theta(x) = 0$ if $x < 0$ and $\theta(x) = 1$ for $x \geq 0$). If side **A** is in majority then $\lambda = 1$, otherwise $\lambda = 0$.

Every agent j has a set of S randomly drawn strategies, $s_{j,l}, l = 1, 2, \ldots, S$, $j = 1, 2, \ldots, N$, from the full pool of 2^P strategies, which map the global history space to prediction, $s_{i,l} : \mathbb{P} \longrightarrow \{0, 1\}$, and indirectly to actions. The agent keeps a performance score $U_{j,l}(t)$ for its strategies, which evolve according to:

$$U_{j,l}(t) = U_{j,l}(t-1) + 1 - [\lambda(t) - s_{i,l}(\mu(t-1))]^2,$$
$$j = 1, \ldots, N, \ l = 1, \ldots, S, \tag{2}$$

thus after t steps it can randomly select a strategy from the set of strategies that share the highest score:

$$l^*(j, t) \in \underset{l=1,\ldots,S}{\mathrm{argmax}}(U_{j,l}(t)). \tag{3}$$

The agents base their predictions on their best scoring strategies:

$$p_j(t) = s_{j,l^*(j,t)} , \tag{4}$$

where $p_j(t) \in \{0, 1\}$ denotes the prediction of agent j at time t, for what the next global bit $\lambda(t+1)$ should be. Every agent j thus has a prediction success (or agent score), denoted by $R_j(t)$, which is just a counter for how many times agent j predicted correctly the new bit λ in the past. These scores evolve according to

$$R_j(t) = R_j(t-1) + 1 - [\lambda(t) - p_j(t-1)]^2 \tag{5}$$

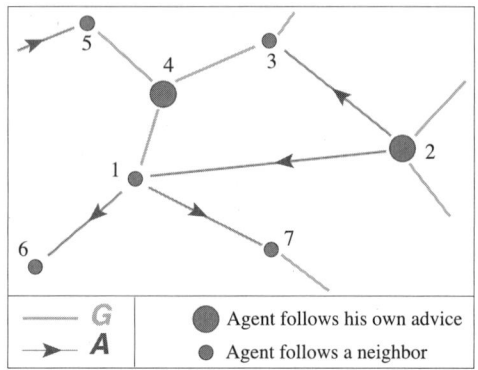

Figure 1. The substrate network and the active network.

for all agents. Let us denote by $\overline{\Gamma}_i$ the closed neighborhood of i, which includes the set of nearest-neighbor vertices on **G** of i, and i himself. The agent $j^*(i, t) \in \overline{\Gamma}_i$ whom advice i will follow through action (for the (t+1)th step) is a randomly chosen element of the set:

$$j^*(i, t) \in \underset{j \in \overline{\Gamma}_i}{\mathrm{argmax}}(R_j(t)) . \qquad (6)$$

The collection of directed edges $i \leftarrow j^*(i, t), i = 1, 2, \ldots, N$, is the active network **F** at time t. Figure 1 shows in a schematic diagram an example of the directions of influence on the substrate network. Agents 1 and 3 follow the advice of agent 2, who follows its own advice. This means that $R_2 \geq \max\{R_1, R_6, R_7, R_4\}$, and $R_2 \geq \{R_4, R_3, \ldots\}$. However, agent 4 follows itself, which implies $R_4 \geq \{R_1, R_3, R_5\}$.

The *action* $a_i(t + 1) \in \{0, 1\}$ at the $t + 1$th step taken by agent i will therefore be:

$$a_i(t + 1) = 1 - p_{j^*(i,t)}(t) = 1 - s_{j^*(i,t),l^*} \qquad (7)$$

because if it is predicted that side **A** will be in majority (bit one), then the agent better choose side **B**, so its presence at **A** is the bit zero, and vice versa. The total attendance at side **A** just after the $t + 1$th step can thus be written as:

$$A(t) = \sum_{i=1}^{N} a_i(t + 1) = N - \sum_{i=1}^{N} p_{j^*(i,t)}(t) = N - \sum_{i=1}^{N} s_{j^*(i,t),l^*}. \qquad (8)$$

Equations 1–8 form a strongly nonlinear coupled set of equations describing the microscopic dynamics of the minority game on an arbitrary network **G**.

The reward received by agent i just after the $t + 1$th step is thus:

$$g_i(t + 1) = [\lambda(t + 1) - a_i(t + 1)]^2 \qquad (9)$$

(it is zero if the agent was in the majority side and unity if it was in the minority side).

We do not, in general, know the precise topology of the social network. However, it is known that social networks have a small-world character [9, 14, 15, 21, 22]. Here we take **G** to be an Erdős–Rényi (ER) random graph with link probability p. An ER random graph shows the small-world effect, because the diameter of the graph increases only logarithmically with the number of vertices [15] and the nodes also have a well-defined average degree, pN, which results from cognitive limitation [9]. Studies using other types of network topologies, which are more suited to describe social networks (one drawback of ER is its low clustering coefficient [22]) will be presented in future publications.

The game is initialized by fixing at random S strategies (Boolean functions) for each agent, an arbitrary initial history string, and a fixed instance of the substrate network **G**. After many iterations the game evolution becomes insensitive to the particular initial history string, however it may remain sensitive to the quenched disorders in the strategy space of the NS strategies that are used and in the social network. There are four relevant parameters in this game: N, S, m, and $p \in [0, 1]$. The substrate network in reality can also change (we make new friends and others fade away). However, its dynamics may be assumed much slower than that of **F**, and in a first approximation it is neglected here

In [2] we presented two rather interesting effects that this model produces, namely: (1) the statistics of outlinks (leadership level) is supported on a $1/k$, scale-free law [1] and (2) if the average connectivity on the substrate network of an agent (pN) is in a particular range of values (approx. 15 to 20, which is a rather natural number for the average number of active acquintances one has), and the trait diversity is small ($m \simeq 2$), then the networked collective can be more efficient than in the standard MG, making this effect wordy for further systems design studies [23].

Next we present further results that refer to the information content of the global history string when interagent communications are present and to the stability of a leadership position (see the introduction or [2]).

3 Predictability and Persistence

The history string of m bits contains information about the past evolution of the collective, and in principle, some of that information can be used by an agent to better coordinate and improve its next move. The virtual scores of their strategies incorporate the projection of that information onto their individual strategy spaces, and similarly, the virtual scores of agents' predictions incorporate the projection of that information onto the local neighborhood on the social network.

In the classical MG, the agents could only exploit the information in the history string through the virtual scores of their strategies. The standard game can be divided in two main regimes [?, 4, 18], depending on whether $\alpha < \alpha_c$ or $\alpha > \alpha_c$, where $\alpha = P/N = 2^m/N$ is the scaling variable of the MG, and $\alpha_c \simeq 0.3374\ldots$ (for $S = 2$) is the critical point separating the two regimes. The domain $\alpha < \alpha_c$ is called the symmetric regime where no agent can on average make gains over other agents, and most importantly, all the useful information from the history string has been arbitraged away; see [?,4] for more details. The point α_c is where this symmetry brakes, and the agents develop the maximum amount of cooperation (as a collective), making the game the most efficient (where the volatility σ has a minimum). For $\alpha > \alpha_c$, the history string will have nonexploited useful information, which for fixed N will not be arbitraged away [?,4]. (Normally, such information would attract more agents into the game, thus increasing N and decreasing α, pushing it down into the symmetric regime.) A possible measure for the information contained in the history string is the square of the average of the new bit λ conditional on the history string ν that just preceeds it, minus $1/2$: $(\langle \lambda | \nu \rangle - 1/2)^2$. If all information is arbitraged away from the history string, then the bit 0 appears as frequently as the bit 1 and so this quantity is zero for all histories; otherwise it is a nonzero positive number at least for some histories. Here, for simplicity, we represent a history string ν by its integer representation $\nu \in 0, 1, 2, \ldots, P - 1$. An overall measure therefore is:

$$\theta(m) = \lim_{T \to \infty} \sum_{\nu=0}^{P-1} (\langle \lambda | \nu \rangle - 1/2)^2 f_\nu, \tag{10}$$

where f_ν is the frequency of the history string ν in the time series

$$f_\nu = \sum_{t=1}^{T} \delta_{\mu(t),\nu} / T.$$

Figure 2 shows $\theta(m)$, which quantifies the amount of predictability left in the history string, for various substrate network connectivities. The classical MG corresponds to $p = 0$. As expected, in the symmetric phase, there is no useful information left in the history string for the agents to exploit, when $p = 0$. For $\alpha > \alpha_c$ (or $m > m_c$), i.e., in the antisymmetric regime, $\theta > 0$ and there is valuable information left in the history string. As p is increased, the symmetric regime remains almost

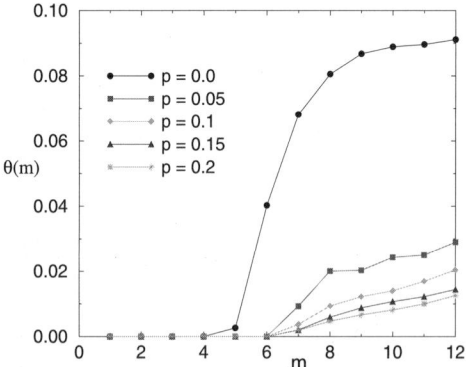

Figure 2. Predictability left in the history string for various substrate connectivities. Here $N = 101$, $S = 2$, and thus $m_c \simeq 5.1$ for the standard MG. Each point was obtained after averaging over 32 time series realizations, keeping the random network fixed and varying the strategy space disorder. $T = 2 \cdot 10^5$, and the first $2 \cdot 10^5$ iterations were discarded as transients.

unchanged (apart from a slight shift of α_c to larger values). The antisymmetric domain remains, however, with θ values considerably *lower* than for the classical MG, as p increases. This means that the agents actually use their network acquintances to arbitrage away *some* of the useful information left in the global history string, and therefore one could say that the network improves on the *information efficiency* of the game. The quantity θ, however, does not have enough resolution to give us dynamical information about the MG. A better quantity for that is the persistence of outcomes as calculated by the correlation between the global outcome $\lambda(t)$ at time t and that at time $t + \tau$, $\lambda(t + \tau)$, given that the same history strings preceeded these outcomes:

$$Z(\tau) = \sum_{v=0}^{P-1} f_v \langle [\lambda(t) - 1/2][\lambda(t + \tau) - 1/2] | \mu(t) = \mu(t + \tau) = v \rangle \qquad (11)$$

as was introduced in [5].

Figure 3 shows the time correlations versus τ, as the connectivity of the substrate network, p, is increased. The curves with $p = 0$ in Figures 3a and b correspond to the classical MG. In Figure 3a, $\alpha < \alpha_c$ and the behavior is anti-persistent in the symmetric phase: The agents' action is periodic with period $2P$ and on average they choose opposite actions compared to previous times for the same history strings. This is an information that could be arbitraged away, except that the agents do not sense this opportunity [4]. If a smarter agent is introduced in this collective (with larger m), it can take advantage of this [4] and make profits. Introducing agent-agent communications across the substrate network ($p > 0$) completely makes the antipersistent behavior disappear, already for low connectivities ($p = 0.05$) as seen in Figure 3a! In the antisymmetric phase, $\alpha > \alpha_c$, which is Figure 3b, the classical MG has a persistent behavior, namely agents will likely repeat their actions given the same history string. As substrate connectivity is increased, this persistent behavior disappears, and the correlations will tend to zero (when the average connectivity, $pN = \mathcal{O}(1)$). This is in concordance with the behavior of θ, namely the history string will have much less useful information left in it to be exploited because of the presence of the social network. The only case in the classical MG where the correlations vanish, is at the critical point $\alpha = \alpha_c$ when the game is maximally efficient (from the point of view

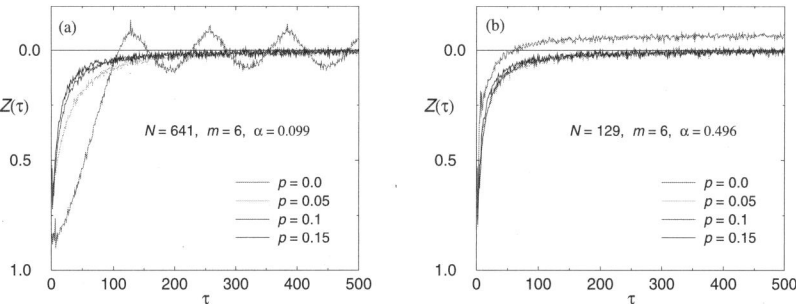

Figure 3. The function $Z(\tau)$. Here 10^6 transients were discarded, $S = 2$, and $T = 1 \cdot 10^5$.

of attendance fluctuations, i.e., volatility). In contrast, when on a random network, these correlations vanish for most of the cases, but this does not mean that the game is efficient! None of the quantities θ and $Z(\tau)$ is able to resolve that kind of information, because they do not describe the statistics of the *local* information flow *on the network*. It means that the network information flow is more important from the point of view of collective efficiency (in the sense of volatility) than the information encased in the global history string.

4 Stability of a Leadership Position

In this section we estimate the persistence of the agents in the leadership structure by computing the time correlations in the number of outlinks (followers) that the agents have. Due to the glassiness shown by the system, we first estimate for each agent the average number of outlinks, i.e.,

$$\langle k_j^{\text{out}} \rangle = \frac{1}{T} \sum_{t=1}^{T} k_j^{\text{out}}(t), \tag{12}$$

where $k_j^{\text{out}}(t)$ is the number of followers that agent j has at time t. Then we analyze the statistical behavior of its leadership position by computing the time correlations in the fluctuations present in the number of outlinks:

$$C_j(\tau) = \frac{1}{T} \sum_{t=1}^{T} (k_j^{\text{out}}(t + \tau) - \langle k_j^{\text{out}} \rangle)(k_j^{\text{out}}(t) - \langle k_j^{\text{out}} \rangle). \tag{13}$$

The overall leadership correlations are then defined as averages over all the agents in the society,

$$C(\tau) \equiv \frac{1}{N} \sum_{j=1}^{N} C_j(\tau)/C_j(0). \tag{14}$$

Figure 4 shows the correlation function $C(\tau)$ versus τ for different m values. The curves correspond to different realizations of randomness in both strategy and network disorder spaces. Figures 4a and b are drawn with dots, for better visibility. Both the correlation functions are periodically oscillating; see the insets where the data is drawn with line markers. Note the glassy character of the system for low memory values ($m = 2$, $m = 3$) in Figures 4a and b. These oscillations are tied to the oscillatory behavior in the attendance of the standard MG; see [7]. For large memory, the oscillations disappear and the correlation function has power law–like decay with an exponential cutoff, see the insets in Figures 4c and d. The average over the disorders in this case behave similarly, as shown in Figure 5. The nondecaying behavior of $C(\tau)$ for low-memory regimes suggests that there are leaders whose position is the same in average, i.e., their position is more stable than in the case of large memory, as claimed in the main article. Figure 6 shows the dynamics of the influence,

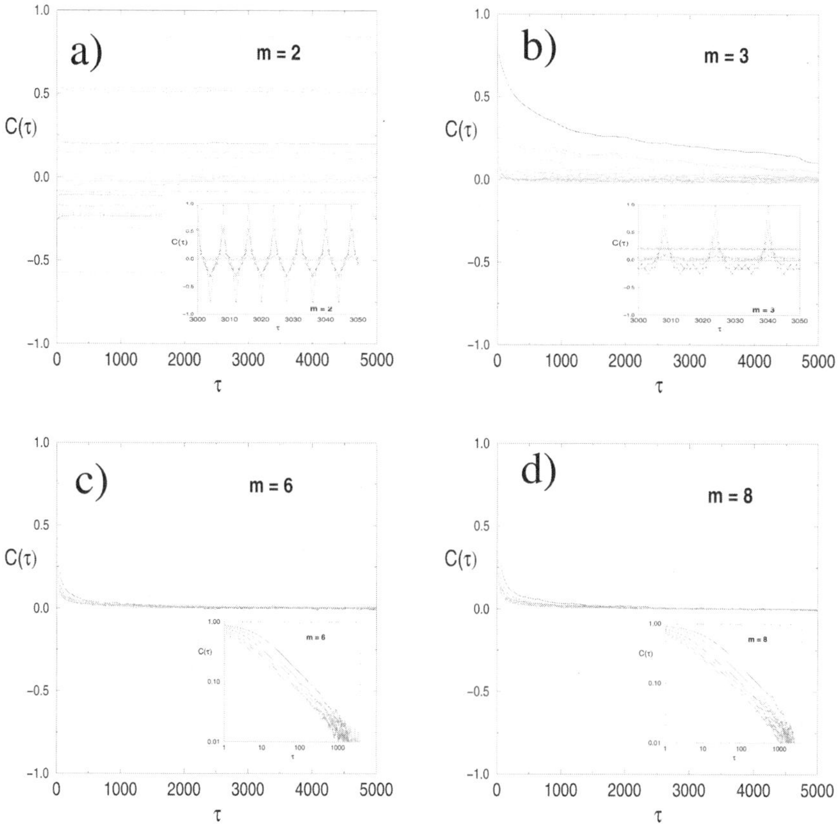

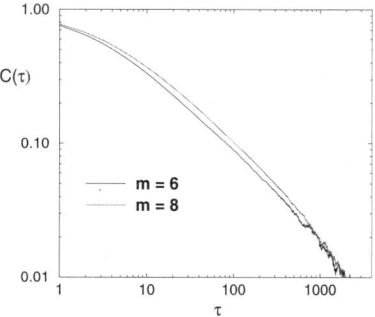

Figure 4. The temporal out-link correlation function $C(\tau)$. For all cases $N = 101$, $S = 2$, $5 \cdot 10^5$ transients have been discarded, and $T = 10^5$. The insets in a) and b) are magnifications of corresponding pieces from the main figures with data drawn with lines-markers to show the oscillatory character of the correlations. The insets in c) and d) are the same plots as the main figures, shown on a log-log scale.

Figure 5. The temporal outlink correlation function $C(\tau)$ after averaging over both strategy space and network space disorders for $m = 6$ and $m = 8$.

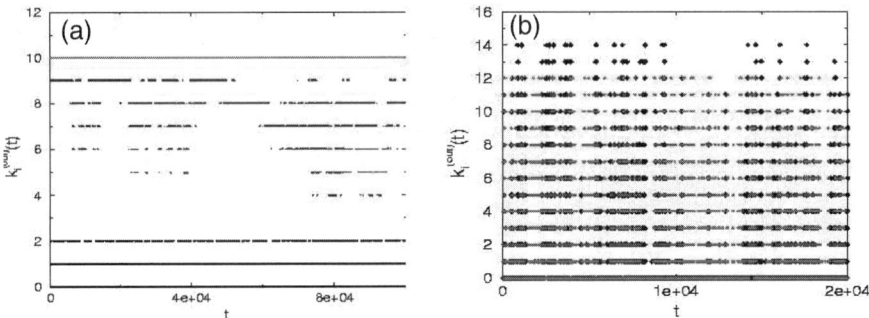

Figure 6. Influence fluctuations for some arbitrarily chosen leaders in the low trait diversity, $m = 3$ regime (a), and large trait diversity regime $m = 8$, (b). Different markers correspond to different agents. Here $N = 101$, $S = 2$.

i.e., the outlinks of a few specific, arbitrarily chosen agents, in both the low-memory ($m = 3$) and large-memory ($m = 8$) cases. Low memory means low trait diversity in the strategy space and large memory implies large trait diversity. Notice that for the large trait diversity case the influence of a particular agent fluctuates rather wildly, but the leadership position is more stable in the case of low trait diversity, where agents tend to keep their influences (in average) across time.

5 Discussion and Outlook

We have shown (also in [2]) that the evolution of multiagent games can strongly depend on the nature of the agent's information resources, including local information gathered on the social network, a network whose structure in turn is influenced by the fate of the game itself. In our study, we allowed for this dynamic coupling between the game and the network by using reinforcement learning as an ubiquitous mechanism for inter-agent communications. In addition to the results presented in [2], here we have shown that information obtained through the social network can override the information content of the global source, and thus directly affect the evolution of the collective. Low trait diversity systems seem to produce more stable links in the active network and thus more effective stability to the leaders (similarly to dictatorships, where the space of allowed action for the agents is rather limited).

Certainly, one might ask: How general are these observed effects, and how much are they artifacts of the particular model? We have to count for such artifacts, and ultimately experiments will decide which effects are generic and which are not. However, these models can teach us how to deal in general with the novel complexities presented by multiagent systems. Very much in the same vein as the dynamical system $x_{n+1} = r x_n (1 - x_n)$ (the logistic map) has taught us how to deal with nonlinearities generating chaos (Feigenbaum, a physicist, could probably care less about the fate of the rabbits' population amids wolfs, which this equation is supposed to describe). The main message learned from this little artificial model is the set of *allowed or sensible questions* one might ask about such systems.

Science is defined by no-go statements or theorems: Even though we know how a single molecule behaves in a box or how to describe collisions of Newtonian particles in the same box, the methods of statistical mechanics were ultimately needed to derive from such knowledge the phenomenologically obtained laws of thermodynamics for a mol of gas in a box. Here the no-go statement was that one cannot effectively describe the *collective* of 10^{23} Newtonian particles in a box by coupling on the order of 10^{23} equations of motions. Another example of a no-go statement is from quantum mechanics: One cannot determine with infinite precision simultaneously the position and momentum of a quantum particle. Yet another example comes from computer science: One cannot solve in polynomial time NP-hard problems, such as the traveling salesman problem. The chapter of chaos and nonlinear dynamical systems serves another no-go statement: One cannot predict the fate of a trajectory beyond time scales determined by the inverse of the average positive Lyapunov exponent. It seems as if when there is a novel type of complexity on the table, no-go statements are generated. It is also a signature of the fact that one is dealing with a new chapter of science. From the difficulty of describing these systems, it is apparent that multiagent systems and collectives theory *is a new chapter* of science. We know how to describe the two-agent interaction process via game theory, in the same way we were able to describe the collision process of two particles in a gas. This knowledge, however, becomes less useful when trying to describe interacting many-agent systems, in the same way the collision theory was less useful in describing a mol of gas in a box. What are this novel chapter's other no-go statements? What kind of questions can one ask sensibly and how? These we can only begin to learn from "playing" with simple models such as the ones presented in this chapter, with the hope that we will eventually find the "logistic map" of collectives.

References

1. R. Albert and A.-L. Barabási. Statistical Mechanics of Complex Networks, *Rev. Mod. Phys.* **74**, 47 (2002).
2. M. Anghel, Z. Toroczkai, K. E. Bassler, and G. Korniss. Competition-Driven Network Dynamics: Emergence of a Scale-Free Leadership Structure and Collective Efficiency, *Phys. Rev. Lett.* **92**, 058701 (2004)
3. B. W. Arthur. Inductive Reasoning and Bounded Rationality, *Am. Econ. Rev.* **84(2)**, 406 (1994).
4. D. Challet, *Modelling markets dynamics: Minority games and beyond.* Ph.D. Thesis (2000).
5. D. Challet and M. Marsili. Phase transition and symmetry breaking in the minority game, *Phys. Rev. E* **60**, 6271 (1999).
6. D. Challet and Y.-C. Zhang. Emergence of cooperation and organization in an evolutionary game, *Physica A* **246**, 407 (1997).
7. M. A. R. de Cara, O. Pla, and F. Guinea. Competition, efficiency and collective behavior in the "El Farol" bar model *Eur.Phys. J. B* **10**, 187 (1999).

8. V. M. Eiguiluz and M. G. Zimmermann. Transmission of Information and Herd Behavior: An Application to Financial Markets, *Phys. Rev. Lett.* **85**, 5659 (2000).
9. E. M. Jin, M. Girvan, and M. E. J. Newman. Structure of growing social networks, *Phys. Rev. E* **64**, 046132 (2001).
10. N. F. Johnson, M. Hart, and P. M. Hui. Crowd effects and volatility in markets with competing agents, *Physica A* **269**, 1 (1999).
11. L. P. Kaelbing, M. L. Littman, and A. W. Moore. Reinforcement learning: A survey, *J. Artif. Intell. Res.* **4**, 237 (1996).
12. T. Kalinowski, H.-J. Schulz, and M. Birese. Cooperation in the Minority Game with local information, *Physica A*, **277**, 502 (2000).
13. R. Manuca, Y. Li, R. Riolo, and R. Savit. The structure of adaptive competition in minority games, *Physica A* **282**, 559 (2000).
14. S. Milgram. Small-World problem, *Psychol. Today* **2**, 61 (1967).
15. M. E. J. Newman, Models of the small world, *J. Stat. Phys.* **101**, 819 (2000).
16. M. A. Nowak and R. M. May, Evolutionary games and spatial chaos, *Nature* **359**, 826 (1992).
17. M. Paczuski, K. E. Bassler, and A. Corral. Self-organized networks of competing Boolean agents, *Phys. Rev. Lett.* **84**, 3185 (2000).
18. R. Savit, R. Manuca, and R. Riolo. Adaptive Competition, Market Efficiency, and Phase Transitions, *Phys. Rev. Lett.* **82**, 2203 (1999).
19. B. Skyrms and R. Pemantle. A dynamic model of social network formation, *Proc. Natl. Acad. Sci. USA*, **97**, 9340 (2000).
20. F. Slanina. Harms and benefits from social imitation, *Physica A*, **299**, 334 (2000).
21. D. J. Watts, *Small Worlds* (Princeton, NJ: Princeton University Press, 1999).
22. D.J . Watts and S. H. Strogatz. Collective dynamics of 'small-world' networks, *Nature* **393**, 440 (1998).
23. D. H. Wolpert and K. Tumer, Optimal payoff functions for members of collectives, *Advances in Complex Systems*, **4(2/3)** 265 (2001).

8

Man and Superman: Human Limitations, Innovation, and Emergence in Resource Competition

Robert Savit,* Katia Koelle,[†] Wendy Treynor,[‡] and Richard Gonzalez[‡]

1 Introduction

This conference is devoted to the theme of the design, prediction, and control of collectives. Many of the collectives that we are implicitly concerned with (and for good reason) are collectives composed of software agents or combinations of software and hardware agents. Collectives of agents that remotely gather information from distant planets and then transmit that information to Earth are one example. Of interest to the military are collectives of small, cheap sensors distributed on a battlefield or in a city that measure some aspect of local conditions and then relay that information to a central repository near a command center. Another example is a collection of sensors and actuators that control the flow of oil or electricity through a complex network by sensing local conditions and responding to them. One common architecture for the interaction of these local agents is through some sort of analogy with economic systems. Here it is supposed that the local agents compete for some scarce resource (bandwidth in the case of agents whose job it is to transmit information, or fluid pressure in the case of those agents whose job it is to regulate oil flow), possibly by a bidding mechanism or by some other strategic architecture that rewards agents for "buying low" or "selling high."

In all these cases, the local (software and hardware) agents rely on adaptive algorithms associated with that agent to make choices and execute actions. But in many cases the situation is more complicated. There will often be situations in which a human (or humans) can intervene in the workings of an otherwise automated, engineered system and change its behavior radically. Thus, a controller in Houston may decide to alter the mission or location of a set of remote sensors in space. A board of directors of an oil company may decide to intervene or countermand the actions of a network of local controllers on pipelines for the purpose of maximizing short-term

---
* Physics Department and Center for Theoretical Physics, University of Michigan, Ann Arbor, MI 48109

[†] Biology Department, University of Michigan, Ann Arbor, MI 48109

[‡] Psychology Department, University of Michigan, Ann Arbor, MI 48109

profit. In still other systems of great importance the system may be entirely composed of human agents competing for a scarce resource. The archetypical example of such a system is financial markets, but there are others. Academics may compete for the scarce resource of tenure (or once tenure is secured, fame and a higher salary) by making a seminally important discovery before anyone else. Pharmaceutical companies (composed of humans) devote many resources to drug discovery in the hopes of patenting a lucrative (and, of course, beneficial) drug before their competitors.

These scenarios and many others like them naturally raise the question of how human agents behave when placed in competition for scarce resources. There are, generically, two ways in which such competition can proceed: conformity (or majority seeking) and innovation (or minority seeking). Examples of the dynamics of conformity include wars (the winner is usually the one with the bigger army, so it pays to be in the majority) and the acquisition of political power in a democracy. It is much better to belong to the party in control (i.e., the one that garnered the most votes and is thus the majority party). The examples cited in the previous paragraph, on the other hand, are largely examples of innovation or minority seeking. It only pays to discover and patent a drug if you're the first one to do it, and it's the one who *first* proves (and publishes) that great theorem who gets tenure.

Of course, in real systems it is the interplay between majority and minority seeking that gives them their richness and complexity. So, in war it is usually, but not always, the bigger army that wins. Sometimes David can beat Goliath by being innovative. In financial markets it pays to be innovative, but generally only if the crowd follows your example a little later. You want to buy IBM only if everyone else does—but does it the next day.

Nevertheless, in order to begin to develop a basis for understanding the complexities of competition in the real world, it is useful to look at very simple systems in which the naked dynamics of majority or minority seeking is exposed. In this paper we will concern ourselves with the dynamics of minority seeking, and, specifically, with the dynamics of minority seeking (or innovation) when it involves humans.

The minority game, first introduced by Challet and Zhang, and subsequently studied numerically and analytically[1] is a system in which pure innovation is rewarded. This model has also played a role in a number of other presentations at this conference. Detailed expositions of the model have appeared elsewhere, so I will not spend much time describing it. Most of the work done on the minority game has been in the context of either analytic treatments or computer simulations. In particular, there have, heretofore, been no controlled studies of how *humans* actually behave when faced with the need to place themselves in the minority. In this chapter I will discuss experiments we performed at the University of Michigan with human subjects playing the minority game.

---

[1] D. Challet and Y.-C. Zhang, *Physica A*, **246**, 407 (1997). R. Savit, R. Manuca, and R. Riolo, *Phys. Rev. Lett.* **82**, 2203 (1999). D. Challet, M. Marsili, and R. Zecchina, *Phys. Rev. Lett.* **84**, 1824 (2000). See also the references on the excellent Web site http://www.unifr.ch/econophysics/ minority.

2 Basic Features of the Minority Game

2.1 The Standard Minority Game

Definition

The simplest version of the minority game consists of N (odd) agents playing a game as follows: At each time step of the game, each of the N agents joins one of two groups, labeled 0 or 1. Each agent in the minority group at that time step is awarded a point, and each agent belonging to the majority group gets nothing. An agent chooses which group to join at a given time step based on the prediction of a strategy. The strategy uses information from the historical record of which group was the minority as a function of time. A strategy of memory m is a table of two columns and 2^m rows. The left column contains all the 2^m possible combinations of m 0s and 1s; each entry in the right column is a 0 or a 1. To use this strategy, an agent observes which groups were the minority groups during the immediately preceding m time steps and finds that string of 0s and 1s in the left column of the table. The corresponding entry in the right column contains that strategy's determination of which group (0 or 1) the agent should join during the current time step. An example of an $m = 3$ strategy is shown here:

Recent History	Predicted Next Minority Group
000	0
001	1
010	1
011	0
100	0
101	0
110	1
111	1

In the simplest version of the minority game, all strategies used by all agents have the same value of m. At the beginning of the game each agent is randomly assigned s (>1) of the 2^{2^m} possible strategies, chosen with replacement. For its current play the agent chooses its strategy that would have had the best performance over the history of the game up to that time. Ties between strategies are decided by a coin toss. In the games we will discuss in this section, each agent has two strategies ($s = 2$). Because the agents have more than one strategy, the game is adaptive in that agents can choose to play different strategies at different moments of the game in response to changes in their environment, that is, in response to new entries in the time series of minority groups as the game proceeds. Note, however, that in these games agents must play with the strategies they were assigned at the beginning of the game. There is no evolution in these games. Evolution will be discussed later.

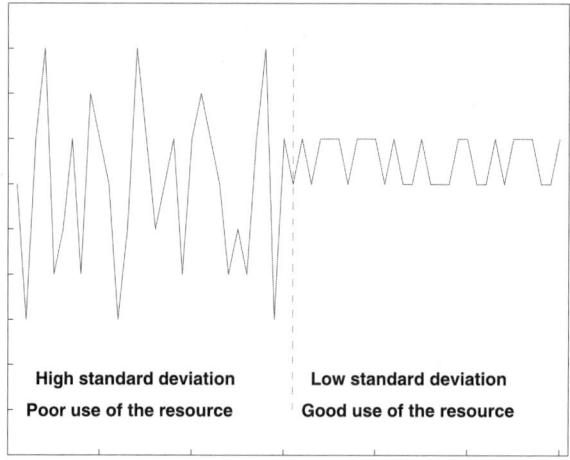

Figure 1.

Results—Analytic and Numerical

One of the interesting questions to address with the minority game is what the typical experience of the agents is. To put it another way, membership in the minority group is a limited resource. We might ask whether that resource is well used. If the minority groups are typically large (i.e., just less than $N/2$), then the limited resource is well used and a relatively large number of points are awarded to the agents in general. If, on the other hand, the minority groups are relatively small, then the limited resource is not well used, and not many points are awarded in toto. A convenient inverse measure of resource use is σ, the standard deviation of the number of agents in one of the groups, say, group 1. This may be thought of as a measure of inefficiency of the system at distributing resources. To see this, look at Figure 1. Because the game is symmetric, the expectation value of the number of agents in each group averaged over time is close to $N/2$.[2] If σ is large then the minority groups typically will be small, and if σ is small the minority groups will be large.

The basic result of the standard minority game is illustrated in Figure 2. Here we have plotted σ^2/N as a function of $z = 2^m/N$. Detailed discussion of this result can be found in the literature.[3] Here we only point out the most important features. First, all games lie on the same scaling curve. Second, if z is too small, then typically the system does poorly at allocating resources. If z is very large the system also does relatively poorly at allocating resources. In fact, for large z the aggregate behavior of the system, in the sense of resource distribution, is the same as if the agents were making their choices randomly. The dynamics here are somewhat different than sim-

---

[2] It is not quite N/2 in a given game because there are biases built into the game due to the particular (random) strategies that were assigned to the agents at the beginning of the game. This bias is not important for our discussion here.

[3] See note 1.

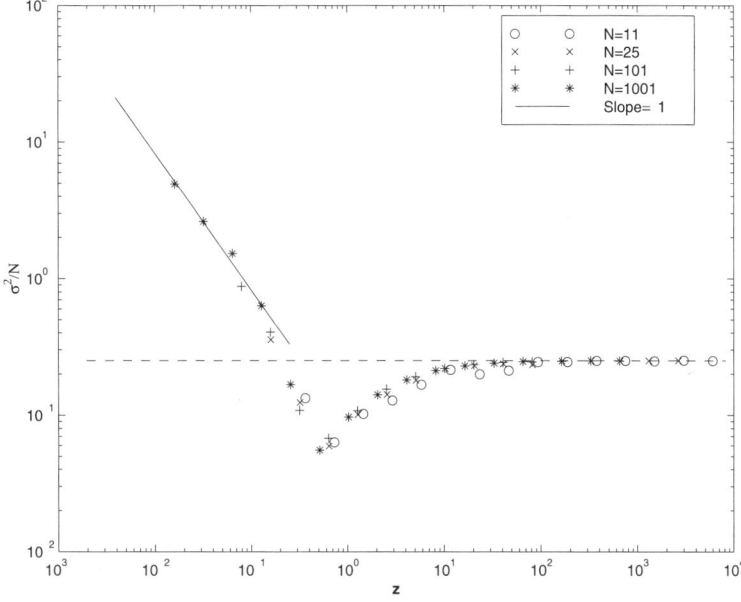

Figure 2.

ple independent random choices between the two groups, but the typical size of the minority group is the same as such a random choice game (RCG). For intermediate values of z we see emergent coordination in the agents' choices. That is, σ is significantly smaller than it would be if the agents were making uncoordinated or random choices, and the size of the typical minority group is relatively high. Note also that there is a minimum and an apparent cusp at a particular value of $z \equiv z_c$. At z_c there is a bona fide phase transition separating two phases with very different structure. Extensive discussions of this counterintuitive result can be found in a number of places in the literature.[4]

2.2 The Minority Game with Evolution

Before turning to a discussion of the human experiments, I want to describe one variation of the standard minority game that will be important for our subsequent discussion.[5] In the standard game, agents are assigned strategies at the beginning of the game and they retain those strategies during the entire game. However, in addition to adaptivity (being able to alter among established strategies in response to changes in the environment), agents in various systems can also manifest evolutionary capabilities. That is, agents can evolve their strategies, developing new ones

---

[4] See note 1.
[5] Y. Li, R. Riolo, and R. Savit, *Physica A* **276**, 234 (2000); *Physica A* **276**, 265 (2000).

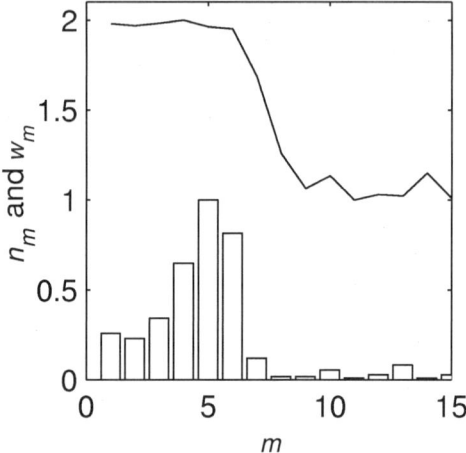

Figure 3.

and jettisoning old, poorly performing strategies. To model this dynamic, we modify the standard minority game in the following way: After playing the game for T time steps, a selection of the poorest performing agents are chosen, their strategies are discarded, and they are give two new (randomly generated) strategies. In a typical experiment, $T = 500$ time steps and half the agents from the bottom 20% of performers are chosen at random to have their strategies exchanged. The two new strategies can have a different memory, m, from the ones they are replacing so that the game now becomes one of competition among agents, each of whom may have a different memory. (Although one agent may play with strategies with different memory from another agent, the two strategies that a given agent has will have the same m as each other. That is, a given agent's two strategies always have the same memory during a given generation.) The results we describe here do not qualitatively depend on these parameter choices. This evolutionary process is repeated for a substantial number of generations (typically 20–50).

As one might expect, σ^2/N for the games with evolution is typically considerably smaller than σ^2/N for the nonevolutionary games. There is an additional important feature of these games illustrated in Figure 3. Here we plot some features of the population of agents after 50 generations in a typical minority game with evolution. In this case, $N = 101$. On the horizontal axis is m, the memory of the strategies of a given agent. Two types of data are plotted on this graph. The first, illustrated by the bar chart, shows the relative number of agents playing with a given memory. Note that almost all the agents play with memories of 6 or less.[6] The curve in this figure represents the average wealth of agents playing with a given memory. Note that

---

[6] The fact that there is a dramatic fall-off in the wealth per agent and in the number of agents playing with a given memory at $m = 6$ is not an accident. The value of m at the fall-off depends on N and is related to the value of z_c in the games played with fixed N and m. See Y. Li, R. Riolo, and R. Savit, *Physica A* **276,** 265 (2000), for more details.

the wealthiest agents (i.e., those that were most often in the minority group) were those playing with the *simplest* strategies, that is, the strategies that used the shortest memories. We will come back to these results later in this chapter.

3 The Human Experiments

3.1 The Setup

The human minority game experiments were conducted with volunteers from the University of Michigan and the Ann Arbor area. A room was set up containing 25 PCs. Partitions were placed between the computer screens so that players could not see what was on neighboring screens. Each player's screen contained two buttons that could be clicked with the mouse. Clicking the left button placed that player in group 1 and clicking on the right button placed that player in group 2. In addition, the screen contained a sequential list of which were the minority groups for all past time steps of the game. Each screen also contained a graph that showed that player's total winnings as a function of time. The history of minority groups and the graph of that player's winnings were updated after each time step of the game. No other information was available to the players, and no direct communication was allowed among players. Prior to the game being played, the rules of the game were explained to the volunteers. The volunteers were also told that they would be paid $10.00 for participating in the game and that players would receive $0.05 each time they were in a minority group. Finally, the players were informed that the player with the greatest accumulated wealth in the game would have its name entered into a drawing with nine other highest-scoring players from each of nine other games for a $50.00 bonus. This bonus was instituted to ensure that players would continue to focus and actively participate in the game. The volunteers were also told that they would be asked to complete a short questionnaire at the end of the game.

Each game was played for 400 time steps and took about 45 minutes. Players were allowed five seconds to make their choices in a given time step. A two-second grace period followed the five-second decision interval. A counter appeared on the screen so that the players would know the time remaining to make their choices. If at the end of seven seconds a player did not make a choice, the computer entered a random choice for the player. In different sessions, games were played with different numbers of players, N, ranging from 5 to 23.

3.2 Results

Among the most intriguing results of the computer simulations (and the analytic analyses) of the minority game is the observation of emergent coordination among the agents' choices. As shown in Figure 2, in games played with a fixed agent memory, for a range of values of memory, minority groups are typically larger than they would be if the agents were making random choices leading to greater generated average wealth. In the evolutionary versions of the game, in which agents' strategies

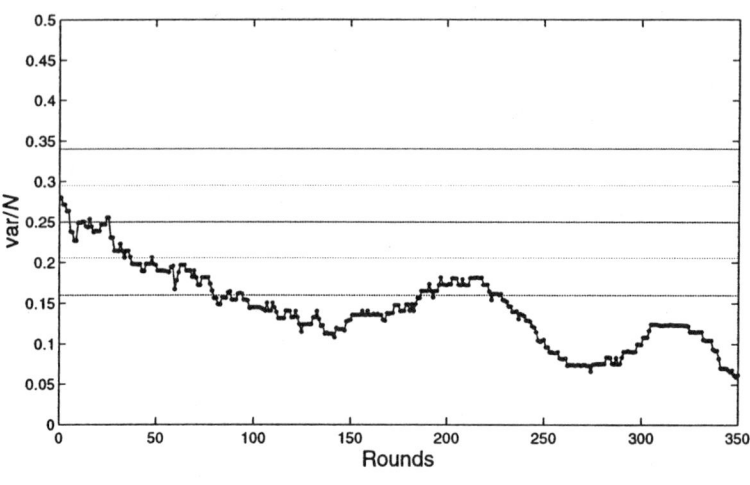

Figure 4.

and memories are allowed to evolve over time the emergent coordination is even more marked and the limited resource (minority group membership) is even better used. Or, to put it another way, more wealth is generated.

What happens when the game is played with humans? In Figure 4 we plot, for one of the games (in this case $N = 5$) σ^2/N as a function of time steps in the game. This result is qualitatively typical of the outcomes of our games. In this plot, σ^2/N is computed over a moving window of 50 time steps. The horizontal line at 0.25 indicates the expected value of σ^2/N for a random choice game (RCG). The lines at 0.2 and 0.3 (0.15 and 0.35) indicate one (two) standard deviation(s) about that expectation value under the RCG assumption. We see that at the beginning of the game σ^2/N has the value we would expect if the players were making their choices randomly and with equal probability. As time goes by, however, players' choices become more coordinated and the average size of the minority group increases, resulting in increased generated wealth. This is quite a remarkable finding. One might have supposed a priori that players, lacking information about the choices and strategies of other players, would have effectively made random choices of group membership. It appears, however, that this is not the case and that players effectively coordinate their choices based solely on the aggregate information provided by the time series of minority groups. One additional noteworthy feature is the occurrence of oscillations in σ^2/N with a period of 50 to 100 time steps. As we shall report in detail elsewhere,[7], these oscillations are the result of nonstationarity in the strategies of the players. In particular, players evolve their heuristics over time until a quasiequilibrium state is reached. Then one player, feeling that he can do better, will dramatically change his strategy. Because the game is endogenous, the other players must accommodate their strategies to the qualitatively new environment (i.e., the one generated by a qualitatively different strategy being played by one of the participants). During the period of

---

[7] R. Savit, K. Koelle, Y. Li, and R. Gonzalez, to appear.

adjustment overall efficiency of the systems degrades until a new quasiequilibrium state is reached, leading to oscillations in σ^2/N.

The results of Figure 4 are typical of results for most games played with various numbers of players. It is interesting to compare these results with similar ones generated by computer simulations. In Figure 5 we show some typical analogous results for computer simulation games played with evolution and with $N = 5, 17$, and 101 agents. In these examples the poorest agents are allowed to change their strategies every 20 time steps. Specifically, half of the least successful 30% of agents are chosen at random for strategy replacement. Their existing strategies are discarded and they are given two new strategies. The m value of the new strategies may be different than that of the old strategies, but the two new strategies share the same m value. Note the qualitative similarity to Figure 4, both in the decrease of σ^2/N over time and in the existence of oscillations.

The existence of emergent coordination in the human experiments, qualitatively similar to that observed in the computer simulations, is remarkable. Remember that the ways in which the computer agents choose their strategies is quite different from the ways in which humans develop and evolve heuristics. Nevertheless, the systemwide performance of the collectives is remarkably similar.

An equally remarkable observation concerns the behavior of individual agents and their strategies. Recall from Figure 3 that in computer simulations agents tended to adopt simpler strategies (as measured by the memory of the strategies) as the game progressed. Moreover, those agents with relatively simple strategies tended to fare better than agents with more complex strategies. Remarkably, with regard to simplicity, we find the same qualitative behavior in the human experiments.

Before presenting the results on individual players in the human experiments, it is useful to spend a moment discussing the definition of simplicity. There are at least two aspects of agent strategies that contribute to "simplicity." First is the amount of information agents use to make their decisions. In the context of the computer simulations, m is a simple measure of this component. The second aspect is the degree to which an agent's choice, given a certain amount of information, is deterministic. One simple way to measure this is to consider quantities like $A_m \equiv [P(1 \mid s_m) - 1/2]^2$. Here s_m is a specific string (of minority groups) of length m, and $P(1 \mid s_m)$ is the conditional probability that the agent in question chooses group 1 following the occurrence of the string s_m. If, given s_m, an agent's choice is completely deterministic then $A_m = 1/4$. If, on the other hand an agent's choice given s_m is completely stochastic, then $A_m = 0$. In the case of the computer simulations, agents with low memories (for example, in the case of Figure 3, agents with memories less than or equal to 6) generally have one of their strategies consistently more highly ranked than the other, so that $A_m \approx 1/4$ for all s_m associated with the memory of their strategies. On the other hand, agents with strategy memories above 6 have more closely ranked pairs of strategies. These agents bounce relatively often between these closely ranked strategies and so the associated A_ms for these agents tend to be relatively small.

In the human experiments we capture all the key strokes of the players, so we are able to impute effective strategies to the players and determine something about their

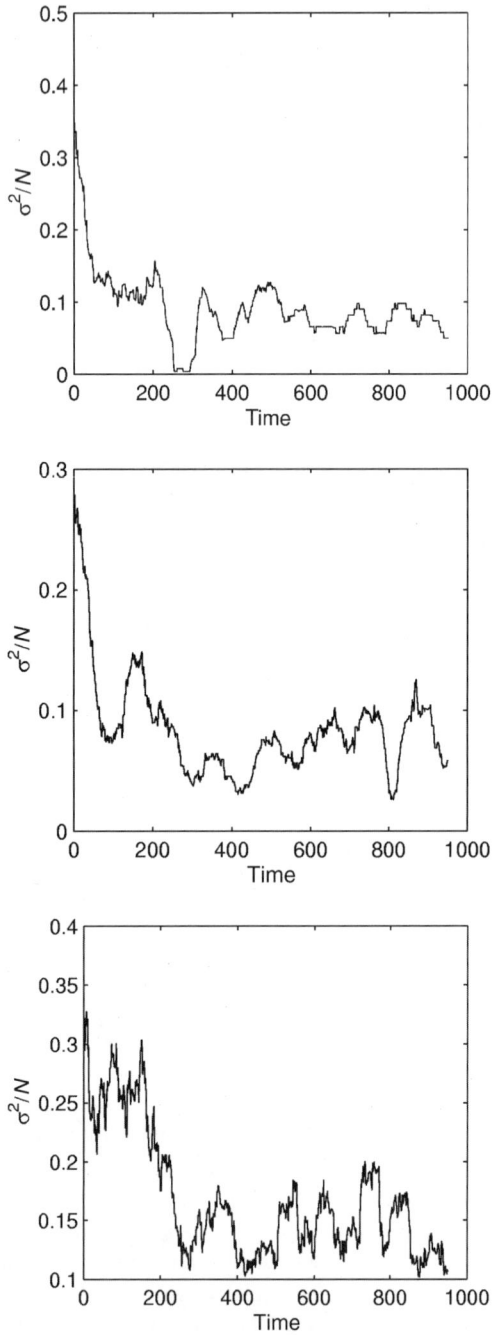

Figure 5.

simplicities. In a forthcoming publication we will discuss this question in detail,[8] but here we present one simplified measure that indicates the relationship between simplicity and accumulated wealth. Consider

$$I_m \equiv \sum_{s_m} P(s_m) A_m$$

where $P(s_m)$ is the probability that the string s_m appears in the history of minority groups. If we assume that a player bases his choice of which group to join on information contained in no more than m lags of the time series of minority groups, then, I_m is a measure of the simplicity of the strategy. In particular, the larger I_m is the simpler the strategy is, in the sense that the strategy is more deterministic. Assume that the players in human experiments consider, at most, information from the last three time steps in deciding which group to join.[9] (We have also studied the m dependence of a player's strategy and have found that small m is also associated with greater wealth. This will be discussed in detail in a forthcoming publication.)

In Figure 6 we present a scatter plot of agent wealth versus I_m for a game with $N = 5$ players. In this figure, each shade of gray represents a different player. Each dot represents wealth versus I_m for that player over a 50-time-step window. Note first the obvious positive slope of the points indicating that, in general, there is a positive correlation between agent wealth and the simplicity (more properly, here, the degree of determinism) of an agent's strategy. Note also that there is a spread in the points of a given shading. In particular, one finds that, generally, points of a given shading that are further to the right (higher values of I_m) and consequently, in general, associated with greater wealth, occur later in the game. This is not too surprising because, generally later epochs of the game result in greater average wealth (see Figure 4). Finally, note that some players perform qualitatively better than others, and again, those players that perform better tend to adopt simpler strategies.

The general features of Figure 6 are found in nearly all the games we have studied for all values of N. In fact, the player who did the best out of all games was, I am sorry to say, an economist who pressed 1 all the time.

We have, therefore, two main observations. First, as in the computer simulations, humans playing the minority game demonstrate emergent group coordination. As the game is played, people learn about the actions of other agents through the medium of the publicly available aggregate information of the time series of past minority groups. Second, like the agents in the computer simulation of the minority game with evolution, there is a generally monotonic relation between the simplicity of a player's strategy and accumulated wealth.

There are several comments we would like to make about these observations. First, if we accept the observation that humans can generally pay attention to about

---

[8] See note 7.

[9] There is good reason to suppose that $m = 3$ is about the largest value of m that most people will use in making their decisions. There is a famous notion in psychology called 7 ± 2 that asserts that people typically can pay attention to between five and nine different pieces of information. Because $m = 3$ encompasses eight pieces of information, this is a reasonable value to take as a maximum number of lags that can be used to determine a person's choice.

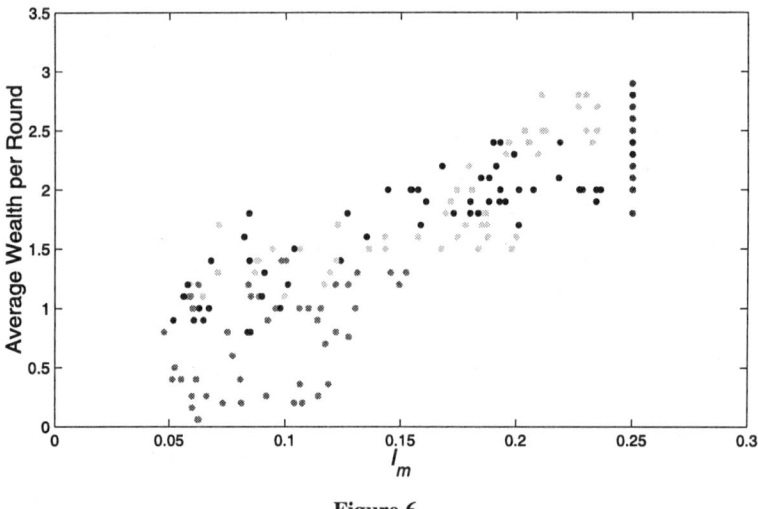

Figure 6.

seven different pieces of information (7 ± 2), then we expect that we can get good coordination of players' choices, and consequently good average wealth generation, if no player is forced to rely on strategies that use more than about seven pieces of information. Roughly, this means paying attention to no more than three previous time steps. If we further make the reasonable assumption that humans will pay the most attention to the most recent events, then we are led to deduce an upper limit on group size that can result in good wealth generation. Recall (see, for example, Figure 3) that in an evolutionary game in which different agents can use different memories, the wealthy agents have a memory, m less than some value m_t. If the processing power of the agents is not restricted, then $m_t = m_c - 1$. But in the case of humans, processing power is restricted, so we expect that $m_t \approx 3$. The effective dimension of the strategy space is therefore $\sum_{m=1}^{m_t} 2^m \approx 2^{m_t+1}$. For the best emergent coordination, the number of agents should be no greater than a number proportional to the effective dimension of the strategy space, with a proportionality constant of about 3.[10] Therefore, the number of agents that can be accommodated with a maximum memory of 3, in a game with agents with different memories, such that that collective achieves the best emergent coordination is $N \approx 3 \times 2^{m_t+1} \approx 40$. We thus expect that, for groups of fewer than about 40 players, we will see emergent coordination qualitatively similar to that which we have seen in our experiments to date. But for games played with groups larger than about 40 under the same circumstances, we expect that emergent coordination will degrade as group size increases.

Second, based on some of our exit polls, we noted that, although most people playing the game continued to be engaged during the entire duration of the game, some people became bored. When they became bored they tended to play very simple strategies, such as always joining the same group. This raises the interesting if

---

[10] See note 5.

somewhat speculative (note emphasis) idea that boredom may be an evolutionarily adaptive strategy. We may tend to get bored when we are engaged in an activity that is not particularly rewarding. Under at least some circumstances, namely those in which innovation can lead to success, the feeling of boredom and the attendant simple actions that it promotes may, in fact, lead to greater individual and group success.

Third, we have noted that there are oscillations in both the computer simulations and the human experiments. With regard to the human experiments, the period and nature of these oscillations tell us something about the nonstationarity of human strategic decisions. In particular, they go directly to the issue of exploration versus exploitation. When a player ceases being satisfied with his exploitation of the system he will begin to explore, and by that exploration (because the system is endogenous) he will upset the near equilibrium state of play, resulting in the performance oscillations we have observed. A closer analysis of these oscillations, their nature, and genesis, will shed light on the relationship between exploration versus exploitation in humans.

Finally, the research project of which these human experiments are a part involves direct confrontation of those experiments with computer simulations of similar games. We do not believe that all the subtleties of human behavior can be captured in simple computer games. However, there are clearly aspects of human and group behavior that have clear analogues in simple computer games. As we have seen in this chapter, taking the results of these computer games seriously affects the kinds of questions that we are led to ask about the human groups and individual behavior in those groups. This suggests a new epistemological thrust in psychology, and perhaps in the other social sciences. The *serious* confrontation with simple computational models can lead to a broader set of questions for the psychological community, and answers to those questions can generate a deeper understanding of individual and group behavior.

The primary observations reported here, namely the existence of emergent coordination and the correlation between strategy simplicity and agent wealth are particularly remarkable given the great difference in the ways in which agents choose their strategies in the human experiments compared to the computer simulations. The fact that both these features—emergent coordination and the dominance of simpler strategies—occur in such different settings, one computational and the other biological is striking. It suggests that there is a deeper, more general dynamic that underlies both these systems. This directly supports the implicit assumptions underlying this conference, namely that there are general underlying principles that are independent of the details of a particular collective and that can be used to guide the design and control of such collectives. More concretely, our observations point us in the direction of formulating at least tentative hypotheses concerning the general emergent group and individual behavior of agents, whether silicon- or carbon-based, competing for limited resources by being in the minority.

Acknowledgments. We are grateful to Yi Li for help with some of the calculations and data analysis. This work was supported, in part, by the University of Michigan's Office of the Vice-President for Research.

Design Principles for the Distributed Control of Modular Self-Reconfigurable Robots

Arancha Casal[1] and Tad Hogg[2]

Summary. Modular self-reconfigurable (MSR) robots consist of many identical modules that can move, attach, and detach relative to each other, thereby changing the robot's overall shape. This chapter presents general design techniques for the distributed multiagent control algorithms of MSR robots, based on local rules. These techniques are illustrated with simulation experiments on two types of MSR robots: Proteo and TeleCube.

1 Introduction

1.1 Multiagent Control of Complex Systems

Multiagent control techniques or agent-based simulations are widely used to study complex systems. Complex systems typically encompass large numbers of components, or agents, where interaction and communication between the simple components result in complex global behavior. Most natural systems come under the category of complex systems, including social insects, multicellular organisms, ecologies, and human societies (e.g., market economies and systems of common law). Examples of synthetic complex systems are teams of robots, the Internet, artificial ecologies, and the stock market. The main characteristic underlying the multiagent complex systems approach is that the local interactions of large numbers of agents lead to the bottom-up emergence of global complex behavior, unpredictable with current mathematical techniques. Often, the individual agents are relatively simple, and the "intelligence" of the system resides in the underlying network of communications and interactions. This is in sharp contrast to traditional control systems, which typically study a limited number of relatively complex components, and assume a centralized, top-down approach. However, the rising ubiquity of networked large-scale systems (the Internet and collections of robots being two prime examples) has focused attention on complex systems approaches.

[1] Stanford University cas@cs.stanford.edu
[2] HP Laboratories, Palo Alto, CA 94304 thogg@exch.hpl.hp.com

A defining characteristic of the multiagent control methodology we propose here for the shape control, or self-reconfiguration, of MSR robots is the fact that the resulting shapes are "imprecise." That is, the emergent shapes we obtain have the desired functionality, for example, particular locomotion or manipulation abilities, but the resulting exact geometry is irrelevant. In this respect, the results we obtain are more "organic" than controls giving precisely defined shapes. This is analogous to natural evolution, which characteristically produces such imprecise components, driven by the demand for robustness to uncertain environments [8]. For example, in the context of reconfiguration, imprecise shapes have a distinct advantage when grasping objects of unknown shape, size, or location (see Section 3).

1.2 Modular Self-Reconfigurable Robots

Modular self-reconfigurable (or metamorphic) robotics is a relatively new concept [7, 19, 26–29, 37, 38]. Such robotic systems consist of many simple identical modules that can attach and detach from one another to change their overall topology. These systems can dynamically adapt their shapes to suit the needs of the task at hand, e.g., for manipulation, locomotion, and creation of static structures. For instance, shapes for locomotion include wheels for flat surfaces, snakes for small tunnels, and multiple legs for rough surfaces. Another advantage arises from the fact that all modules are identical, resulting in robustness with respect to a task (because no module is critical, if any breaks down it can be easily replaced by another). In addition, because typical systems consist of a large number of modules (hundreds or thousands) reductions in manufacturing costs can be brought about through mass production.

From a planning and control viewpoint, metamorphic robots pose several interesting research challenges. Self-reconfiguration, or how to change shape automatically, is a new and thus far little-studied problem. The problem of self-reconfiguration is unique to MSR robots.[3] Decentralized control is a useful approach to this problem due to the large number of modules in a typical robot and the fact that each module is a self-contained unit with its own processing, sensing, and actuation. This observation means the large body of work on distributed multiagent control is particularly relevant.

Ideally, reconfiguration should occur with minimum cost, typically measured by the number of steps (module moves). Such an optimal solution to reconfiguration, a combinatorial optimization problem, involves searching the space of all possible reconfiguration sequences for the optimal one. The space of robot configurations corresponds to all the possible arrangements of a set of labeled connected modules, which grows exponentially with the number of modules [13]. Therefore, for robots with hundreds of modules or more, the size of the search space makes finding a globally optimal solution intractable.

A number of algorithms use heuristics to find near-optimal solutions for different robot systems [6, 16, 19, 26, 28, 29, 38]. These methods all require determining and defining, ahead of time, a desired shape appropriate to solve the task at hand.

---

[3] A similar problem is the classic transportation problem in operations research [32].

This target shape becomes the goal input to the reconfiguration algorithm and requires an exact (geometrical or otherwise) description. However, there are instances when defining an exact target shape may not be suitable or even possible. This may arise when there is uncertainty about the environment or the task, for example, when grasping an object of unknown size or shape.

1.3 Approach

Our approach differs from these self-reconfiguration algorithms in several respects. Even though reconfiguration is achieved, the algorithm does not aim at attaining an exact predefined shape. Rather, the goal is to create a structure with the correct *properties* (structural, morphological, etc) required to achieve the task. Any stable "emergent" structure that exhibits the desired properties is considered satisfactory, with no regard for the optimality or details of the resulting geometry. In this respect, our approach is more akin to the biologically inspired ideas found in artificial life than to traditional control theory.

Distributed or multiagent control is applied to teams of robots cooperating to achieve a common task [5, 11, 14, 18, 30, 33]. These methods usually apply to independently mobile robots that are, in general, not connected to one another. In most current modular robot systems the modules remain attached to one another forming a single connected whole, so these methods are not directly applicable. Biologically inspired algorithms for distributed control studied in artificial life [4, 25] tend to concentrate on how complex natural organisms achieve sophisticated crowd behaviors or deal with abstract agents that were not intended to, or could not, be physically constructed [1, 11, 12]. Our work helps bridge the gap between robot control and these artificial life concepts.

Specifically, we explore the use of very *simple*, purely *local* rules to produce control algorithms for accomplishing tasks such as forming complex connected structures, object manipulation, and dynamic adaptation under changing external conditions (e.g., weight). We will use the term *behaviors* for the specific control algorithms. The assumptions we make are as follows:

- Modules have limited computational capabilities. We allow a module to have limited memory (a few bits) and run a simple finite-state machine (FSM) in which state transitions are driven by the local state, the states of neighboring modules, their locations, and some external sensor information. The state of a module includes the FSM state as well as the memory state, and state transitions can update the memory state of a module or its neighbors.
- Communication is limited to immediate neighbors, and a limited number of bits are exchanged at each step. We specifically disallowed modules from being able to broadcast messages globally, because the power required would likely not scale well if the size of modules shrinks. In addition, with this assumption we have remained true to a local-only control philosophy.
- Modules are constrained to form a fully connected whole at all times. That is, a module or group of modules is not allowed to secede from the rest of the robot.

This may impose tight motion constraints and requires treatment other than more conventional teams of disconnected mobile robots.

The approach we propose is particularly well-suited for systems of large numbers of modules (100s and 1000s) that operate with some degree of uncertainty. Although untested, we expect the approach to scale well to both larger numbers of modules (tens and hundreds of thousands) and to smaller size scales (micro, nano) than the current centimeter scale.

2 Control Primitives

Modules can only directly access local information, but many control tasks involve properties of the cluster as a whole. An example is identifying or manipulating an object much larger than a module. Furthermore, even knowing these properties may not easily allow determining a suitable response, let alone an optimal one according to some global performance measure, due to the combinatorics of possible module motions. Thus it is useful to have some general design techniques for developing agent rules to give robust, reasonably good behavior, especially allowing for noise and unreliable modules. In the context of modular robots interacting with the physical world, such techniques include virtual force fields, asynchronous randomized decisions, dynamic equilibrium, and thresholds with hysteresis. The remainder of this section discusses these techniques.

A number of reconfiguration tasks involve a property that some modules in the cluster can detect, but then require other distant modules to address. A conceptually simple control technique uses *virtual force fields* through the cluster, which then guide module motions. These forces result from gradient values created by propagating certain messages throughout a cluster. These messages carry a value that is incremented as they pass between modules. Each module records the minimum value it receives from its neighbors, so the net result gives each module a value equal to its distance (in terms of a shortest path through the graph of connections within its cluster) to the originator of the message. Messages can originate from multiple sources, in which case recording the minimum value gives modules the distance to the closest originator. As an elaboration, the message propagation can be restricted to modules with certain properties, e.g., those on the surface of a cluster or with specified values of previously created gradients. These messages can have a maximum number of iterations to prevent them passing among modules indefinitely.

Once the gradient values are defined, an agent can compare its value with that of its neighbors to find the direction in which the gradient most rapidly decreases, thereby defining a vector for each module. These vectors can be viewed as a force field, specifying desired motions for the modules. Of course modules may not be able to move directly as specified by these vectors (e.g., due to obstructions of other modules) so these virtual forces act as guides rather than definite instructions: Each agent can modify the instruction in light of its local environment. Force fields can position and orient objects, even without sensor feedback [2]. Agents can adjust their

 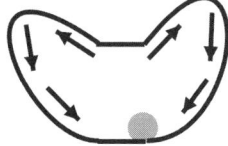

Figure 1. Virtual forces produced by gradients sent from the gray module. The messages propagate through all modules in the cluster (left) or only those on the boundary (right). Using all modules gives a local minimum if the cluster is compact, preventing modules from moving through it. Using the boundary gives longer paths but allows motion toward the originating module even in dense clusters.

response based on their local environment giving more general behaviors. In particular, when combined with some randomness and asynchronous operation, following gradients allows MSR robots to form various shapes (e.g., chains, sparse treelike structures or dense clusters), coordinate motion and manipulate objects [3, 20, 31].

A second technique creates structures as resulting from the *dynamic equilibrium* of continual probabilistic changes by the modules. For instance, instead of a complicated computation to globally determine when to build or destroy a structure, modules can randomly add themselves to, or remove themselves from, a structure with probabilities depending on their local environment or messages received. An overall equilibrium between addition and removal can result, giving stable large-scale structures. Changing probabilities, due to shifts in the local environment, can alter the equilibrium without any explicit decision by the robot as a whole. As an example, this technique can build legs to support weight as it moves over the modules [3].

As a third technique, thresholds allow local rules to determine when to switch task modes, e.g., between diffuse structures to cover large areas and compact structures for object manipulation. Producing a decision for the cluster as a whole could then activate some further activity such as repairs that require the full cluster to be in place. Such rules avoid the need to globally determine when a task is complete and then broadcast commands to switch between tasks. They are especially useful if several robots are engaged in similar tasks in a region, at differing stages of completion, so a single broadcast command would have to wait for the last to finish. Specifically, switching uses thresholds based on average properties sent through the cluster. That is, if there is some measurable property available within the cluster whose value indicates when the task is complete, testing that value can provide a signal for task completion. Selecting a threshold for this signal as part of the agent design may also allow trading off the quality of the task with how long it will take, on average. To make definite decisions, the thresholds can be used with hysteresis: A decision is made when a property increases above one threshold but not reversed unless the property subsequently is below a somewhat lower threshold. This reduces the likelihood of oscillations in the decision due to sensor errors or other noise. Using time-averaged values can further reduce sensitivity to noise, although it also makes the MSR robot slower to adjust to changes.

Specifically, our approach uses the following concepts:

- **Growth** is the process that creates structures. It is important to provide a mechanism for focusing the movement of modules to specific spots. Otherwise, if the movement is too random, it could take a long time before any reasonably good structure is grown.

- **Seeds** are the main agents that cause growth. A seed is a module that attracts other modules in order to further grow the structure. As more modules are attracted to a seed, they can in turn become seeds themselves and thus propagate the growth process.

- **Scents** are the means of global communication among modules. Scents are propagated through the system in a distributed breadth-first fashion as follows. Each module keeps a number in its memory representing the strength of the scent at its location. At each time step modules look at their neighbors and update this number to be the minimum value plus one. Modules that emit the scent set their own value to zero at each time step. Thus, smaller values indicate a stronger scent, and a scent gradient is created throughout the structure. Scents values are an approximation of the minimum distance to a scent-emitting module in the system. We typically use either one or two different scents in our experiments. Seeds emit a scent to attract modules, and modules that are searching for seeds move along the surface gradient of the scent to find them.

- The **mode** of a module is its present FSM state. For instance, seeds are usually denoted by the SEED mode, modules that search for seeds are in the SEARCH mode, modules that are part of the finished structure are in the FINAL mode, and modules that cause branching are in NODE mode. The mode in turn will determine the rules of behavior of a module.

3 Simulation Experiments

3.1 Proteo

Proteo is a modular self-reconfigurable, or metamorphic, robot developed at Xerox PARC. The modules are rhombic dodecahedra (polyhedrons with twelve identical faces, each of which is a rhombus). Modules attach to one another along their faces forming general three-dimensional solids. To achieve a change of shape modules on the outer surface roll over the substrate of other modules to new positions. This type of reconfiguration has been called "substrate reconfiguration," in contrast to other existing reconfiguration classes [6].

The rhombic dodecahedron can be thought of as the 3D analog of the hexagon; it has several useful properties. Notably, these polyhedra result in maximum internal volume for a given surface area [34], meaning more room for packing electronic and mechanical components. Also, all module-on-module rotations are always 120 degrees, unlike the cube, which requires 180-degree rotations in certain cases. This uniformity simplifies actuator and control design. A main disadvantage of this structure is that twelve faces per module need to be actuated, increasing the complexity and expense of the hardware. For a target module size in the centimeter scale, current

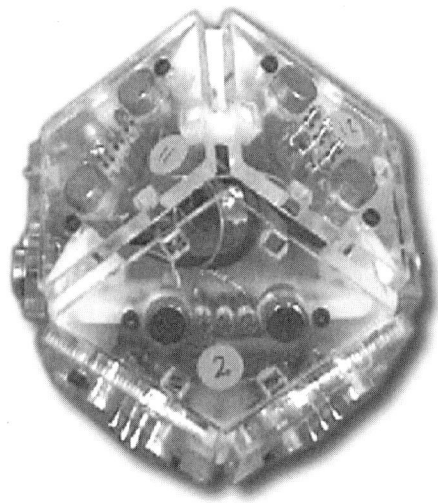

Figure 2. A Proteo module, consisting of 12 rhombic faces.

actuator technologies result in large weight-to-power ratios and high cost per module. A manually actuated version of Proteo has been built and is shown in Figure 2.

Substrate Reconfiguration

Other substrate reconfiguration robots have been built besides Proteo, including [16, 19]. In substrate robots a module needs a substrate of other modules to move over in order to get to a new location (by rolling or sliding over the substrate, for example). The modules can be seen to occupy discrete positions in a lattice, or grid, and are constrained to move over the exterior surface or inside cavities. No internal motions are possible when the modules are closely packed. The module geometries tend to be space-filling polyhedra, or "axial" approximations. These robots can closely approximate solids and 3D surfaces, much like Lego bricks, and are well suited to creating static and deformable solid structures.

Each module is independently capable of moving to a neighboring location in the grid; therefore, reconfiguration proceeds as a series of individual module motions to a neighboring position that gets increasingly closer to the goal location. Moving to a neighboring grid location typically involves a very simple module trajectory. This greatly simplifies some planning considerations such as external collisions, overall stability, and kinematics.

Locomotion and manipulation in substrate robots typically require reconfiguration, that is, making and breaking connections, due to the small range of motion of each module. Therefore, when moving, these robots somewhat resemble fluids, with the underlying pieces flowing to their new positions.

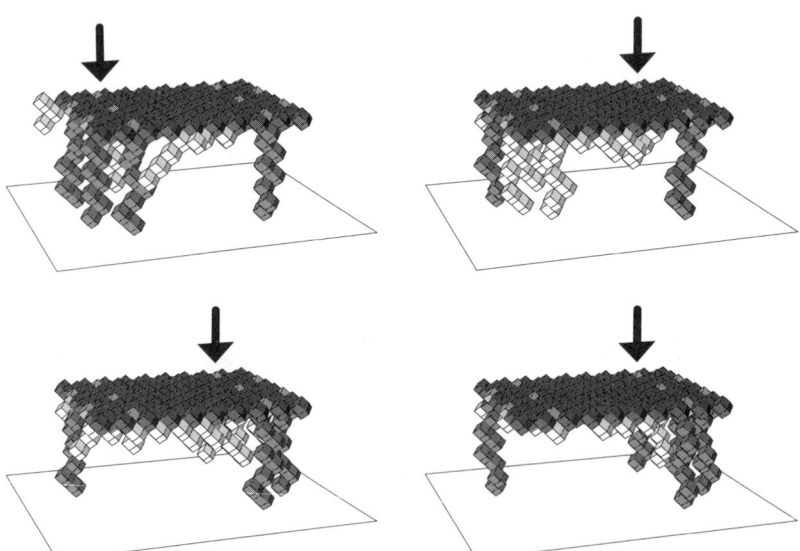

Figure 3. Adaptive behavior. Arrows indicate where the weight is placed. Initially, the right side receives little stress, so it has only one leg (leftmost picture). The weight is shifted to the right, and the table adapts by disbanding most of the legs on the left and growing more legs on the right side (next three pictures). Gray modules are available for additional legs if needed. On the top of the table, modules are in FIXED mode. In this example, the probabilities for a root to create or disband legs are $p_{max} = p_{min} = 0.05$. The weight thresholds were $F_{max} = 2$ to create new legs and $F_{min} = 1$ to disband legs. The board was a 19 by 15 square with five roots in each half of the board, separated by a distance of three modules in each direction.

Control Example

One important task for reconfigurable robots is to adjust themselves in response to environmental forces. For instance, a collection of such robots supporting a weight on a set of "legs" should be able to change the location and density of the legs when the weight shifts. As a simple example of this task, we examined the formation of legs to support a flat structure with an additional imposed force whose location could change over time. For simplicity, we neglect the weights of the modules themselves, i.e., we assume their weights are small compared to the weight of the additional objects they are supporting on top of the flat structure or "table."

For this behavior [3], we form some of the modules into a "board" (the top of the table) that supports the additional weight. These modules, which never move, are of two types. The first, always in FIXED mode, only transmits scent. The second type are "root" modules, which are uniformly spaced over the board and can communicate with each other, e.g., through signals sent locally through the fixed modules. We assume these signals propagate much faster than the physical movements of the modules. The roots are grouped into regions on the board (in the experiments reported here, we use two regions: the two halves of the board).

For examining dynamic adjustment to force changes using local rules, we are not concerned with rules to form the initial table structure. The modules to be in the table structure could be positioned with a global broadcast of module positions [38] or rules to form lattice structures similar to those forming the branching structure given earlier. Following creation of the table structure, one module could randomly become a seed and then spread scent with a specific value indicating an appropriate distance to form other "root" modules in the table.

We assume modules are equipped with a force sensor that allows them to measure the weight they are supporting. Furthermore, we assume the modules can either determine the direction in which gravity acts or this direction toward the ground is prespecified when creating the roots in the board. Roots within a region monitor the total weight supported in that region by communicating their sensor readings.

The root modules on the board can be in one of three modes: ROOT, IROOT, or AROOT. Initially the root modules are in IROOT mode, which monitors the weight they are supporting and may start growing a leg. AROOT mode emits a scent to attract other modules to start growing a leg, in much the same way as growing a single chain. Once the leg starts growing, the root shifts to ROOT mode, where it remains until the weight it supports drops below a specified threshold in which case it probabilistically causes its leg to disband. Thus the root modules grow or disband legs probabilistically according to how much weight is experienced in their part of the table. We refer to root modules in ROOT or AROOT mode as "active" roots.

The fixed and root modules are set at the beginning and don't change throughout the experiment. All other modules are initially in SLEEP mode. The structure first grows legs, then disbands some of them and creates new ones according to shifts in weight (controlled interactively by the user of the simulator).

The rules for this behavior for the root modules are:

- If in IROOT mode, if average weight per active root in its region is above a certain threshold F_{max}, with a small probability p_{max}: Go to AROOT mode.
- If in AROOT mode, emit scent.
- If in ROOT mode, if average weight per active root in its region is below a certain threshold F_{min}, with a small probability p_{min}: Set all FINAL and SEED neighbors to DISBAND mode, go to IROOT mode.

Although similar adaptive behaviors can occur with a range of values for the thresholds, one important issue is to prevent the disbanding of a single leg supporting a minimal weight in a region. In our experiments, this minimal value is one unit of weight, so we should have $F_{min} \leq 1$. The rules for the remaining modules are:

- If in SLEEP mode, if a scent is detected, go to SEARCH mode.
- If in SEARCH mode, propagate scent and move along its gradient; If there is a neighboring SEED or AROOT module and location is toward the ground with respect to this neighbor:
  - If this neighbor is a SEED, set it to FINAL mode; otherwise set it to ROOT mode.
  - Go to SEED mode

- If in SEED mode, if touching the ground, go to FINAL mode.
- If in FIXED or FINAL mode, transmit scent.
- If in DISBAND mode, set all FINAL and SEED neighbors to DISBAND mode, go to SEARCH mode.

Figure 3 illustrates how, once created, a supporting structure can adapt in response to changes in external forces. The behavior dynamically adapts the location and number of its legs to accommodate changes in the supported weight. In this example, we suppose weight W_1 is applied to the first half of the table and W_2 applied to the second half, with an arbitrary choice of units giving $W_1 + W_2 = 10$. In each half of the table, active roots communicate their sensory information to determine how much of this weight is supported by those in their half of the table. The result is the average weight supported by each active root in each half of the table, i.e., $w_1 = W_1/N_1$ for the first half (where N_1 is the number of active roots in the first half), and similarly for w_2 as the average weight supported per active root on the second half.

The probabilistic growing and disbanding of legs avoids possible oscillations in root behavior: If deterministic, when the weight shifts, many roots could decide to grow legs, then disband them on the next step, thus oscillating between the two without doing anything useful. Such oscillations are common for systems with synchronous updates [17, 24]: Randomization is a simple technique to prevent spurious synchronization of agent activity.

After a root r decides to grow a leg, some time is required for the modules to move to that root and produce the leg. However, because a root's decision to grow a leg is based on the weight in its region averaged over the active roots, once root r starts the process of growing a leg by emitting scent, the average weight per active root drops immediately and proportionately with the number of supporting modules. This change, rapidly communicated among the roots, gives feedback to other roots in the region and prevents other legs from growing nearby unnecessarily. In practice, this implies that the weight must be shifted slowly; the system will not be able to respond quickly to sudden changes.

An indication of how fast the modules react to external conditions is the number of steps after a weight shift until a new stable configuration is achieved. In the examples shown here, this time is on the order of 200 cycles. This includes the time needed to disband some legs and construct some new ones. Although the modules know about the shifted weight immediately, some time is needed until some roots decide to disband their legs and some inactive roots decide to grow legs. These decisions are probabilistic: Each root decides to change its state (go from active to inactive or vice versa) with a probability we chose to be on the order of $1/R$, where R is the total number of roots in the structure. Thus it is unlikely that many roots will decide to switch state at the same time step, thereby avoiding unstable or oscillating system behavior. We depend on the rough assumption that decisions to disband or grow legs have immediate effect on the strain felt by the modules in the system. This assumption is questionable for real-world applications, especially with larger structures. This is reasonable when weights move slowly compared to module re-

Figure 4. The TeleCube hardware: two connected modules, shown with arms retracted.

sponse times. More generally, the trade-off will be between fast response with a risk of oscillating behavior and a slow but stable response to external conditions.

Other Control Examples

We have shown a number of other control examples with Proteo. These include the creation of static structures suitable for different tasks such as a snake, scaffold, recursive branching and sponge, and a dynamic "hand" capable of grasping objects of unknown shape and size. These examples and their corresponding local rules are discussed in [3].

3.2 TeleCube

TeleCube is an MSR robot where each module is a cube that can prismatically extend each of its six faces independently up to a factor of two times its fully retracted length (Figure 4). A 2D analogue was previously developed at Dartmouth [29]. Each module can communicate with its immediate neighbors in all six directions. When a module extends an arm and makes contact with an object, it can exert a force on that object. This design allows modules bound inside a group to move, so TeleCube can perform tasks inside the aggregate, such as internal object manipulation and density changes.

Prismatic Reconfiguration

In prismatic reconfiguration MSR robots, the modules use prismatic, or telescoping, degrees of freedom to move, attach, and detach from one another. Aside from TeleCube, the 2D crystalline robot [29] is another hardware design. The underlying concept was first inspired by elastic biological systems, such as muscle cells, that can change shape and size by continuously deforming their enveloping membrane, rather than through the reordering of discrete pieces as in substrate robots. These systems achieve module relocation by retracting a module into the interior of the set and then extruding another module at the desired goal location on the surface, or vice versa. Overall reconfiguration can be achieved by a repeated number of these operations, which effectively change the shape of the surface. The visual effect is one of a deformable surface, even though most of the necessary rearrangements are actually happening inside the robot. These systems tend to form closed-packed solid structures, like substrate robots. The ability to move and deform internally, however, is in marked contrast to substrate robots, where module motions can only take place on the outside surface or internal cavities. This has the effect of possibly removing a lot of the motion constraints present in substrate systems, potentially facilitating and speeding up reconfiguration. As is also the case for substrate robots, kinematic, gravitational stability, and 3D collision avoidance considerations are, for the most part, trivial.

This category of MSR robot is characterized by the fact that internal motions within the robot can take place. This can potentially increase the speed of reconfiguration by allowing shorter-distance routes to goal locations. However, moving inside the robot incurs important motion constraints. A module moving internally requires cooperation from other modules around it in order to be able to advance to a new position; for example, surrounding modules need to squeeze out of the way of the moving module. This means a simple module move within the robot requires coordinating several modules at once, which is not the case in substrate robots.

The required cooperation for single-module motion also leads to an additional problem, not present in substrate robots: The tendency for groups of modules to "shed off" from the rest of the robot. In order to avoid module shedding and to still obtain the required cooperation we introduced new message types in addition to scents. The additional message types we defined were: impulses (direct messages to neighbors only), queries (requests for information from neighbor modules), and commands (forcible messages to neighbors, such as "contract arm").

Control Example

The TeleCube architecture allows manipulating objects inside a group of modules [20]. This can be accomplished by growing around a supported object or, more generally, opening gaps within the structure and pushing an object into them.

Internal object manipulation requires translational and rotational motions. In both cases, a module that is not in direct contact with an object moves based on the gradient of messages it receives from its neighbors, determined by comparing the relative numerical values of the "scent" messages. Namely, if possible, a module will move in the direction of the positive gradient. If the module does not sense a gradient, it will try to move to restore an "optimal" density of modules in its neighborhood. This means moving away from a neighbor that is too close or toward a distant neighbor.

Internal manipulation uses **shell** and **tissue** states, and one *stimulus* message propagated among neighbors to form a gradient scent. The process starts with a broadcast of the desired movement direction. Modules on the outside of the structure enter the **shell** state and do not move under the influence of gradients or density adjustments. Thus, these modules form a rigid support structure off which inside modules can push, i.e., MSR robots cannot only form tools shaped to their task, but can also provide dynamic support structures for using those tools. Interior modules enter the **tissue** state.

Translational 2D motion uses a simple stimulus-based response. Given the desired direction of motion, modules in contact with the object use the following rules:

- If a module is in front of the object (i.e., touching it with an arm extending from the module in a direction going against the desired direction of object movement), it releases a negative *stimulus* message and then tries to move away from the object. If possible, it moves in the direction opposite to the arm touching the object. If that direction is blocked by other modules, it tries to move instead perpendicular to that direction. Either motion tends to move the module out of the object's way. Furthermore, the negative *stimulus* message creates a scent gradient among neighbors causing them to also move away and make room for the module to move.

- If a module is behind the object (i.e., touching it with an arm in a direction aligned with the desired direction of object movement), it releases a positive *stimulus* and tries to move toward and push the object. If the module has more than one arm in contact with the object, this rule applies to the arm most closely aligned with the desired direction of motion.

Rotation requires the approximate location of the object's center to allow relating individual module forces to the overall torque imposed on the object. Estimating this location via a distributed local algorithm can be difficult if the modules are much smaller than the object and, on the scale of the modules, the object is not smooth. Instead, we assume the higher-level controller broadcasts the approximate location of the object's center. Another possibility is to use open-loop force fields to position the object in a known starting configuration, as demonstrated on a micromachined surface [2]. In either case, for the behavior described here we suppose knowledge of the approximate center. That is, any error in the center's specified location is small compared to the object's size but not necessarily small compared to the size of the modules. The modules act in the same way as the translation modules, except they move away from or toward the object if they are in front of a corner that should be turned toward or away from them, respectively, as determined by their relative location to the specified center and the desired direction of rotation. Again, they release positive and negative *stimulus* messages when moving toward and away from the object, respectively, and push the object when they move toward it. This behavior gives 2D rotation in a plane.

Figure 5 includes both types of motion. First the modules are told to move the object in one direction, then to rotate it, and finally move in the perpendicular direction. These instructions cause modules to switch between translation and rotation rules, giving desired motions without the higher-level control specifying individual module motions. We found the local rules could produce a variety of trajectories. The combination of translation and rotation rules allows achieving arbitrary planar position and orientation of the object.

Modules move the object by exerting forces on it. They could also exert compressive forces on the object by simply replacing the negative *stimulus* messages with

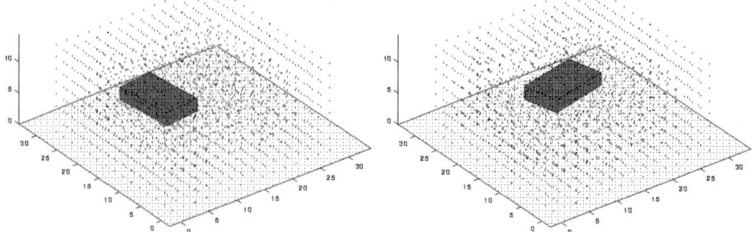

Figure 5. Internally manipulating an object. The modules form a $15 \times 15 \times 8$ structure and are shown simply as points to allow seeing the internally manipulated object. The full sequence, consisting of 138 simulation steps, shows the object gradually shifted from its initial to its final position in response to instructions to move the object in an L-shaped path. The figure shows steps 15 and 80.

positive ones so modules on all sides move toward the object. This behavior could be used to push parts together. Shear forces could arise from tangential motion, provided friction between the arms of the modules and the object was sufficient. The modules then can be viewed as a material surrounding the object with forces under programmed control, changing from rigid support to fluidlike flow as needed. This behavior is a useful programming abstraction for higher levels of control, similar to programmable force fields in two dimensions [2]. By giving different instructions to different regions, a higher-level control could use the modules to move multiple objects along different paths or, through feedback based on the position of the objects (rather than details of the much larger number of modules), bring objects together.

Other Control Examples

One of the most involved examples we have shown with TeleCube is a complex navigation task where the robot is required to reach a goal location by navigating an environment with obstacles. This example combined reconfiguration, locomotion (with turning), and path planning (with obstacle avoidance). Details and local rules can be found in [21].

4 Limitations

4.1 Robustness

An important open question is the robustness of our approach to a variety of failures. For instance, the examples shown here assume that seed modules stop creating their gradient when the rules change the module to a different mode. However, if a seed module fails not by becoming inactive (e.g., due to loss of power) but rather by failing to switch off its gradient when it should, the resulting signals may confuse other modules.

One approach to the "SEED staying on" error is to replace our notion of single-module seeds with signals from a compact cluster acting together as a seed, each with a different identifier with their signal. Then modules far away could look for gradients in the average value of several nearby scent values rather than just picking the absolute minimum value (which might be from a broken single seed module somewhere else). Although a bit more complicated for the local rules, it would give some statistical robustness against single failures. More generally, this is an application of achieving reliable behavior from unreliable components [35] (e.g., by majority voting).

More generally, this example highlights the difference between individual modules failing in their own actuations and failures leading to sending the wrong signals to others. Robustness with respect to the latter failure mode requires modules to be somewhat skeptical of signals, hence treating other modules as possibly noncooperative even for tasks with an overall design goal. This illustrates an important issue for designing collectives: In spite of common overall goals, noise and failures may cause some components to act against the desired global behavior even when the agent rules themselves would, if correctly implemented, work toward the overall goal. In this respect, these cooperative systems become similar to groups of self-interested agents in which designs must account for the possibility, even the likelihood, of noncooperative behavior on the part of other agents.

4.2 Generality

Our examples require that modules be exactly registered on a global grid. With large numbers of modules, such a global coordinate system is unrealistic. Motion along gradients could handle gradual variations in the coordinates (e.g., due to a drooping extended chain of modules). Alternatively, modules could introduce defects into the grid structure to adjust to external forces, analogous to dislocations in crystals.

We focus on achieving static shapes in which module motions are fairly slow, with no need to explicitly account for inertial effects as modules move. This should be particularly appropriate for tiny modules, dominated by friction and viscous forces rather than gravity. However, dynamics can be important for large aggregates. Examples include forming a bridge across some region without falling over, or a walking-type gait (e.g., for a spiderlike shape) in which leg motions may need to be fast enough to prevent the robot from falling over.

We have presented a variety of examples with local rules leading to useful global behaviors for two types of modular robots. An important question is how well these techniques generalize to other tasks, particularly because local rules could lead to some modules becoming stuck for long periods of time in unfavorable configurations. The randomness we introduce with our rules is sufficient to avoid this problem for the tasks treated here but would fail in cases requiring nearly simultaneous rearrangement of many modules to escape from some local minima. Theoretical analyses based on stochastic choices of many independent agents can provide insight into the range of possible global dynamics and general local approaches to modify this dynamics [15]. Such approaches can even quantitatively model small teams of robots [23], but it remains to be seen how well such methods apply to the tightly coupled behaviors of modular robots.

5 Conclusions

We presented a biologically inspired method for the control of MSR robots that is flexible (we showed different tasks for two different MSR platforms, substrate and prismatic) and robust (the tasks were dynamic and included uncertainty and randomness), as well as scalable from tens to hundreds of modules. With this method we obtain imprecise structures with desired global properties, despite local-only control. This has the distinct advantage of avoiding the need to specify a precise target shape a priori, something impractical or impossible in uncertain environments and tasks. Our main assumptions were limited module capabilities and full connectivity.

Aside from the design of new rules for more tasks, there are a number of other possible extensions to this work. Most of the difficulty with this method lies in translating a global goal or constraint on desired behavior into local rules, the key design issue for collectives [36]. Genetic algorithms can be used to evolve new rules automatically [22], although to be successful they must be "pointed in the right direction," avoiding purely random searches.

Rule composition could be used for more complex functionality, such as gait generation or complex manipulation. Also, in hierarchical control schemes the local rules can be invoked at low levels of control, simplifying the overall design effort.

The method could be extended to relax the global connectivity constraint. Small groups of several modules could disconnect from the rest, perform independent or cooperative tasks among them, and rejoin later. We could also try to scale up to thousands of modules, here the effects of gravity and limits on actuator performance and relative strength should be considered.

The method could have applications to smaller systems performing shape formation or cooperative actions, with the required scalability modifications. For example, biological systems (slime mold, immune cells, cancer cells) and synthetic systems (nanorobots, MEMS, molecular machines) or applications requiring a combination of biological and synthetic systems, such as nanomedicine [9]. Here, very different physical forces (internal and external) and motion constraints would need to be considered.

Finally, verification of the viability of these methods will require implementation on real hardware, when this becomes feasible.

Acknowledgments. We thank H. Bojinov and J. Kubica for many useful discussions and implementations of the examples presented here. The Palo Alto Research Center's Modular Robotics team provided the motivation for this work.

References

1. H. Abelson et al. Amorphous computing. Technical Report 1665, MIT Artificial Intelligence Lab, August 1999.
2. K. F. Bohringer et al. Computational methods for design and control of MEMS micromanipulator arrays. *Computational Science and Engineering*, 4(1):17–29, January–March 1997.
3. H. Bojinov, A. Casal, and T. Hogg. Multiagent control of modular self-reconfigurable robots. *Artificial Intelligence*, 142:99–120, 2002. Preprint available at Los Alamos archive cs.RO/0006030.
4. N. Bowden, A. Terfort, J. Carbeck, and G. M. Whitesides. Self-assembly of mesoscale objects into ordered two-dimensional arrays. *Science*, 276:233–5, 1997.
5. P. Caloud et al. Indoor automation with many mobile robots. In *Proc. of the Intl. Workshop on Intelligent Robots and Systems*. IEEE, 1990.
6. A. Casal and M. Yim. Self-reconfiguration planning for a class of modular robots. In *SPIE Symposium on Intelligent Systems and Advanced Manufacturing: Sensor Fusion and Decentralized Control in Robotic Systems*, pages 246–57, 1999.
7. A. Castano, W. M. Shen, and P. Will. CONRO: Towards miniature self-sufficient metamorphic robots. *Autonomous Robots*, 8:309–24, 2000.
8. M. E. Csete and J. C. Doyle. Reverse engineering of biological complexity. *Science*, 295:1664–9, 2002.
9. R. A. Freitas, Jr. *Nanomedicine*, volume 1. Landes Bioscience, Georgetown, TX, 1999. Available at www.nanomedicine.com.
10. T. Fukuda and Y. Kawauchi. Cellular robotic system (cebot) as one of the realizations of self-organizing intelligent universal manipulator. In *Proc. of the IEEE Conference on Robotics and Automation*, pages 662–7, 1990.
11. S. Hackwood and G. Beni. Self-organization of sensors for swarm intelligence. In *Proc. of the Conference on Robotics and Automation (ICRA92)*. IEEE, 1992.
12. J. Storrs Hall. Utility fog: The stuff that dreams are made of. In B. C. Crandall, editor, *Nanotechnology*, pages 161–84. MIT Press, Cambridge, MA, 1996.
13. F. Harary and E. M. Palmer. *Graphical Enumeration*. Academic Press, New York, 1973.
14. B. Hasslacher and M. W. Tilden. Living machines. In L. Steels, editor, *Robotics and Autonomous Systems: The Biology and Technology of Intelligent Autonomous Agents*. Elsivier, 1995.
15. T. Hogg and B. A. Huberman. Achieving global stability through local controls. In *Proc. of the 6th IEEE Symposium on Intelligent Control (ISIC 91)*, pages 67–72, 1991.
16. K. Hosokawa et al. Self-organizing collective robots with morphogenesis in a vertical plane. In *Proc. of the Conference on Robotics and Automation (ICRA98)*. IEEE, 1998.
17. B. A. Huberman and N. S. Glance. Evolutionary games and computer simulations. *Proceedings of the National Academy of Science USA*, 90:7716–8, August 1993.
18. H. Kitano, editor. *Robocup-97: Robot Soccer World Cup I*, volume 1395 of *Lecture Notes in Computer Science*. Springer, Berlin, 1998.
19. K. Kotay, D. Rus, M. Vona, and C. McGray. The self-reconfiguring robotic molecule: Design and control algorithms. *Algorithmic Foundations of Robotics*, 1998.
20. J. Kubica, A. Casal, and T. Hogg. Agent-based control for object manipulation with modular self-reconfigurable robots. In *Proc. of the 17th Intl. Joint Conf. on Artificial Intelligence (IJCAI-2001)*, pages 1344–9, San Francisco, 2001. Morgan Kaufmann.
21. J. Kubica, A. Casal, and T. Hogg. Complex behaviors from local rules in modular self-reconfigurable robots. In *Proc. of IEEE Conference on Robotics and Automation (ICRA2001)*, 2001.

22. J. Kubica and E. Rieffel. Creating a smarter membrane: Automatic code generation for modular self-reconfigurable robots. In *Proc. of ICRA-2002*, 2002.

23. K. Lerman et al. A macroscopic analytical model of collaboration in distributed robotic systems. *Artificial Life*, 7:375–93, 2001.

24. W. G. Macready, A. G. Siapas, and S. A. Kauffman. Criticality and parallelism in combinatorial optimization. *Science*, 271:56–8, 1996.

25. R. J. Metzger and M. A. Krasnow. Genetic control of branching morphogenesis. *Science*, 284:1635–9, 1999.

26. S. Murata et al. A 3-D self-reconfigurable structure. In *Proc. of the Conference on Robotics and Automation (ICRA98)*, p. 432. IEEE, 1998.

27. S. Murata, H. Kurokawa, and S. Kokaji. Self-assembling machine. In *Proc. of the Conference on Robotics and Automation (ICRA94)*, pp. 441–8, Los Alamitos, CA, 1994. IEEE.

28. A. Pamecha, I. Ebert-Uphoff, and G. S. Chirikjian. Useful metrics for modular robot motion planning. *IEEE Transactions on Robotics and Automation*, 13:531–45, 1997.

29. D. Rus and M. Vona. Self-reconfiguration planning with compressible unit modules. In *Proc. of the Conference on Robotics and Automation (ICRA99)*. IEEE, 1999.

30. J. R. Rush, A. P. Fraser, and D. P. Barnes. Evolving cooperation in autonomous robotic systems. In *Proceedings of the IEEE International Conference on Control*, March 21–24 1994.

31. B. Salemi, W.-M. Shen, and P. Will. Hormone controlled metamorphic robots. In *Proc. of the Intl. Conf. on Robotics and Automation (ICRA2001)*, 2001.

32. A. Schrijver. *Theory of Linear and Integer Programming*. John Wiley, 1987.

33. L. Steels. Cooperation between distributed agents through self-organization. *Journal on Robotics and Autonomous Systems*, 1989.

34. D. W. Thompson. *On Growth and Form*. Cambridge University Press, Cambridge, 1992.

35. J. von Neumann. Probabilistic logics and the synthesis of reliable organisms from unreliable components. In C. E. Shannon and J. McCarthy, editors, *Automata Studies*, volume 34 of *Ann. of Math. Stud.*, pages 43–98. Princeton University Press, 1956.

36. D. H. Wolpert and K. Tumer. Collective intelligence, data routing and braess' paradox. *J. of Artificial Intelligence Research*, 16:359–87, 2002.

37. M. Yim. *Locomotion with a Unit-Modular Reconfigurable Robot*. Ph.D. thesis, Stanford University, 1994.

38. M. Yim, Ying Zhang, John Lamping, and Eric Mao. Distributed control for 3D metamorphosis. *Autonomous Robots*, 10:41–56, 2001.

Two Paradigms for the Design of Artificial Collectives

Kristina Lerman* and Aram Galstyan*

Summary. Artificial collectives are systems composed of multiple autonomous information or software agents, mobile robots, or nodes in a sensor or communication network. In the future, such systems will be responsible for many important tasks, such as highway traffic control, disaster response, toxic spill monitoring and cleanup, and exploration of other planets. Because such systems will have to function in environments with unreliable communication channels, where agents are likely to fail, they will have to be reliable, scalable, robust, adaptable, and amenable to quantitative mathematical analysis. The last property is important because analysis is crucial to understanding the issues of the design, control, adaptability, and dynamics of collective behavior. We describe two approaches to distributed control of artificial collectives and study them quantitatively. The first, biologically based control, relies on local interactions among many simple agents to create desirable collective behavior. The second approach allows collectives to maximize their world utility using market-based mechanisms. We present two applications—foraging in a group of robots and resource allocation in dynamic environments—that use these control paradigms and perform an analysis of each problem.

1 Introduction

Artificial collectives, also known as multiagent systems, are systems composed of multiple autonomous agents, e.g., software agents, mobile robots, or nodes in a sensor network, and have become a focus of intense study by the artificial intelligence and networks communities. The interest is easy to understand: in the future, many tasks such as directing traffic flow on roads and highways, coordinating a response to a disaster or emergency, toxic spill monitoring and cleanup, and exploration of other planets, to name just a few, will be delegated to swarms of simple (and cheap) units, be they information or software agents, mobile embodied agents, or nodes in a sensor or communications network. These multiagent swarms will have to function in dynamic environments where communication channels are unreliable and agents are likely to fail. Therefore, to be useful, they will have to satisfy the following criteria: they will have to be (1) reliable, show good performance in uncertain dynamic

* Information Sciences Institute, University of Southern California, 4676 Admiralty Way, Marina del Rey, CA 90292 lerman@isi.edu galstyan@isi.edu

environments; (2) scalable, work equally well for systems composed of tens or thousands of agents; (3) robust, be tolerant of individual agent error or failure; and (4) adaptable, be tolerant of changing environment or task requirements.

Distributed control schemes in systems composed of simple agents, which *collectively* accomplish some desired task, satisfy these requirements and are preferable to alternative system architectures. Here, by simple agents, we mean agents that are not deliberative, i.e., that do not have the capacity to reason, plan action, or negotiate with other agents. Simple agents are less likely to fail or produce errors than more complex deliberative agents, making the system more robust. Although deliberative agents are also capable of collective action in the absence of central control, these agents require detailed knowledge about the capabilities and states of other agents with which they may interact. Acquiring the knowledge necessary to coordinate collective behavior and carrying out the requisite computation may be expensive and impractical, especially for systems containing more than a dozen agents.

Several tools are available for studying the behavior of artificial collectives. In the robotics domain, experiment is the most direct way to observe the behavior of the system. Sensor-based simulators that attempt to realistically model the environment and the robots' imperfect sensing of and interaction with it, offer another investigation tool. However, experiments and even grounded simulations, are very costly and time-consuming to implement and often do not scale well as the size of the system grows. Numeric simulations and analytic models are examples of a mathematical approach that offers an alternative to experiment and grounded simulations. Analysis allows us to efficiently study the behavior of collectives, even very large ones, and gain insight into system design, (e.g., what parameters optimize performance or prevent instability). Despite its power, the mathematical approach has so far not often been used to study artificial collectives (see [24, 52] and our own [34, 35] for exceptions).

One of the obstacles to wider implementation of artificial collectives is the difficulty of the inverse problem, i.e., specifying the local rules that will lead to desirable collective behavior, by which we mean the behavior that will maximize the value of the collective's global utility. This problem has been exacerbated by lack of analysis tools to evaluate different designs. In this paper we discuss two approaches to the design of distributed control for multiagent systems and present two analysis tools used to study them. The first approach, referred to as biologically based control (Section 2), uses local interactions among many simple agents to create desirable collective behavior. The second approach to distributed control uses market-based mechanisms (Section 3) for coordination and adaptation between agents. We describe two applications that use these control paradigms and perform a quantitative analysis of each problem. We use two different analysis techniques: The biologically inspired system is studied analytically, and the market-based system is studied numerically. The former is a general analytic approach that can be applied to other artificial collectives satisfying simple criteria, which we will define.

2 Biologically Based Control

Biologically based control [9], sometimes referred to as swarm intelligence [6], is modeled on social insects (and other species), in which complex collective behavior arises out of local interactions among simple agents [48]. This approach takes advantage of the minimalist design [8, 36] of the individual agents and the inherent distributedness of the collective exploiting either direct (agent-to-agent) or indirect (through the environment) local interactions. In the last few years, this control paradigm has been successfully applied in the collective robotics domain: aggregation [5, 36, 39, 52] and segregation [23], beacon and odor localization [20, 21], collaborative mapping [7], collaborative transportation [27, 33], work division and task allocation [1, 32], flocking and foraging [18, 42]. All these works have been performed using groups of simple, autonomous reactive or behavior-based [2] robots or embodied simulated agents, exploiting local communication forms among teammates (implicit, through the environment, or explicit, wireless communication), and fully distributed control. The simplicity of agents and their interactions makes the collective behavior of the system amenable to quantitative mathematical analysis. In this chapter we present a methodology for creating a mathematical model of an artificial collective using biologically based control. We use the well-known (outside of computer science) theory of stochastic systems and show how this analysis applies to a general class of Markov, or memoryless, agents. We illustrate the approach by using it to study collaboration in a group of robots and qualitatively compare the predictions of the mathematical model to the results of experiment and sensor-based simulations.

2.1 Mathematical Analysis of Collectives

A mathematical model of a collective comes in two flavors: *microscopic* or *macroscopic*. A microscopic description treats individual agents as the fundamental unit of the model and describes the agent's interactions with other agents and the environment. There are several variations of the microscopic approach. A common method employed by physicists consists of writing down the microscopic equations of motion for each agent and solving them to study the behavior of the system. For large systems, however, solving equations with many degrees of freedom is often impractical. Microscopic simulations, such as molecular dynamics, cellular automata [57] and particlehopping models [14], are popular tools for studying dynamics of large multiagent systems. In these simulations, agents change state stochastically or depending on the state of their neighbors. Another example of the microscopic approach are the probabilistic models developed by Martinoli and coworkers [25,37,38] to study collective behavior in groups of robots. Rather than compute the exact trajectories and sensory information of individual robots, Martinoli et al. model each robot's interactions with other robots and the environment as a series of stochastic events, with probabilities determined by simple geometric considerations. Running several series of stochastic events in parallel, one for each robot, allows them to study the group behavior of the multirobot system.

Unlike microscopic models, macroscopic models directly describe collective behavior. A macroscopic description offers several advantages over the microscopic approach. It is more computationally efficient, because it uses many fewer variables. The macroscopic descriptions also tend to be more universal and, therefore, more powerful: The same mathematical description can be applied to other systems governed by the same abstract principles. Of course, the two descriptive levels are related, and it may be possible in some cases to exactly derive the parameters of the macroscopic model from microscopic theory. Schweitzer and coworkers [50] have done just that in their analytic study of trail formation by ants and people.

Our approach is based on viewing collectives as stochastic systems; therefore, it is inherently probabilistic. Though the microscopic description of such systems may be very complex, we will show that a macroscopic description takes a very simple (probabilistic) form.

Stochastic Systems Approach: A Tutorial

The behavior of individual agents in a collective has many complex influences, even in a controlled laboratory setting. Agents are influenced by external, often unanticipated, forces. For robots, external forces include friction, which may vary with the type of surface on which the robot is moving, battery power, sound, and ambient light. Even if all the forces are known in advance, the agents are still subject to random events: fluctuations in the environment, noise in the robot's sensors and actuators. Each agent will interact with other agents that are influenced by these and other events. In most cases it is difficult to predict the agents' exact trajectories and thus to know which agents will come in contact with one another. Finally, the agent designer can take advantage of the unpredictability and incorporate it directly into the agent's behavior. For example, the simplest effective policy for obstacle avoidance in robots is for them to turn a random angle and move forward. In summary, the behavior of agents in a collective is so complex, the collective itself may best described probabilistically, as a stochastic system.

We will present a tutorial on mathematical analysis of stochastic systems. For details we refer the reader to the excellent text by Van Kampen [29]. We begin by defining some concepts. *State* labels a set of related agent behaviors required to accomplish some task. Each of the high-level states may consist of a single action or behavior or a set of behaviors. For example, when the robot is in the *searching* state, it is wandering around the arena, detecting objects and avoiding obstacles. In the course of accomplishing the task, the robot will transition from one state to another, and on completion of the task it may return to the initial state to repeat the cycle. It is clear that during a sufficiently short time interval, each agent in a collective is in exactly one of a finite number of states. Note that there can be one-to-one correspondence between agent actions and behaviors and states. However, in order to keep the mathematical model compact and tractable, it is often useful to *coarse-grain* the system by choosing a smaller number of states, each incorporating a set of related agent actions or behaviors. Coarse-graining is even more desirable because we are often interested in finding the *minimal* model that explains observed features of the collective.

We associate a unit vector $\hat{q}_k$ with each state $k = 1, 2, \ldots, L$. The configuration of the system is defined by the occupation vector

$$\mathbf{n} = \sum_{k=1}^{L} n_k \hat{q}_k, \tag{1}$$

where n_k is the number of agents in state k. The probability distribution $P(\mathbf{n}, t)$ is the probability that the system is in configuration $\mathbf{n}$ at time t. The time evolution of this probability distribution is described by the stochastic master equation.

For systems that obey the Markov property, the future is determined only by the present not the past. Clearly, agents that plan or use memory of past actions to make decisions will not meet this criterion; however, many artificial collectives, specifically those based on reactive and behavior-based robots, satisfy the Markov property. The Markov property can be restated more precisely: The configuration of a system at time $t + \Delta t$ depends only on the configuration of the system at time t. This fact allows us to rewrite the marginal probability density $P(\mathbf{n}, t + \Delta t)$ in terms of conditional probabilities:

$$P(\mathbf{n}, t + \Delta t) = \sum_{\mathbf{n}'} P(\mathbf{n}, t + \Delta t | \mathbf{n}', t) P(\mathbf{n}', t).$$

We can, therefore, write the change in probability density as

$$
\begin{aligned}
P(\mathbf{n}, t + \Delta t) &- P(\mathbf{n}, t) \\
&= \sum_{\mathbf{n}'} P(\mathbf{n}, t + \Delta t | \mathbf{n}', t) P(\mathbf{n}', t) - \sum_{\mathbf{n}'} P(\mathbf{n}', t + \Delta t | \mathbf{n}, t) P(\mathbf{n}, t). \quad (2)
\end{aligned}
$$

In the continuum limit, as $\Delta t \to 0$, Equation 2 becomes

$$\frac{\partial P(\mathbf{n}, t)}{\partial t} = \sum_{\mathbf{n}'} W(\mathbf{n} | \mathbf{n}'; t) P(\mathbf{n}', t) - \sum_{\mathbf{n}'} W(\mathbf{n}' | \mathbf{n}; t) P(\mathbf{n}, t) \tag{3}$$

with transition rates defined as

$$W(\mathbf{n} | \mathbf{n}'; t) = \lim_{\Delta t \to 0} \frac{P(\mathbf{n}, t + \Delta t | \mathbf{n}', t)}{\Delta t}. \tag{4}$$

Equation 3 is known as the master equation, and it fully determines the evolution of a stochastic system. Once the probability distribution $P(\mathbf{n}, t)$ is found, we can calculate system properties. Sometimes, however, it is more useful to study the system's average quantities. The rate equation, which can be derived from the master equation (see, e.g., [29]), governs the time evolution of average occupation numbers:

$$\frac{\partial}{\partial t} \langle n_k \rangle = \sum_j w_{jk}(\langle \mathbf{n} \rangle) \langle n_j \rangle - \langle n_k \rangle \sum_j w_{kj}(\langle \mathbf{n} \rangle), \tag{5}$$

where $w_{ij}(\langle \mathbf{n} \rangle)$ is the transition rate from state j to state i (for simplicity, we allow only individual transitions between states). This equation has the following interpretation: Occupation number n_k will increase in time (first term in Equation 5) due to transitions from other states to state k, and it will decrease in time due to the transitions from the state k to other states (second term).

The rate equation has been used to model dynamic processes in a wide variety of systems. The following is a short list of applications: In chemistry, it has been used to study chemical reactions [17]; in physics, the growth of semiconductor surfaces [4]; and in ecology to study population dynamics including predator-prey systems [19]; and in biology to model the behavior of ant colonies [46]. The rate equation has also found applications in the social sciences [22]. However, with the exception of the work by Huberman and Hogg [24] on computational ecologies and Sugawara and coworkers [53,54] on foraging in a group of communicating robots, the rate equation approach has not been used in the robotics and AI communities.

The rate equation is usually derived from the phenomenological finite difference equation describing the change in the instantaneous value of a dynamic variable (e.g., U.S. population) over some time interval Δt (e.g., a decade is used by the Census Bureau). By taking the limit $\Delta t \to 0$, one recovers the differential form of the rate equation. For stochastic Markov systems, the rate equation simply describes the evolution of the first moment (mean) of the probability distribution. How closely the mean tracks the behavior of a dynamic variable depends on the magnitude of its fluctuations (higher moments of the distribution). The larger the system, the smaller the (relative) fluctuations, the more accurately the rate equation describes the evolution of dynamic variables. In a small system, the experiment may be repeated many times to average out the effect of fluctuations; therefore, the (continuous) occupation number in the rate equation can be thought to represent an (integer) dynamic variable averaged over repeated experiments. Pacala et al. [46] showed that in models of task allocation in ants, the exact stochastic and the average deterministic models *quantitatively* agree in systems containing as few as ten ants. The agreement increases as the size of the system grows.

Rate Equation and Artificial Collectives

The rate equation approach presented here is valid for Markov and semi-Markov systems, in which the agent's future state depends only on its present state and, for semi-Markov systems, on how much time it has spent in that state, not on any past states. While many systems, including reactive and behavior-based robotics and some software agent systems and sensors, clearly obey the Markov property, other systems composed of agents with memory, learning, or deliberative capabilities do not and therefore cannot be described by the simple models presented here. However, the rate equations are useful for studying swarmlike systems of simple agents. Finding an appropriate mathematical form for the transition rates is the main challenge in applying the rate equations to real systems. Usually, the transition is triggered when an agent encounters some stimulus—be it another agent in a particular state, an object, its location, etc. For simplicity, we will assume that agents and triggers are dilute and uniformly distributed in space (though we will consider systems where agents interact in space, it does not necessarily have to be physical space, but a network, the Web, etc.). The assumption of spatial uniformity may be reasonable for agents that randomly explore space (e.g., searching behavior in robots tends to smooth out any inhomogeneities in the robots' initial distribution); however, it fails for systems that are strongly localized, for instance, where all the objects to be collected by robots are located in the center of the arena. In these anomalous cases, the transition rates will have a more complicated form and in some cases it may not be possible to express them analytically. Crowding effects will also make calculation of transition rates difficult. If the transition rates cannot be calculated from first principles, it may be expedient to leave them as parameters in the model and estimate them by fitting the model to data. Another potential limitation of the approach is that, as a mean-field-type approach, it is better suited for larger systems, where fluctuations are relatively less important. However, as shown by work of Pacala et al., the rate equations approach becomes a good quantitative description of systems as small as ten agents. We have obtained excellent quantitative agreement with simulations data for systems containing as few as two to ten agents [34].

Despite these limitations, we believe that the rate equation is a useful tool for mathematical analysis of macroscopic dynamics of artificial collectives. To facilitate the analysis, we begin by drawing the macroscopic state diagram of the system. The state diagram can be constructed from the details of the individual agent's behavior, specified by its controller (often represented as a finite state machine). Clearly, in the worst case, the macroscopic diagram will be represented by the same finite state machine (FSM) as the microscopic controller. However, it is often useful to coarse-grain the system by merging related blocks into a single state, thereby reducing the complexity of the macroscopic diagram. For example, we may take the searching state of robots to consist of the actions *wander in the arena, detect objects,* and *avoid obstacles.* When it is necessary to explicitly take obstacle avoidance into account, e.g., when the density of robots becomes high, the searching state may be split into three states, one for each behavior. In most cases, however, we are interested in the *minimal* model that captures the important behavior of the system. Coarse-graining presents a way to construct such a minimal model. In addition to the modeler's intuition, a simple rule of thumb can be used as a guide for proper coarse-graining— merge only contiguous states of the FSM. This is easily done (programmatically, if necessary) by drawing a box around these states. To complete the model, we must also specify transitions between states. These will be represented as arrows leading from one state to another.

Each state in the macroscopic state diagram corresponds to a dynamic variable in the mathematical model—the average number of agents in that state—and it is coupled to other variables via transitions between states. The mathematical model will consist of a series of coupled rate equations, one for each state, which describe how the number of agents in those states changes in time. Every transition will be accounted for by a term in each equation, with transition rates specified by the details of the interactions between agents. Note that the macroscopic state diagrams bear a resemblance to Markov chains [45]. Indeed, our models can be considered instances of continuous-time Markov chain models. However, we are not interested in studying the characteristics of Markov chains per se (e.g., identifying recurrent states, or communicating classes); rather, we use them as a guide for constructing a model of the collective and studying its dynamics. In the next section we illustrate our approach by applying it to study collaboration in a group of robots.

2.2 Collaboration in Robots

Collaboration can significantly improve the performance of a collective. In "strictly collaborative" systems [36], collaboration is an explicit requirement, because no single agent can successfully complete the task on its own. Such systems are common in insect as well as human societies, e.g., transport of objects too heavy or awkward to be lifted by a single ant, flying the space shuttle, and playing a soccer match. Collaboration in a group of robots has been studied by several groups [25,33,40,41,54,55]. We will focus on a specific case study initiated by Martinoli and collaborators [40] and studied in detail by Ijspeert et al. [25]. In this system collaboration in a group of reactive robots was achieved entirely through local interactions, i.e., without explicit global communication or coordination among robots. This system, therefore, is a compelling and effective model of how collaboration may arise in natural systems, such as insect societies. In addition, the simplicity of the robots' interactions lends itself to mathematical analysis. In this section we study an analytical model of collaboration in a group of robots.

Stick-Pulling Experiments in Groups of Robots

The stick-pulling experiments were carried out by Ijspeert et al. to study the dynamics of collaboration among locally interacting simple reactive robots. Figure 1 is a

Figure 1. Physical setup of the stick-pulling experiment showing six Khepera robots (courtesy of A. Martinoli).

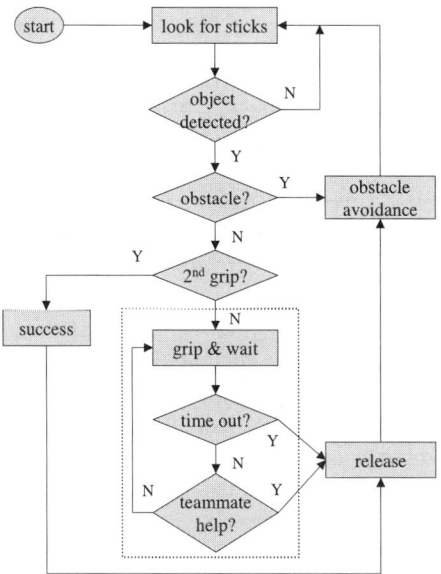

Figure 2. Flowchart of the robots' controller (from [25].

snapshot of the physical setup of the experiments. The robots' task was to locate sticks scattered around the arena and pull them out of their holes. A single robot cannot complete the task on its own (because the stick is too long)—a collaboration between two robots is necessary for the task to be successfully completed. In a general case, a collaboration between an arbitrary number of robots may be required to successfully complete the task (because sticks may be of varying length). A collaboration occurs in the following way: One robot finds a stick and waits for a second robot to find it, partially lifting the stick out of its hole. When a second robot finds it, it will grip the stick and pull it out of the ground, successfully completing the task. (In the general case, a group of some size has to accumulate at the site of the stick before the required number of robots necessary to complete the task is present.)

The actions of each robot are governed by a simple controller, outlined in Figure 2. The robot's default behavior is to wander around the arena looking for sticks and avoiding obstacles, which could be other robots or walls. When a robot finds a stick that is not being held by another robot, it grips it, lifts it halfway out of the ground, and waits for a period of time specified by the *gripping time parameter*. If no other robot comes to its aid during the waiting period, the robot releases the stick and resumes the search for other sticks. If another robot encounters a robot holding a stick, a successful collaboration will take place during which the second robot will grip the stick, pulling it out of the ground completely, while the first robot releases the stick and resumes the search. After the task is completed, the second robot also releases the stick and returns to the search mode, and the experimenter replaces the stick in its hole.

Real Robots, Embodied Simulations, and Microscopic Modeling

Ijspeert et al. [25] studied the dynamics of collaboration in the stick-pulling experiment at three different levels: by conducting experiments with physical robots; using a sensor-based simulator of robots; and using a microscopic probabilistic model. The physical experiments were carried out in groups of two to six Khepera robots in an arena containing four sticks. Because experiments with physical robots are very time consuming, Webots [43], the sensor-based simulator of Khepera robots, was used to systematically explore parameters affecting the dynamics of collaboration. The Webots simulator attempts to faithfully model the environment and replicate the experiment by reproducing the robots' (noisy) sensory input and the (noisy) response of the on-board actuators in order to compute the trajectory and interactions of all the robots in the arena. The probabilistic microscopic model, on the other hand, does not attempt to compute trajectories of individual robots. Rather, it is a numerical model in which the robot's actions—encountering a stick, a wall, another robot, a robot gripping a stick, or wandering around the arena—are represented as a series of stochastic events, with probabilities based on simple geometric considerations and systematic tests with one or two real robots. For example, the probability of a robot encountering a stick is equal to the product of the number of ungripped sticks and the detection area of the stick normalized by the arena area. Probabilities of other interactions can be similarly calculated. The microscopic simulation consists of running several processes in parallel, one for each robot, while keeping track of the global state of the environment, such as the number of gripped and ungripped sticks. According to Ijspeert et al. the acceleration factor for Webots and real robots can vary between one and two orders of magnitude for the experiments presented here. Because the probabilistic model does not require calculations of the details of the robots' trajectories, it is about 300 times faster than Webots for this experiment.

Experimental and Simulation Results

Ijspeert et al. systematically studied the collaboration rate (the number of sticks successfully pulled out of the ground in a given time interval), its dependence on the group size, and the gripping time parameter. They found very good qualitative and quantitative agreement between the three different levels of experiments, as shown in Figure 3. Their main observation was that, depending on the ratio of robots to sticks (or workers to the amount of work), there appear to be two different regimes in the collaboration dynamics. When there are fewer robots than sticks, the collaboration rate decreases to zero as the value of the gripping time parameter grows. In the extreme case, when the robot grabs a stick and waits indefinitely for another robot to come and help it, the collaboration rate is zero, because after some period of time each robot ends up holding a stick, and no robots are available to help. When there are more robots than sticks, the collaboration rate remains finite even in the limit the gripping time parameter becomes infinite, because there will always be robots available to help pull the sticks out. Another finding was that when there are fewer robots than sticks, there is an optimal value of the gripping time parameter that maximizes the collaboration rate. In the other regime, the collaboration rate appears to

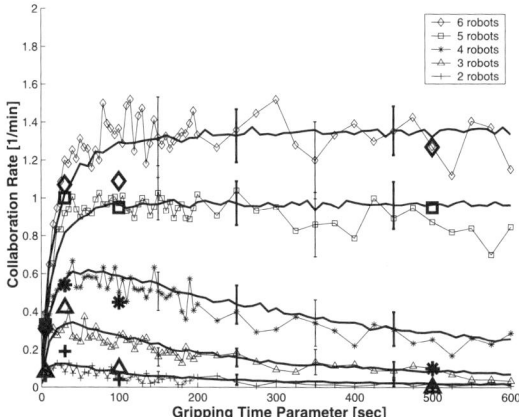

Figure 3. Collaboration rate vs. the gripping time parameter for groups of two to six robots and four sticks (from [25]). Heavy symbols represent experimental results, symbols connected by lines are the results of sensor-based simulations, and the smooth heavy lines are the result of the probabilistic microscopic model.

be independent of the gripping time parameter above a specific value, so the optimal strategy is for the robot to grip a stick and hold it indefinitely.

A Mathematical Model of Collaboration

In the following sections we present a macroscopic analytical model of the stick-pulling experiments in a homogeneous multirobot system. Such a model is useful for the following reasons. First, the complexity of a macroscopic model is independent of the system size, i.e., the number of robots: Therefore, the time required to obtain solutions for a system of 5,000 robots is as long as that to obtain solutions for a system of five robots, whereas for a microscopic description the time required for computer simulation scales at least linearly with the number of robots. Second, our approach allows us to derive analytic expressions for certain important parameters, (e.g., those for which performance is optimal). It also enables us to study the stability properties of the system and see whether solutions are robust under external perturbation or noise. These capabilities are important for the design and control of large multiagent systems.

In order to construct a mathematical model of stick-pulling experiments, it is helpful to draw the state diagram of the system. On a macroscopic level, during a sufficiently short time interval, each robot will be in one of two states: *searching* or *gripping*. Using the flowchart of the robots' controller, shown in Figure 2, we include in the search state the set of behaviors associated with the looking-for-sticks mode, such as wandering around the arena ("look for sticks" action), detecting objects, and avoiding obstacles; while the gripping state is composed of decisions and an action inside the dotted box. We assume that actions "success" (pull the stick out completely) and "release" (release the stick) take place on a short enough time scale that

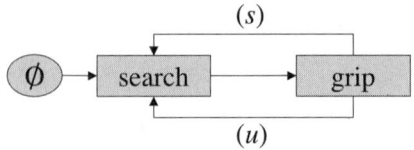

Figure 4. Macroscopic state diagram of the multirobot system. The arrow marked s corresponds to the transition from the gripping to the searching state after a successful collaboration; the arrow marked u corresponds to the transition after an unsuccessful collaboration, i.e., when the robots time out.

they can be incorporated into the search state. Of course, there can be a discrete state corresponding to every action depicted in Figure 2, but this would complicate the mathematical analysis without adding much to the descriptive power of the model. While the robot is in the obstacle avoidance mode, it cannot detect and try to grip objects; therefore, avoidance serves to decrease the number of robots that are searching and capable of gripping sticks. We studied the effect of avoidance in [35] and found that it does not qualitatively change the results of the simpler model. For now, we are interested in the *minimal* model that reproduces main experimental results.

In addition to states, we must specify all possible transitions between states. When it finds a stick, the robot makes a transition from the search state to the gripping state. After both a successful collaboration and when it times out (unsuccessful collaboration) the robot releases the stick and makes a transition into the searching state, as shown in Figure 4. These arrows correspond to the arrow entering and the two arrows leaving the dotted box in Figure 2. We will use the macroscopic state diagram as the basis for writing the rate equations that describe the dynamics of the stick-pulling experiments. Note that the system is a semi-Markov system, because the transition from gripping to the searching state depends not only on the present state (gripping) but also on how long the robot has been in the gripping state, i.e., whether the waiting has timed out. This property of the system is captured by time-dependent transition rates.

The dynamic variables of the model are $N_s(t)$, $N_g(t)$, the number of robots in the searching and gripping states respectively. Also, let $M(t)$ be the number of unextracted sticks at time t. The latter variable does not represent a macroscopic state, rather it tracks the state of the environment. The rate equations governing the dynamics of the system read:

$$\frac{dN_s}{dt} = -\alpha N_s(t)\Big(M(t) - N_g(t)\Big) + \tilde{\alpha} N_s(t) N_g(t)$$

$$+ \alpha N_s(t-\tau)\Big(M(t-\tau) - N_g(t-\tau)\Big)\Gamma(t;\tau), \tag{6}$$

$$N_g = N_0 - N_s, \tag{7}$$

$$\frac{dM}{dt} = -\tilde{\alpha} N_s(t) N_g(t) + \mu(t), \tag{8}$$

where α, $\tilde{\alpha}$ are the rates at which a searching robot encounters a stick and a gripping robot, respectively; τ is the gripping time parameter; and $\mu(t)$ is the rate at which new sticks are added. The parameters α, $\tilde{\alpha}$, and τ connect the model to the experiment; α and $\tilde{\alpha}$ are related to the size of the object, the robot's detection radius, or footprint, and the speed at which it explores the arena; $\Gamma(t; \tau)$, the fraction of failed collaborations at time t, is the probability no robot came "to help" during the time interval $[t - \tau, t]$. It corresponds to the time-dependent transition rates (marked u in Figure 4) in this semi-Markov system.

To calculate $\Gamma(t; \tau)$ let us divide the time interval $[t - \tau, t]$ into K small intervals of length $\delta t = \tau/K$. The probability that no robot comes to help during the time interval $[t - \tau, t - \tau + \delta t]$ is simply $1 - \tilde{\alpha} N_s (t - \tau) \delta t$. Hence, the probability for a failed collaboration is

$$\Gamma(t; \tau) = \prod_{i=1}^{K}[1 - \tilde{\alpha}\delta t N_s(t - \tau + i\delta t)]\Theta(t - \tau)$$

$$\equiv \exp\left[\sum_{i=1}^{K} \ln[1 - \tilde{\alpha}\delta t N_s(t - \tau + i\delta t)]\right]\Theta(t - \tau). \tag{9}$$

The step function $\Theta(t - \tau)$ ensures that $\Gamma(t; \tau)$ is zero for $t < \tau$. Finally, expanding the logarithm in Equation 9 and taking the limit $\delta t \to 0$ we obtain

$$\Gamma(t; \tau) = \exp[-\tilde{\alpha}\int_{t-\tau}^{t} dt' N_s(t')]\Theta(t - \tau). \tag{10}$$

The three terms in Equation 6 correspond to the three arrows between the states in Figure 4. The first term accounts for the decrease in the number of searching robots because some robots find and grip sticks, the second term describes the successful collaborations between two robots, and the third term accounts for the failed collaborations, both of which lead to an increase in the number of searching robots. We do not need a separate equation for N_g, because this quantity may be calculated from the conservation-of-robots condition, Equation 7. Equation 8 states that the number of sticks, $M(t)$, decreases in time at the rate of successful collaborations but also increases at the rate new sticks are added. The equations are subject to the initial conditions that at $t = 0$ the number of searching robots is N_0 and the number of sticks is M_0.

To proceed further, let us introduce $n(t) = N_s(t)/N_0$, $m(t) = M(t)/M_0$, $\beta = N_0/M_0$, $R_G = \tilde{\alpha}/\alpha$, $\tilde{\beta} = R_G\beta$, and a dimensionless time $t \to \alpha M_0 t$, $\tau \to \alpha M_0 \tau$. μ' is the dimensionless rate at which new sticks are added. $n(t)$ is the fraction of robots in the search state and $m(t)$ is the fraction of unextracted sticks at time t. Due to the conservation of number of robots, the fraction of robots in the gripping state is simply $1 - n(t)$. Equations 6–8 can be rewritten in dimensionless form as:

$$\frac{dn}{dt} = -n(t)[m(t) + \beta n(t) - \beta] + \tilde{\beta}n(t)[1 - n(t)] + n(t - \tau)[m(t - \tau)$$
$$+ \beta n(t - \tau) - \beta] \times \gamma(t; \tau), \tag{11}$$

$$\frac{dm}{dt} = -\beta\tilde{\beta}n(t)[1 - n(t)] + \mu',$$ (12)

$$\gamma(t; \tau) = \exp\left[-\tilde{\beta}\int_{t-\tau}^{t} dt' n(t')\right].$$ (13)

Equations 11–13, together with initial conditions $n(0) = 1$, $m(0) = 1$, determine the dynamical evolution of the system. Note that only two parameters, β and τ, appear in the equations and thus determine the behavior of solutions. The third parameter $\tilde{\beta} = R_G\beta$ is fixed experimentally and is not independent. Note that we do not need to specify α and $\tilde{\alpha}$—they enter the model only through R_G (throughout this chapter we will use $R_G = 0.35$, the value reported in [25]).[1] We will provide a detailed analysis of the equations.

Results

In [35] we studied the steady-state properties of the system (Equations 11–13) for the case of a static environment, $m(t) = const = 1$. Experimentally this was realized by replacing sticks in their holes after they were pulled out, $\mu(t) = \tilde{\alpha}N_s(t)N_g(t)$. Particularly, it was found that for $\beta < \beta_c \equiv 2/(1+R_G)$ the steady-state collaboration rate, given by $R(\tau, \beta) = \beta\tilde{\beta}n(\tau, \beta)(1-n(\tau, \beta))$, has a maximum for a certain value of the gripping time parameter τ.

We will provide an analysis for the case of a dynamically changing environment. There are no new sticks added to the system, $\mu(t) = 0$; therefore, the number of unextracted sticks decreases monotonically. First, we consider the case of $\tau = \infty$, which corresponds to robots gripping the sticks and holding them partway out of the ground indefinitely. Solving Equations 11–13 yields the number of robots in the search state, Figure 5(a), and the number of unextracted sticks, Figure 5(b), as a function of time for two values of β. A qualitatively different solution is obtained for small and large values of the parameter β. For small βs, the fraction of searching robots exponentially decreases to zero and the fraction of unextracted sticks "saturates" at $m(t) \rightarrow m \neq 0$ as $t \rightarrow \infty$. For sufficiently large β's, however, all the robots are in the searching mode and all the sticks are collected in the long time limit. This different behavior is illustrated in Figure 5. For ($\beta = 0.5$), the number of searching robots drops to zero as all robots end up gripping a stick and only a small fraction of the sticks is collected (solid lines). For $\beta = 1$, however, the number of searching robots first decreases as robots find sticks, but then it increases because successful

---

[1] The parameter α can be easily calculated from experimental values quoted in [25]. As a robot travels through the arena, it sweeps out some area during time dt and will detect objects that fall in that area. This detection area is $V_R W_R dt$, where $V_R = 8.0$ cm/s is robot's speed, and $W_R = 14.0$ cm is robot's detection width. If the arena radius is $R = 40.0$ cm, a robot will detect sticks at the rate $\alpha = V_R W_R/\pi R^2 = 0.02$ s^{-1}. According to [25], a robot's probability to grab a stick already being held by another robot is 35% of the probability of grabbing a free stick. Therefore, $R_G = \tilde{\alpha}/\alpha = 0.35$. R_G is an experimental value obtained with systematic experiments with two real robots, one holding the stick and the other approaching the stick from different angles.

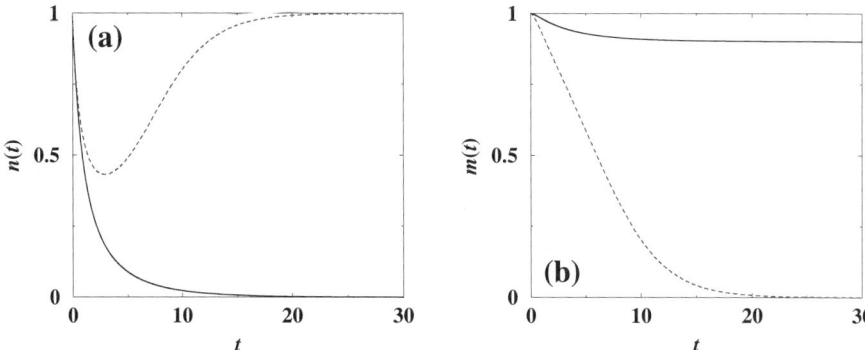

Figure 5. (a) Fraction of robots in searching state and (b) fraction of unextracted sticks as a function of time for $\tau = \infty$, $\beta = 0.5$ (solid), and $\beta = 1$ (dashed), where τ is the gripping time parameter and β is the ratio of robots to sticks.

collaborations return the gripping robots back to the searching state. Eventually, all the sticks are collected (dashed lines), and all the robots are in the searching state.

When the gripping time parameter τ is finite, the solution to Equation 11 displays characteristic oscillations (Figure 6(a)), which die out as the solution approaches its steady-state value $n(t \to \infty) = 1$, $m(t \to \infty) = 0$. Note that the steady-state solution for this case is trivial in the sense that all the sticks are eventually collected and all the robots are in the searching state after some transient time. Consequently, we modify the measure of collaboration as the inverse of the time it takes to collect certain fraction of sticks (e.g., 0.9 in our analysis). Collaboration rate versus the gripping time parameter for different values of β is shown in Figure 6(b). As for the static case studied in the experiments, an optimal behavior is seen for small β, i.e., for these cases there exists a gripping time parameter that maximizes the collaboration

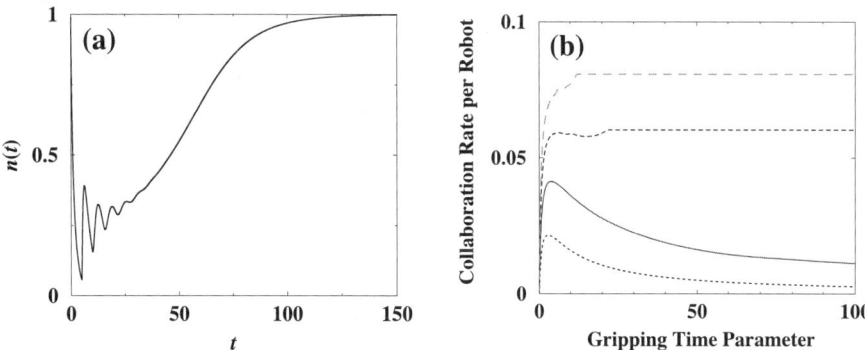

Figure 6. (a) Fraction of searching robots for $\tau = 5$ and $\beta = 0.4$. (b) Collaboration rate per robot vs. gripping time parameter τ for $\beta = 0.25, 0.5, 0.75, 1$, for the bottom to top curves, respectively. Collaboration rate is defined as the inverse of the time needed to collect 90% of the sticks.

rate. Note also that the kinks in the graph are not numeric artifacts but are due to our definition of the collaboration rate. Because $n(t)$ oscillates in the transient regime, the time to collect $100f\%$ of the sticks will vary significantly if it falls within this regime. We have checked that these kinks disappear as $f \to 1$.

3 Market-Based Control

Previous research has shown that market-based (or game-dynamical) control strategy, in which agents make "economically" motivated decisions with the goal of maximizing individual payoff but that result in the optimization of some global system property, e.g., world utility, is a feasible distributed control mechanism for artificial collectives (see, e.g., [56] for an overview).

We will present a model of distributed coordination of agents in non-stationary environments. Specifically, we consider a network of interconnected Boolean agents that compete for a resource with a limited capacity using a form of minority game. At each time step the agents face a choice of whether to use the resource, and the agents in the winning group are rewarded and those in the losing group are punished. The winning group is the one whose size is less than resource capacity: thus, this game penalizes overcrowding. We will consider the case where the resource capacity changes in time and demonstrate that under certain conditions our model shows globally adaptive and coordinated behavior, resulting in efficient resource utilization.

3.1 Minority Games

The minority game [12] (MG) is a simple model of competing agents that has a very rich dynamics. It was introduced by Challet and Zhang as a simplification of Arthur's El Farol Bar attendance problem [3]. The MG consists of N agents with bounded rationality that repeatedly choose between two alternatives labeled 0 and 1 (e.g., staying at home or going to the bar). At each time step, agents who made the minority decision win. In the generalized minority game [26], the wining group is 1 (0) if the fraction of the agents who chose "1" is smaller (greater) than the capacity level η, $0 < \eta < 1$. For $\eta = 0.5$, the game reduces to the traditional MG. Each agent uses a set of S strategies to decide its next move and reinforces strategies that would have predicted the winning group. A strategy is simply a lookup table that prescribes a binary output for all possible inputs. In the original version of the game, the input is a binary string containing the last m outcomes of the game, so the agents interact by sharing the same global signal. If the agents choose either action with probability $1/2$ (the random choice game), then, on average, the number of agents choosing "1" (henceforth referred to as utilization) is $(N-1)/2$ with standard deviation $\sigma = \sqrt{N}/2$ in the limit of large N. The most interesting phenomenon of the minority model is the emergence of a coordinated phase, where the standard deviation of utilization, the volatility, becomes smaller than in the random choice game. The coordination is achieved for memory sizes for which the dimension of the reduced strategy space is comparable to the number of agents in the system, $2^m \sim N$ [13, 49]. It was later pointed out that the dynamics of the game remains mostly unchanged if one replaces the string with the actual histories with a random one [10], provided that all the agents act on the same signal. Analytical studies based on this simplification have revealed many interesting properties of the minority model [11, 44].

In addition to the original MG, different versions of the game where the agents interact using local information only (cellular automata [28], evolving random Boolean networks [47], personal histories [15]), have been studied. In particular, it was established that coordination still arises out of local interactions, and the system as a whole achieves "better than random" performance in terms of the utilization of resources.

In all previous studies the capacity level has been fixed as an external parameter, so the environment in which the agents compete is stationary. As we mentioned, however, we are interested in a situation where the environment is changing. It is interesting to see if a coordinated behavior still emerges and to what degree agents can adapt to the changing environment. Namely, we study a system of Boolean agents playing a generalized minority game, assuming that the capacity level is not fixed but varies with time, $\eta(t) = \eta_0 + \eta_1(t)$, where $\eta_1(t)$ is a time-dependent perturbation. The framework of the interactions is based on Kauffman NK random Boolean nets [30], where each agent gets its input from K other randomly chosen agents and maps the input to a new state according to a Boolean function of K variables, which is also randomly chosen and quenched throughout the dynamics of the system. The generalization we make is that agents are allowed to adapt by having more than one Boolean function, or strategy, and the use of a particular strategy is determined by an agent based on how often it predicted the winning group throughout the game. Note that this approach is very different from adaptation through evolution studied previously in the context of the minority model [47].

3.2 The Model

We consider a set of N Boolean agents described by "spin" variables $s_i = \{0, 1\}$, $i = 1, \ldots, N$. Each agent gets its input from K other randomly chosen agents and maps the input to a new state:

$$s_i(t + 1) = F_i^j(s_{k_1}(t), s_{k_2}(t), \ldots, s_{k_K}(t)), \qquad (14)$$

where s_{k_i}, $i = 1, \ldots, K$ are the set of neighbors, and F_i^j, $j = 1, \ldots, S$ are randomly chosen Boolean functions (called strategies hereafter) used by the ith agent. For each strategy F_i^j, the agent keeps a score that monitors the performance of that strategy, adding (subtracting) a point if the strategy predicted the winning (losing) side. Let the "utilization" $A(t)$ be the cumulative output of the system at time t, $A(t) = \sum_{i=1}^{N} s_i(t)$. Then the winning choice is "1" if $A(t) \leq N\eta(t)$, and "0" otherwise. Those in the winning group are awarded a point and the others lose one. Agents play the strategies that have predicted the winning side most often, and the ties are broken randomly.

As a global measure of performance, the world utility, we define efficient utilization as one that has the smallest cumulative resource "waste." If $\delta(t) = A(t) - N\eta(t)$ describes the deviation from the optimal resource utilization, cumulative "waste" over a certain time window is

$$\sigma = \sqrt{\frac{1}{T} \sum_{t=t_0}^{t_0+T} \delta(t)^2}. \tag{15}$$

For $\eta_1(t) = 0$ this quantity is simply the volatility as defined in the traditional minority game.

We compare the performance of our system to a default random choice game, defined as follows: Assume that the agents are told what the capacity $\eta(t)$ is at time t and they choose to go to the bar with probability $\eta(t)$. In this case the main utilization will be close to $\eta(t)N$ at each time step, and the fluctuations around the mean are given by the standard deviation

$$\sigma_0^2 = N\frac{1}{T} \int_{t_0}^{t_0+T} dt' \eta(t')[1 - \eta(t')]. \tag{16}$$

3.3 Results

We performed intensive numerical simulations of the system just described, with the number of agents ranging from 100 to 10^4 and for network connectivity K ranging from 1 to 10. Although in our simulations we used different forms for the perturbation $\eta_1(t)$, in this chapter we consider periodic perturbations only. For each K, a set of strategies was chosen for each agent randomly and independently from a pool of 2^{2^K} possible Boolean functions and was quenched throughout the game. In all simulations we used $S = 2$ strategies per agent. Starting from a random initial configuration, the system evolved according to the specified rules. The duration of the simulation T_0 was determined by the particular choice of $\eta(t)$. Depending on the amplitude of the perturbation, we run the simulations for 10 to 20 periods and usually use the data for the last two periods to determine σ.

Our main observation is that networks with $K = 2$ show a tendency toward self-organization into a phase characterized by small fluctuations, hence, an effective utilization of the resource, even for relatively large variations in the capacity level $\eta(t)$. Note that in the Kauffman nets with $K > 2$ the dynamics of the system is chaotic with an exponentially increasing length of attractors as the system size grows, while for $K < 2$ the network reaches a frozen configuration. The case $K = 2$ corresponds to a phase transition in the dynamical properties of the network and is often referred as the "edge of the chaos." We would like to reiterate, however, that our system is different from a Kauffman network because the agents have an internal degree of freedom, characterized by their strategies. Specifically, our system does not necessarily have periodic attractors, but in Kauffman nets periodic attractors are guaranteed to exist due to the finite phase space and quenched rules of updating.

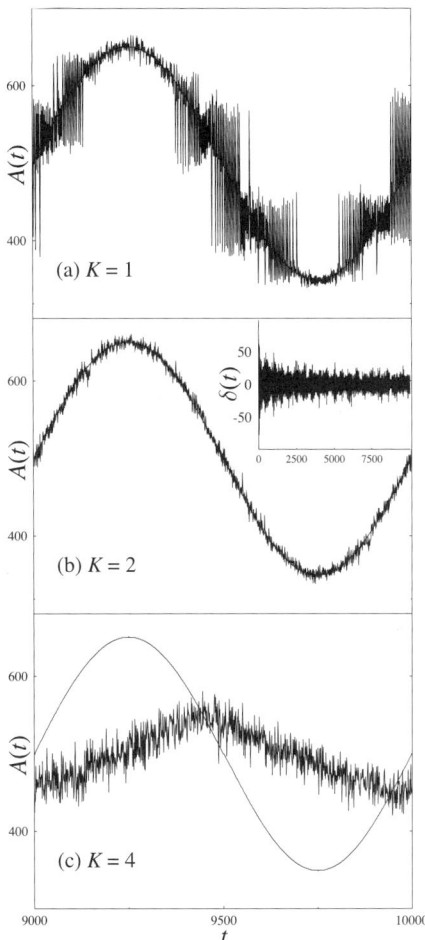

Figure 7. A segment of the utilization time series for $\eta(t) = 0.5 + 0.15\sin(2\pi t/T)$, $T = 1000$, and different network connectivity K.

Figure 7 shows a typical segment of the time series of the utilization $A(t)$ for a system of size $N = 1000$, a sinusoidal perturbation $\eta_1(t)$, and different network connectivities. For $K = 1$ the agents react to the changes in the capacity level, however, there are strong fluctuations in the utilization series. For $K = 4$, on the other hand, response of the system to the environmental dynamics is very weak, and, as our results indicate, it becomes even weaker for larger K. Remarkably, the system with $K = 2$ adapts very efficiently to changes in the capacity level. The inset of Figure 7 (b) shows the time series of the deviation $\delta(t)$ for $K = 2$. Initially there are strong fluctuations, hence poor utilization of the resource, but after some transient time the system as a whole adapts and the strength of the fluctuations decreases. In fact, the standard deviation of the fluctuations is considerably smaller than in

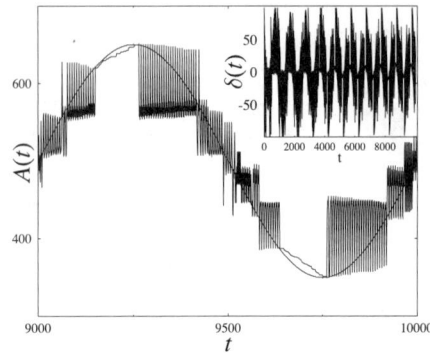

Figure 8. Same as in Figure 7 for the traditional MG (global histories) with memory size $m = 5$.

the random choice game as defined by Equation 16. Note also that the agents have information only about the winning choice, but not the capacity level. This suggests that the particular form of the perturbation may not be important as long as it meets some general criteria for smoothness.

For comparison, we also studied the effect of the changing capacity level in the traditional (generalized) minority model with publicly available information about the last m outcomes of the game. We plot the utilization and deviation time series for a system with a memory size $m = 6$ (corresponding to the minimum of σ) in Figure 8. One can see that in this case also the system reacts to the external change. However, the structure of adaptation is very different from the previous case. Indeed, an analysis of Figure 8 shows that even though the total "wealth," i.e., the total points accumulated by the agents in the system, increases with time, the overall performance in terms of resource allocation as described by σ is much poorer than the previous case. Another important difference is that in the traditional system the distribution of wealth among the players is much wider than in the system with local information exchange, i.e., the later mechanism of adaptation is socially more "fair."

In Figure 9 we plot the variance per agent versus network connectivity K, for system sizes $N = 100, 200, 500, 1000$. For each K we performed 32 runs and averaged results. Our simulations suggest that the details of this dependence are not very sensitive to the particular form of the perturbation $\eta_1(t)$, and the general picture is the same for a wide range of functions, provided that they are smooth enough. As we already mentioned, the variance attains its minimum for $K = 2$, independent of the number of agents in the system. For bigger K it saturates at a value that depends on the amplitude of the perturbation and on the number of agents in the system. We found that for large K the time series of the utilization closely resembles the time series in the absence of perturbation. This implies that for large K the agents do not "feel" the change in the capacity level. Consequently, the standard deviation increases linearly with the number of agents in the system, $\sigma \propto N$. For $K = 2$, on the other hand, σ increases considerably slower with the number of agents in the system,

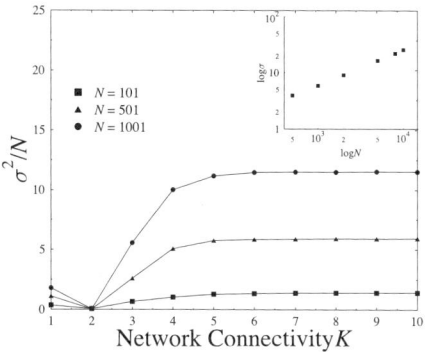

Figure 9. σ^2/N vs. the network connectivity for different system sizes and $\eta(t) = 0.5 + 0.15\sin(2\pi t/T)$, $T = 1000$. Inset plot shows the scaling relationship between σ and N for $K = 2$. Average over 16 runs has been taken.

$\sigma \propto N^\gamma$, $\gamma < 1$ (see the inset in Figure 9). Our results indicate that the scaling (i.e., the exponent γ) is not universal and depends on the perturbation.

We do not currently have an analytic theory for the observed emergent coordination. In contrast to the traditional minority game, where global interactions and the Markovian approximation allow one to construct a mean field description, our model seems to be analytically intractable due to explicit emphasis on local information processing. We strongly believe, however, that the adaptability of the networks with $K = 2$ is related to the peculiar properties of the corresponding Kauffman nets, particularly to the phase transition between the chaotic and frozen phases. It is known [16] that the phase transition in the Kauffman networks can be achieved by tuning the homogeneity parameter P, which is the fraction of 1s or 0s in the output of the Boolean functions (whichever is the majority), with the critical value given by $P_c = 1/2 + 1/2\sqrt{1 - 2/K}$. To test our hypothesis, we studied the properties of networks with $K = 3$ for a range of homogeneity parameter P. In Figure 10

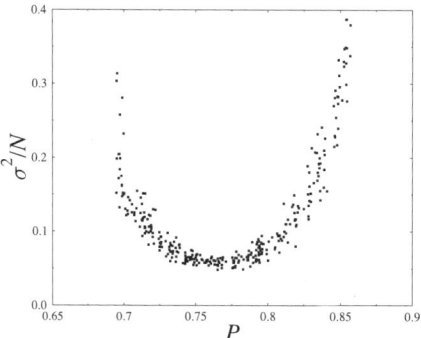

Figure 10. Standard deviation per agent vs. homogeneity coefficient P for $K = 3$ networks: $N = 1000$, $\eta(t) = 0.5 + 0.15\sin(2\pi t/T)$, $T = 1000$.

we plot σ^2/N versus the homogeneity parameter P. One can see that the optimal resource allocation is indeed achieved in the vicinity of the $P_c \sim 0.78$, indicating that the properties of Kauffman networks at the phase transition might be responsible in this emergent coordination. Recent investigation of the coordinated phase using information-theoretic analysis [51] suggests that emergence of the coordinated phase coincides with the growth of clusters of synchronous agents. More analysis is required to illuminate this insight.

4 Related Work

With the exceptions noted later, there has been very little prior work on mathematical analysis of artificial collectives. The closest in spirit to this chapter is the work by Huberman, Hogg, and coworkers on computational ecologies [24,31]. These authors mathematically studied collective behavior in a system of agents, each choosing between two alternative strategies. They derived a rate equation for the average number of agents using each strategy from the underlying probability distributions. Our approach is consistent with theirs—in fact, we can easily write these rate equations directly from the macroscopic state diagram of the system, without having to derive them from probability distributions. Therefore, computational ecologies can be considered another application of the methodology we described here.

Sugawara and coworkers [52,54] carried out quantitative studies of cooperative foraging in a group of communicating and noncommunicating robots in different environments. They have developed a simple state-based analytical model and analyzed it under different conditions. In their system, when a robot finds a puck or a collection of pucks, it may broadcast a signal for a period of time to other robots, which move toward it. The robots pick up pucks and bring them home. Sugawara et al. did not take the interaction into account explicitly but in an approximate manner. In our model of collaboration, we include the duration of the interaction explicitly, resulting in a better description of the system. Another difference between their work and ours is that their system is not strictly collaborative—collaboration via signaling improves foraging performance but is not a requirement for task completion.

5 Conclusion

Distributed control is a superior paradigm for control of artificial collectives that has a number of advantages over alternative designs, namely, robustness, scalability, reliability, and adaptability. However, the "inverse" problem of distributed control is notoriously difficult to solve: It is hard to identify the local rules that will lead to desirable collective behavior. Lack of analysis tools to evaluate different designs has been one of the major obstacles to progress in this area.

We presented two approaches to the *design* of distributed control mechanisms for artificial collectives, as well as two *analysis* tools used to study these mechanisms. The first design approach is biologically based control, which uses local interactions among many simple agents to create desirable collective behavior. We presented a general methodology for mathematical analysis of artificial collectives designed according to these principles.

Our analysis applies to a class of systems known as stochastic Markov systems in which the state of an agent at a future time depends only on the current state (and perhaps on how much time the agent has spent in this state). Though each agent's actions are unpredictable in stochastic systems, the probabilistic description of the collective behavior is surprisingly simple. It is given by the rate equation, which describes how the average macroscopic (collective) system properties change in time.

We illustrated our approach by applying it to study collaboration in a homogeneous group of reactive robots. The robots' task was to pull sticks out of their holes, and it could be successfully achieved only through collaboration between two robots. The system we modeled was slightly different from the one studied by Ijspeert et al. [25] in that the number of sticks was not constant, but decreased as robots pulled them out. Detailed analysis of the Ijspeert et al. experiments and simulations is presented in a separate paper [35].

Mathematical analysis shows that the performance of the system where the number of sticks changes in time is qualitatively similar to the performance of the system in the static environment, where the number of sticks remains constant (see Figure 3). Indeed, we were able to reproduce some of the conclusions of the Ijspeert et al. work; namely, the different dynamical regimes for different values of the ratio of robots to sticks (β) and the optimal gripping time parameter for β less than the critical value. Moreover, some conclusions, such as the importance of the parameter β, fall directly out of simple analysis of the model, without requiring any time-consuming simulations or experiments. In [35] we reported qualitative agreement between the predictions of the model and results of the experiment and simulation. In the simple state-based model we studied, the robot's future state depends only on its current state (and on how much time it has spent in that state). Although the reactive and behavior-based robots clearly obey the Markov property, other systems composed of agents with memory, learning, or deliberative capabilities do not, and therefore, they cannot be described by the simple models presented here. Creating a mathematical model that addresses these issues is our next challenge.

The second approach to distributed control uses market-based mechanisms for adaptation of an artificial collective to a dynamically changing environment. We studied a network of Boolean agents playing minority games and competing for use of a resource with a dynamic capacity. We studied the problem numerically, by simulating games in systems of different sizes, network connectivities K, and capacity functions. We established that networks with connectivity $K = 2$ can be extremely adaptable and robust with respect to capacity level changes. For $K > 2$ the coordination can be achieved by tuning the homogeneity parameter to its critical value. The adaptation happens without the agents knowing the capacity level. Remarkably, the system that uses local information is much more efficient in a dynamic environment than a system that uses global information.

Acknowledgments. The authors wish to thank the following people for insights and useful discussions: Alcherio Martinoli, Maja Matarić, Richard Ross, Dmitry Tsigankov, Jim Crutchfield, and Cosma Shalizi. The research reported here was supported in part by the Defense Advanced Research Projects Agency (DARPA) under contract number F30602-00-2-0573, in part by the National Science Foundation under Grant No. 0074790, and by the ISI/ISD Research Fund Award. The views and conclusions contained herein are those of the authors and should not be interpreted as representing the official policies or endorsements, either expressed or implied, of any of these organizations or any person connected with them.

References

1. W. Agassounon, A. Martinoli, and R. M. Goodman. A scalable, distributed algorithm for allocating workers in embedded systems. In *Proc. of the IEEE Conf. on System, Man and Cybernetics SMC-01, October 2001, Tucson, AR, USA,* to appear. 2001.
2. R. C. Arkin. *Behavior-Based Robotics.* The MIT Press, Cambridge, MA, 1999.
3. B. W. Arthur. Inductive reasoning and bounded rationality. *Am. Econ. Assoc. Papers Proc.,* 84:406, 1994.
4. A.-L. Barabasi and H. E. Stanley. *Fractal Concepts in Surface Growth.* Cambridge University Press, 1995.
5. R. Beckers, O. E. Holland, and J. L. Deneubourg. From local actions to global tasks: Stigmergy and collective robotics. In Rodney A. Brooks and Pattie Maes, editors, *Proc. of the 4th International Workshop on the Synthesis and Simulation of Living Systems Artificial Life IV*, pages 181–9, Cambridge, MA, USA, July 1994. MIT Press.
6. G. Beni and J. Wang. Swarm intelligence. In *Proc. of the Seventh Annual Meeting of the Robotics Society of Japan, Tokyo, Japan*, pages 425–8, Tokyo, Japan, 1989. RSJ Press.
7. A. Billard, A.J. Ijspeert, and A. Martinoli. A multi-robot system for adaptive exploration of a fast changing environment: Probabilistic modelling and experimental study. *Connection Science*, 11(3/4):359–79, 1999.
8. K. Boehringer, R. Brown, B. Donald, J. Jennings, and D. Rus. Distributed robotic manipulation: Experiments in minimalism. In O. Khatib and J. K. Salisbury, editors, *Proc. of the Fourth Int. Symp. on Experimental Robotics, Stanford*, pages 11–25. Lecture Notes in Control and Information Sciences, Springer-Verlag, 1995.
9. E. Bonabeau, M. Dorigo, and G. Theraulaz. *Swarm Intelligence: From Natural to Artificial Systems.* Oxford University Press, New York, 1999.
10. A. Cavagna. Irrelevance of memory in the minority game. *Phys. Rev.,* E59:R3783, 1998.
11. D. Challet and M. Marsili. Phase transition and symmetry breaking in the minority game. *Phys. Rev.,* E60:R6271, 1999.
12. D. Challet and Y.-C. Zhang. Emergence of cooperation and organization in an evolutionary game. *Physica,* A246:407, 1997.
13. D. Challet and Y.-C. Zhang. On the minority game: Analytical and numerical studies. *Physica,* A256:514, 1998.
14. D. Chowdhury, L. Santen, and A. Schadschneider. Statistical physics of vehicular traffic and some related systems. *Physics Reports*, 329:199, 2000.
15. M. A. R. de Cara, O. Pla, and F. Guinea. Learning, competition and cooperation in simple games. *Eur. Phys. J.,* B13:413, 2000.
16. B. Derrida and Y. Pomeau. Random networks of automata: A simple annealed approximation. *Eur. Phys. Lett.,* 1:45, 1986.
17. C. W. Garnier. *Handbook of Stochastic Methods.* Springer, New York, NY, 1983.

18. D. Goldberg and Maja J Matarić. Robust behavior-based control for distributed multi-robot collection tasks. Technical Report IRIS-00-387, USC Institute for Robotics and Intelligent Systems, 2000.

19. R. Haberman. *Mathematical Models: Mechanical Vibrations, Population Dynamics, and Traffic Flow*. Society of Industrial and Applied Mathematics (SIAM), Philadelphia, PA, 1998.

20. A. T. Hayes, A. Martinoli, and R. M. Goodman. Comparing distributed exploration strategies with simulated and real autonomous robots. In L. E. Parker, G. Bekey, and J. Bahren, editors, *Proc. of the Fifth Int. Symp. on Distributed Autonomous Robotic Systems DARS-00, October, 2000, Knoxville, TN*, pp. 261–70. Springer-Verlag, 2000.

21. A. T. Hayes, A. Martinoli, and R. M. Goodman. Swarm robotic odor localization. In *Proc. of the IEEE Conf. on Intelligent Robots and Systems IROS-01, October–November 2001, Maui, HI, USA*. 2001.

22. D. Helbing. *Quantitative Sociodynamics: Stochastic Methods and Models of Social Interaction Processes*, volume 31 of *Theory and Decision Library B: Mathematical and Statistical Methods*. Kluwer Academic, Dordrecht, 1995.

23. O. Holland and C. Melhuish. Stigmergy, self-organization, and sorting in collective robotics. *Artificial Life*, 5:173–202, 1999.

24. B. A. Huberman and T. Hogg. The behavior of computational ecologies. In B. A. Huberman, editor, *The Ecology of Computation*, pages 77–115, Amsterdam, 1988. Elsevier (North-Holland).

25. A. J. Ijspeert, A. Martinoli, A. Billard, and L. M. Gambardella. Collaboration through the exploitation of local interactions in autonomous collective robotics: The stick pulling experiment. *Autonomous Robots*, 11(2):149–71, 2001.

26. N. F. Johnson, P. M. Hui, D. Zheng, and C. W. Tai. Minority game with arbitrary cuttoffs. *Physica*, A269:493, 1999.

27. P. J. Johnson and J. S. Bay. Distributed control of simulated autonomous mobile robot collectives in payload transportation. *Autonomous Robots*, 2:43–63, 1995.

28. T. Kalinowski, H.-J. Schulz, and M. Briese. Cooperation in the minority game with local information. *Physica*, A277:502, 2000.

29. N. G. Van Kampen. *Stochastic Processes in Physics and Chemistry*. Elsevier Science, Amsterdam, revised and enlarged edition, 1992.

30. S. A. Kauffman. *The Origins of Order*. Oxford University Press, New York, 1993.

31. J. O. Kephart, T. Hogg, and B. A. Huberman. Collective behavior of predictive agents. *Physica*, D 42:48–65, 1990.

32. M. J. B. Krieger and J.-B. Billeter. The call of duty: Self-organised task allocation in a population of up to twelve mobile robots. *Robotics and Autonomous Systems*, 30(1–2):65–84, 2000.

33. C. R. Kube and E. Bonabeau. Cooperative transport by ants and robots. *Robotics and Autonomous Systems*, 30(1–2):85–101, 2000.

34. K. Lerman and A. Galstyan. Mathematical model of foraging in a group of robots: Effect of interference. *Autonomous Robots*, 13(2), 2002.

35. K. Lerman, A. Galstyan, A. Martinoli, and A. Ijspeert. A macroscopic analytical model of collaboration in distributed robotic systems. *Artificial Life Journal*, 7(4):375–93, 2001.

36. A. Martinoli. *Swarm Intelligence in Autonomous Collective Robotics: From Tools to the Analysis and Synthesis of Distributed Control Strategies*. Ph.D. thesis, No. 2069, EPFL, 1999.

37. A. Martinoli. *Swarm Intelligence in Autonomous Collective Robotics: From Tools to the Analysis and Synthesis of Distributed Control Strategies*. Ph.D. thesis, No. 2069, EPFL, 1999.

38. A. Martinoli, A. J. Ijspeert, and L. M. Gambardella. A probabilistic model for understanding and comparing collective aggregation mechanisms. In Dario Floreano, Jean-Daniel Nicoud, and Francesco Mondada, editors, *Proc. of the 5th European Conference on Advances in Artificial Life (ECAL-99)*, volume 1674 of *LNAI*, pp. 575–84, Berlin, September 13–17 1999. Springer.

39. A. Martinoli, A.J. Ijspeert, and F. Mondada. Understanding collective aggregation mechanisms: From probabilistic modelling to experiments with real robots. *Robotics and Autonomous Systems*, 29:51–63, 1999.

40. A. Martinoli and F. Mondada. Collective and cooperative group behaviors: Biologically inspired experiments in robotics. In O. Khatib and J. K. Salisbur, editors, *Proc. of the Fourth Int. Symp. on Experimental Robotics ISER-95*. Springer Verlag, June–July 1995.

41. M. J. Matarić, M. Nilsson, and K. Simsarian. Cooperative multi-robot box pushing. In *Proc. of the 1995 IEEE/RSJ International Conference on Intelligent Robots*, 1995.

42. Maja Matarić. *Interaction and Intelligent Behavior*. Ph.D. thesis, Dept. of Electrical Engineering and Computer Science, MIT, Cambridge, MA, 1994.

43. O. Michel. Webots: Symbiosis between virtual and real mobile robots. In J.-C. Heudin, editor, *Proc. of the First Int. Conf. on Virtual Worlds, Paris, France,* pp. 254–63. Springer-Verlag, 1998. See also http://www.cyberbotics.com/webots/

44. See http://www.unifr.ch/econophysics/minority/ for an extensive collection of articles and references.

45. J. R. Norris. *Markov Chains*. Cambridge Series in Statistical and Probabilistic Mathematics. Cambridge University Press, Cambridge, UK, 1997.

46. S. W. Pacala, D. M. Gordon, and H. C. J. Godfray. Effects of social group size on information transfer and task allocation. *Evolutionary Ecology*, 10:127–65, 1996.

47. M. Paczuski and K. E. Bassler. Self-organized networks of competing Boolean agents. *Phys. Rev. Lett.*, 84:3185, 2000.

48. J. K. Parrish and W. M. Hamner. *Animal Groups in Three Dimensions*. Cambridge University Press, 1997.

49. R. Savit, R. Manuca, and R. Riolo. Adaptive competition, market efficiency, phase transition. *Phys. Rev. Lett*, 82(10):2203, 1999.

50. F. Schweitzer, K. Lao, and F. Family. Active random walkers simulate trunk trail formation by ants. *BioSystems*, 41:153–66, 1997.

51. C. Shalizi. private communication.

52. K. Sugawara and M. Sano. Cooperative acceleration of task performance: Foraging behavior of interacting multi-robots system. *Physica*, D100:343–54, 1997.

53. K. Sugawara, M. Sano, and I. Yoshihara. Cooperative acceleration of task performance: Analysis of foraging behavior by interacting multi-robots. In *Proc. IPSJ Int. Symp. on Information Systems and Technologies for Network Society*, pp. 314–17, Fukuoka, Japan, September 1997.

54. K. Sugawara, M. Sano, I. Yoshihara, and K. Abe. Cooperative behavior of interacting robots. *Artificial Life and Robotics*, 2:62–7, 1998.

55. R. T. Vaughan, K. Støy, G. S. Sukhatme, and M. J. Matarić. Blazing a trail: Insect-inspired resource transportation by a robot team. In *Proc. of the 5th International Symposium on Distributed Autonomous Robotic Systems (DARS), Knoxville, TN*, 2000.

56. M. P. Wellman. Market-oriented programming: Some early lessons. In S. H. Clearwater, editor, *Market-Based Control: A Paradigm for Distributed Resource Allocation*, pp. 74–95. World Scientific, January 1996.

57. S. Wolfram. *Cellular Automata and Complexity*. Addison-Wesley, Reading, MA, 1994.

11

Efficiency and Equity in Collective Systems of Interacting Heterogeneous Agents

Akira Namatame* and Saori Iwanaga*

Summary. In this chapter we address the issue realizing efficient and equitable utilization of limited resources by collective decision of interacting heterogeneous agents. There is no presumption that collective action of interacting agents leads to collectively satisfactory results without any central authority. How well agents do in adapting to their environment is not the same thing as how satisfactory an environment they collectively create. Agents normally react to others' decisions, and the resulting volatile collective decision is often far from being efficient. By means of experiments, we show that the overall performance of the system depends on the types of interaction and the heterogeneity of preferences. We also show that the most crucial factor that considerably improves the performance is the way of information presentation to agents. It is shown that if each agent adapts to global information the performances are poor. The optimal guidance strategy to improve both efficiency and equity depends on the way of interaction. With symmetric interaction, the local information of the same type realizes the highest performance. With asymmetric interaction, however, the local information of the opposite preference type realizes the highest performance.

1 Introduction

The question of how it is possible for a group of independent individuals to achieve both their own goals and a common goal has been addressed in many fields. By a common goal, we mean a goal achievable by a group to require cooperation. The key element that distinguishes a common goal from an individual goal is that it requires collective action. Collective action, however, poses difficult problems and requires cooperation to overcome them. Coordination is a different concept from cooperation, which does not assume the existence of the common goal shared by members. Coordination is necessary to achieve individuals' independent goals efficiently. The design of efficient collective action from the bottom up becomes a crucial issue in many disciplines [1, 2, 20]. Another interesting problem is under what circumstances a collection of interacting agents could realize efficient coordination from

---

* Department of Computer Science, National Defense Academy, Yokosuka, JAPAN
nama@nda.ac.jp

the bottom up [9, 10, 20]. There are strong interests in many disciplines to answer the following questions: How do agents with heterogeneous micromotives generate self-organized global macroscopic orders or regularities? However, there has been no natural methodology for systematically studying the dynamics of highly interacting heterogeneous agents. Some models treat adaptive processes with the assumption of the homogeneous payoff. Interdependent situations, in which an agent's decision depends on the decisions of other agents, are the ones that usually don't permit any simple summation or extrapolation to the aggregate. To make that connection we usually have to look at the system of collective interaction among individuals, which is also treated as the relation between individuals and the collectivity. *Collective* means any pair of a complex system of autonomous components, together with a performance criterion by which we rank the behavior of the overall system. Wolpert and Tumer propose that the fundamental issue is to focus on improving our formal understanding of two closely related issues concerning collective [26]:

1. The forward problem of how the fine-grained structure of the system underlying a collective determines its complex emergent behavior and therefore its performance.
2. The inverse problem of how to design the structure of the system underlying a collective to induce optimal performance.

In examining collectives, we shall draw heavily on the individual decisions. Indeed, an organization or society does not make decisions, individuals do. It might be argued that understanding how individuals make decisions is sufficient to understand and improve collective action. Much of the literature on collectives has reacted against the older notion that irrationality is the key to explanation. They agree that collectives often result from rational and calculated action. In this chapter, we take a different view. Although individual decision is important to understand, it is not sufficient to describe how a collection of agents arrives at specific decisions. These situations, in which an agent decision depends on the decisions of the others, are the ones that usually do not permit any simple summation or extrapolation to the aggregates. To make that connection we usually have to look at the system of interactions between agents and the collectivity. Sometimes the analysis of the collective is difficult and inconclusive [2, 7, 11, 15, 16, 22]. But even an inconclusive analysis warned against jumping to conclusions about the behavior of aggregates from what one knows or can guess about agent interests or motivations or jumping to conclusions about agent intentions from the observations of aggregates. We are also interested in how the society gropes toward equilibrium in an imperfect world of locally interacting agents. There is no presumption that the self-interested behavior of agents usually leads to collectively satisfactory results [8, 12, 13, 18, 19]. How well each agent does in adapting to its social environment is not the same thing as how satisfactory a social environment they collectively create for themselves. Although all agents understand that the outcome is inefficient, agents acting independently are powerless to manage this collective about what to do and how to decide. The question of whether interacting heterogeneous agents self-organize efficient macroscopic orders from the bottom up depends on how they interact with each other. We attempt to probe this issue by specifying how agents adapt to each other. We consider two types of interaction, symmetric and asymmetric interaction. With *symmetric interaction* an agent receives a payoff if it chooses the same action as the majority. With *asymmetric interaction* an agent receives a payoff if it chooses the same action as the minority. Agents myopically adapt their behavior based on their idiosyncratic rule to others' behaviors. We analyze adaptive dynamics that relate the collective with the underlying individual adaptive behaviors. There are many parameters to be considered, among them, we examine the heterogeneity of utility and the configuration of locating agents. We evaluate emergent collectives from the criteria of efficiency and equity. We show that interacting agents outperform when they adapt to local information rather than to global information.

2 Formalism of the Model

2.1 Collective Systems with a Micro-Macro Loop

If the system consists of many interacting components, called agents, the system performance should be described on two different levels: the microscopic level, where the decisions of the individual agents occur, and the macroscopic level, where collective decision can be observed. Understanding the role of a link between these two levels remains one of the challenges of complex system theory as shown in Figure 1. Among many factors that may influence the performance of the overall system we focus on the information about others' decisions that are available to each agent. The greatest promise lies in analysis of situations where agents behave in ways contingent on one another, and these situations are central in theoretical analysis of linking micro to macro levels of collective decision. We aim at discovering fundamental local or micro mechanisms that are sufficient to generate the macroscopic order of efficiency. This type of self-organization is often referred to as collective orders from the bottom up [3].

2.2 Examples of Collectives with Interacting Agents

We address specific problems of collectives with interacting agents. Social interactions pose many coordination problems to individuals. There are many situations

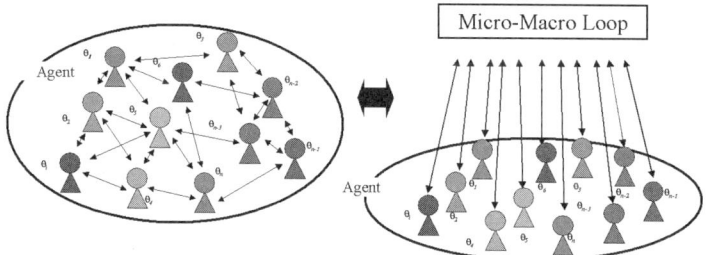

Figure 1. The systems of collective as a micro-macro loop.

where interacting agents can benefit from coordinating their action. Agents face problems of sharing and distributing limited resources in an efficient way.

1. *Network formation by heterogeneous agents.* We consider a collection of agents $G = \{A_i :\leq i \leq N\}$ in which each agent faces the binary decision problem. Agents periodically have to make the decision to join the network or sever from it. Agents try to establish links to achieve higher payoffs. If more agents join the network, they receive a higher payoff; this property is referred to as network externality [5,6]. Perhaps an essential point to make is that networks induce a special interdependency and a specific heterogeneity, which can affect network structure and aggregate phenomena in ways that are out of reach without them. To capture the intuition of this, it is enough to accept an agent's rational decision, depending on the agents with which it is directly linked. This interdependence with heterogeneity in decisions may influence the evolution of the networks. Here, each agent $A_i \in G$ has the following two strategies:

S_1: joins to the network.

S_2: does not join the network.

The number of agents to choose S_1 (trade) is denoted by n ($0 \leq n \leq N$). Agent Ai acquires a benefit of $a_i(n/N)$, a fixed value a_i multiplied by the proportion of agents who join the network. If agent A_i adds to the network, a cost c_i is incurred. An agent can get a benefit as a spillover effect by $b_i(n/N)$, even if it does not add to the network. The payoff of agent A_i when it chooses S_1 or S_2 is given as follows.

The utility of agent A_i to choose S_1 or S_2 is illustrated as the function of (n/N) in Figure 2. The utility of each agent is an increasing function of the population of agents in the network n/N:

$$U_i(S_1) = a_i(n/N) - c_i,$$
$$U_i(S_2) = b_i(n/N). \qquad (1)$$

2. *Route selection by heterogeneous agents.* There is another type of interaction in which we have to use different methodology. We consider a competitive routing

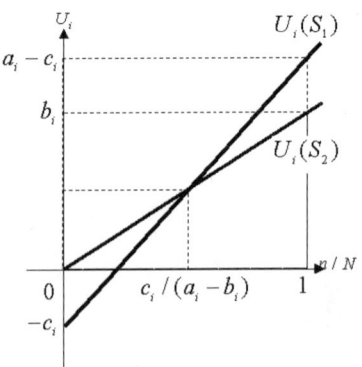

Figure 2. The utility of agent A_i under S_1 or S_2 as a function of (n/N).

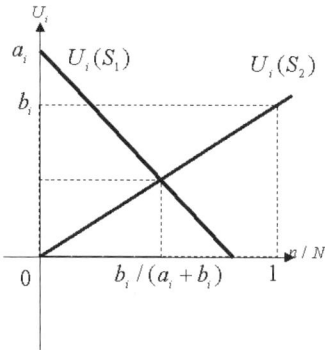

Figure 3. The utility of agent A_i under S_1 or S_2 as a function of (n/N).

problem of networks, in which the paths from sources to destinations have to be established by independent agents. For example, in the context of traffic networks, agents have to determine their route independently. In telecommunication networks, they have to decide what fraction of their traffic to send on each link of the network. Consider two parallel routes A and B; each agent has to choose independently one of the two routes. As shown in Figure 3, each agent has the following two strategies:

S_1: chooses route A.

S_2: chooses route B.

The utility of each agent is determined by what the majority does, and each agent gains utility only if it chooses the opposite route of the majority. The utility function of agent A_i, if it chooses S_1 or S_2, is given as follows:

$$U_i(S_1) = a_i(1 - n/N),$$
$$U_i(S_2) = b_i(n/N). \tag{2}$$

The payoff of agent A_i, if it chooses S_1, is a linearly decreasing function of the proportion of the same decision. On the other hand, the payoff if it chooses S_2 is a linearly increasing function of the proportion of agents with the opposite decision. The utility of an agent when it chooses S_1 or S_2 is illustrated as the function of (n/N) in Figure 4.

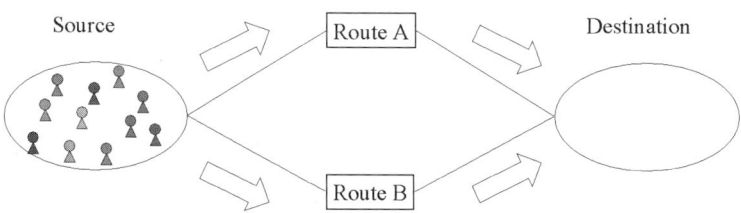

Figure 4. A competitive route selection.

Table 1. The payoff matrix of agent A_i.

		Choice of Other Agents	
		S_1	S_2
Choice of Agent A_i	S_1	$a_i - c_i$	$-c_i$
	S_2	b_i	0

Table 2. The payoff matrix of agent A_i.

		Choice of Other Agents	
		S_1	S_2
Choice of Agent A_i	S_1	$1 - \theta_i$	0
	S_2	0	θ_i

Large-scale interactions with N persons can be decomposed into the problem of the interaction between an individual and the aggregate. In the network formation problem in the previous section, we define the payoff matrix of each agent as given in Table 1.

The expected payoff of agent Ai if it chooses S_1 or S_2 is given as follows:

$$U_i(S_1) = (a_i - c_i)(n/N) - c_i(1 - n/N) = a_i(n/N) - c_i,$$
$$U_i(S_2) = b_i(n/N). \tag{3}$$

Therefore, we have the same utility function with Equation 2.2. Because the matrix of the two-person game is invariant for the affine transformation [25], the payoff matrix of Table 1 can be equivalently transformed into the matrix of Table 2, where $\theta_i = c_i/(a_i - b_i)$. Similarly, the payoff matrix of agent A_i in the route selection problem can be given as in Table 3. The matrix of Table 3 can be equivalently transformed into the matrix of Table 4, where $\theta_i = b_i/(a_i + b_i)$.

Agents have to coordinate their decisions with others to improve their utility. We distinguish the two types of interactions as symmetric and asymmetric interactions [16, 17]. *Interaction* usually implies that increased effort by some agents leads the remaining agents to follow suit, which gives multiplier effects [14]. We call this

Table 3. The payoff matrix of agent A_i.

		Choice of Other Agents	
		S_1	S_2
Choice of Agent A_i	S_1	0	a_i
	S_2	b_i	0

Table 4. The payoff matrix of agent A_i.

		Choice of Other Agents	
		S_1	S_2
Choice of Agent A_i	S_1	0	θ_i
	S_2	$1 - \theta_i$	0

type of interaction symmetric interaction. On the other hand, in the route-selection problem, agents receive a payoff if they select the opposite strategy from the majority. This type of interaction is called asymmetric interaction. This type of interaction is also referred to as minority games, in which agents receive payoff if they select the same strategy as the minority [1, 17, 21]. For realizing efficient and equitable distributions of limited resources, agents normally react to aggregates of others' decisions. The resulting volatile collective decision is often far from being efficient. The overall performance depends on the type of interaction and the heterogeneity of agent preferences.

3 Global Adaptation versus Local Adaptation

In examining collective decisions, we shall draw heavily on the individual adaptive decisions. Within the scope of our model, we treat models in which agents make deliberate decisions by applying rational procedures, which also guide their reasoning. In order to describe the adaptation process at the individual level, we may have two fundamental models, global adaptation and local adaptation. It is important to consider with whom an agent interacts and how each agent decides its action depending on others' actions. Agents may adapt based on the aggregate information representing the current status of the whole system (global adaptation) as shown in Figure 5 (a). In this case, each agent chooses an optimal decision based on aggregate information about how all other agents behaved in the past. An agent calculates her reward and plays her best response strategy. An important assumption of global adaptation is that agents receive knowledge of the aggregate. In many situations, agents are not assumed to know or correctly guess or anticipate other agents' actions, or they are less sophisticated and they do not know how to calculate the best replies [9]. With local adaptation each agent is modeled to adapt to its neighbors [12]. The hypothesis of local adaptation also reflects the limited ability of agents' to receive, decide, and act based on information they receive in the course of interaction. As a specific model, we consider the lattice structure as shown in Figure 5 (b), in which each agent interacts with its neighbors. The main point is that an agent's decision depends on what it

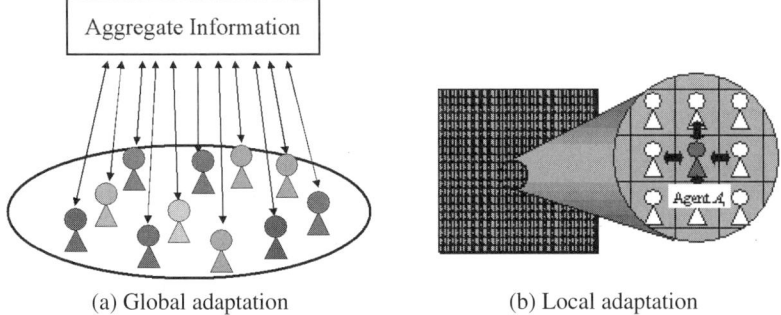

(a) Global adaptation   (b) Local adaptation

Figure 5. Two basic adaptation models of agents.

knows about others. At each period of time, each agent decides whether to add to or sever the network given the knowledge. An agent thinks strategically, knowing that everyone else is also making a rational decision given global or local information.

1. Global adaptation and symmetric interaction. We obtain the adaptive rule of each agent as the best response. We denote the proportion of agents who chose S_1 at time t in a population by $p(t)$. Agent A_i of the payoff parameter θ_i in Table 2, calculates its expected utilities as follows:

$$U_i(S_1) = p(t)(1 - \theta_i),$$
$$U_i(S_2) = (1 - p(t))\theta_i. \tag{4}$$

By comparing the expected utilities under the optimal adaptive rule of the agent is obtained as the function of the aggregate information on collectives and its idiosyncratic payoff (defined as threshold) as follows:

$$p(t) \geq \theta_i \rightarrow S_1,$$
$$p(t) < \theta_i \rightarrow S_2. \tag{5}$$

2. Local adaptation and symmetric interaction. The local adaptive rule is obtained as follows. Denote the proportion of the neighbors of agent A_i that chose S_1 at time t by $p_i(t)$. The optimal adaptive rule with local adaptation is obtained as follows:

$$p_i(t) \geq \theta_i \rightarrow S_1,$$
$$p_i(t) < \theta_i \rightarrow S_2. \tag{6}$$

3. Global adaptation and asymmetric interaction. We obtain the adaptive rules of agents with asymmetric interaction. Denote the proportion of agents that chose S_1 at time t in a population by $p(t)$. The agent of the payoff parameter in Table 3 calculates its expected utilities as follows:

$$U_i(S_1) = (1 - p(t))\theta_i,$$
$$U_i(S_2) = p(t)(1 - \theta_i). \tag{7}$$

By comparing the expected utilities under the optimal adaptive rule of the agent is obtained as the function of the aggregate information on collectives and its idiosyncratic threshold as follows:

$$p(t) \leq \theta_i \rightarrow S_1,$$
$$p(t) > \theta_i \rightarrow S_2. \tag{8}$$

4. Local adaptation and asymmetric interaction. The adaptive rule with local adaptation is obtained as follows. Denote the proportion of the neighbors of agents who have chosen at time t by $p_i(t)$. The optimal adaptive rule with local adaptation is obtained as follows:

$$p_i(t) \leq \theta_i \rightarrow S_1,$$
$$p_i(t) > \theta_i \rightarrow S_2. \tag{9}$$

4 Heterogeneity in Preferences and Representation of Diversity

The crucial concept for describing heterogeneity of agents is their preference characterized by their threshold. Threshold models choose the elements of collectives which game theory handles only with difficulty and makes central: substantial heterogeneity of preferences and interdependence of decisions over time. This is possible because the payoff matrix is replaced by a one-dimensional vector of threshold for each agent, which allows enormous simplification in the ensuing analysis. In this section, we consider several collections of heterogeneous agents. We also characterize the diversity of heterogeneous agents from both threshold distribution and the configuration of their locations. Each agent has an idiosyncratic threshold, and the diversity of heterogeneous agents is represented by the distribution of the threshold. We classify heterogeneous agents into the following two types:

1. Type 1. Agent with the threshold $\theta_i < 0.5$. (Such an agent prefers the strategy S_1 to S_2.)
2. Type 2. Agent with the threshold $\theta_i > 0.5$. (Such an agent prefers the strategy S_2 to S_1.)

We also classify interaction types as follows:

1. Random neighbor. Each agent interacts with neighbors of any type.
2. Homogeneous neighbor. Each agent interacts with neighbors of the same type.
3. Heterogeneous neighbor. Each agent interacts with neighbors of the opposite type.

We assume that the proportions of agents of Type 1 and Type 2 in a collection of agents $G = \{A_i : 1 \leq i \leq N\}$ are the same. We denote the number of agents with the same threshold θ in G by $n(\theta)$. We define the density of θ by $f(\theta)$, which is obtained by $n(\theta)$ divided by the total number of agents N,

$$f(\theta) = n(\theta)/N. \tag{10}$$

We also assume that the threshold distribution $f(\theta)$ is symmetric, with the property

$$f(\theta) = f(1 - \theta). \tag{11}$$

As specific examples, we consider the distribution functions shown in Figure 6. In these cases, the average of the threshold is 0.5, i.e.,

$$\int_0^1 \theta f(\theta) = 0.5. \tag{12}$$

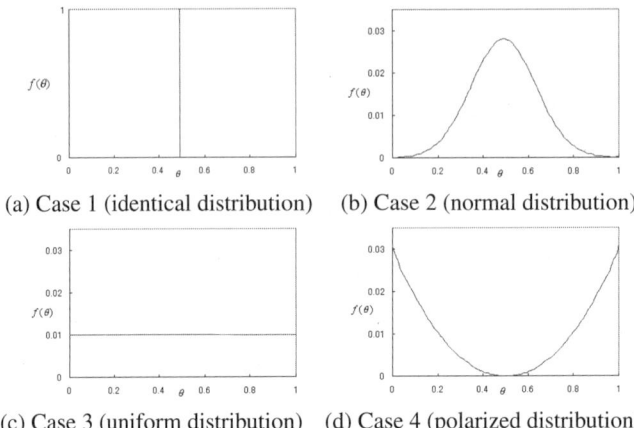

(a) Case 1 (identical distribution)   (b) Case 2 (normal distribution)

(c) Case 3 (uniform distribution)   (d) Case 4 (polarized distribution)

Figure 6. Several distribution functions of threshold $f(\theta)$.

○Type1: An agent who prefer S_1 to S_2 ◆Type2: An agent who prefer S_2 to S_1

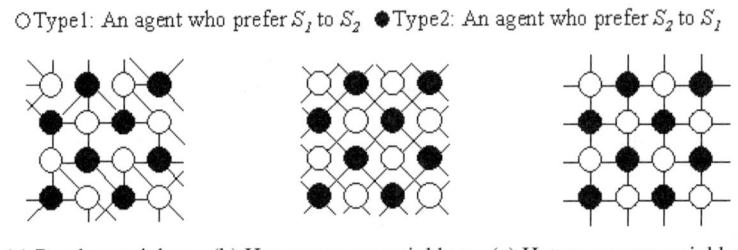

(a) Random neigbor   (b) Homogeneous neighbor   (c) Heterogeneous neighbor

Figure 7. Configurations of neighbor.

5 Evaluation of the Systems of Collective

In this section, we evaluate collectives of interacting heterogeneous agents with three criteria: stability, efficiency, and equity. The stability of collectives is from the point of the path-dependency of collectives. We obtain and evaluate the proportion of agents who choose each strategy staring from any initial condition. Efficiency is evaluated by obtaining the average utility, which also stands for the measure of the desirability at the macro level. Equity is evaluated by obtaining the utility distribution, which stands for the measure of the desirability at the micro level.

5.1 Collectives under Symmetric Interaction

1. Efficiency

We characterize collectives at equilibrium by p^*, which represents the proportion of agents to choose S_1 at equilibrium. The efficiency of global adaptation is evaluated as follows. The adaptive rule of each agent at equilibrium is given by Equation 3.2. Agents with the threshold θ less than or equal to S_1 receive the utility at the level of

$$u = p^*(1 - \theta) \quad (0 \le \theta \le p^*).$$ (13)

Agents whose thresholds are greater than S_1 receive their utility at the level of:

$$u = (1 - p^*)\theta \quad (p^* \le \theta \le 1).$$ (14)

Therefore, the average utility is obtained as:

$$\bar{U} = \int_0^{p^*} (1 - \theta)p^* f(\theta)d\theta + \int_{p^*}^1 \theta(1 - p^*)f(\theta)d\theta.$$ (15)

From this equation, the average payoff (efficiency) $\bar{U}$ depends on a collective at equilibrium p^* and the threshold distribution $f(\theta)$. We consider the following typical cases:

1. All agents choose the same strategy, $S_1(p^* =1)$ (or $S_2(p^* =0)$).
2. Half of the agents choose S_1 and the rest of agents choose S_2 ($p^* =0.5$).

   Efficiencies of the above two cases are obtained as

1. $p^* =1$ (or $p^* =0$): $\bar{U} = 0.5$,
2. $p^* =0.5$: $\bar{U} = 0.5 - \int_0^{0.5} \theta f(\theta)d\theta$.

   2. Equity
The proportion of agents who gain the utility u by choosing S_1 is given as $f(1 - \theta)$. Therefore, we have the utility distribution as follows:

$$g_1(u) = f(1 - \theta) = f(u/p^*) \quad (0 \le \theta_i \le p^*, \; p^* \ne 0).$$ (16)

The proportion of agents who gain the utility by choosing is given by the distribution as follows. Therefore, we have the utility distribution.

$$g_2(u) = f(1 - \theta) = f(u/1 - p^*) \quad (p^* \le \theta_i \le 1, \; p^* \ne 1).$$ (17)

Therefore, the overall utility distribution is obtained as:

$$g(u) = g_1(u) + g_2(u).$$ (18)

The utility distribution of collective equilibrium is obtained as:

1. $p^* = 1$ (or $p^* = 0$): $g(u) = f(u)$ $(0 \le u \le 1)$.
2. $p^* = 0.5$: $g(u) = 2f(2u)$ $(0.25 \le u \le 0.5)$.

   The Gini ratio ψ $(0 \le \psi \le 1)$ is often used to measure the extent to which the utility distribution of a society. The Gini ratio can be obtained from a Lorenz curve. The Gini ratio is obtained by measuring the area surrounded by the Lorenz curve $L(x)$ in Figure 8. The x-axis represents the cumulative proportion of agents and the y-axis represents the cumulative proportion of the total utility $L(x)$, which is

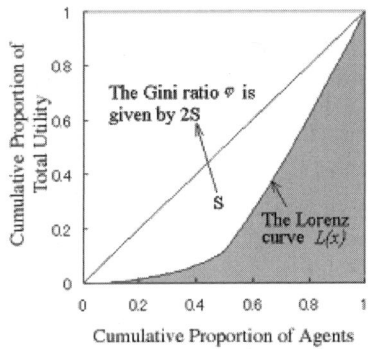

Figure 8. The Lorenz curve and the Gini ratio.

cumulated to the proportion at the level x, starting with the poorest agents. The Gini ratio ψ is then defined as

$$\psi = 1 - 2 \int_0^1 L(x)dx. \qquad (19)$$

The measure of equity of global adaptation is then obtained as follows:

$$E = 1 - \psi = 2 \int_0^1 L(x)dx. \qquad (20)$$

Using the proportion of agents who obtain the utility level, the Lorenz curve is given as follows:

$$L(x) = \int_0^x \tau g(\tau)d\tau / \int_0^1 \tau g(\tau)d\tau, \qquad (21)$$

where x is defined as the parameter satisfying $x = \int_0^w g(\tau)d\tau$.

5.2 Collectives under Asymmetric Interaction

The adaptive rule of an agent who faces asymmetric interaction is given by Equation 3.5. in Ref. (8) Agents whose threshold is less than or equal to equilibrium receive the utility at the level of

$$u = (1 - p^*)\theta \qquad (p^* \le \theta \le 1). \qquad (22)$$

Agents whose threshold is greater than chosen receive utility

$$u = p^*(1 - \theta) \qquad (0 \le \theta \le p^*). \qquad (23)$$

The average utility U (efficiency) is obtained as given in Equation 5.3 in Ref. (20), and the efficiency and equity are the same as the case of symmetric interactions.

6 Simulation Results

We arrange a collection of heterogeneous agents in the area of 50×50 (2500 agents in total) with no gap, four corners, and an edge of an area connects it with an opposite side. The consequence of their actions also effects agents with whom they are not directly linked. We are interested in the long-run behavior of collectives when heterogeneous interacting agents adapt their decisions over time. We especially investigate how agents' decisions combine with the decisions of others to produce the macro behavior. We impose only a weak monotonic condition reflecting the inertia and myopia hypotheses on the dynamics, which describe the changes in the number of agents playing each strategy.

6.1 Collectives of Symmetric Interaction

1. Global Adaptation

The simulation results of global adaptation are shown in Figure 9. In Figure 9 (a), the x-axis represents the proportion of agents that chose S_1 initially and the y-axis represents collective p^* at equilibrium. Collective decision p^* at equilibrium depends

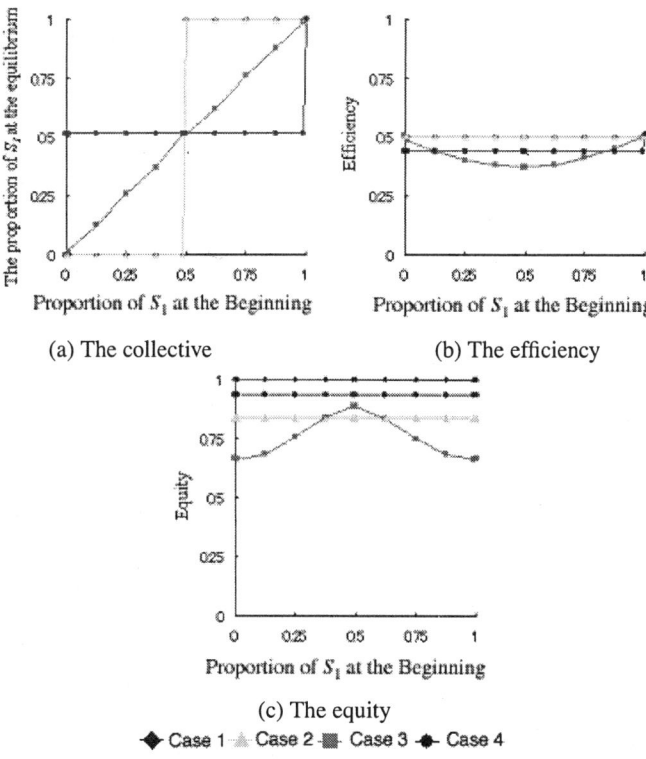

Figure 9. Simulation results of global adaptation.

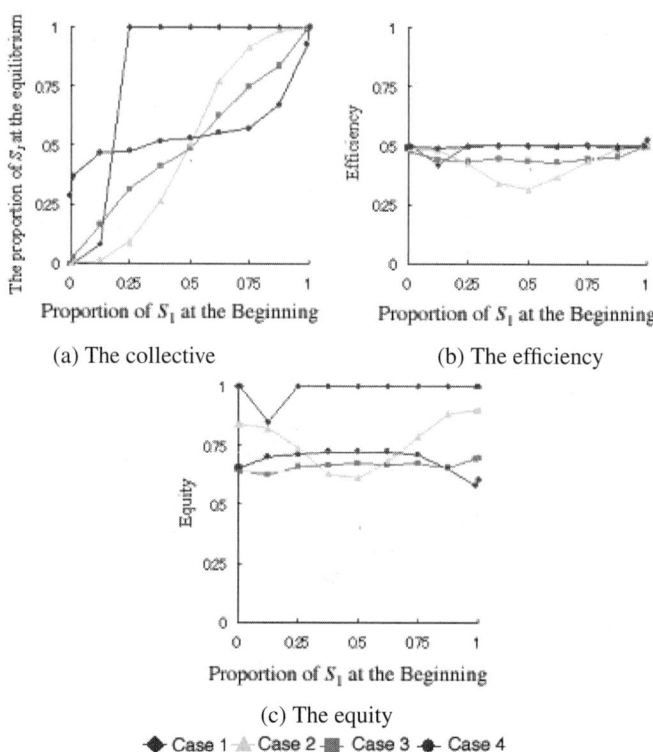

(a) The collective

(b) The efficiency

(c) The equity

◆ Case 1 ▲ Case 2 ■ Case 3 ● Case 4

Figure 10. Simulation results of local adaptation.

on both the population structure and the initial value. In Figure 9 (b), the y-axis represents the average utility $\bar{U}$ at equilibrium. In all cases, efficiencies $\bar{U}$ are less than 0.5. In Figure 9 (c), the y-axis represents the equity E at equilibrium.

2. Local Adaptation to Random neighbors
The simulation results of local adaptation with random neighbors are shown in Figure 10. Collective behavior is similar to the global adaptation model in Figure 9 (a), although the turning point is dull in all cases, as shown in Figure 10 (a). The average utilities $\bar{U}$ of all cases are almost 0.5 (Figure 10 (b)). Efficiency is also close to the case of global adaptation (Figure 9 (b)).

3. Local Adaptation to Homogeneous Neighbors
The simulation results with homogeneous neighbors are shown in Figure 11. Collective behavior p^* at equilibrium is about 0.5 starting from any initial point in Cases 2, 3, and 4 (Figure 11 (a)). The simulation result of Case 1 is the same as adaptation to random neighbors. The average utilities $\bar{U}$ of all cases become more than 0.5 (Figure 11 (b)), and equity E is also high (Figure 11 (c)). From these results, local adaptation to homogeneous neighbors results in desirable behavior.

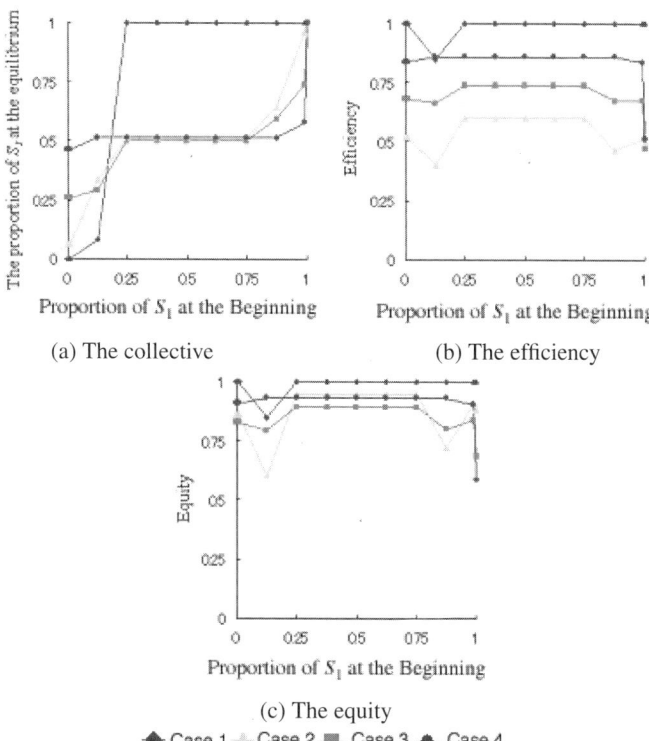

(a) The collective   (b) The efficiency

(c) The equity

◆ Case 1 ▲ Case 2 ■ Case 3 ● Case 4

Figure 11. Simulation results of local adaptation under homogeneous neighbors.

4. Efficiency and Equity

In Figure 12, we summarize the simulation results. The x-axis represents equity E and the y-axis represents efficiency, in terms of the average utility U. With the global adaptation model, we obtain: Case 1: $(E, \bar{U})$= (1.0, 0.5), Case 2: (0.84, 0.5), Case 3: (0.89, 0.38), and Case 4: (0.94, 0.44). For the local adaptation model with random neighbors, we obtain: Case 1:$(E, \bar{U})$ = (1.0, 0.5), Case 2: (0.61, 0.31), Case 3: (0.67, 0.44), and Case 4: (0.73, 0.50). With the local adaptation model with homogeneous

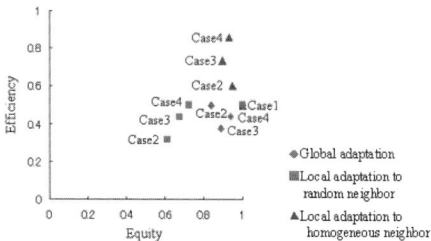

Figure 12. Efficiency and equity (the initial proportion is 0.5).

neighbors, we obtain: Case 1: $(E, \bar{U}) = (1.0, 0.5)$, Case 2: $(0.95, 0.6)$, Case 3: $(0.89, 0.73)$, and Case 4: $(0.93, 0.86)$. Efficiency and equity are different, depending on the interaction, although collectives are almost the same. For a population of identical agents (Case 1), all agents have the same payoff and equity is the highest, but the efficiency is moderate. In global adaptation with a diverse population, efficiency is moderate and equity is high. In local adaptation with random neighbors, both efficiency and equity are low, and diversity tightens the gap in efficiency and equity. With homogeneous neighbors, both efficiency and equity become high.

6.2 Collectives of Asymmetric Interactions

1. Global Adaptation
The simulation results of global adaptation are shown in Figure 13. Oscillation appears, with asymmetric interaction, and we describe both maximum and minimum values of $p(t)$ in Figure 13 (a). However, in Cases 3 and 4, oscillations are suppressed and efficiency U and equity E become high.

2. Local Adaptation to Random Neighbors

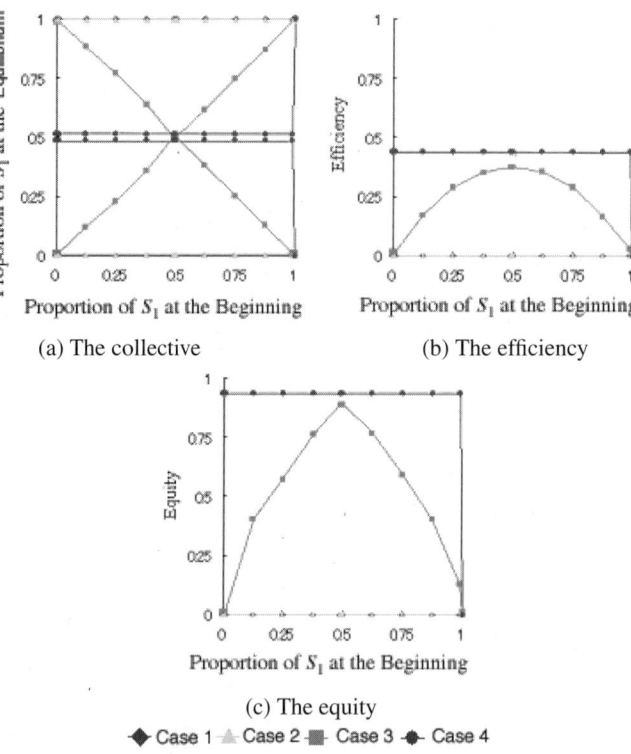

(a) The collective   (b) The efficiency

(c) The equity
◆ Case 1 ▲ Case 2 ■ Case 3 ◆ Case 4

Figure 13. Simulation results of global adaptation.

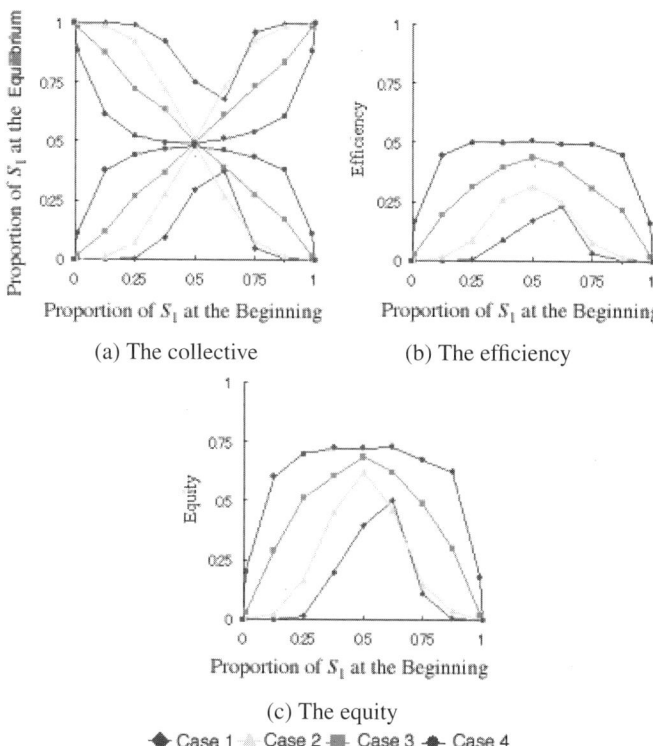

(a) The collective   (b) The efficiency

(c) The equity

◆ Case 1 ▲ Case 2 ■ Case 3 ● Case 4

Figure 14. Simulation results of local adaptation.

The simulation results of local adaptation to random neighbors are shown in Figure 14. Collective behavior is similar to the global adaptation model, as shown in Figure 13 (a), although the turning point is dull in all cases. In any case, there are huge discrepancies among agents; the average utilities U are less than 0.5 and equities E are low. From these results, the local adaptation model with random neighbors becomes the same as the global adaptation model.

3. Local Adaptation to Heterogeneous Neighbors
The simulation results of local adaptation to homogeneous neighbors are shown in Figure 15. The collective behavior p^* at equilibrium is obtained as about 0.5 starting from any initial condition in Cases 2, 3, and 4 as shown in Figure 15 (a). In spite of diverse preferences, they show the same as collectives with the local adaptation to homogeneous neighbors. From these results, homogeneous interaction gives rise to the most desirable collective behavior by overcoming diversity of preferences.

4. Efficiency and Equity
In Figure 16, we summarize the simulation results in terms of equity and efficiency. The x-axis represents equity E and the y-axis represents efficiency, the average utility is U. For the global adaptation model, we obtain: Case 1: $(E, \bar{U}) = (0.0, 0.0)$,

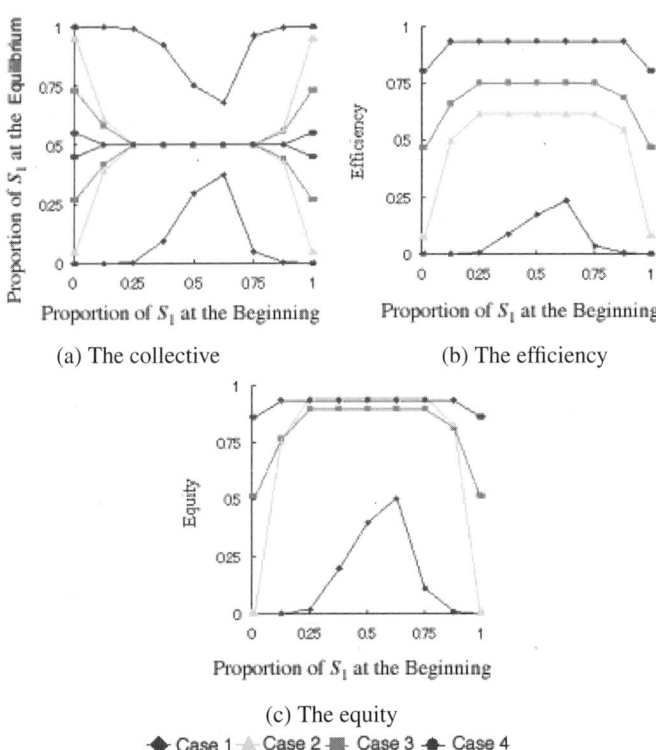

(a) The collective

(b) The efficiency

(c) The equity

◆ Case 1 ▲ Case 2 ■ Case 3 ● Case 4

Figure 15. Simulation results of local adaptation under heterogeneous neighbors.

Case 2: (0.0, 0.0), Case 3: (0.89, 0.38), and Case 4: (0.94, 0.44). For the local adaptation model to random neighbors, we obtain: Case 1: $(E, \bar{U}) = (0.69, 0.17)$, Case 2: (0.56, 0.31), Case 3: (0.66, 0.44), and Case 4: (0.73, 0.51). For the Local adaptation model with homogeneous neighbors, we obtain: Case 1: $(E, \bar{U}) = (0.69, 0.17)$, Case 2: (0.73, 0.51), Case 3: (0.95, 0.75), and Case 4: (0.93, 0.87). For a collection of identical agents (Case 1), almost all agents choose the same strategy; their utilities are 0 and efficiency is low. In other diverse populations, they have different properties.

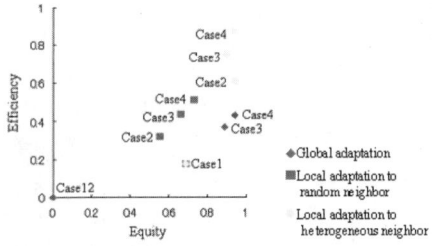

Figure 16. Efficiency and equity (the initial proportion is 0.5).

In global adaptation, efficiency is moderate and equity is high. In local adaptation to random neighbors, both efficiency and equity are low. With the heterogeneous neighbors, both efficiency and equity become high.

7 Conclusion

In this chapter we addressed the issue of collective decisions by heterogeneous agents in which they have to realize both efficient and equitable utilization of limited resources. Agents normally react to aggregate of others' decisions, and the resulting volatile collective decision is often far from efficient. By means of experiments, we showed that the overall performance depends on the types of interacting decisions as well as the heterogeneity of agents in terms of their preferences. We considered two different types of interaction, symmetric and asymmetric. We showed that the most crucial factor that considerably improves the overall system is information presentation to agents. It was shown that the global information presentation on the whole is inefficient. The optimal guidance strategy to improve the efficiency and fairness depends on the interactions. With symmetric coordination, the local information presentation regarding neighbors of the same type realizes the highest performance. With asymmetric coordination, however, the local information regarding neighbors of different types realizes the highest performance.

8 Acknowledgments

We would like to thank the Grant-in-Aid for Scientific Research (c) No. 1460815 Japan Society for the Promotion of Science (JSPS). We would like to thank our hosts for the warm hospitality we experienced at the workshops organized by Dr. Tumer and Dr. Wolpert. We are grateful for fruitful collaboration with and comments from Dr. Hiroshi Sato and Dr. Masao Kubo.

References

1. W. B. Arthur. Complexity in economic theory: Inductive reasoning and bounded rationality. *The American Economic Review*, 84(2):406–11, May 1994.
2. S. Bakhchandani, D. Hirshleifer, and I. D. Welch. Conformism and diversity under social learning. *Economic Theory*, 17:101–120, 2001.
3. V. Bala and S. Goyal. Self-organization in communication networks. *Econometrica*, 68: 1181–1230, 2000.
4. V. Bala and S. Goyal. Learning from neighbours. *Review of Economic Studies*, 65:595–621, 1998.
5. V. Bala and S. Goyal. A non-cooperative model of network formation. *Econometrica*, 68: 1181–1229, 2000.
6. S. Banerjee. *Efficiency and Stability in Economic Networks*. mimeo: Boston University, 1999.

7. S. N. Durlauf and H. P. Young. *Social Dynamics*. Brookings Institution Press, 2001.
8. B. Dutta and M. O. Jackson. The stability and efficiency of directed communication networks. *Review of Economic Design*, 5:251–72, 2000.
9. G. Ellison. Learning local interaction and coordination. *Econometrica*, 61:1047–71, 1993.
10. D. Fudenberg and D. Levine. *The Theory of Learning in Games*. MIT Press, 1998.
11. M. Granovetter. Threshold models of collective behavior. *American Journal of Sociology*, 183, 1420–33, 1978.
12. J. Harsarnyi and R. Selten. *A Game Theory of Equilibrium Selection in Games*. MIT Press, 1988.
13. D. Helbing. *Quantitative Sociodynamics*. Kluwer Academic, 1995.
14. J. Hofbauer and K. Sigmund. *Evolutionary Games and Population Dynamics*. Cambridge Univ. Press, 1998.
15. B. Huberman and N. Glance. *Diversity and Collective Action*. Interdisciplinary Approaches to Nonlinear Systems, Springer, 1993.
16. S. Iwanaga and A. Namatame. Asymmetric coordination of heterogeneous agents. *IEICE Trans. on Information and Systems*, E84-D:937–44, 2001.
17. S. Iwanaga and A. Namatame. The Complexity of Collective Decision. *Journal of Nonlinear Dynamics and Control*, 6:2:137–58, 2002.
18. C. Johnson and R. P. Gilles. Spatial social networks. *Review of Economic Design*, 5:273–300, 1999.
19. Y. Kaniovski, A. Kryazhimskii, and H, Young. Adaptive dynamics in games played by heterogeneous populations. *Games and Economics Behavior*, 31:50-96,2000.
20. A. Kirman. The economy as an evolving network. *Journal of Evolutionary Economics*, 7:339–53, 1997.
21. M. Matteo. Toy models of markets with heterogeneous interacting agents. *Lecture Notes in Economics and Mathematical Systems*, 503:161–81, Springer, 2001.
22. M.A. Nowak and R.M. May. Evolutionary games and spatial chaos. *Nature*, 359:826–9, 1992.
23. A. Rubinstein. *Modeling Bounded Rationality*. The MIT Press, 1998.
24. T. Schelling. *Micromotives and Macrobehavior*. Norton, 1978.
25. J. Weibull. *Evolutionary Game Theory*. The MIT Press, 1996.
26. D. Wolpert, K. Wheeler, and K. Tumer. Collective intelligence for control of distributed dynamical systems, *Europhysics Letters*, 49:6, 2000.

12

Selection in Coevolutionary Algorithms and the Inverse Problem

Sevan Ficici,[1] Ofer Melnik,[2] and Jordan Pollack[3]

Summary. The *inverse problem* in the collective intelligence framework concerns how the private utility functions of agents can be engineered so that their selfish behaviors collectively give rise to a desired world state. In this chapter we examine several selection and fitness-sharing methods used in coevolution and consider their operation with respect to the inverse problem. The methods we test are truncation and linear-rank selection and competitive and similarity-based fitness sharing. Using evolutionary game theory to establish the desired world state, our analyses show that variable-sum games with polymorphic Nash are problematic for these methods. Rather than converge to polymorphic Nash, the methods we test produce cyclic behavior, chaos, or attractors that lack game-theoretic justification and therefore fail to solve the inverse problem. The private utilities of the evolving agents may thus be viewed as *poorly factored*—improved private utility does not correspond to improved world utility.

1 Introduction

Hillis' seminal paper on the coevolution of sorting networks against input sequences [16] was among the first to suggest the potential of coevolution as an approach to optimization. Since then, a number of subsequent results have further demonstrated the capacity of coevolution to outperform static fitness functions and provide high-quality solutions for machine-learning problems, for example, [1, 2, 18]. Unfortunately, the many successful applications of coevolution are balanced by a number of well-known and frequently encountered modes of failure.

The undesirable outcomes of coevolutionary optimization include cyclic dynamics, loss of fitness gradient, mediocre stable states, and evolutionary forgetting. A number of papers illustrate and investigate these issues, for example, [3, 4, 6, 8, 18, 22–24, 30]. Apart from these well-studied modes of failure, however, there exists

* Department of Computer Science Brandeis University, Waltham MA, 02454
  sevan@cs.brandeis.edu
† DIMACS, Rutgers University, Piscataway, NJ 08854 melnik@dimacs.rutgers.edu
‡ Computer Science Department, Center for Complex Systems, Brandeis University, Waltham MA 02454 pollack@cs.brandeis.edu

another, much less appreciated class of pathology that involves the *selection* step in coevolution. This pathology involves certain methods used in coevolutionary algorithms that can prevent the attainment of game-theoretically justifiable results, and it is particularly well captured by the *inverse problem* of the collective intelligence (COIN) framework [29, 31].

COIN assumes a collection of self-interested adaptive agents, each trying to maximize its own private utility, and a world utility function that indicates which states of the world are most desired. The *inverse problem* concerns how one is to engineer the agents' private utilities such that their selfish behavior naturally gives rise to the desired world state. We will show that certain algorithms used in coevolution can fail to solve the inverse problem, specifically in variable-sum games where polymorphic Nash equilibria are desired world states.

To describe a coevolutionary system in terms of COIN we need to identify: (1) a collection of agents, (2) their adaptive mechanism(s), (3) their private utility functions, and (4) a world utility function, most particularly a goal world state. Clearly, the coevolving population provides our collective of agents, and the adaptive mechanism used by the agents is simulated evolution. The problem domain, to which coevolutionary optimization is applied, defines both the space of possible agent strategies (behaviors), and the outcomes of all possible strategy interactions. This interactive aspect of the domain suggests that game theory is the appropriate formalism with which to construct our world utility function; particularly, any goal world-state we wish to obtain should at minimum agree with the game-theoretic solution concept of Nash equilibrium [12]. The innovation of *evolutionary* game theory (EGT) [20] showed that simple replicator dynamics are capable of driving a population of agents to a Nash equilibrium; thus, the private utilities of our agents also follow from the problem domain and appear *factored*—that is, improvement in agents' utilities coincide with improvement in world utility, ultimately resulting in our goal state (a Nash equilibrium).

Unfortunately, evolutionary game theory makes several strong assumptions that generally do not obtain in an operating coevolutionary algorithm. Chief among these assumptions is that the entire strategy space is known a priori, for standard evolutionary game theory concerns itself strictly with strategy *selection*, not search. In contrast, the initial population in a coevolutionary algorithm will contain only a small fraction of the possible strategies for all but the most trivial of strategy spaces. Indeed, both coevolutionary algorithms and the COIN framework assume that agents must learn, i.e., search the strategy space.

The typical evolutionary algorithm iterates a sequence of *evaluation*, *selection*, and *reproduction* operations [13]. The evaluation of agents' performance yields fitness values that determine which agents are selected for reproduction, during which offspring agents are generated using variation operators. Many methods have been devised for evolutionary algorithms (some specifically for coevolution) to improve their ability to search. Several of these methods operate in connection with the selection step of the algorithm to prevent premature genetic convergence and maintain genetic diversity. This chapter illustrates how methods affecting the selection step in coevolution can prevent the population of agents from reaching our goal state, that is,

Nash equilibrium. Instead, we find cyclic dynamics, non-Nash attractors, and even chaos. From the point of view of COIN, the methods we investigate can be understood to distort the agents' private utility functions such that they are poorly factored with respect to our world utility.

The specific methods we examine are truncation and linear rank selection (Section 4), and competitive and similarity-based fitness sharing (Sections 5 and 6). Because these methods pertain to the selection step, we can demonstrate their behavior in a simple selection-only system, such as that used in evolutionary game theory. Therefore, Section 2 precedes our analyses with a brief discussion of EGT. Section 3 discusses the properties of a simple replicator system (i.e., without the various modifications we examine later) in the context of the *Hawk-Dove* game. Section 8 offers final remarks and a conclusion.

2 Evolutionary Game Theory

A central achievement of evolutionary game theory was the introduction of a method by which agents come to play "optimal" strategies in the absence of agent rationality [20]. Through a process of Darwinian selection, a population of agents can converge to an *evolutionary stable strategy* (ESS), which is a Nash equilibrium with an additional "stability" criterion. Despite the name, Maynard-Smith's definition of evolutionary stability is actually a static concept, and since its introduction many other solution concepts have been proposed [19], including those that are more properly rooted in dynamical systems theory [25]. Nevertheless, for the game studied in this paper (Hawk-Dove), the ESS corresponds to a dynamical attractor [17, 28].

2.1 Assumptions and Operation

A symmetric two-player game consisting of m "pure" strategies is described by an m by m payoff matrix $\mathbf{G}$. If Player 1 plays strategy i and Player 2 plays strategy j, then their payoffs are given by matrix entries $\mathbf{G}_{i,j}$ and $\mathbf{G}_{j,i}$, respectively. We assume a single infinitely large population of agents, where each agent plays some pure strategy. The state of a population is represented by column vector $\mathbf{p}$, of length m, where element $\mathbf{p}_i$ represents the proportion with which game strategy i appears in the population of agents. Thus, each element $\mathbf{p}_i$ has a value between zero and one (inclusive), and the elements must sum to one.

We assume *complete mixing*: All possible pair-wise interactions between agents take place at each time step (i.e., generation). We define the *cumulative payoff* received by an agent playing strategy i to be the sum of (1) payoffs obtained upon interacting with all other agents (computed by the inner product of row i of the payoff matrix and the proportion vector $\mathbf{p}$), and (2) a constant baseline fitness w_0 (derived in Equation 2) endowed to each agent before interaction takes place. The vector $\mathbf{w}$ gives the cumulative payoffs for all strategies and is calculated by matrix multiplication and vector addition, as shown in Equation 1; $\mathbf{w}_i$ is the cumulative payoff of strategy i and hence of all agents that play strategy i. (Note: $\mathbf{w_0}$ is either a column vector or matrix, as appropriate, where all elements are w_0.)

Given the population state and cumulative payoff vectors at time t, $\mathbf{p}^t$, and $\mathbf{w}^t$, we compute the new state of our evolving population, $\mathbf{p}^{t+1}$, with Equation 3. This difference equation is known as a *replicator* and causes the number of agents playing each strategy to increase (replicate) in proportion to cumulative payoff. We then renormalize strategy proportions such that they again sum to one. Note that strategies absent from the initial population cannot appear at later time steps, because we are describing a selection-only system—no variational operators (i.e., mutation or recombination) exist to introduce strategies not already present.

$$\mathbf{w} = \mathbf{Gp} + \mathbf{w_0} \tag{1}$$

$$w_0 = |\min(\min(\mathbf{G}), 0)| + k, \qquad k \geq 0 \tag{2}$$

$$\mathbf{p}^{t+1} = \text{normalize}(\text{diag}(\mathbf{p}^t)\mathbf{w}^t) \tag{3}$$

Agent *fitness* is defined to be proportional to reproductive success. Because an agent can have no fewer than zero offspring, an agent's fitness value f must be $f \geq 0$. Because the standard replicator used in EGT specifies that agents reproduce offspring in proportion to cumulative payoff, we may interpret cumulative payoff to be synonymous with fitness. Thus, we define w_0 to be large enough to ensure that fitness values are nonnegative, even if complete mixing leaves an agent with a negative net payoff. As we examine alternatives to the standard replicator equation, we will find that the relationship between cumulative payoff and fitness loses its linearity.

Finally, as shown in Equation 4, the baseline fitness w_0 can instead be added to each element in the payoff matrix $\mathbf{G}$ before multiplication with vector $\mathbf{p}$ to achieve the same fitness values as in Equation 1 (recall that the elements of $\mathbf{p}$ sum to one). Therefore, given a game $\mathbf{G}$ (with payoffs $a, b, \ldots$) and a baseline fitness w_0, we can define a new game $\mathbf{G}'$ (with payoffs $A, B, \ldots$), as shown in Equation 5.

$$\mathbf{w} = (\mathbf{G} + \mathbf{w_0})\mathbf{p} = \mathbf{Gp} + \mathbf{w_0}\mathbf{p} = \mathbf{Gp} + \mathbf{w_0} \tag{4}$$

$$\mathbf{G}' = \begin{pmatrix} A & B \\ C & D \end{pmatrix} = \mathbf{G} + \mathbf{w_0} = \begin{pmatrix} a + w_0 & b + w_0 \\ c + w_0 & d + w_0 \end{pmatrix} \tag{5}$$

2.2 Nash Equilibrium

In a symmetric two-player game (e.g., the Hawk-Dove game defined later), a strategy s^* creates a Nash equilibrium iff it is its own *best reply* [12]:

$$\forall s \in \mathcal{S}: \quad E(s, s^*) \leq E(s^*, s^*), \tag{6}$$

where $\mathcal{S}$ is the set of possible pure and mixed strategies and $E(s_1, s_2)$ is the expected payoff given to strategy s_1 after interaction with strategy s_2.

That is, if Player 2 chooses to play s^*, then the maximal expected payoff that Player 1 can achieve is acquired by also playing strategy s^*, and vice versa. The strategy s^* may be pure or "mixed" (a probability distribution over the set of pure strategies). If s^* is a unique best reply, that is, if there exists no other strategy that does as well when interacting with s^* as s^* itself, then the Nash equilibrium is *strict*. Otherwise, it is *weak*. All finite games have at least one mixed Nash equilibrium (pure Nash equilibria being degenerate mixtures).

3 Standard Replicator

We are interested in how the dynamics and equilibria of the standard discrete-time replicator (Equation 3) change when the calculation of strategy fitness is modified to implement various selection methods and forms of fitness sharing. In this section, we note the replicator's normative behavior, that is, in the absence of modifications.

The results we present throughout this chapter are illustrated with the Hawk-Dove game, the payoff matrix for which is shown in Equation 7. This is a symmetric, variable-sum game for two players that has two pure strategies (Hawk and Dove). Such games always cause the standard replicator to converge to a point attractor that is an ESS, and hence a Nash equilibrium [20]. Point attractors are either *monomorphic* or *polymorphic*. A monomorphic attractor is a population state comprised of a single pure strategy (where all the other strategies are driven to "extinction," that is, an infinitely small proportion of the infinitely large population). A polymorphic attractor is a population state comprising more than one pure strategy, where the surviving strategies have reached a *fitness equilibrium* at some particular strategy proportion. As we will see, the Hawk-Dove game has a polymorphic attractor.

$$G = \begin{array}{c|cc} & H & D \\ \hline H & -25 & 50 \\ D & 0 & 15 \end{array} \tag{7}$$

3.1 Equilibrium

Given an arbitrary game of two pure strategies x and y, the population state vector is composed of two scalars $\mathbf{p} = [p_x \ p_y]^T$, as is the fitness vector $\mathbf{w} = [w_x \ w_y]^T$. We can find the proportion at which the strategies reach fitness equilibrium (assuming that such a proportion exists) by setting $w_x = w_y$ and solving for p_x; the solution is given by Equation 8. If the game in question does not have a polymorphic equilibrium, then Equation 8 will give a value outside the interval $(0, 1)$ or have a zero denominator. Because a two-strategy game yields a one-dimensional system, the value of p_y can be inferred: $p_y = 1 - p_x$.

The important feature of Equation 8 is that the fitness equilibrium ratio between p_x and p_y does not depend on the value of w_0. Indeed, the polymorphic equilibria of Equation 3 are independent of w_0 regardless of the number of strategies [25]. If this is the case, we may ask why we need w_0. Though the value of w_0 is unimportant at fitness equilibrium, it is important when the population state is away from equilibrium—recall that we need it to prevent negative fitness values. Thus, there exist uncountably many games with the same set of fitness equilibria.

The Hawk-Dove game has a polymorphic Nash equilibrium; the proportion of Hawks at this equilibrium is $p_H = (15 - 50)/(-25 - 50 - 0 + 15) = 7/12$. For population states $p_H < 7/12$, Equation 1 shows that $w_H > w_D$; for population states $p_H > 7/12$, we find $w_H < w_D$.

$$p_x = \frac{D - B}{A - B - C + D}$$
$$= \frac{d + w_0 - b - w_0}{a + w_0 - b - w_0 - c - w_0 + d + w_0}$$
$$= \frac{d - b}{a - b - c + d} \tag{8}$$

3.2 Dynamics

Because two-strategy games give one-dimensional systems, we can depict the dynamics of the Hawk-Dove game with a *return map*; the x-axis represents the state of the population p_H (proportion of Hawks in the population) at time t and the y-axis represents p_H at time $t + 1$. Figure 1 shows the return map of the Hawk-Dove game at two different values of w_0. Both curves intersect the diagonal line at the same three points; each of these intersections represents a *fixed point* of the dynamical system, where the population state does not change from one time step to the next. The fixed point in the middle of the graph is the polymorphic Nash equilibrium of the Hawk-Dove game, where $w_H = w_D$.

The slope of the curve at a fixed point determines the fixed point's *stability*. If the absolute value of the slope is less than one, then the fixed point is stable. We see

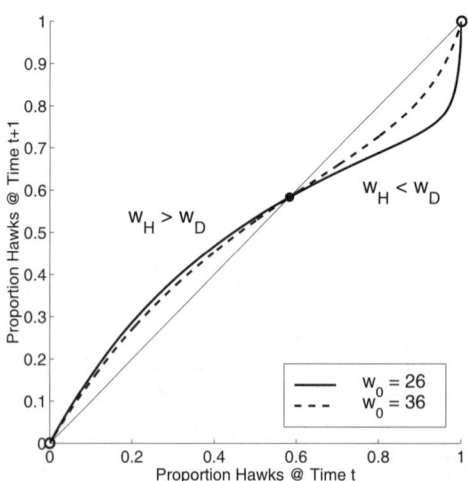

Figure 1. Return map of Hawk-Dove game using different values of w_0.

that both curves in Figure 1 meet this requirement where $p_H = 7/12$, and so the polymorphism is an (indeed, the only) attractor of the dynamical system. Though w_0 affects neither the stability nor the location of the polymorphism, we see that larger values of w_0 bring the curve closer to the diagonal, which results in a dynamical system that moves more slowly to the attractor.

4 Selection Methods

The behaviors of various selection methods have been studied in the context of "ordinary" evolutionary algorithms (i.e., not coevolution) [14,15]. But, how might alternatives to standard fitness-proportionate selection (the replicator specified by EGT) behave in the context of coevolution? Do they exhibit similar dynamics and promote the same fixed points and attractors? In variable-sum games with polymorphic Nash attractors (such as the Hawk-Dove game), we find that many alternative selection methods impose a fixed-point dynamic virtually unrelated to the payoffs of the game matrix, give cyclic behavior, or induce chaos. Here, we examine the properties of two popular alternative selection methods, *truncation* and *linear ranking*; we analyze additional selection methods in [5].

4.1 Truncation Selection

Truncation selection is frequently used in a variety of evolutionary computation known as *evolutionary programming* [9]. Truncation operates by first sorting the population according to fitness and then removing the worst k % of the population and replacing them with variations of the best k %; the value k expresses a selection pressure. For example, given a population of size 200 and selection pressure of $k = 25$, we will remove the worst 50 individuals and replace them with variations of the best 50 individuals. This approach requires a selection pressure range of $0 \leq k \leq 50$, where higher values of k give higher selection pressure. Because evolutionary game theory assumes selection only, we exclude variation operators and simply replace the worst $k\%$ with exact copies of the best $k\%$.

We can easily implement truncation selection for the infinite population that evolutionary game theory assumes. All agents that play the same strategy receive the same cumulative payoff; therefore, we need only sort the strategies by their cumulative payoffs, given the state of the population, and note the proportions with which each strategy appears in the population.

More precisely, given the population state $\mathbf{p}$, strategy i exists with proportion $\mathbf{p}_i$ and receives a cumulative payoff of $\mathbf{w}_i$. We sort the strategies of the game according to cumulative payoffs and obtain a new vector $\mathbf{q}$. The element $\mathbf{q}_{s_j}$ is the proportion with which strategy s_j (the strategy with sorted rank j) appears in the population; the index j ranges between 1 and m, and s_1 signifies the strategy with the highest cumulative payoff.

We construct a vector $\mathbf{r}$ to indicate the proportion of each strategy we are to remove from the population; with $\mathbf{r}$ we represent the worst k % of the population.

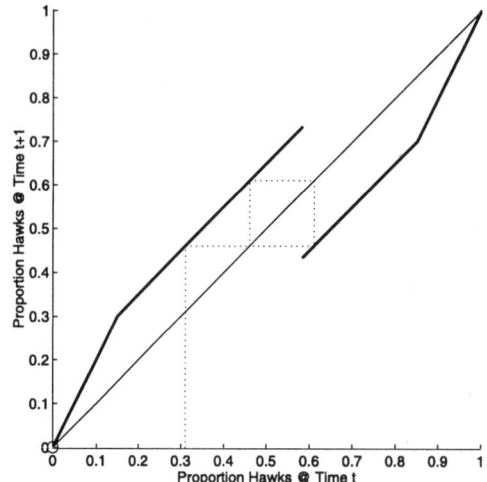

Figure 2. Truncation selection on an infinite population.

We construct a similar vector **b** to indicate the proportion of each strategy we are to add to the population; we use **b** to represent the best k % of the population. The new strategy proportions are $\mathbf{q}' = \mathbf{q} - \mathbf{r} + \mathbf{b}$.

Figure 2 illustrates a game of three strategies where each strategy initially occupies 1/3 of the population; truncation is applied with maximum selection pressure ($k = 50$). The worst half of the population contains all of the agents that play strategy s_3 and half of those that play s_2; the best half contains all of the agents that play s_1 and the other half of those who play s_2 (note that we do not make special accommodations for ties). After truncation, the new proportions $\mathbf{q}'$ indicate that s_1 and s_2 compose 2/3 and 1/3 of the population, respectively; strategy s_3 has been eliminated.

What does truncation selection do at a fixed point that involves more than one strategy, such as the polymorphic Nash equilibrium of the Hawk-Dove game? Recall that at a fixed point all strategies present in the population receive the same fitness. Because no special accommodation is made for fitness equilibria (ties), the result of sorting, and therefore truncation selection, is ill-defined. Truncation selection is unable to maintain arbitrary fixed points unless special precautions are taken to deal with fitness equilibria.

When we use truncation selection instead of the standard replicator, we observe three regimes of behavior as selection pressure is varied. For higher selection pressures, in the range 42% $\leq k \leq$ 50%, truncation selection causes the system to converge onto a new attractor of all Hawks. Figure 3 (top) shows the return map produced by truncation when $k = 50$. We find a large discontinuity precisely at the population state where the attractive Nash equilibrium should be. The example orbit eventually converges to the state of all Hawks.

Equation 1 gives both strategies the same cumulative payoff at the Nash equilibrium proportion of $p_H = 7/12$; below this proportion, the Hawks outscore the

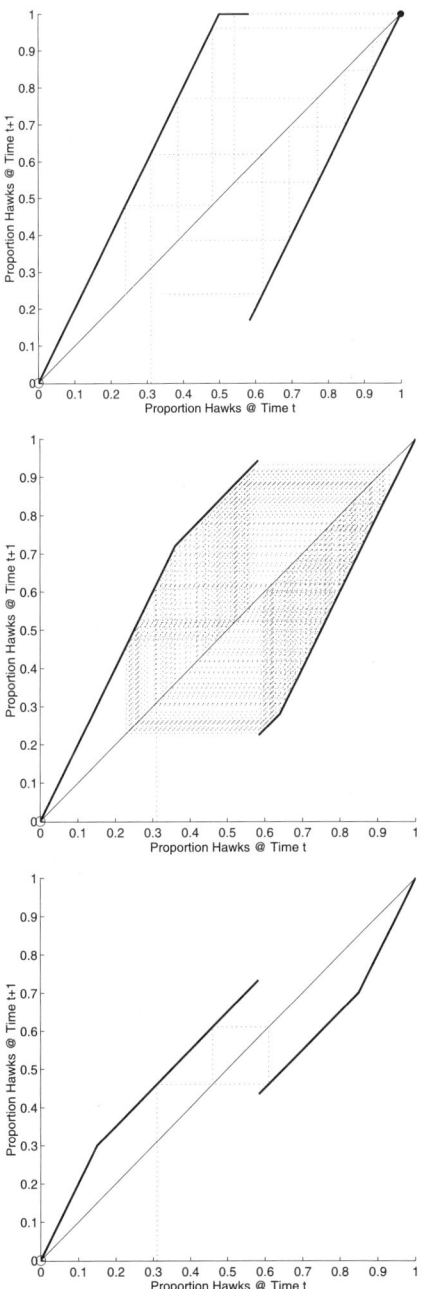

Figure 3. Return maps of truncation selection method with selection pressure at 50% (top), 36% (middle), and 15% (bottom).

Doves and above this proportion the Doves outscore the Hawks. By virtue of this payoff relationship, the standard replicator enables a simple feedback mechanism that gives the Nash its stability. But truncation selection breaks this feedback mechanism. As an illustration, let us consider a population state where the proportion of Hawks is $1/2 \leq p_H < 7/12$. Because p_H is below the Nash equilibrium proportion, the Hawks receive higher cumulative payoff than the Doves. But the Hawks also comprise more than half of the population. Thus, the best 50% of the agents in the population can only be playing the Hawk strategy, and the next generation will be 100% Hawks. The orbit of most initial conditions $0 < p_H^0 < 1$ will eventually fall into the critical interval $1/2 \leq p_H < 7/12$ and converge to the non-Nash attractor of all Hawks. Nevertheless, cyclic behavior is possible as well; for example, unstable period-two and period-three cycles exist. If the population state begins at the Nash equilibrium, then we must account for fitness ties and maintain the proper ratio of Hawks and Doves in the **r** and **b** vectors; otherwise, the fixed point will be lost.

For moderate selection pressures $31\% \leq k \leq 41\%$, truncation selection produces chaos. Figure 3 (middle) shows one such chaotic orbit where $k = 36$. The *Liapunov exponent* of a dynamical system is a measure of sensitivity to initial conditions and is an indicator of chaotic behavior if it is greater than zero. To calculate the Liapunov exponent, we normally measure the derivative of the map at each time step of an orbit. But the truncation map has a discontinuity and so is not differentiable. The map is piecewise linear, however, and the lack of smoothness is negligible. Therefore, we use the slope of the line segment. This yields a Liapunov exponent of $\lambda = 0.69$.

For lower selection pressures, $0 < k \leq 30\%$, truncation selection gives neutrally stable cycles. Figure 3 (bottom) provides a sample orbit where $k = 15$. The discontinuity at the Nash proportion remains; for $p_H < 7/12$ the map is above the diagonal, and for $p_H > 7/12$ the map is below. Therefore, all of the cycles go around the Nash proportion. The exact location of the cycle is determined by where the orbit first enters the cycle-inducing region of the map. As selection pressure decreases, the limit cycles exhibit tighter orbits around 7/12.

4.2 Linear Rank Selection

A common selection method used in genetic algorithms is *ranking* [13]; we sort agents according to score and then assign fitness values according to their rank, such that superior ranks yield higher fitness values. In *linear* ranking, fitness changes linearly with rank; agents are then selected in proportion to fitness. Ranking methods are used to reshape the population's fitness distribution. In the absence of ranking, differences between agents' fitnesses can become too small for the standard roulette wheel to resolve, given a finite population; superior genetic material may be lost or insufficiently exploited. Alternatively, a very large difference in fitness may lead to premature convergence to local optima. With ranking, however, excessively large fitness differences are attenuated and very small differences are expanded.

We implement linear ranking for our infinite population with ease; we simply rank the strategies' cumulative payoffs and then assign each agent a fitness value according to the rank of the strategy it is playing. In the case of the Hawk-Dove

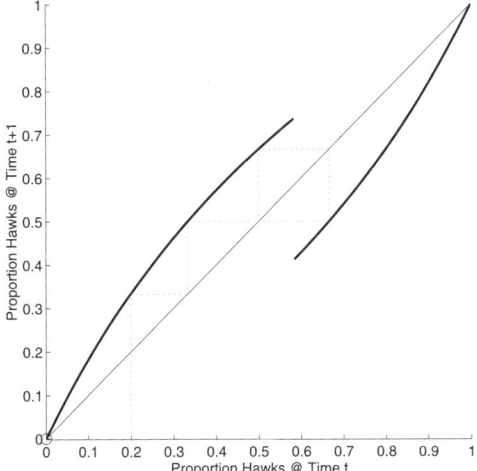

Figure 4. Return map of linear rank selection.

game, we have only two strategies; whichever of the two strategies obtains the higher cumulative payoff for the given population state provides its agents a fitness of two, while the other strategy provides a fitness of one. After normalization, the fitness values will either be $f_H = 1/3$, $f_D = 2/3$, or $f_H = 2/3$, $f_D = 1/3$; if special care is taken to handle ties (at Nash equilibrium), then we obtain $f_H = 1/2$, $f_D = 1/2$. Selection then proceeds in proportion to these fitness values.

Figure 4 shows the return map for linear rank selection. Again, at the population state that is the Nash equilibrium ($p_H = 7/12$), we find a discontinuity instead of an attractor. Further, we find that linear ranking produces neutrally stable cycles around the Nash equilibrium proportion; this is the only behavior that linear ranking produces. Because the fitnesses, and hence rates of growth, of the two strategies are exactly inverted as the Nash proportion is crossed, a period-two cycle must result.

Ranking maps all possible fitness proportions to a single proportion. As a result, rates of growth can never approach equality, which makes attractive polymorphic fixed points impossible, as is visually obvious in Figure 4. Another version of rank-based selection assigns fitness values that vary exponentially with rank. This method has the same properties as linear ranking that prevent convergence to polymorphisms.

5 Competitive Fitness Sharing

Competitive fitness sharing is a diversity maintenance technique for coevolution proposed by Rosin [24]. The games Rosin considers are a subset of zero-sum games—a strategy either wins or loses to another strategy. When an agent α defeats an opponent β, the reward given to α is $1/n$, where n is the total number of agents capable of defeating β.

5.1 Equilibrium

We can easily extend competitive fitness sharing to variable-sum games. The payoff agent α (playing strategy i) receives from interacting with agent β (playing strategy j) is $\mathbf{G}'_{i,j}/d$, where d is the total payoff awarded to all agents by interacting with agent β. In a two-strategy game, we calculate the "shared" fitnesses for strategies x and y, as shown in Equation 9.

Given these equations, we set $w_x = w_y$ and solve for p_x to find the proportion at which the strategies achieve fitness equilibrium, assuming an equilibrium exists; the solution for p_x is given by Equation 10. As with the standard replicator, if a polymorphism does not exist, then Equation 10 will give a value outside of the interval $(0, 1)$. Rosin [24] proves that the equilibria for shared and nonshared fitness are the same in win-lose games. But, as Equation 10 shows, this is not true in the general case. We see instead that, for an arbitrary two-strategy game, the equilibrium point depends on the value of w_0. Further, as w_0 gets larger, the equilibrium approaches that of the standard replicator (i.e., nonshared fitness).

$$w_x = \frac{p_x A}{p_x A + p_y C} + \frac{p_y B}{p_x B + p_y D}$$

$$w_y = \frac{p_x C}{p_x A + p_y C} + \frac{p_y D}{p_x B + p_y D} \tag{9}$$

$$p_x = \frac{C(D - B)}{BA - 2BC + CD} \tag{10}$$
$$\frac{c(d - b) + w_0(d - b)}{ab - 2bc + cd + w_0(a - b - c + d)} \tag{10}$$

5.2 Dynamics

Figure 5 shows the return map of the Hawk-Dove game under competitive fitness sharing with the same two values of w_0 used in Figure 1. Unlike the selection methods we examined earlier, the map in Figure 5 is continuous; further, the fitness equilibrium is an attractor, though it is not the Nash equilibrium of the game. As Equation 10 indicates, the fitness equilibrium moves closer to 7/12 as w_0 increases. Again we see that the curves approach the diagonal as w_0 increases, meaning that the difference between two consecutive population states becomes smaller and the population dynamic slows. A value of w_0 sufficiently large to reasonably approximate the equilibrium of 7/12 will cause the dynamics to move very slowly, indeed.

6 Similarity-Based Sharing

An older method for diversity maintenance discounts an agent's fitness based on how genotypically or phenotypically redundant it is with respect to the rest of the population. This method is known as *similarity-based sharing* [13] and was originally used

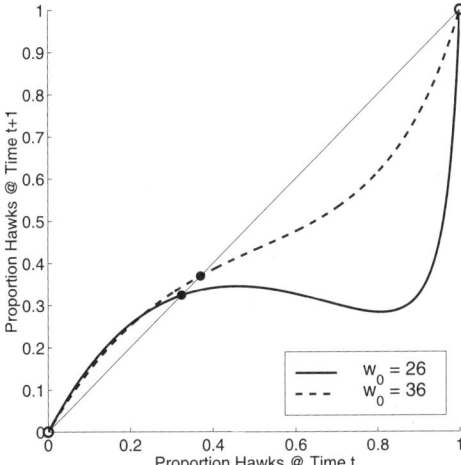

Figure 5. Return map of Hawk-Dove game with competitive fitness sharing using different values of w_0.

in noncoevolutionary algorithms. Because this method requires a similarity metric to measure redundancy and we can imagine a number of similarity metrics, there exist many ways to formulate this procedure. Here we investigate one very simple formulation that considers two agents to be similar only if they are playing the same strategy. This metric is analytically convenient but unlikely to be used in real-world domains.

6.1 Equilibrium

Given a game of m pure strategies $\mathbf{G}'$, the shared fitness of an agent playing strategy i is the inner product of payoff matrix row i and population state vector $\mathbf{p}$, divided by the number of agents playing strategy i, thus $\mathbf{w}_i = (\sum_j \mathbf{G}'_{i,j}\mathbf{p}_j)/\mathbf{p}_i$. Equation 11 shows how we calculate shared fitness based on similarity in a two-strategy game.

$$w_x = \frac{p_x A + p_y B}{p_x} = A + \frac{p_y}{p_x} B$$
$$w_y = \frac{p_x C + p_y D}{p_y} = \frac{p_x}{p_y} C + D \tag{11}$$

Given Equation 11, we can solve for p_x to find the proportion at which two strategies reach fitness equilibrium, if they do at all. This is somewhat more complex than in competitive fitness sharing because we must find the roots of the polynomial in Equation 12. Using the quadratic equation, we get Equation 13. We again find that the location of the fitness equilibrium is dependent on the magnitude of w_0.

Indeed, as w_0 approaches infinity, p_x approaches 1/2 regardless of the payoffs in the game. For this to be true, the square-root term must behave as shown in Equation 14. The $(a - d)^2$ term in Equation 14 becomes insignificant as w_0 grows, so we concentrate on the remaining terms, as shown in Equation 15. The square root of Equation 15 is approximated by the square root of Equation 16 as w_0 increases, which is the right side of Equation 14. We use our approximation to simplify Equation 13 and obtain Equation 17; thus, at $w_0 = \infty$, we get $p_x = 1/2$.

$$\mathbf{p}_x^2(-A + B - C + D) + \mathbf{p}_x(A - 2B - D) + B = 0 \tag{12}$$

$$\mathbf{p}_x = \frac{-a + 2b + d + 2w_0}{2(-a + b - c + d)} \pm \frac{\sqrt{(a - d)^2 + (2b + 2w_0)(2c + 2w_0)}}{2(-a + b - c + d)} \tag{13}$$

$$\sqrt{(a - d)^2 + (2b + 2w_0)(2c + 2w_0)} \equiv_{w_0 \to \infty} b + c + 2w_0 \tag{14}$$

$$(2b + 2w_0)(2c + 2w_0) = 4bc + 4bw_0 + 4cw_0 + 4w_0^2 \tag{15}$$

$$(b + c + 2w_0)^2 = b^2 + bc + c^2 + 4bw_0 + 4cw_0 + 4w_0^2 \tag{16}$$

$$\frac{-a + 2b + d + 2w_0 - (b + c + 2w_0)}{2(-a + b - c + d)} = \frac{1}{2} \tag{17}$$

6.2 Dynamics

Figure 6 shows the return map for the Hawk-Dove game using our formulation of similarity-based fitness sharing. The values of w_0 we use are 26 and 56; we see that the polymorphic equilibrium moves toward 1/2 as w_0 increases. Like the map for competitive fitness sharing, the map in Figure 6 is continuous at the fitness equilibrium; the equilibrium is an attractor, but not the Nash equilibrium of the game. Because the slope of the curve is negative at fitness equilibrium, this system approaches equilibrium via a damped oscillation rather than a monotonic convergence. Another feature of this map is that it is discontinuous at $p_x = 0$ and $p_x = 1$, unlike the previous maps.

7 Discussion

What generalizations can we make from the two-strategy Hawk-Dove game? Because truncation and rank selection use sorting, their dynamics are unable in principle to converge to a polymorphism, regardless of the number of strategies involved. Rather, these selection methods introduce discontinuities where attractors should be.

The behavior of a selection method reflects (or, more accurately, is a proxy for) the agents' private utility functions, for it indicates which strategies offer selective advantage and are therefore more preferable for an agent to adopt. Viewed in this

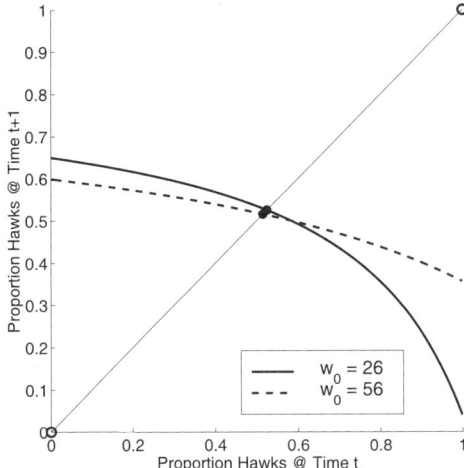

Figure 6. Return map of Hawk-Dove game with similarity-based fitness sharing using different values of w_0.

way, we can interpret the effects of truncation and rank selection as distortions of the agents' private utility functions. Further, the distortions are such that the agents' private utilities become poorly factored with respect to our world utility function, which seeks a population state that is a Nash equilibrium.

The importance of understanding that certain mechanisms distort the expected evolutionary dynamics is appreciated with the following case study (which stimulated the work we report here). Because the strong assumptions made by evolutionary game theory are, of course, not to be found in the real world, D. Fogel and G. Fogel et al. [10,11] investigate the effects of finite populations, noisy payoffs, and incomplete mixing on the equilibria and dynamics that EGT predicts. They use the Hawk-Dove game in their simulations, but they also use truncation selection for several of their experiments. The results they report are consistent with those we discussed, but they attribute their results to the factors they study, such as finite populations. We know from our experiments that truncation violates the expected outcome even when the strong assumptions of evolutionary game theory are met. Many studies that concern the iterated prisoner's dilemma also use mechanisms that prevent proper convergence to polymorphisms. For example, in [21] (μ, λ)-ES selection is used, which has properties very similar to truncation selection [5].

The purpose of fitness-sharing methods is to maintain genetic diversity and thereby provide the evolutionary algorithm more raw material with which to perform variation and search. The methods we reviewed achieve their goal by manipulating the proportions with which the various genotypes, and hence phenotypes, appear in the population. By doing so, fitness-sharing methods may easily act contrary to the requirements of the solution, or world state, we seek.

We should note that the degree of distortion introduced by competitive fitness sharing depends on not only the magnitude of w_0, but also the number of strategies in the polymorphism. We see considerable distortion when the polymorphism involves only two strategies. But, as more strategies become involved, we get more equations like those in Equation 9 and the divisors of those equations involve more terms; more importantly, the shared-fitness equations for any two strategies (involved in the polymorphism) will have more of their divisor terms in common. Thus, as the polymorphism includes more strategies, the divisors tend to become more similar, leaving us with an approximation of nonshared fitness. The quality of the approximation still depends on the payoffs of the game, however, and one generally does not know a priori the size of the polymorphism(s) a game will have.

8 Summary and Conclusion

With the Hawk-Dove game as a backdrop, we used evolutionary game theory to establish the normative behavior and outcome for a coevolutionary algorithm. The Hawk-Dove game has a single polymorphic Nash equilibrium that is an attractor of the standard replicator dynamic used in EGT. Against this norm we contrast the operation of a coevolutionary algorithm using one of four alternatives to the standard replicator equation; these methods are truncation and linear rank selection and competitive and similarity-based fitness sharing.

When applied to variable-sum games with attractive polymorphic Nash, these methods alter selection pressures such that the system either fails to converge or converges to solutions that lack game-theoretic justification. Truncation and linear rank selection cannot attain Nash equilibria that involve more than one strategy. Instead, these methods exhibit cyclic behavior, chaos, or fixed points that are not related to the values of the payoff matrix. The fitness-sharing procedures cause the polymorphic attractor of the Hawk-Dove game to deviate such that it is no longer Nash. We believe that our results are particularly relevant to the vast body of research on the iterated prisoner's dilemma, which is also a variable-sum game that can have polymorphisms, given a finite sample of strategies.

Viewed in the COIN framework, our analyses reveal that a coevolutionary algorithm that uses certain selection and fitness-sharing methods does not solve the inverse problem. Because the agents are given full knowledge of the strategy space, the pathologies we illustrate cannot be due to a lack of *learnability* of agents' private utility functions. Instead, the methods we examine distort the private utilities of the agents such that they become poorly factored and prevent the desired world state—a polymorphic Nash equilibrium—from being attained.

Acknowledgments. The authors thank David Fogel, Kagan Tumer, David Wolpert, and the members of the DEMO Lab for valuable feedback and discussions.

References

1. P. J. Angeline and J. B. Pollack. Competitive environments evolve better solutions for complex tasks. In Stephanie Forrest, editor, *Proc. of the Fifth International Conference on Genetic Algorithms*, pages 264–70. Morgan Kaufmann, 1994.

2. K. Chellapilla and D. B. Fogel. Anaconda defeats Hoyle 6–0: A case study competing an evolved checkers program against commercially available software. In Zalzala et al. [32], pages 857–63.

3. D. Cliff and G. F. Miller. Tracking the red queen: Measurements of adaptive progress in co-evolutionary simulations. In Frederico Moran et al., editors, *Third European Conference on Artificial Life*, pages 200–18, Berlin; New York, 1995. Springer Verlag.

4. A. Eriksson and K. Lindgren. Evolution of strategies in repeated stochastic games with full information of the payoff matrix. In Spector et al. [27], pages 853–59.

5. S. G. Ficici, O. Melnik, and J. B. Pollack. A game-theoretic investigation of selection methods used in evolutionary algorithms. In Zalzala et al. [32], pages 880–7.

6. S. G. Ficici and J. B. Pollack. Challenges in coevolutionary learning: Arms-race dynamics, open-endedness, and mediocre stable states. In Chris Adami et al., editors, *Artificial Life VI (1998)*, pages 238–47. MIT Press, 1998.

7. S. G. Ficici and J. B. Pollack. Game theory and the simple coevolutionary algorithm: Some results on fitness sharing. In Robert Heckendorn, editor, *2001 Genetic and Evolutionary Computation Conference Workshop Program*, pages 2–7, 2001.

8. D. Floreano, S. Nolfi, and F. Mondada. Competitive co-evolutionary robotics: From theory to practice. In Rolf Pfeifer et al., editors, *From Animals to Animats V*, pages 515–24. MIT Press, 1998.

9. D. B. Fogel. An overview of evolutionary programming. In L. D. Davis, K. De Jong, M. D. Vose, and L. D. Whitley, editors, *Evolutionary Algorithms*, pages 89–109. Springer, 1997.

10. D. B. Fogel and G. B. Fogel. Evolutionary stable strategies are not always stable under evolutionary dynamics. In *Evolutionary Programming IV*, pages 565–77, 1995.

11. G. B. Fogel, P. C. Andrews, and D. B. Fogel. On the instability of evolutionary stable strategies in small populations. *Ecological Modelling*, 109:283–94, 1998.

12. D. Fudenberg and D. K. Levine. *The Theory of Learning in Games*. MIT Press, 1998.

13. D. E. Goldberg. *Genetic Algorithms in Search, Optimization, and Machine Learning*. Addison-Wesley, 1989.

14. D. E. Goldberg and K. Deb. A comparative analysis of selection schemes used in genetic algorithms. In G. J. E. Rawlins, editor, *Foundations of Genetic Algorithms (FOGA 1)*, pages 69–93, 1991.

15. P. J. B. Hancock. An empirical comparison of selection methods in evolutionary algorithms. In T. C. Fogarty, editor, *Evolutionary Computing (AISB '94)*, pages 80–94, 1994.

16. D. Hillis. Co-evolving parasites improves simulated evolution as an optimization procedure. In C. Langton, C. Taylor, J. Farmer, and S. Rasmussen, editors, *Artificial Life II (1990)*. Addison-Wesley, 1991.

17. J. Hofbauer and K. Sigmund. *Evolutionary Games and Population Dynamics*. Cambridge University Press, 1998.

18. H. Juillé and J. B. Pollack. Coevolving the "ideal" trainer: Application to the discovery of cellular automata rules. In *Proc. of the Third Annual Genetic Programming Conference*, 1998.

19. S. Lessard. Evolutionary stability: One concept, several meanings. *Theoretical Population Biology*, 37:159–70, 1990.

20. J. Maynard-Smith. *Evolution and the Theory of Games*. Cambridge University Press, 1982.

21. N. Meuleau and C. Lattaud. The artificial evolution of cooperation. In J.-M. Alliot, E. Lutton, E. Ronald, M Schoenauer, and Snyers D., editors, *Aritificial Evolution (AE 95)*, pages 159–80. Springer-Verlag, 1995.

22. B. Olsson. *NK*-landscapes as test functions for evaluation of host-parasite algorithms. In Schoenauer et al. [26], pages 487–96.

23. J. Paredis. Towards balanced coevolution. In Schoenauer et al. [26], pages 497–506.

24. C. D. Rosin. *Coevolutionary Search Among Adversaries*. Ph.D. thesis, University of California, San Diego, 1997.

25. G. W. Rowe, I. F. Harvey, and S. F. Hubbard. The essential properties of evolutionary stability. *Journal of Theoretical Biology*, 115:269–85, 1985.

26. M. Schoenauer et al., editors. *Parallel Problem Solving from Nature VI*. Springer-Verlag, 2000.

27. L. Spector et al., editors. *Proc. of the 2001 Genetic and Evolutionary Computation Conference (GECCO 2001)*, 2001.

28. S. H. Strogatz. *Nonlinear Dynamics and Chaos*. Addison-Wesley, 1994.

29. K. Tumer and D. H. Wolpert. Collective intelligence and Braess' paradox. In Henry Kautz and Bruce Porter, editors, *Proc. of the Seventeenth National Conference on Artificial Intelligence*, pages 104–9, 2000.

30. R. A. Watson and J. B. Pollack. Coevolutionary dynamics in a minimal substrate. In Spector et al. [27], pages 702–9.

31. D. H. Wolpert and K. Tumer. Optimal payoff functions for members of collectives. *Advances in Complex Systems*, 4(2/3):265–79, 2001.

32. Ali Zalzala et al., editors. *Proc. of the 2000 Congress on Evolutionary Computation*. IEEE Press, 2000.

Dynamics of Large Autonomous Computational Systems

Tad Hogg* and Bernardo A. Huberman*

Summary. Distributed large-scale computation gives rise to a wide range of behaviors, from the simple to the chaotic. This diversity of behaviors stems from the fact that the agents and programs have incomplete knowledge and imperfect information on the state of the system. We describe an instantiation of such systems based on market mechanisms, which provides an interesting example of autonomous control. We also show that when agents choose among several resources, the dynamics of the system can be oscillatory and even chaotic. Furthermore, we describe a mechanism for achieving global stability through local controls.

1 Introduction

It is by now an established fact that computation has become widely distributed over the world, as both networked computers and embedded systems, such as the processing power available in automobiles, mobile phones, and robots. And in distributed form, the capabilities of the system as a whole are much greater than those of single components. This is because of the ability of a distributed system to share information and resources and to parcel the computation in efficient ways.

The effective use of distributed computation is a challenging task, because the processes must obtain resources in a dynamically changing environment and be designed to collaborate despite a variety of asynchronous and unpredictable changes. For instance, the lack of global perspectives for determining resource allocation requires a very different approach to system-level programming and the creation of suitable languages. Even implementing reliable methods whereby processes can compute in machines with diverse characteristics is difficult.

As these distributed systems grow, they become a community of concurrent processes, or a *computational ecosystem* [9], which, in their interactions, strategies, and lack of perfect knowledge, are analogous to biological ecosystems and human economies. Because all of these systems consist of a large number of independent

* HP Laboratories Palo Alto, CA 94304 thogg@exch.hpl.hp.com; huberman@exch.hpl.hp.com

actors competing for resources, this analogy can suggest new ways to design and understand the behavior of these emerging computational systems. In particular, these existing systems have methods to deal successfully with coordinating asynchronous operations in the face of imperfect knowledge. These methods allow the system as a whole to adapt to changes in the environment or disturbances to individual members, in marked contrast to the brittle nature of most current computer programs, which often fail completely if there is even a small change in their inputs or error in the program itself. To improve the reliability and usefulness of distributed computation, it is therefore of interest to examine the extent to which this analogy can be exploited.

Statistical mechanics, based on the law of large numbers, has taught us that many universal and generic features of large systems can be quantitatively understood as approximations to the average behavior of infinite systems. Although such infinite models can be difficult to solve in detail, their overall qualitative features can be determined with a surprising degree of accuracy. Because these features are universal in character and depend only on a few general properties of the system, they can be expected to apply to a wide range of actual configurations. This is the case when the number of relevant degrees of freedom in the system, as well as the number of interesting parameters, is small. In this situation, it becomes useful to treat the unspecified internal degrees of freedom as if they are given by a probability distribution. This implies assuming a lack of correlations between the unspecified and specified degrees of freedom. This assumption has been extremely successful in statistical mechanics. It implies that although degrees of freedom may change according to purely deterministic algorithms, the fact that they are unspecified makes them appear to an outside observer as effectively random.

Consider, for instance, massively parallel systems that are desired to be robust and adaptable. They should work in the presence of unexpected errors and with changes in the environment in which they are embedded (i.e., fail-soft). This implies that many of the system's internal degrees of freedom will be allowed to adjust by taking on a range of possible configurations. Furthermore, their large size will necessarily enforce a perspective that concentrates on a few relevant variables. Although these considerations suggest that the assumptions necessary for a statistical description hold for these systems, experiments will be necessary for deciding their applicability.

Although computational and biological systems such as social insects and multicellular organisms share a number of features, we should also note that there are a number of important differences. For instance, in contrast to biological individuals, computational agents are programmed to complete their tasks as soon as possible, which implies a desirability for their earliest death. This task completion may also involve terminating other processes spawned to work on different aspects of the same problem, as in parallel search, where the first process to find a solution terminates the others. This much more rapid turnover of agents can be expected to lead to dynamics at much shorter time scales than seen in biological or economic counterparts.

Another interesting difference between biological and computational ecologies lies in the fact that for the latter the local rules (or programs for the processes) can be arbitrarily defined, whereas in biology those rules are fixed. Moreover, in distributed computational systems the interactions are not constrained by a Euclidean metric, so that processes separated by large physical distances can strongly affect each other by passing messages of arbitrary complexity between them. And last but not least, in computational ecologies the rationality assumption of game theory can be explicitly imposed on their agents, thereby making these systems amenable to game-dynamic analysis, suitably adjusted for their intrinsic characteristics. On the other hand, computational agents are considerably less sophisticated in their decision-making capacity than people, which could prevent expectations based on observed human performance from being realized.

There are by now a number of distributed computational systems that exhibit many of these characteristics and that offer increased performance when compared with traditional operating systems. For instance, a number of market-based systems have been developed [3]. *Enterprise* [12] is a marketlike scheduler where independent processes or agents are allocated at run time among remote idle workstations through a bidding mechanism. A more evolved system, *Spawn* [16], is organized as a market economy composed of interacting buyers and sellers. The commodities in this economy are computer processing resources; specifically, slices of CPU time on various types of computers in a distributed computational environment. The system has been shown to provide substantial improvements over more conventional systems, while providing dynamic response to changes and resource sharing.

Another interesting application of distributed control for autonomous systems is *smart matter*. These are mechanical systems with embedded microscopic sensors, computers, and actuators that actively monitor and respond to their environments in precisely controlled ways. These are microelectromechanical systems (MEMS) [1, 2], where the devices are fabricated together in single silicon wafers. A robust control approach for such systems uses a collection of distributed autonomous processes, or *agents*, that each deal with a limited part of the overall control problem [8]. Individual agents can be associated with each sensor or actuator in the material or with various aggregations of these devices to provide a mapping between agents and physical location.

From a scientific point of view, the analogy between distributed computation and natural ecologies brings to mind the spontaneous appearance of organized behavior in biological and social systems, where agents can engage in cooperating strategies while working on the solution of particular problems. In some cases, the strategy mix used by these agents evolves toward an asymptotic ratio that is constant in time and stable against perturbations. This phenomenon sometimes goes under the name of evolutionarily stable strategy (ESS). Recently, it has been shown that spontaneous organization can also exist in open computational systems when agents can choose among many possible strategies while collaborating in the solution of computational tasks. In this case, however, imperfect knowledge and delays in information introduce asymptotic oscillatory and chaotic states that exclude the existence of simple ESSs. This is an important finding in light of studies that resort to notions of evolutionarily stable strategies in the design and prediction of the performance of open systems.

In what follows we will describe a market-based computational ecosystem and a theory of distributed computation. The theory describes the collective dynamics of computational agents, while incorporating many of the features endemic to such systems, including distributed control, asynchrony, resource contention, and extensive communication among agents. When processes can choose among many possible strategies while collaborating in the solution of computational tasks, the dynamics leads to asymptotic regimes characterized by complex attractors. Detailed experiments have confirmed many of the theoretical predictions, while uncovering new phenomena, such as chaos induced by overly clever decision-making procedures.

Next, we will deal with the problem of controlling chaos in such systems, for we have discovered ways of achieving global stability through local controls inspired by fitness mechanisms found in nature. Furthermore, we will show how diversity enters into the picture, along with the minimal amount of such diversity that is required to achieve stable behavior in a distributed computational system.

2 Computational Markets for Resource Allocation

Allocating resources to competing tasks is one of the key issues for making effective use of computer networks. Examples include deciding whether to run a task in parallel on many machines or serially on one and whether to save intermediate results or recompute them as needed. The similarity of this problem to resource allocation in market economies has prompted considerable interest in using analogous techniques to schedule tasks in a network environment. In effect, a coordinated solution to the allocation problem is obtained using Adam Smith's "invisible hand" [14]. Although unlikely to produce the optimal allocation that would be made by an omniscient controller with unlimited computational capability, it can perform well compared to other feasible alternatives [4, 11]. As in economics [6], the use of prices provides a flexible mechanism for allocating resources, with relatively low information requirements: A single price summarizes the current demand for each resource, whether processor time, memory, communication bandwidth, use of a database, or control of a particular sensor. This flexibility is especially desirable when resource preferences and performance measures differ among tasks. For instance, an intensive numerical simulation's need for fast floating-point hardware is quite different from an interactive text editor's requirement for rapid response to user commands or a database search's requirement for rapid access to the data and fast query matching.

As a conceptual example of how this could work in a computational setting, suppose that a number of database search tasks are using networked computers to find items of interest to various users. Furthermore, suppose that some of the machines have fast floating-point hardware but all are otherwise identical. Assuming the search tasks make little use of floating-point operations, their performance will not depend on whether they run on a machine with fast floating-point hardware. In a market-based system, these programs will tend to value each machine based on how many other tasks it is running, leading to a uniform load on the machines. Now suppose some floating-point-intensive tasks arrive in the system. These will definitely prefer the specialized machines and consequently bid up the price of those particular resources. The database tasks, observing that the price for some machines has gone up, will then tend to migrate toward those machines without the fast floating-point hardware. Importantly, because of the high cost of modifying large existing programs, the database tasks will not need to be rewritten to adjust for the presence of the new tasks. Similarly, there is no need to reprogram the scheduling method of a traditional central controller, which is often very time-consuming.

This example illustrates how a reasonable allocation of resources could be brought about by simply having the tasks be sensitive to current resource price. Moreover, adjustments can take place continually as new uses are found for particular network resources (which could include specialized databases or proprietary algorithms as well as the more obvious hardware resources) and do not require all users to agree on, or even know about, these new uses, thus encouraging an incremental and experimental approach to resource allocation.

While this example motivates the use of market-based resource allocation, a study of actual implementations is required to see how large the system must be for its benefits to appear and whether any of the differences between simple computer programs and human agents pose additional problems. In particular, a successful use of markets requires a number of changes to traditional computer systems. First the system must provide an easily accessible, reliable market so that buyers and sellers can quickly find each other. Second, individual programs must be price-sensitive so they will respond to changes in relative prices among resources. This implies that the programs must, in some sense at least, be able to make choices among various resources based on how well suited they are for the task at hand.

A number of marketlike systems have been implemented over the years [12, 15, 16]. Most instances focus on finding an appropriate machine for running a single task. While this is important, further flexibility is provided by systems that use market mechanisms to also manage a collection of parallel processes contributing to the solution of a single task. In this latter case, prices give a flexible method for allocating resources among multiple competing heuristics for the same problem based on their perceived progress. It thus greatly simplifies the development of programs that adjust to unpredictable changes in resource demand or availability. Thus we have a second reason to consider markets: Not only may they be useful for flexible allocation of computational resources among competing tasks, but also the simplicity of the price mechanism could provide help with designing cooperative parallel programs.

One such system is Spawn [16], in which each task, starting with a certain amount of money corresponding to its relative priority, bids for the use of machines on the network. In this way, each task can allocate its budget toward those resources most important for it. In addition, when prices are low enough, some tasks can split into several parts that run in parallel, as shown in Figure 1, thereby adjusting the number of machines devoted to each task based on the demand from other users. From a user's point of view, starting a task with the Spawn system amounts to giving a command to execute it and giving it the necessary funding to buy resources. The Spawn system manages auctions on each of the participating machines and the use of resources by each participating task and provides communication paths among

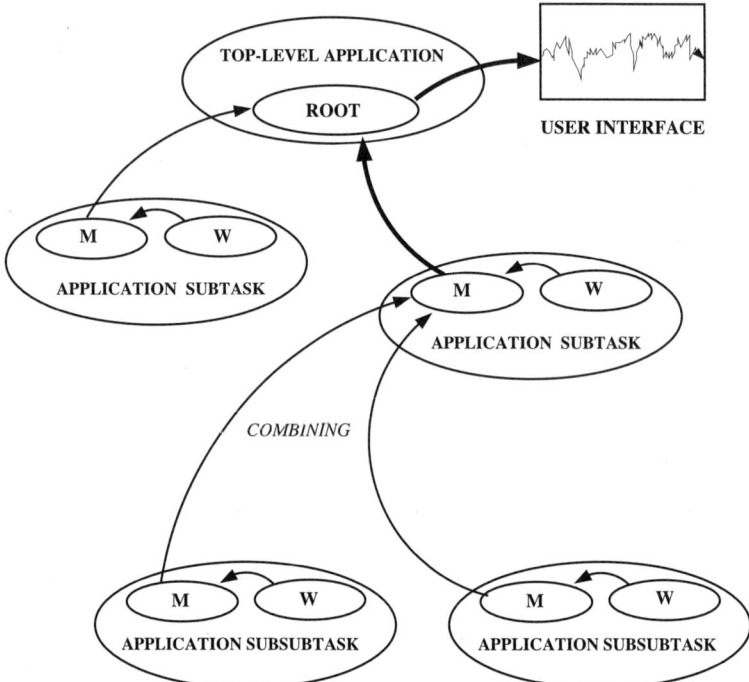

Figure 1. Managing parallel execution of subtasks in Spawn. Worker processes (W) report progress to their local managers (M), who in turn make reports to the next higher level of management. Upper management combines data into aggregate reports. Finally, the root manager presents results to the user. Managers also bid for the use of additional machines and, if successful, spawn additional subtasks on them.

the spawned processes. It remains for the programmer to determine the specific algorithms to be used and the meaningful subtasks into which to partition the problem. That is, the Spawn system provides the price information and a market, but the individual programs must be written to make their own price decisions to effectively participate in the market. To allow existing, nonprice-sensitive, programs to run within the Spawn system without modification, we provided a simple default manager that simply attempted to buy time on a single machine for that task. Users could then gradually modify this manager for their particular task, if desired, to spawn subtasks or use market strategies more appropriate for the particular task.

Studies with this system show that an equilibrium price can be meaningfully defined with even a few machines participating. A specific instance is shown in Figure 2. Despite the continuing fluctuations, this small network reaches a rough price equilibrium. Moreover, the ratio of prices between the two machines closely matches their relative speeds, which was the only important difference between the two types of machine for these tasks. An additional experiment studied a network with some lengthy, low-priority tasks to which was added a short, high-priority task. The new

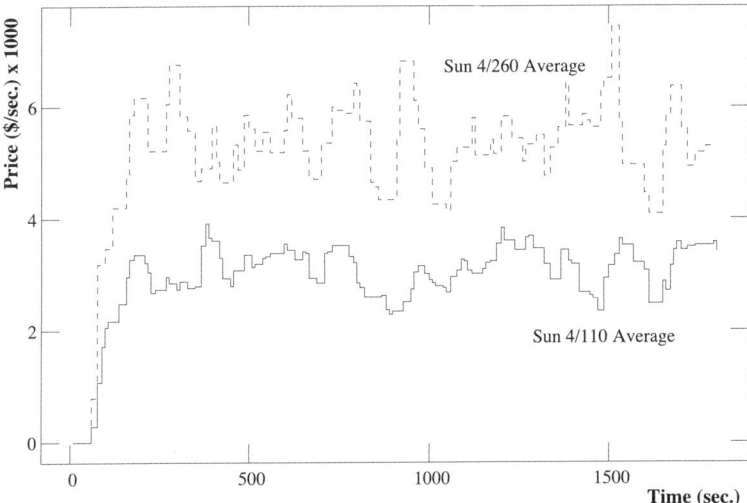

Figure 2. Price as a function of time (in seconds) in an inhomogeneous Spawn network consisting of three Sun 4/260s and six Sun 4/110s running four independent tasks. The average price of the 260s is the dashed line, the less powerful 110s are solid.

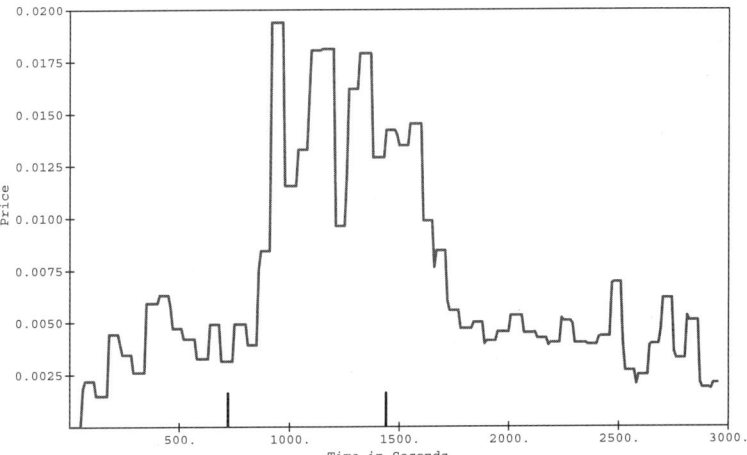

Figure 3. Price as a function of time (in seconds) when a high-priority task is introduced into a Spawn network running low-priority jobs. The first vertical line segment on the time axis marks the introduction of the high-priority task, the second one the termination of its funding.

task rapidly expands throughout the network by outbidding the existing tasks and driving the price of CPU time up, as shown in Figure 3. It is therefore able to briefly use a large number of networked machines and illustrates the inherent flexibility of market-based resource allocation. Although the very small networks used in these experiments could be adequately managed centrally, these results do show that expected market behavior can emerge even in small cases.

Computer market systems can be used to experimentally address a number of additional issues, for instance, understanding what happens when more sophisticated programs begin to use the network, e.g., processes that attempt to anticipate future loads to maximize their own resource use. Such behavior can destabilize the overall system. Another area of interest is the emergence of diversity or specialization from a group of initially similar machines. For example, a machine might cache some of the routines or data commonly used by its processes, giving it a comparative advantage in bids for similar tasks in the future. Ultimately this could result in complex organizational structures embedded within a larger market framework [13]. Within these groups, some machines could keep track of the kinds of problems for which others perform best and use this information to guide new tasks to appropriate machines. In this way the system could gradually learn to perform common tasks more effectively.

These experiments also highlighted a number of more immediate practical issues. In setting up Spawn, it was necessary to find individuals willing to allow their machines to be part of the market. While it would seem simple enough to do so, in practice a number of incentives were needed to overcome the natural reluctance of people to have other tasks running on their machines. This reluctance is partly based on perceived limitations on the security of the network and the individual operating systems; for it was possible that a remote procedure could crash an individual machine or consume more resources than anticipated. In particular, users with little need for compute-intensive tasks saw little benefit from participating because they had no use for the money collected by their machines. This indicates the need to use real money in such situations so that these users could use their revenues for their own needs. This, in turn, brings the issue of computer security to the forefront so users will feel confident that no counterfeiting of money takes place and tasks will in fact be limited to only use resources for which they have paid.

Similarly, for those users participating in the system as buyers, they need to have some idea of what amount of money is appropriate to give a task. In a fully developed market, there could easily be tools to monitor the results of various auctions and hence give a current market price for resources. However, when using a newly created market with only a few users, tools are not always available to give easy access to prices, and even if they are, the prices have large fluctuations. Effective use of such a system also requires users to have some idea of what resources are required for their programs, or, better yet, to encode that information in the program itself so it will be able to respond to available resources, e.g., by spawning subtasks, more rapidly than the users can. Conversely, there must be a mechanism whereby sellers can make available information about the characteristics of their resources (e.g., clock speed, available disk space, or special hardware). This can eventually allow for more complex market mechanisms, such as auctions that attempt to sell simultaneous use of different resources (e.g., CPU time and fast memory) or future use of currently unavailable resources to give tasks a more predictable use of resources. Developing and evaluating a variety of auction and price mechanisms that are particularly well suited to these computational tasks is an interesting open problem.

Finally, these experimental systems help clarify the differences between human and computer markets. For instance, computational processes can respond to events much more rapidly than people, but are far less sophisticated. Moreover, unlike the situation with people, particular incentive structures, rationality assumptions, and the like can be explicitly built into computational processes, allowing for the possibility of designing particular market mechanisms. This could lead to the ironic situation in which economic theory has greater predictability for the behavior of computational markets than for that of the larger, and more complex, human economy.

3 Chaos in Computational Ecosystems

The Spawn system highlights the need to understand the dynamical behaviors of simple agents with fast response times, compared to humans in economic settings, which are complex and slower. To this end we present a dynamical model of resource contention in the presence of imperfect information and delays [9].

In this model, agents independently and asynchronously select among the available choices based on their perceived payoff. These payoffs are actual computational measures of performance, such as the time required to complete a task, accuracy of the solution, and amount of memory required. In general, the payoff G_r for using resource r depends on the number of agents already using it. In a purely competitive environment, the payoff for using a particular resource tends to decrease as more agents make use of it. Alternatively, the agents using a resource could assist one another in their computations, as might be the case if the overall task could be decomposed into a number of subtasks. If these subtasks communicate extensively to share partial results, the agents will be better off using the same computer rather than running more rapidly on separate machines and then being limited by slow communication. As another example, agents using a particular database could leave index links that are useful to others. In such cooperative situations, the payoff of a resource would then increase as more agents use it, until it became sufficiently crowded.

Imperfect information about the state of the system causes each agent's perceived payoff to differ from the actual value, with the difference increasing when there is more uncertainty in the information available to the agents. This type of uncertainty concisely captures the effect of many sources of errors such as some program bugs, heuristics incorrectly evaluating choices, errors in communicating the load on various machines, and mistakes in interpreting sensory data. Specifically, the perceived payoffs are taken to be normally distributed, with standard deviation σ, around their correct values. In addition, information delays cause each agent's knowledge of the state of the system to be somewhat out of date. Although for simplicity we will consider the case in which all agents have the same effective delay, uncertainty, and preferences for resource use, we should mention that the same range of behaviors is also found in more general situations [7].

As a specific illustration of this approach, we consider the case of two resources so the system can be described by $P(n, t)$, the probability to have n agents selecting the first resource at time t. Its dynamics over a small time interval Δt is governed by [9]

$$\frac{P(n, t + \Delta t) - P(n, t)}{\Delta t} = \sum_{n'} \left(W(n|n') P(n', t) - W(n'|n) P(n, t) \right), \quad (1)$$

where $W(n'|n)$ is the transition probability per unit time that the state changes from n to n'. To derive an expression for the transition rates, notice that in the time interval Δt, the probabilities that a given agent using resource 1 switches to resource 2 and vice versa are given by

$$P(2 \to 1) = \alpha \Delta t \, \rho, \quad (2)$$
$$P(1 \to 2) = \alpha \Delta t \, (1 - \rho),$$

where α is the rate at which agents reevaluate their resource choice and ρ is the probability an agent prefers resource 1 over resource 2. For a system with network externalities, ρ depends on the number of agents using each resource.

For very short time intervals, the asynchronous decisions mean one can assume that only one of the agents reevaluates the option to switch. This means that $W(n|n') = 0$ unless $n - n' = 0, 1$, or -1. Taking these three cases into account, the transition probabilities become

$$W(n|n') \Delta t = \delta_{n, n'-1} (n' \alpha \Delta t (1 - \rho(n'))) \quad (3)$$
$$+ \delta_{n, n'+1} ((N - n') \alpha \Delta t \rho(n'))$$
$$+ \delta_{n, n'} (1 - n' \alpha \Delta t (1 - \rho(n')) - (N - n') \alpha \Delta t \rho(n')).$$

As $\Delta t \to 0$, the probability of any changes in the agent choices goes to zero, making $W(n|n) \Delta t \to 1$. In this limit, the right-hand side of the equation correctly gives 1 for $n = n'$. Substituting this into Equation 1 and letting $\Delta t \to 0$ gives

$$\frac{\partial P(n, t)}{\partial t} = \alpha P(n, t)[-n(1 - \rho(n)) - (N - n)\rho(n)] \quad (4)$$
$$+ \alpha P(n + 1, t)[(n + 1)(1 - \rho(n + 1))]$$
$$+ \alpha P(n - 1, t)[(N - n + 1)\rho(n - 1)].$$

We can now compute the dynamics for the average number of agents by using the identity

$$\frac{d}{dt} \langle n \rangle = \sum_{n'=0}^{N} n' \frac{\partial P(n', t)}{\partial t}. \quad (5)$$

Using Equation 1 to evaluate the sum on the right hand side gives the evolution of the average number of agents as

$$\frac{d\langle n\rangle}{dt} = \alpha\,\langle(N-n)\rho(n) - n(1-\rho(n))\rangle \tag{6}$$

$$= \alpha(N\,\langle\rho(n)\rangle - \langle n\rangle).$$

The first line is simply interpreted as the difference between the number of agents using resource 2 who switch to resource 1 and those using resource 1 who switch to resource 2. This expression can be further simplified by invoking the mean field approximation $\langle\rho(n)\rangle \approx \rho(\langle n\rangle)$ and defining the fraction $f \equiv n/N$ of agents using resource 1 at any given time:

$$\frac{df}{dt} = \alpha(\rho - f). \tag{7}$$

With this formulation, it is convenient to treat ρ as a function of f. It can be expressed in terms of the payoffs G_1, G_2 associated with each resource and the uncertainty in the information available to the agents. Specifically for a normally distributed error around the true value of the payoff, ρ becomes

$$\rho = \frac{1}{2}\left(1 + \mathrm{erf}\left(\frac{G_1(f) - G_2(f)}{2\sigma}\right)\right), \tag{8}$$

where σ quantifies the uncertainty. Notice that this definition captures the simple requirement that an agent is more likely to prefer a resource when its payoff is relatively large. Finally, delays in information are modeled by supposing that the payoffs that enter into ρ at time t are the values they had at a delayed time $t - \tau$.

For a typical system of many agents with a mixture of cooperative and competitive payoffs, the kinds of dynamical behaviors exhibited by the model are shown in Figure 4. When the delays and uncertainty are fairly small, the system converges to an equilibrium point close to the optimal obtainable by an omniscient central controller. As the information available to the agents becomes more corrupted, the equilibrium point moves further from the optimal value. With increasing delays, the equilibrium eventually becomes unstable, leading to the oscillatory and chaotic behavior shown in the figure. In these cases, the number of agents using particular resources continues to vary so that the system spends relatively little time near the optimal value, with a consequent drop in its overall performance. This can be due to the fact that chaotic systems are unpredictable, hence making it difficult for individual agents to automatically select the best resources at any given time.

4 The Uses of Fitness

We will now describe an effective procedure for controlling chaos in distributed systems [7]. It is based on a mechanism that rewards agents according to their actual performance. As we shall see, such an algorithm leads to the emergence of a diverse community of agents out of an essentially homogenous one. This diversity eliminates chaotic behavior through a series of dynamical bifurcations, which render chaos a transient phenomenon.

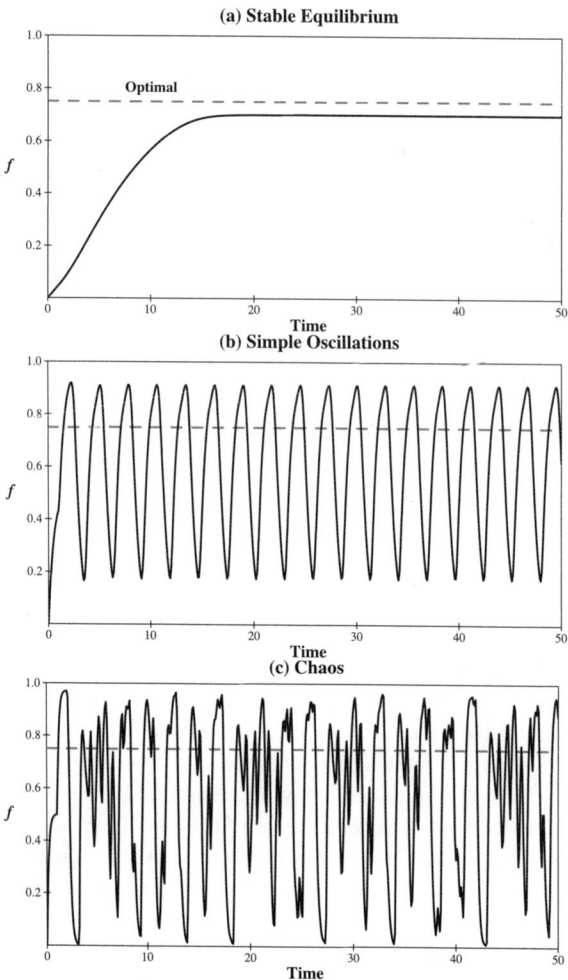

Figure 4. Typical behaviors for the fraction f of agents using resource 1 as a function of time for successively longer delays: (a) relaxation toward stable equilibrium, (b) simple persistent oscillations, and (c) chaotic oscillations. The payoffs are $G_1 = 4 + 7f - 5.333 f^2$ for resource 1 and $G_2 = 4 + 3f$ for resource 2. The time scale is in units of the delay time τ, $\sigma = 1/4$ and the dashed line shows the optimal allocation for these payoffs.

The actual performance of computational processes can be rewarded in a number of ways. A particularly appealing one is to mimic the mechanism found in biological evolution, where fitness determines the number of survivors of a given species in a changing environment. This mechanism is used in computation under the name *genetic algorithms* [5]. Another example is provided by computational systems modeled on ideal economic markets [13, 16], which reward good performance in terms of profits. In this case, agents pay for the use of resources, and they are paid for completing their tasks. Those making the best choices collect the most currency and are able to outbid others for the use of resources. Consequently they come to dominate the system.

While there is a range of possible reward mechanisms, their net effect is to increase the proportion of agents that are performing successfully, thereby decreasing the number of those who do not do as well. It is with this insight in mind that we developed a general theory of effective reward mechanisms without resorting to the details of their implementations. Because this change in agent mix will change the choices made by every agent and their payoffs, those that were initially most successful need not be so in the future. This leads to an evolving diversity whose eventual stability is by no means obvious.

Before proceeding with the theory, we point out that the resource payoffs that we will consider are instantaneous ones (i.e., shorter than the delays in the system), e.g., work actually done by a machine or currency actually received. Other reward mechanisms, such as those based on averaged past performance, could lead to very different behavior from the one exhibited here.

In order to investigate the effects of rewarding actual performance we generalize the previous model of computational ecosystems by allowing agents to be of different types, a fact that gives them different performance characteristics. Recall that the agents need to estimate the current state of the system based on imperfect and delayed information in order to make good choices. This can be done in a number of ways, ranging from extremely simple extrapolations from previous data to complex forecasting techniques. The different types of agents then correspond to the various ways in which they can make these extrapolations.

Within this context, a computational ecosystem can be described by specifying the fraction of agents, f_{rs}, of a given type s using a given resource r at a particular time. We will also define the total fraction of agents using a resource of a particular type as

$$f_r^{res} = \sum_s f_{rs},$$ (9)

$$f_s^{type} = \sum_r f_{rs},$$

respectively.

As mentioned previously, the net effect of rewarding performance is to increase the fraction of highly performing agents. If γ is the rate at which performance is rewarded, then Equation 7 is enhanced with an extra term that corresponds to this reward mechanism. This gives

$$\frac{df_{rs}}{dt} = \alpha \left(f_s^{type} \rho_{rs} - f_{rs} \right) + \gamma \left(f_r^{res} \eta_s - f_{rs} \right),$$ (10)

where the first term is analogous to that of the previous theory, and the second term incorporates the effect of rewards on the population. In this equation ρ_{rs} is the probability that an agent of type s will prefer resource r when it makes a choice, and η_s is the probability that new agents will be of type s, which we take to be proportional to the actual payoff associated with agents of type s. As before, α denotes the rate at which agents make resource choices and the detailed interpretation of γ depends on the particular reward mechanism involved. For example, if they are replaced on the basis of their fitness, it is the rate at which this happens. In a market system, on the other hand, γ corresponds to the rate at which agents are paid. Notice that in this case, the fraction of each type is proportional to the wealth of agents of that type.

Because the total fraction of agents of all types must be one, a simple form of the normalization condition can be obtained if one considers the relative payoff, which is given by

$$\eta_s = \frac{\sum_r f_{rs} G_r}{\sum_r f_r^{res} G_r}. \tag{11}$$

Note that the numerator is the actual payoff received by agents of type s given their current resource use and the denominator is the total payoff for all agents in the system, both normalized to the total number of agents in the system. This form assumes positive payoffs, e.g., they could be growth rates. If the payoffs can be negative (e.g., currency changes in an economic system), one can use instead the difference between the actual payoffs and their minimum value m. Because the η_s must sum to 1, this will give

$$\eta_s = \frac{\sum_r f_{rs} G_r - m}{\sum_r f_r^{res} G_r - Sm}, \tag{12}$$

which reduces to the previous case when $m = 0$.

Summing Equation 10 over all resources and types gives

$$\frac{df_r^{res}}{dt} = \alpha \left(\sum_s f_s^{type} \rho_{rs} - f_r^{res} \right), \tag{13}$$

$$\frac{df_s^{type}}{dt} = \gamma \left(\eta_s - f_s^{type} \right),$$

which describe the dynamics of overall resource use and the distribution of agent types, respectively. Note that this implies that those agent types that receive greater than average payoff (i.e., types for which $\eta_s > f_s^{type}$) will increase in the system at the expense of the low-performing types.

Note that the actual payoffs can only reward existing types of agents. Thus in order to introduce new variations to the population an additional mechanism is needed (e.g., corresponding to mutation in genetic algorithms or learning).

5 Results

In order to illustrate the effectiveness of rewarding actual payoffs in controlling chaos, we examine the dynamics generated by Equation 10 for the case in which

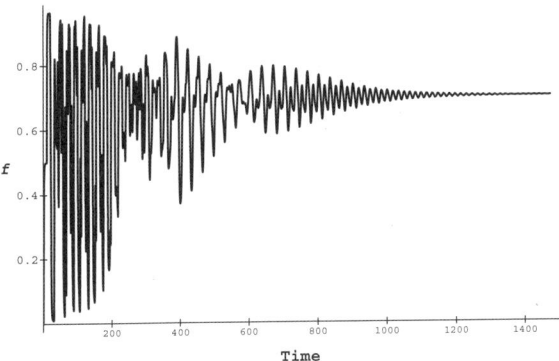

Figure 5. Fraction of agents using resource 1 as a function of time with adjustment based on actual payoff. These parameters correspond to Figure 4(c), without the adjustment the system would remain chaotic.

agents choose among two resources with cooperative payoffs, a case we have shown to generate chaotic behavior in the absence of rewards [9, 10]. As in the particular example of Figure 4c, we use $\tau = 10$, $G_1 = 4 + 7f_1 - 5.333f_1^2$, $G_2 = 7 - 3f_2$, $\sigma = 1/4$, and an initial condition in which all agents start using resource 2.

One kind of diversity among agents is motivated by the simple case in which the system oscillates with a fixed period. In this case, those agents that are able to discover the period of the oscillation can use this knowledge to reliably estimate the current system state in spite of delays in information. Notice that this estimate does not necessarily guarantee that they will keep performing well in the future, for their choice can change the basic frequency of oscillation of the system.

In what follows, we take the diversity of agent types to correspond to the different past horizons, or extra delays, that they use to extrapolate to the current state of the system. These differences in estimation could be due to having a variety of procedures for analyzing the system's behavior. Specifically, we identify different agent types with the different assumed periods that range over a given interval. Thus, we take agents of type s to use an effective delay of $\tau + s$ while evaluating their choices.

The resulting behavior is shown in Figure 5, which should be contrasted with Figure 4(c). We used an interval of extra delays ranging from 0 to 40. As shown, the introduction of actual payoffs induces a chaotic transient that, after a series of dynamical bifurcations, settles into a fixed point that signals stable behavior. Furthermore, this fixed point is exactly that obtained in the case of no delays. That this equilibrium is stable against perturbations can be seen by the fact that if the system were perturbed again (as shown in Figure 6), it rapidly returns to its previous value. In additional experiments, with a smaller range of delays, we found that the system continued to oscillate without achieving the fixed point.

This transient chaos and its eventual stability can be understood from the distribution of agents with extra delays as a function of time. As can be seen in Figure 7 actual payoffs lead to a highly heterogeneous system, characterized by a diverse

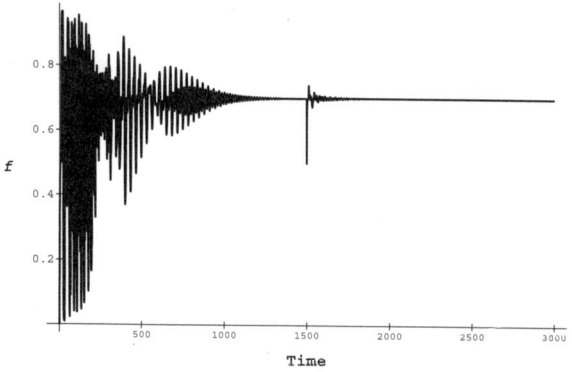

Figure 6. Behavior of the system shown in Figure 5 with a perturbation introduced at time 1500.

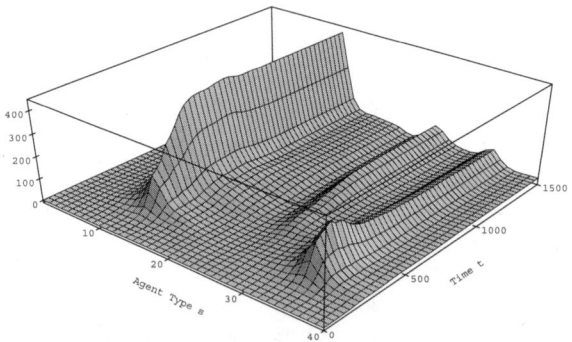

Figure 7. Ratio $f_s^{\text{type}}(t)/f_s^{\text{type}}(0)$ of the fraction of agents of each type, normalized to their initial values, as a function of time. Note there are several peaks, which correspond to agents with extra delays of 12, 26 and 34 time units. Because $\tau = 10$, these match periods of length 22, 36, and 44, respectively.

population of agents of different types. It also shows that the fraction of agents with certain extra delays increases greatly. These delays correspond to the major periodicities in the system.

6 Stability and Minimal Diversity

As we showed in the previous section, rewarding the performance of large collections of agents engaging in resource choices leads to a highly diverse mix of agents that stabilizes the system. This suggests that the real cause of stability in a distributed system is that provided by sufficient diversity and that the reward mechanism is an efficient way of automatically finding a good mix. This raises the interesting question of the minimal amount of diversity needed to have a stable system.

The stability of a system is determined by the behavior of a perturbation around equilibrium, which can be found from the linearized version of Equation 10. In our case, the diversity is related to the range of different delays that agents can have. For a continuous distribution of extra delays, the characteristic equation is obtained by assuming a solution of the type $e^{\lambda t}$ in the linearized equation, giving

$$\lambda + \alpha - \alpha \rho' \int ds \, f(s) e^{-\lambda(s+\tau)} = 0. \tag{14}$$

Stability requires that all the values of λ have negative real parts so that perturbations will relax back to equilibrium. As an example, suppose agent types are uniformly distributed in $(0, S)$. Then $f(s) = 1/S$, and the characteristic equation becomes

$$\lambda + \alpha - \alpha \rho' \frac{1 - e^{-\lambda S}}{\lambda S} e^{-\lambda \tau} = 0. \tag{15}$$

Defining a normalized measure of the diversity of the system for this case by $\eta \equiv S/\tau$, introducing the new variable $z \equiv \lambda \tau (1 + \eta)$, and multiplying Equation 15 by $\tau(1 + \eta)z e^z$ introduces an extra root at $z = 0$ and gives

$$(z^2 + az)e^z - b + be^{rz} = 0, \tag{16}$$

where

$$a = \alpha \tau (1 + \eta) > 0, \tag{17}$$

$$b = -\rho' \frac{\alpha \tau (1 + \eta)^2}{\eta} > 0,$$

$$r = \frac{\eta}{1 + \eta} \in (0, 1).$$

The stability of the system with uniform distribution of agents with extra delays thus reduces to finding the condition under which all roots of Equation 16, other than $z = 0$, have negative real parts. This equation is a particular instance of an *exponential polynomial*, whose terms consist of powers multiplied by exponentials. Unlike regular polynomials, these objects generally have an infinite number of roots and are important in the study of the stability properties of differential-delay equations. Established methods can then be used to determine when they have roots with positive real parts. This defines the stability boundary of the equation. The result for the particular case in which $\rho' = -3.41044$, corresponding to the parameters used in Section 5, is shown in the top half of Figure 8.

Similarly, if we choose an exponential distribution of delays, i.e., $f(s) = (1/S)e^{-s/S}$ with positive S, the characteristic equation acquires the form

$$(z^2 + pz + q)e^z + r = 0, \tag{18}$$

where

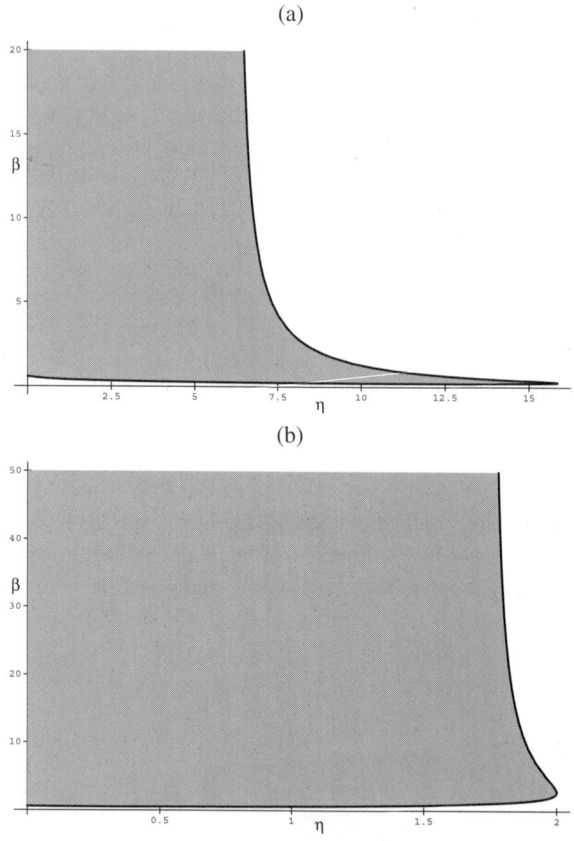

Figure 8. Stability as a function of $\beta = \alpha\tau$ and $\eta = S/\tau$ for two possible distributions of agent types: (a) $f(s) = 1/S$ in $(0, S)$, and (b) $f(s) = (1/S)e^{-s/S}$. The system is unstable in the shaded regions and stable to the right and below the curves.

$$p = \alpha\tau + \frac{1}{\eta} > 0, \qquad (19)$$

$$q = \frac{\alpha\tau}{\eta} > 0,$$

$$r = -\frac{\alpha\tau\rho'}{\eta} > 0,$$

and $z \equiv \lambda\tau$. An analysis similar to that for the uniform distribution case leads to the stability diagram shown in the bottom half of the figure.

Although the actual distributions of agent types can differ from these two cases, the similarity between the stability diagrams suggests that regardless of the magnitude of β one can always find an appropriate mix that will make the system stable. This property follows from the vertical asymptote of the stability boundary. It also illustrates the need for a minimum diversity in the system in order to make it stable when the delays aren't too small.

Having established the right mix that produces stability one may wonder whether a static assignment of agent types at an initial time would not constitute a simpler and more direct procedure to stabilize the system without resorting to a dynamic reward mechanism. Although this is indeed the case in a nonfluctuating environment, such a static mechanism cannot cope with changes in both the nature of the system (e.g., machines crashing) and the arrival of new tasks or fluctuating loads. It is precisely to avoid this vulnerability by keeping the system adaptive that a dynamic procedure is needed.

Having seen how sufficient diversity stabilizes a distributed system, we now turn to the mechanisms that can generate such heterogeneity, as well as the time that it takes for the system to stabilize. In particular, the details of the reward procedures determine whether the system can even find a stable mix of agents. In the cases described, the reward was proportional to the actual performance, as measured by the payoffs associated with the resources used. One might also wonder whether stability would be achieved more rapidly by giving greater (than their fair share) increases to the top performers.

We have examined two such cases: (1) rewards proportional to the square of their actual performance, and (2) giving all the rewards to top performers (e.g., those performing at the 90th percentile or better in the population). In the former case we observed stability with a shorter transient, whereas in the latter case the mix of changes continued to change through time, thus preventing stable behavior. This can be understood in terms of our earlier observation that whereas a small percentage of agents can identify oscillation periods and thereby reduce their amplitude, a large number of them can no longer perform well.

Note that the time to reach equilibrium is determined by two parameters of the system. The first is the time that it takes to find a stable mix of agent types, which is governed by γ, and the second is the rate at which perturbations relax, given the stable mix. The latter is determined by the largest real part of any of the roots, λ, of the characteristic equation.

7 Discussion

We have presented a case for treating distributed computation as an ecosystem, an analogy that turns out to be quite fruitful in the analysis, design, and control of such systems. In spite of the many differences between computational processes and organisms, resource contention, complex dynamics, and reward mechanisms seem to be ubiquitous in distributed computation, making it also a tool for the study of natural ecosystems.

Because chaotic behavior seems to be the natural result of interacting processes with imperfect and delayed information, the problem of controlling such systems is of paramount importance. We discovered that rewards based on the actual performance of agents in a distributed computational system can stabilize an otherwise chaotic or oscillatory system. This leads to greatly improved system performance.

In all these cases, stability is achieved by making chaos a transient phenomenon. In the case of distributed systems, the addition of the reward mechanism has the effect of dynamically changing the control parameters of the resource allocation dynamics in such a way that a global fixed point of the system is achieved. This brings the issue of the length of the chaotic transient as compared to the time needed for most agents to complete their tasks. Even when the transients are long, the results of this study show that the range gradually decreases, thereby improving performance even before the fixed point is achieved.

A particularly relevant question for distributed systems is the extent to which these results generalize beyond the mechanism that we studied. We considered the specific situation of a collection of agents with different delays in their appraisal of the system evolution. Similar behavior is also observed if the agents have a bias for a particular resource. It is of interest to inquire whether using rewards to increase diversity works more generally than in these cases.

Because we considered only agents choosing between two resources, it is important to understand what happens when there are many resources from which the agents can choose. One may argue that because diversity is the key to stability, a plurality of resources provides enough channels to develop the necessary heterogeneity, which is what we observed in situations with three resources. Another note of caution has to do with the effect of fluctuations on a finite population of agent types. While we have shown that sufficient diversity can, on average, stabilize the system, in practice a fluctuation could wipe out those agent types that would otherwise be successful in stabilizing the system. Thus, we need either a large number of each kind of agent or a mechanism, such as mutation, to create new kinds of agents.

Another issue concerns the time scales over which rewards are assigned to agents. In our treatment, we assumed the rewards were always based on the performance at the time they were given. Because in many cases this procedure is delayed, there is the question of the extent to which rewards based on past performance are also able to stabilize chaotic distributed systems.

Finally, the validity of this approach will have to be determined by actual implementations and measurements of distributed systems. This will present some challenges in identifying the relevant variables to be measured and aggregated to correspond to quantities used in the theory.

The fact that these simple resource-allocation mechanisms work and produce a stable environment provides a basis for developing more complex software systems that can be used for a wide range of computational problems.

References

1. A. A. Berlin, H. Abelson, N. Cohen, L. Fogel, C. M. Ho, M. Horowitz, J. How, T. F. Knight, R. Newton, and K. Pister. Distributed information systems for MEMS. Technical report, Information Systems and Technology (ISAT) Study, 1995.

2. J. Bryzek, K. Petersen, and W. McCulley. Micromachines on the march. *IEEE Spectrum*, 20–31, May 1994.

3. S. H. Clearwater, editor. *Market-Based Control: A Paradigm for Distributed Resource Allocation*. World Scientific, Singapore, 1996.

4. D. Ferguson, Y. Yemini, and C. Nikolaou. Microeconomic algorithms for load balancing in distributed computer systems. In *International Conference on Distributed Computer Systems*, pages 491–9. IEEE, 1988.

5. D. E. Goldberg. *Genetic Algorithms in Search, Optimization and Machine Learning*. Addison-Wesley, New York, 1989.

6. F. A. Hayek. Competition as a discovery procedure. In *New Studies in Philosophy, Politics, Economics and the History of Ideas*, pages 179–90. University of Chicago Press, Chicago, 1978.

7. T. Hogg and B. A. Huberman. Controlling chaos in distributed systems. *IEEE Trans. on Systems, Man and Cybernetics*, 21(6):1325–32, November/December 1991.

8. T. Hogg and B. A. Huberman. Controlling smart matter. *Smart Materials and Structures*, 7:R1–R14, 1998. Los Alamos preprint cond-mat/9611024.

9. B. A. Huberman and T. Hogg. The behavior of computational ecologies. In B. A. Huberman, editor, *The Ecology of Computation*, pages 77–115. North-Holland, Amsterdam, 1988.

10. J. O. Kephart, T. Hogg, and B. A. Huberman. Dynamics of computational ecosystems. *Physical Review A*, 40:404–21, 1989.

11. J. F. Kurose and R. Simha. A microeconomic approach to optimal resource allocation in distributed computer systems. *IEEE Transactions on Computers*, 38(5):705–17, 1989.

12. T. W. Malone, R. E. Fikes, K. R. Grant, and M. T. Howard. Enterprise: A market-like task scheduler for distributed computing environments. In B. A. Huberman, editor, *The Ecology of Computation*, pages 177–205. North-Holland, Amsterdam, 1988.

13. M. S. Miller and K. E. Drexler. Markets and computation: Agoric open systems. In B. A. Huberman, editor, *The Ecology of Computation*, pages 133–76. North-Holland, Amsterdam, 1988.

14. A. Smith. *An Inquiry into the Nature and Causes of the Wealth of Nations*. University of Chicago Press, Chicago, 1976. Reprint of the 1776 edition.

15. I. E. Sutherland. A futures market in computer time. *Communications of the ACM*, 11(6): 449–51, June 1968.

16. C. A. Waldspurger, T. Hogg, B. A. Huberman, J. O. Kephart, and W. S. Stornetta. Spawn: A distributed computational economy. *IEEE Trans. on Software Engineering*, 18(2):103–17, February 1992.

Index

agent-based system, 186
air space management, 6
allocative efficiency, 111, 123
ambiguity, 58–67, 69–74, 76, 79, 87, 88, 90–92, 101–5
aristocrat utility (AU), 45, 76–8, 80, 81
artificial life, 215
asymmetric interaction, 259, 263, 264, 268, 272, 275
asynchronous, 295, 296, 303, 304
asynchronous decisions, 216
asynchronous learning, 138
asynchronous play, 137
attractor, 279
  monomorphic, 281
  non-Nash, 279
  polymorphic, 281
auction, 15, 107, 133
autonomous agents, 295

bar problem, 161–3, 247
  grand canonical bar problem, 164, 172, 174 176, 181
Bayesian-Nash equilibrium, 110
behavior-based robots, 231, 233, 235, 237, 253
biologically based control, 231–233, 253
Boltzmann learning, 125
bots, 134
bounded rationality, 113, 186

catastrophe, 161, 162, 181

central equation, 44, 48, 49, 51, 52, 64, 67, 69, 80, 83, 96, 102
chaos, 279, 298, 302, 306, 308, 309, 313
clamping factor, 118, 119
clustered volatility, 295
coevolution, 278
  selection, 278
collaboration, 233, 238–46, 252, 253
collapsed utility, 45, 68
collective, 1, 187
  analysis, 187
  charateristics, 2
  definition, 2
  design, 187, 227
  evolution, 185
  examples, 5
  experimental domains, 5
  large fluctuations, 186
  network, 188
  robustness, 227
  statistical physics, 186
collective action, 258, 259
collective intelligence (COIN), 119, 278, 279
  aristocrat utility, 26
  central equation, 24
  clamping, 27
  coevolution, 278
  coevolutionary algorithm, 292
  difference utility, 26
  factored, 116
  intelligence, 25, 26
  learnability, 26

COIN (*Continued*)
  wonderful life utility, 27
communication
  centralized, 187
  global, 218
  interagent, 188
competition, 200, 204, 296, 298, 299, 303, 306
complex networks, 114
complex social network, 185
complex system, 213
computational ecology, 19, 297
computational economies, 15, 17
confidence, 164, 167, 173, 177
congestion, 141
congestion control, 134
congestion game, 119
connectivity, 248, 251, 253
constrained optimization, 96, 103
control
  adaptive, 24
  agent-based, 213
  artificial life, 215
  biologically inspired, 215
  centralized, 4, 187
  complex system, 213
  congestion, 134
  constellations of satellites, 6
  distributed, 213, 215
  multiagent, 213
  planetary exploration vehicles, 6
  routing, 6
convergence guaranteed, 138
cooperation, 203, 206, 207, 209–11, 258, 297, 299, 303, 306, 308
coordinate, 258, 260, 263, 275
coordinate utility, 46, 49, 50, 52, 64, 83
coordination, 203, 206, 207, 209–11
cumulative distribution function, 82
cyclic dynamics, 278

data network, 141
De Bruijn, 174, 175, 181
delays, 297, 302, 303, 305–11, 313, 314
design coordinate, 48, 52, 75, 94
discontinuity, 284, 287
disorder, 167, 168, 176, 177, 181
distributed
  AI, 8

computation, 295–8, 313
distributed control, 231–3, 246, 252, 253
diversity, 265, 272, 273
dynamics, 295, 296, 298, 303, 304, 308, 313
  cyclic, 278
  replicator, 278

ecosystem, 7
efficiency, 266
El Farol Bar problem, 21, 119, 188
emergence, 199
emergent coordination, 252
emergent structure, 215
endogenous, 161, 162, 174, 181, 207, 211
equilibrium
  dynamic, 217
  fitness, 281
  polymorphic, 281
equity, 266
evolution, 204–7, 209–11
evolutionary algorithm, 279
evolutionary programming, 283

factored, 49–52, 59, 64–8, 73, 75, 76, 78–81, 86, 88, 91, 92, 95–8, 101, 102
factoredness, 26, 108
fair queuing, 141
finite population, 291
first premise, 59–63, 65, 67, 94, 96, 100, 101
fitness, 298, 306, 307
fitness equilibrium, 281
fitness sharing, 281, 291, 292
  competitive, 287
  inverse problem, 292
  similarity-based, 290
  variable-sum games, 288
fixed point, 282
  Nash equilibrium, 282
  stability, 283
forage, 231, 233, 236, 252
forward problem, 2, 3, 135

game theory, 11, 109, 133, 186
  cooperative, 12
  evolution and learning, 13
  evolutionary, 278, 279
  extensive form game, 11
  multi-stage game, 11
  noncooperative, 11

game theory (*Continued*)
  normal-form game, 11
  perfect rationality, 12
  single-stage game, 11
general equilibrium theory, 14
generalized coordinates, 44, 46, 53, 79, 84
generalized cumulative distribution function, 82
global adaptation, 264, 266, 268, 270, 272, 273, 275
gradient ascent for categorical variables, 45, 97, 98
grand canonical, 164, 172, 181
group behavior, 211
Groves mechanism, 111

Hawk-Dove game, 279, 281, 291
  dynamics, 282
  Nash equilibrium, 282
heterogeneity, 258–60, 263, 265, 266, 269, 275
history, 163, 164, 166–8, 171, 174, 176, 177, 181
history space, 190
homogeneity, 258, 270, 272, 273, 275
human, 199
hysteresis, 216, 217

immunize, 162
incentive design, 7
individual rationality, 112, 121
information, 199, 201, 205, 207, 209, 210, 295, 297, 298, 300–4, 306–8, 313
  global, 166, 168, 175
innovation, 199
intelligence, 47–50, 52, 53, 55, 57, 59, 60, 64–7, 69, 71, 73, 74, 76, 77, 80–3, 85, 86, 91, 94–6
inverse problem, 2, 3, 140, 141, 278, 292
iterated dominance, 136
iterated game, 77, 81, 94, 96, 97

learnability, 26, 57, 69–73, 75–8, 80, 81, 90–2, 292
learnable, 108
learning
  asynchronous play, 138
  PAC, 137
limited rationality, 108, 129

linear rank selection, 287
  private utility, 291
local adaptation, 264, 270, 272, 273, 275

macrolearn, 95
macroscopic order, 259
manager, 181
market, 231, 232, 246, 253, 295, 297–302, 306, 307
master equation, 235
mean field, 304
mechanism, 135
  Groves, 111
  incentive compatible, 110
  VCG-WLU, 120
  Vickrey-Clarke-Groves, 111
mechanism design, 15, 107, 109, 134
  learnable, 120
  automated, 129
  COIN-inspired, 120
  decentralized, 142
  efficient, 111
  online, 113
memory, 166, 171, 181
microlearn, 95
minority game, 21, 162, 188, 200–6, 209, 246–8, 253, 263
  persistence, 193
  predictability, 193
  substrate network, 189
move, 44, 50, 53–6, 59, 63, 67, 68, 71, 77, 79–81, 84, 88, 92–103, 105
multiagent systems, 9, 161–4, 185, 232, 233, 241, 242, 295
  design, 9
  reinforcement learning, 10
  social agents, 10
  team game agents, 10
multistage game, 65, 83, 94, 96
multistep game, 45, 93, 95, 96, 105
multiplier effect, 263

nanocomputer, 7
Nash equilibrium, 10, 12, 25, 26, 50, 51, 94–6, 110, 115, 278, 279, 281
  Hawk-Dove game, 282
  monomorphic, 281
  polymorphic, 278, 281, 282
  variable-sum game, 292

network, 295, 298–303
    complex, 114
    formation, 113
network formation, 262
NK model, 247, 248, 252
nodal weight, 174, 176, 177, 181

overwhelmed strategy, 139

PAC learning, 137
personal utility function, 133
phase transition, 203, 248, 252
planning, 214
    long-term, 186
Poisson process, 141
polymorphism, 283
population biology, 19
power grid management, 6
predict, 161, 163, 164, 167, 169, 171, 174–6, 178, 181
pricing, 142
prisoner and altruist game, 136
prisoner's dilemma, 135
private utility, 43–5, 48, 52, 54–6, 59, 61, 63–7, 69, 71, 73, 76, 77, 80, 81, 94–6, 99–102
private utility function, 2, 278, 279
protocell, 7
protocol fair share, 141

quench, 167, 168, 176, 177, 181

rate equation, 235–8, 242, 243, 252, 253
reactive robots, 233, 235, 237–9, 253
reconfiguration
    growth, 218
    mode, 218
    prismatic, 224
    scents, 218
    seeds, 218
    substrate, 218
reinforcement learning, 9, 187
repeated game, 79, 94, 96
repeating coordinate, 79, 93, 94, 96
replicator, 281
    dynamics, 13, 278
    equation, 280
    standard, 286

resource, 162–5, 174, 199, 200, 202, 203, 206, 211, 231, 246–8, 250, 252, 253, 295–308, 310, 312–4
reward, 306–8, 310, 312–4
robot, 232, 233, 236, 237
    locomotion, 219
    manipulation, 219
    metamorphic, 214
    modular, 214, 215
    self-reconfigurable, 214

second premise, 63, 65, 87, 103, 104
self-organizing systems, 24
self-organization, 258, 259
sensor-based simulation, 232
small world effect, 191
smart matter, 297
social agents, 10
social choice, 107
social choice function, 133, 140
social insects, 213
social network, 189
solution concept, 135
Spawn, 297, 299, 300, 302
spin glass, 44, 45, 68, 76, 81
stability, 266, 295, 298, 306, 309–14
    evolutionary algorithm, 279
    Internet, 134
    leader agent, 188, 196
    Nash equilibrium, 286
Stackelberg
    outcome, 137
statistical mechanics, 186
statistical physics, 20
stochastic fields, 23
stock market, 213
strategy, 109, 163, 164, 167–72, 174–81, 186, 201, 202, 204–7, 209–11
    dominant, 110, 116
    equilibrium, 109
    evolutionary stable, 13, 279
    overwhelmed, 139
    profile, 109
    selection, 278
strategy-proof, 108, 111, 140
swarm intelligence, 20

team game, 117
team game agents, 10

third premise, 66, 67, 73, 88
truncation, private utility, 291
truncation selection, 283, 284
type, 110

uncertainty, 303, 304, 306
utility
    factored, 26
    learnable, 26
    poorly factored, 279
    wonderful life, 108

vaccination, 161, 162
variable sum game, 278, 281, 288
Vickrey-Clarke-Groves mechanism, 111

wealth, 205–7, 209–11
WLU, 45, 77–81, 92, 95
wonderful life utility, 45, 77–81, 92, 95
world utility, 43–6, 50, 75, 79, 81, 99
world utility function, 2, 133, 187, 278, 279
worldview, 54–7, 59–61, 63, 64, 67, 68, 93,
    95, 100

About the Editors

Kagan Tumer is a research scientist at the NASA Ames Research Center. He leads the Control and Coordination in Complex Systems Group and is a member of the Ames Science and Technology Council whose charter is to identify and support innovative research projects.

Dr. Tumer's current research has two main thrusts: The design of collectives, with a particular focus on very large systems of noisy components; and the derivation of quantitative complexity measures that can establish the link between system complexity and risk assessment.

He has published over fifty refereed articles and holds one patent. He received his doctorate degree from the Electrical and Computer Engineering Department of The University of Texas, Austin.

David Wolpert is a senior computer scientist at the NASA Ames Research Center where he formed and led the collective intelligence group. His current primary area of research is collectives and distributed control and optimization. He also does work in complexity measures, multi-argument metrics, and the physics of computation. Previously he has concentrated on machine learning and Bayesian analysis.

Before coming to NASA he was a Research Manager in IBM's Data Mining Solutions group at the Almaden Research Center. He had come to IBM from TXN Inc., a data-mining firm where he was Director of Research. Before that he was a postdoc at the Santa Fe Institute and the Center for Nonlinear Studies at Los Alamos. His degrees are in physics, from the University of California, Santa Barbara and Princeton University.

He is the author of two books, three patents, close to one hundred refereed papers, and numerous awards.